Reframing Difference in
Organizational
Communication
Studies

Reframing Difference in

Organizational Communication Studies

Research, Pedagogy, Practice

Dennis K. Mumby

The University of North Carolina at Chapel Hill

Editor

Los Angeles | London | New Delhi
Singapore | Washington DC

For information:

SAGE Publications, Inc.
2455 Teller Road
Thousand Oaks,
    California 91320
E-mail: order@sagepub.com

SAGE Publications Ltd.
1 Oliver's Yard
55 City Road
London EC1Y 1SP
United Kingdom

SAGE Publications India Pvt. Ltd.
B 1/I 1 Mohan Cooperative
    Industrial Area
Mathura Road, New Delhi 110 044
India

SAGE Publications
    Asia-Pacific Pte. Ltd.
33 Pekin Street #02-01
Far East Square
Singapore 048763

Printed in the United States of America

Library of Congress Cataloging-in-Publication Data

Reframing difference in organizational communication studies: Research, pedagogy, and practice / Dennis K. Mumby, [editor and contributor].
    p. cm.
Includes bibliographical references and index.
ISBN 978-1-4129-7007-5 (cloth)
ISBN 978-1-4129-7008-2 (pbk.)
    1. Communication in organizations. 2. Organizational behavior. I. Mumby, Dennis K.

HD30.3.R45 2011
302.3'5—dc22   2010010921

This book is printed on acid-free paper.

10   11   12   13   14   10   9   8   7   6   5   4   3   2   1

Acquisitions Editor:	Todd R. Armstrong
Editorial Assistant:	Nathan Davidson
Production Editor:	Eric Garner
Copy Editor:	Jenifer Dill
Typesetter:	C&M Digitals (P) Ltd.
Proofreader:	Susan Schon
Indexer:	Terri Corry
Cover Designer:	Candice Harman
Marketing Manager:	Helen Salmon

Contents

Organizing Difference

An Introduction

Dennis K. Mumby

This volume appears at a propitious moment in the evolution of the field of organizational communication. Over the last two decades the field has struggled mightily with how best to address the ways that organizing, power, and communication processes intersect in the context of everyday meaning construction and sense-making practices. This struggle has taken many forms, including interpretive, critical, post-structuralist, and feminist efforts to unpack the processes through which systems of meaning, power, and institutional forms are structured. At the heart of this effort has been the recognition—sometimes explicit, frequently implicit—that difference is both medium and product of the relations of power that organization members communicatively construct. Put in more Batesonian terms, critical organizational communication scholars have for a long time been exploring the ways that "the differences that make a difference" are produced, reproduced, and challenged in organizational life. Difference, as many have argued, is by no means fixed and existing "out there" in the external world, but rather arises through the ability of particular interest groups to marshal discursive, political, and economic resources in order to privilege one system of difference over another. In this sense, it is only through difference that—in the Saussurian sense—a meaningful world becomes possible at all. However, while difference may be arbitrary, it never arises by accident.

Curiously enough, however, critical organization scholars have both embraced difference as a focus of study and held it gingerly at arm's length. Taking on difference as a guiding construct and empirical problematic simultaneously opens up myriad possibilities for exploring organizing and leads one up a conceptual cul-de-sac. Put simply, studying difference in all its complexities is damn hard. We are taught from early in our graduate training that taking on any theoretical framework inevitably means that we can construct only partial, perspectival views of human behavior. All seeing is theory-laden, to paraphrase Norwood Hansen (1958), and such a recognition provides some comfort that we are not expected to do it all; we simply try to carve out our own carefully delineated area of research and leave the rest to others, making the usual disclaimers along the way about contingency, partiality, provisionalism, and so forth.

But somehow these same arguments ring rather hollow when it comes to studying and theorizing difference. Typically, the argument has gone something like this: In the 1980s, critical organization studies theorized power in a relatively generic manner, with occasional references to class or "sectional interests" (Giddens, 1979) as the underlying mechanism for the construction of difference and social inequity. Sometimes there were allusions to the need to expand conceptions of difference to include, for example, discussions of gender. Hearn and Parkin's (1983) review of research on gender and organization, tellingly subtitled "A Selective Review and Critique of a Neglected Area," gives some indication of how marginal the critical study of gender and organizing was back then. Sometimes critical scholars gave rather elaborate and tortured explanations of why gender was excluded as a focus of study. Thus, Alvesson and Willmott (1992), in their widely-read edited collection, *Critical Management Studies,* stated, "Arguably, most if not all social phenomena involve a gender aspect, but it would be reductionistic to capture most aspects of management, production, and consumption basically in feminist terms . . ." (p. 9).

Of course, such a sentiment was rather overwhelmed in the course of the 1990s by efforts to systematically theorize and study the relationships among gender, organization, and power, spurred in many respects by Acker's (1990) landmark essay as well as by early theoretical essays in organizational communication (e.g., Marshall, 1993) that saw gender not simply as an addition to extant organizing processes but as medium and product of everyday organizational sense-making and meaning formations.

But what goes around comes around. It soon became clear that while the broadening of critical organization studies to include gender was a welcome and much-needed move, it also included its own limitations and blind spots. Perhaps most glaringly, little attention was paid to the ways in which race was encoded in everyday organizational life. Indeed, in many ways, and for all its talk about gender as socially constructed, much of this work has tended to essentialize gender as isolated from other, related constructions of difference. Perhaps most frustratingly, many of these studies made frequent calls for the expansion of research to address other difference issues, such as race, but rarely went beyond the expression of a need for such research.

So we see a pattern emerging here. First, a line of research is established that begins to address a neglected aspect of difference; then, the limitations of this work are highlighted as other areas of difference are shown to be marginalized. In other words, the general approach to difference in organization studies can be broadly characterized as additive and piecemeal, with limited efforts to theorize difference in a sustained and coherent manner. Maybe it's time for a different approach to difference.

I'm not going to make any grandiose claims about how this volume solves many of the problems associated with existing research on difference (in any form) and organization. However, I do think that, taken collectively, the essays represent a sustained effort to do justice to the complexities and contradictions that characterize difference as a fundamental and defining feature of organizational life. Moreover, each chapter explores the relationship between difference and organizing *communicatively*, examining how difference is both medium and outcome of the collective sense-making processes of organization members. In other words, difference is both the mechanism through which meanings and identities are organized and the product—intended or unintended—of everyday organizing and collective sense-making. In this context, each of the chapters explores, in various ways, how certain forms of difference are organized into everyday life while others are organized out or marginalized.

Rather than being organized around different forms of difference (which, I think, would defeat the object of theorizing difference in a more systemic, less piecemeal manner), the book is instead structured in three different, but related, sections. In the first section, "Theorizing Difference," contributors explore a number of ways in which difference can be critically examined as a communicative phenomenon; in each chapter, difference is examined as routinely accomplished through everyday organizing processes. Thus, the overarching goal in this section is not to add difference to the list of empirical phenomena that organizational communication scholars must address; rather, the goal is to demonstrate the importance of "difference" as both a construct—a sensitizing device—through which the complexities of organizational communication processes can be examined and as a constitutive feature of everyday organizing. Identities, social realities, and power relations are both medium and outcome of difference.

These chapters explore difference as an organizing mechanism through which these phenomena are produced and reproduced. First, Karen Ashcraft's chapter lays out what, I believe, is an exciting research agenda for the study of difference and organizing; indeed, this initial chapter can be viewed as the conceptual leitmotif for the entire book. Rather than analyzing difference as an individual, group, or organizational phenomenon, Ashcraft instead theorizes it as "an organizing principle of the meaning, structure, practice, and economy of work." With this alternative conception, Ashcraft explores difference not as a manifestation of organizing, but rather as a constitutive mechanism in the organization and understanding of work itself. Next, Linda Putnam, Jody Jahn, and Jane Stuart Baker explore a dialectical approach to difference. Dialectics have played an important part in productively complicating our understanding of communication processes, and Putnam et al.'s chapter frames difference and organizing in ways that move us beyond the rather pervasive tendency to treat difference in a binary manner. The third chapter in this section, by Sarah Dempsey, adopts a transnational feminist approach to difference and organizing. Here, Dempsey looks specifically at the intersectional character of difference, placed in the context of real world globalization processes and the need for praxis-oriented ways to address the effects of globalization. The section ends with Gail Fairhurst, Marthe Church, Danielle Hagen, and Joseph Levi's analysis of the executive coaching literature via a feminist Foucauldian lens. The chapter provides some interesting insights into the gender subtexts that underlie the disciplinary technologies of this movement.

The second section takes up the growing understanding that theorizing difference is inseparable from the need to adequately prepare students for life in an organizational society and its numerous manifestations—corporate, nonprofit, voluntary, nongovernmental, and so forth. In this context, students are increasingly in need of analytic and practical tools that permit them to engage with, and productively participate in, the organization of difference. Such tools are essential if our students are to become self-reflexive and responsive citizens in a democracy. Each of the chapters, then, approaches the intersection of pedagogy and difference in a praxis-oriented manner, drawing on various theoretical constructs to illustrate how dialogues about difference can become integral features of the classroom environment. Teaching (about) difference is one of the biggest challenges that instructors face, and each of these chapters addresses difference and organizing in innovative and provocative ways. One of the most exciting elements of these chapters is that each author self-reflexively explores his or her struggles with teaching difference and each provides concrete, pragmatic recommendations for instructors confronting their own struggles with how to address difference in teaching of organizational communication.

First, Brenda Allen develops *critical communication pedagogy* as a framework that she uses to teach difference. Usefully, she explores in some detail her own experiences teaching a class called "Difference Matters in Organizational Communication." Erika Kirby's chapter uses social identity theory to discuss how she explores the privilege<-> oppression dialectic with her students. One of the most insightful aspects of Erika's chapter is her discussion of the struggle to develop classroom dialogues about difference and privilege<->oppression when the students are overwhelmingly White and privileged. Jennifer Mease's chapter works as an effective complement to Kirby's chapter, addressing how teaching issues of difference to (often privileged) students is partly a question of exploring the relationship between individual and institutional perspectives. As she indicates, her goal in exploring this relationship with students is to show that difference is less individual and more personal—a paradox that I will let you, the reader, unpack as you read her essay. Finally, the section ends with Shiv Ganesh's discussion of teaching difference and organizing in Aotearoa/New Zealand. Using a specific case study (the Josie Bullock case), he provides a deft analysis of how his discussions with Maori and Pakeha (White European) students help to reframe his own sense-making about this case that pivots on the relationship between Maori and Pakeha cultures and customs. Moreover, he explores how bicultural analyses pose their own dialogic problems.

The third and final section of the book takes up difference as a central construct in applied organizational communication research. Continuing the communication orientation, this section explores difference not simply in terms of "workplace diversity" initiatives, but examines it more broadly as a communicative mechanism through which organizations enable some possibilities and exclude others. Each of the chapters in this section adopts an explicitly interventionist and engaged approach to organization and difference. Furthermore, each addresses difference as a constitutive—rather than additive—feature of organizational life.

First, John McClellan, Stephen Williams, and Stanley Deetz's essay examines the National Science Foundation's (NSF) program to advance women in the STEM disciplines (Science, Technology, Engineering, and Mathematics). Beginning with the premise that ways of talking about difference shape meanings and behaviors, they identify four vocabularies that have emerged around implementation of the NSF's intervention program: (1) Diversity, (2) Equity, (3) Advancement, and (4) Development.

The essay shows how each of these discourses constitutes a particular articulation of meaning about difference and, as such, has different—sometimes hidden—interests and consequences. The goal of their essay is to illustrate that, at a very pragmatic level, different ways of talking about difference have concrete consequences in terms of how institutions intervene in diversity efforts. Patricia Parker, Elisa Oceguera, and Joaquín Sánchez provide fascinating insight into how a research team with diverse identities engages in a community-based research project. The authors focus not on the project itself, but rather on the tensions between their roles as academics and social justice advocates engaged in change efforts. The essay beautifully illustrates how each member of the research team struggles self-reflexively with their own sense of identities in relationship to the members of the vulnerable communities with which they are working. For anyone interested in questions of representation (in terms of both voice and epistemology) in politically engaged ethnographic work, this essay effectively interrogates the multiple challenges faced by researchers-activists.

Patrice Buzzanell, Rebecca Dohrman, and Suzie D'Enbeau take as their subject a much-researched phenomenon in organizational communication—the issue of work-life balance and care giving. Here, their focus is not work-life balance per se, but rather the popular and academic discourses that have constructed work-life balance issues in different ways. Adopting a political economy perspective, the essay illustrates how difference is implicated and constructed in a number of ways in relation to work-life issues, privileging some political interests and marginalizing others. The essay concludes with practical and policy recommendations for how work-life balance issues can be more equitably addressed. Finally, Lynn Harter and William Rawlins's essay examines disability and the disabled body as a site of struggle over difference. In a study of "Passion Works," a nonprofit artists' studio within a sheltered workshop, Harter and Rawlins adopt a dialogical aesthetic approach in order to explore Passion Works's "aesthetic celebration of embodied differences." Harter and Rawlins see Passion Works not as an organization that merely accommodates difference, but rather as instantiating a broader model for organizational responses to difference. In this context, difference is not normalized or accommodated, but rather aesthetically and dialogically *answered* and engaged in order to open up possibilities for relationality and meaning construction.

Taken as a whole, then, the twelve essays in this volume represent an important and sustained effort to address the intersection of difference and organizing in a way that does justice to the complexity of the topic. I hope readers will be inspired to contribute to this important conversation.

❖ ACKNOWLEDGMENTS

The origins of this volume lie in a day-long doctoral preconference held at the 2007 International Communication Association conference in San Francisco, where a number of organizational communication scholars and PhD students came together to address the problems and possibilities that inhere in the intersection of organizing and difference. The dynamism of the discussions that day clearly warranted further development and elaboration, and this volume is the result. I'd like to thank Linda Putnam, for first encouraging me to edit a volume based on the conference discussions, as well as the reviewers of the initial proposal: Boris H. J. M. Brummans (Université de Montréal); David Carlone (The University of North Carolina at Greensboro); François Cooren (Université de Montréal); Kristen Lucas (University of Nebraska-Lincoln); Majia Holmer Nadesan (Arizona State University); Jennifer Ziegler (Valparaiso University). At Sage, Todd Armstrong shepherded this project through the various stages of publication with his usual verve and élan, while Nathan Davidson provided invaluable editorial assistance. In the final stages of the project, Jeni Dill proved to be an exceptional copy editor, and Eric Garner ensured the book's timely progress through the production process.

Ultimately, however, an edited volume such as this is only as good as its contributors. I was fortunate enough to be blessed with authors who had important things to say, and who said them in an erudite and insightful manner. Their words stand as eloquent tribute to the success of the preconference.

❖ REFERENCES

Acker, J. (1990). Hierarchies, jobs, bodies: A theory of gendered organizations. *Gender and Society, 4*, 139–158.

Alvesson, M., & Willmott, H. (Eds.). (1992). *Critical management studies.* Newbury Park, CA: Sage.

Giddens, A. (1979). *Central problems in social theory: Action, structure and contradiction in social analysis.* Berkeley: University of California Press.

Hanson, N. (1958). *Patterns of discovery: An inquiry into the conceptual foundations of science.* Cambridge, U.K.: Cambridge University Press.

Hearn, J., & Parkin, W. (1983). Gender and organizations: A selective review and critique of a neglected area. *Organization Studies, 4*, 219–242.

Marshall, J. (1993). Viewing organizational communication from a feminist perspective: A critique and some offerings. In S. A. Deetz (Ed.), *Communication Yearbook* (Vol. 16, pp. 122–141). Newbury Park, CA: Sage.

Part I

Theorizing Difference and Organization

1

Knowing Work Through the Communication of Difference

A Revised Agenda for Difference Studies

Karen Lee Ashcraft

Like many critical theorists of organization, scholars of difference seek to illuminate and revise institutionalized relations of power. They recognize identity as political and central to the configuration and experience of power relations in contemporary organizational life. The distinctive turf of difference research is demarcated by its claim that, however idiosyncratic identity may appear in certain circumstances, it revolves in large part around key cultural formations of difference-sameness, such as gender, race, and class. While this chapter assumes that basic understanding of scope, it aims to establish grounds for a major shift in the current research agenda.

The tacit question guiding most organizational communication scholarship on difference asks: How can diversity be enhanced in professional workplaces? I argue that this is the wrong underlying question, premature and insufficient at best, misleading and self-defeating at worst. I propose an alternative point of departure that asks how communication organizes work through difference—or how we come to know work individually, relationally, organizationally, and culturally through the communication of difference. Accordingly, I advocate shifting our conception of difference from an individual, group, or organizational property (e.g., so-called women's ways of leading, gendered bureaucracies) to an organizing principle of the meaning, structure, practice, and economy of work (i.e., the cultural organization of work via difference). The first section of the chapter builds a rationale for this shift in focus, while the second considers how to do so by confronting theoretical, practical, and political challenges entailed in such a shift.

❖ THE QUESTIONS GUIDING INQUIRY

Difference and "The Workplace": The Current Question

As with most areas of academic study, difference research in organizational communication is characterized by a rich variety of empirical questions. Without minimizing this variety, I suggest that a common underlying question or guiding motive threads through much of it: *How can diversity be enhanced in professional workplaces*—or elongated, *How are various kinds of control based on formations of difference fostered at the workplace, and how might we facilitate greater inclusion and equity?* If this is a fair characterization of shared focus, it is also not surprising. It reflects, for example, the critical orientation of most difference scholars, for whom the purpose of research is not merely to document, describe, or interpret relations of power and difference, but also to transform those relations and move toward some kind of emancipatory vision, however partial and provisional (Alvesson & Willmott, 1992).

My purpose is to examine this guiding question more closely—to consider how relations of difference are already embedded within it, affecting its transformative potential. I seek to reveal key limitations of a shared focus that, at first glance, seems both predictable and appropriate. Toward this end, I take up three key elements that frame the common question, all of which revolve around its focus on "the workplace," variously emphasized. After briefly characterizing each element, I weigh their broader consequences.

A first element entails attention to the workplace. Organizational communication scholars have mostly analyzed difference at the level of organization, conceived in terms of an actual site that *contains* interaction. This trend reflects dominant disciplinary interpretations of the ontology of organizational communication. Much has been said about the limits of the container metaphor of organization historically steering those interpretations (e.g., Putnam, Phillips, & Chapman, 1996; Smith, 1993). It is worth noting, however, that different meanings of *contain* are in circulation among difference researchers. Elsewhere, for example, I have identified two broad strands of gender studies in organizational communication: (1) gender *in* organizations, where the spotlight falls on gendered people and interactions *within* organizational settings; and (b) gender *of* organizations (also known as *gendered organization*), where the setting itself (i.e., organizational forms, cultures, systems) is scrutinized as a consequential agent that facilitates individual identity and interpersonal interaction in particular ways (Ashcraft, 2005, 2006a). To some extent, both approaches retain a sense of organization-as-container, but whereas the container is largely taken for granted in the former, it becomes an object of keen interest in the latter. In other words, research on the gender *of* organization examines the gendered constitution *and* constituting force of organizational systems. Rather than treat organizations as inert, neutral contain*ers* that house lively interactions, this second strand regards organizations as active and political and problematizes their contain*ing* function with respect to interaction. Neither branch, however, has yielded much insight into the actual work of organizations, or the jobs and tasks members perform (Ashcraft, 2006a).

Although notable exceptions have long appeared beside these two strands, only recently have organizational communication scholars commenced sustained research on difference "at work" beyond conventional workplace boundaries—for example, in scholarly representations (Calás, 1992; Calás & Smircich, 1991), popular culture (Carlone & Taylor, 1998; Holmer Nadesan & Trethewey, 2000), occupational associations and public discourse about the professions (Cheney & Ashcraft, 2007), and labor union or social movement activity (Cloud, 2005; Ganesh, 2007). This emerging strain of research—which, for purposes of contrast, might be called the *organization* of work and difference (as opposed to difference *in* or *of* organization)—begins to foreground work itself and cultural notions about it, rather than only the formal sites in which it is conducted. In the process, this research begins to challenge conventional ontologies and epistemologies of organizational communication, revealing multiple sites where work happens (Ashcraft, 2007, 2008).

Although the latter point is explored more fully in the final section, for now I turn to a second element of the common question, latent in the preceding discussion: a focus on the workplace. Certainly, the scope of organizational communication includes interest in organizations whose primary aims are not economic (e.g., Lewis, 2005) and whose primary activities are not designated "work." Indeed, early organizational communication scholars were careful to make this distinction, in part as a way of distancing the field from managerial, business, or corporate biases (Redding & Tompkins, 1988). Simultaneously, the majority of organizational communication scholarship and textbooks representing it accentuate organizations in which employment is the defining relationship and work the defining activity (Ashcraft & Kedrowicz, 2002), even though—as noted above—the spotlight tends not to illuminate work per se. This is all the more true in difference research, wherein arguments for significance often hinge on work in a generic sense: for instance, (a) the central role of work in contemporary formations of identity and power (see Alvesson, Ashcraft, & Thomas, 2008); (b) the growing phenomenon and significance of diversity at work (e.g., invoking the infamous "Workforce 2000" report of demographic trends), and (c) the coordination and productivity implications of diversity as well as other aspects of a so-called business case for difference (for more on the latter two rationales, see Ashcraft & Allen, 2003).

A third key element of the guiding question involves its focus on the workplace, by which I mean its tacit assumption about *which* sort of workplace is most pertinent. To date, the majority of difference research universalizes professional or so-called white-collar settings, as evident when "the workplace" becomes the typical shorthand referent (Ashcraft & Allen, 2003). In gender and organization studies, for example, managerial and professional work/places (i.e., work *and* formal organizational locations thereof) are often taken as the natural or obvious site of women's labor difficulties and empowerment potential (e.g., Buzzanell, 2000). The enormous literatures (in and beyond communication studies) devoted to women in leadership and management and masculine and feminine professional communication styles provide a telling example. Here, problems associated with particular forms of Western, white, middle-class, heterosexual femininity tend to be normalized, taken as representative of women's workplace struggles (for a critical review of these literatures, see Ashcraft, 2004). Yet women of all racial identities are overwhelmingly clustered in other kinds of labor, as documented by the extensive literature on so-called women's work (e.g., Cotter, Hermsen, & Vanneman, 2001). Similarly, research premised on increasing racial diversity at work refers implicitly to demographic changes in white-collar settings. After all, men and women of color have long been present—not to mention disproportionately concentrated—in sites and forms of labor deemed un- or semi-skilled, menial, dirty, and otherwise undesirable (Tomaskovic-Devey, 1993).

With notable exceptions (e.g., Gibson & Papa, 2000; Holmer Nadesan, 1996), difference research in organizational communication has largely neglected such labor sites and forms. It is worth pausing to ask; Why have we stressed "desirable" work/places—the ladder up, the ticket out—rather than also engaging difference in the less enviable work/places where other bodies are historically concentrated, or at least investigating difference in a range of work contexts? Unless one expects a radical redistribution of available jobs, would not the diversification of professional work/places depend on the diversification of others as well?

Some might rightfully interpret the pattern as evidence of the persistent class bias of organizational communication studies (e.g., Cheney, 2000). On the one hand, I concur that the overwhelming focus on professional work/places reflects scholars' (i.e., our own) reproduction of cultural notions about what work is more valuable and worthwhile, what sites are more alluring and potent, and so forth. However, this focus blends relations of difference—not merely of class, but also of race and gender—in a troubling way. Here, I suggest a proposition substantiated below: Gender and race shape the class of work/place; that is, the nature and value of tasks *and* the sites and systems in which they are accomplished are organized around difference (Ashcraft, 2008). Putting the claim in hypothetical terms for now, what if work/places are assessed at least in part on the basis of the bodies with which they are symbolically and materially associated?

If so, then there is an irony in current efforts to enhance relations of difference in professional work/places: namely, to the extent that they are effective, these efforts are likely to induce character and value erosion as well. Consider, for instance, the devaluation of various fields (e.g., clerical and librarian work) that women have entered in a critical mass—a phenomenon suggesting that cultural notions of worthwhile work/places stem at least in part from the historical inclusion and exclusion of certain people (for a review of related issues, see Wright & Jacobs, 1994). It follows that gendered and raced assumptions about the class of work—the labor to which "we all, of course, would aspire"—may be embedded in well-meaning efforts to diversify white-collar work/places. Put bluntly, emphasizing how diversity can be enhanced in professional settings, in the absence of common questions about other labor sites and forms, ironically perpetuates sexist and racist evaluations of work/place. My argument, then, is that despite its evident appeal, the current guiding question may be the wrong one; at least, it is premature and cannot stand alone. The more pressing question seems to be, How does difference play into the organization of work in the first place?

❖ DIFFERENCE AND THE ORGANIZATION OF WORK: AN ALTERNATE QUESTION

Turning difference inquiry toward the latter question requires shifting the conception of difference, from (a) an individual or group feature (as in gender *in* organizations research—for example, so-called feminine styles of leadership communication) or (b) an organizational property (as in gender *of* organization research—gendered bureaucracy, for instance) toward (c) an organizing principle of the meaning, structure, practice, experience, and economy of work itself (as in emerging research on the *organization* of work through difference, mentioned previously). On what grounds might we make such a shift, and how far does it stretch organizational communication as a field? Addressing the first half of that question is the subject of this section, while the second half occupies the remainder of the chapter.

Grounding the Alternative Question

Here, I wish to substantiate the claim that work is *known* (i.e., its nature, character, and value—in a word, *class*—understood) in large part by the gendered and raced bodies with which it becomes aligned. Supporting empirical evidence continues to mount. Most of this research emphasizes material effects of bodily associations and conceives of gender and race in rather basic ways, stressing the habitual social coding of anatomy (e.g., sex categories) or other physical and/or hereditary markers of fixed social identities (e.g., race classifications). Early on, for instance, Phillips and Taylor (1980) showed how institutionalized skill classifications were derived in large part from the sex of those doing the task. In an extensive research program, Tomaskovic-Devey (1993) demonstrated that wage and institutionalized features of the labor process—such as degree of supervision and autonomy, task complexity and routinization, and promotion opportunities—develop around the gender and race profile of the people doing the work. Weeden (2002) also offered compelling evidence that occupational earnings are more affected by social closure (i.e., restricting an occupation to those of a particular gender and race profile) than by the complexity of the occupation's knowledge base.

More recently, symbolic approaches have demonstrated that—alongside, and at times regardless of, gender- and race-coded physical bodies—gender and race discourses are invoked to craft work in consequential ways (for a fuller review, see Ashcraft, 2006a). Studying the prestige of specialties in the medical profession, Hinze (1999) found that medical personnel in diverse physical bodies invoke gender symbolism to explain specialty complexity and value, such that surgical work linked to forceful hands and "sizeable balls" is ranked above the work of pediatrics and psychiatry, which are depicted as softer, easier, and emotionally sensitive. Reversing the usual emphasis on women's *exclusion* from the professions, Davies (1996) argued that women have long been included as silent partners (e.g., semi-skilled support staff) who enable professions in a dual sense: performing the adjunct labor that streamlines professional-client interaction while serving as the ready embodiment of what professionals are not. In this way, she indicted professionalism as "a conceptual frame that requires, but denies it requires, the Other" (p. 672), or as "a specific historical and cultural construction of masculinity" (p. 661). Kirkham and Loft's (1993) historical study of accountants is particularly compelling in this respect. Tracing the professionalization of accounting in England and Wales between 1870 and 1930, they show how gender discourse was the main means of securing the accountant's professional standing, creating a contrast between the elite knowledge of accountants and the simplistic "feminine" tasks of nearby clerks and bookkeepers. As these studies of gender and professions make clear, not only the *horizontal* division of labor (i.e., who does what tasks) but also the *vertical* division (i.e., how tasks are valued in relation to each other) rests on gender and race.

The growing interdisciplinary literature from which these examples are drawn make it difficult to deny that work is configured materially and symbolically in relation to those aligned with it. Organization and management theories that neglect this premise arguably misrecognize the fundamental character of work as a phenomenon independent of the body (Ashcraft, 2008). For scholars of difference, however, neglect comes with particular peril. Since the aim of most difference research is to facilitate work/place justice for those systematically controlled and excluded, it makes little sense to attempt social change primarily in work/places associated with privileged bodies. Especially if those forms and sites of work are valued precisely *for* or largely *on the basis of* that association, such efforts are self-defeating. In this light, the current guiding question (i.e., How can diversity be enhanced in professional workplaces?) not only reflects class bias, it also reflects disproportionate interest in work/places historically aligned with elite (heterosexual, able-bodied, and so forth) white men and relative indifference to labor forms and sites linked with Other bodies. Moreover, these twin habits are tightly linked, for the "class-ification" of work is in large part a function of bodily associations (e.g., as when accounting became professionalized on the grounds that "only elite, educated, masculine men can do this"). To engage this sort of inequity, a different guiding question becomes imperative, one that interrogates the complex historical and ongoing alignment of work with "bodies of difference." The alternative question advocated here asks: *In what ways and to what extent is work materially and symbolically configured in relation to embodied formations of difference, such as—but not limited to—race and gender?*

Engaging the Occupational Segregation Literature

As the previous selective review suggests, there is an ongoing interdisciplinary conversation addressed to this concern, widely known as the study of *occupational segregation* (and affiliated areas, like the sex/gender- and race-typing of work, labor force composition, division and hierarchy of labor). This enormous literature[1] examines various axes (i.e., horizontal and vertical) and levels of segregation, including job, organization (i.e., firm-level), institution (e.g., educational systems), state, regional (e.g., by city), (inter)national comparisons, labor market, industry, specific occupation or family thereof (typically focused on professions and semi-professions, such as medicine), individual selection, and popular culture. Among the recurring factors of interest are occupational prestige or status, preference or choice, and mobility; part- and full-time configurations of labor; and wage differentials. Although the literature is overwhelmingly quantitative, showing a proclivity for longitudinal trend analyses, in-depth qualitative analyses of historical cases have long been part of the scene as well. To date, sociology, economics, history, and (social) psychology are chief among the disciplinary perspectives represented in the literature.

As hinted earlier, most occupational segregation research treats gender and race demographically, or as measurable individual characteristics with corporeal markers and cognitive as well as sociocultural effects. Although scholars have shown abundant interest in both gender and race, these have mostly been studied separately (sometimes even in the same work; see Tomaskovic-Devey, 1993), with notable and mounting exceptions (e.g., Sokoloff, 1992). There can be little doubt, however, that gender has received the lion's share of attention. Indeed, Charles and Grusky's (2004) recent, critically acclaimed meta-review of the sex segregation literature—interestingly titled, *Occupational*

Ghettos—makes an explicit case for this isolated focus. The authors situate the gender division of labor as one of the most defining features of work around the world—a core organizing principle of economies, workplaces, individual and relational choices, as well as a central factor in preserving wage inequities. They argue that, in contrast with race relations, persistent cultural faith in gender essentialism (i.e., the popular belief that men and women are inherently different) has led to an intensification of the horizontal division of labor by gender, or what the authors call "hypersegregation." Specific to the U.S. national case, they observe: "Racist occupational stereotypes were once legion in the U.S. . . . but now are largely discredited and live on in weakened forms . . . This is all to suggest that gender inequality is a uniquely cultural form that rests heavily on essentialist processes" (p. 317).

Against the preponderance of quantitative methods and associated visions of gender and race as fixed-choice variables based on anatomy or ancestry, occupational segregation research more akin to critical organizational communication and critical management studies (or CMS) is on the rise. This research investigates the social and political construction of work realities through discourse and symbols in use (for a fuller review, see Ashcraft, 2006a). Although CMS scholars initially attended to gendered job segregation (e.g., Collinson & Knights, 1986), such projects appear to have declined as concern for the gender *of* organization (i.e., gendered organization) took hold in the field. As symbolic approaches to gendered work resurge, gender becomes less a stable social identity category based on physical and cognitive traits, and more a loose set of evolving cultural discourses (or available narrative prescriptions) about the body, sexual difference, and identity. Gender discourses offer ways of being and acting in the world, which people in diverse physical bodies take up—in more and less creative ways, and toward consequential ends—through their everyday, interactive identity performances. Scholars in this vein examine how mundane interaction maintains the labor divide between so called women's work and men's work (e.g., Benschop, Halsema, & Schreurs, 2001; Monaghan, 2002). They also study discourse tactics through which people cross the gender divide. While the bulk of attention has gone to women in male-dominated work (e.g., Spencer & Podmore, 1987), studies of men in female-dominated work are on a sharp rise (e.g., Cross & Bagilhole, 2002; Williams, 1993).

As this brief characterization suggests, gender has drawn far more attention than race in this emerging critical literature. Here too, as in the broader occupational segregation literature, gender continues to be approached in broadly binary terms, despite increasing acknowledgment of rampant variation in gendered work identities. A strong push toward intersectional analyses—or studies of interaction *among* multiple discourses of difference, like gender, race, sexuality, age, and class—has been a major force in building awareness of variation (e.g., Adib & Guerrier, 2003; Hossfeld, 1993; Mills, 1998). Yet the gender binary persists in scholarly vocabulary and research design and divisions (like studies of masculine and feminine, or women's and men's, work). Moreover, other embodied formations of difference (e.g., race, age, sexuality, physical or mental ability) are rarely considered as organizing principles of work in their own right. As yet, then, we have little sense of how else different bodies of work might factor into the social, political, and material construction of work. The open-ended framing of the alternative guiding question is meant to invite such inquiry.

Until recently, however, organizational communication scholarship on difference has remained mostly silent on matters of occupational segregation, preferring to see difference in terms of work*places* and interaction within them rather than as an organizing premise of labor itself (Ashcraft, 2006a; Medved, in press). I argue that, by taking up the alternate question posed here (i.e., How does difference organize work?), organizational communication scholars could develop meaningful contributions to critical global problems surrounding occupational segregation. Furthermore, bringing communication perspectives into this collaborative interdisciplinary inquiry stands to challenge yet also strengthen the field of organizational communication on at least three levels: (a) theoretically (e.g., the development of "communicational explanations"); (b) practically (e.g., enhancing our role in public and policy dialogue, as well as intervention programs); and thus, (c) politically (i.e., raising the field's profile in interdisciplinary conversations and the public eye). In this sense, communication scholarship on the *organization* of work through difference could exemplify common calls for engagement, which typically imply dual motives: genuinely making a difference while also promoting the integrity and relevance of the field. Elsewhere, Medved (in press) and I (Ashcraft, 2006a) sought to ignite interest within our field by reading occupational segregation literature through a communicative lens. In the remainder of this essay I take on a different task, weighing theoretical, practical, and political challenges entailed in the following question: How (much) would organizational communication scholars need to stretch in order to confront not only difference *in* or *of* organization, but also the *organization* of work through difference?

❖ ORGANIZATIONAL COMMUNICATION "MAKES A DIFFERENCE": FIVE WAYS TO ENGAGE THE ORGANIZATION OF WORK

The call put forth in the previous section asks more of difference researchers than a straightforward shift in research attention or even an expansion of disciplinary scope. As noted at the outset of the previous section, adjusting difference inquiry to accommodate the alternative question requires a change in dominant conceptions of difference, from difference as an individual, group, or organizational property to difference as an organizing principle of work itself, in and beyond the firm level. Moreover, adjusting difference research in this way entails significant shifts in the ontology and epistemology of organizational communication, as hinted in my earlier reference to an emerging strain of studies attuned to difference "at work" beyond conventional workplace boundaries. Shifting what counts as organizational communication and how we go about studying it cannot be taken lightly, because it induces serious theoretical, practical, and political challenges and possibilities that warrant careful consideration. In what follows, I propose five specific ways that organizational communication difference scholars can begin engaging these challenges and realizing the associated potential. To illustrate some of these, I draw on my own work—not because I imagine it as a path to be followed, but because struggles encountered there prompted these reflections.

1: Develop work-specific and site-flexible conceptions of organizational communication (i.e., dis-/re-locating work)

The call issued by this chapter has at least two major implications for how we conceive of organizational communication. First, it necessitates (re)centering work (i.e., jobs, tasks, labor) in studies of difference. As noted above, organizational communication scholars have historically resisted an explicit emphasis on work, and for good reason: to avoid the formation of another academic field in the service of business, managerial, or corporate interests. In response, it is worth noting several points. The sort of inquiry proposed here is avowedly critical, primarily in search of more equitable relations of difference and power, not "diversity management" for better business. This is *not* to say that feasibility drops out of the picture, but that organizations and managers are not presumed to own performance measures.

Rather, the practical questions become the following: Are alternative ways of configuring work more equitable *and* feasible, and in what sense—for whom, for what purposes, serving what and whose interests (Ashcraft, 2002)?

In addition, studying the organization of work does *not* amount to the exclusion of organizations with goals other than economic. After all, work gets done in government and nonprofit organizations as well, and labor is performed in family, leisure, and other enterprises culturally defined against work. In fact, crucial to the organization of work is the cultural (re)production of a split between work and so called labors of love in private, or domestic/family, life. The separation itself reflects relations of difference (e.g., the gendered division and hierarchy of life activities), and so merits close investigation.

I also do not advocate that we cease studying difference at the organization-level. Certainly, workplaces (as conventionally defined) are a pivotal site where work is organized; they are simply not the *only* site. As this implies, nowhere in the previous call is a suggestion that current efforts to understand organizational systems should be *replaced* by an exclusive emphasis on work. Regardless of whether they engage work *per se*, studies of difference *in* or *of* organizations remain vital to understanding the role of individuals, interactions, and firm-level systems. My contention is that we need an equally strong strand of research on the *organization* of work to be developed alongside these other strands.

But perhaps the most serious reservation about a turn toward work is this: What does such a turn mean for the *organizational* in organizational communication, and might it therefore compromise our distinctive analytical turf? Preliminary answers can be found in a similar call for management scholars to "return to work," issued by Barley and Kunda (2001) and modeled in empirical observations of scientists, engineers, technicians, and consultants as they go about their labors. Barley and Kunda (2001) explained that a nuanced understanding of work itself—the "concrete activities" through which people perform tasks amid changing economies and technologies—is indispensable to understanding emerging organizational systems (pp. 76, 84). They go so far as to argue that the drift away from work and toward abstract forms and governance systems in organization theory has hindered our knowledge of contemporary organizational life. Thus far, however, their back-to-work enterprise mostly entails observing the conduct of work at the firm level—studying the *organization* of work *in* organizations, or returning to work in *the* workplace. As the preceding discussion makes clear, I am advocating more.

I propose that we conceive of work not only as a concrete practice occurring amid institutional systems (Barley & Kunda, 2001), but also as a discourse formation that evolves across many sites of cultural activity (Carlone & Taylor, 1998). The latter vision revises the traditional meaning of *workplace*, building a theoretical rationale for studying the cultural (re)production of work in and across multiple arenas. For those concerned about surrendering the spotlight on organizations, it is worth underscoring that the study of multiple work*places* can enrich understanding of how work is organized in the conventional workplace. For example, organization scholars continue to call for greater intersection among sites of organization, occupation, and profession (e.g., Van Maanen & Barley, 1984). A plural conception of work*place* facilitates organization theory on the cusp of those relations (Ashcraft, 2008).

Herein lies the second major implication of the call: The claim that work is organized across cultural sites (i.e., that there are many work*places* not traditionally acknowledged) shatters any residual container metaphor of organizational communication. Instead, it invites us to consider the organizing property of communication (Cooren, 2000) in the myriad sites where work transpires—not only in the formal organizations where people perform tasks, but also in families, educational institutions, popular and trade discourse, legal and regulatory agencies, labor and professional associations, and wherever else we encounter representations, negotiations, and enactments of (who does what) work. In sum, communication becomes the pivotal site of organizing work, evolving in contexts ranging from store rooms and break rooms to living rooms and class rooms to rest rooms and bar rooms. As *evolving* suggests, the call is not simply to *spatially* displace and relocate work, but to do so *temporally* as well (Ashcraft, 2008). Simply put, work as a material notion is also an ongoing historical formation. In Van Maanen and Barley's (1984) terms, work "has a history of its own and, therefore, a context that is not organizationally limited" (p. 291).

Returning to the question of what happens to *organizational* communication, the short answer is that organization begins to traverse time and space, while communication becomes the mechanism of its production. This view can be condensed into the question: Where and how does (or has) communication organize(d) work? Such a move is consistent with a well-established body of scholarship seeking to know organization as a verb (Barley & Kunda, 2001) and as an ongoing process constituted in communication (Taylor & Van Every, 2000). In relation to these developments, the call advocated here entails further dislodging the verb (i.e., organizing) from the noun (i.e., organization).

2: Articulate communicational explanations of occupational segregation

Arguably, the overall aim of organizational communication scholarship is to weigh diverse conceptions of communication as a social practice, toward the articulation of "communicational explanations" of organizing that provide distinctive, useful alternatives to other sorts of accounts (Craig, 1999; Deetz, 1994). Scholars have produced, for example, communicative accounts of organizational culture, power relations, structuration processes, and the emergence of firms. Reviewing such efforts, some colleagues and I recently explored what it means, more precisely, to render a communicational explanation (Ashcraft, Kuhn, & Cooren, 2009). Whereas taking communication seriously once meant accounting for symbolic activity as a generative process, we argue that the bar is now set higher. Communication scholars are increasingly called to account for their apparent elision of materiality, as organization and work clearly exceed symbols and discourse, whatever their constitutive power. In this light, a communicational explanation becomes one that accounts for communication as the ongoing, situated activity through which the representational realm (e.g., symbols, discourses, notions) and the material realm (e.g., physical objects, locations, bodies) become entangled, transforming both realms and (re)producing lived realities in the process.

It is my contention that pursuing the alternate question posed in this chapter—rephrased accordingly, *How does communication organize work symbolically and materially through embodied formations of difference?*—can yield novel and useful communicational explanations of occupational segregation. For instance, the matter of *how* certain bodies become aligned with certain tasks (i.e., the constitution of the workbody relation) remains a highly contested matter in the interdisciplinary occupational segregation literature (for more on this and further support of the argument here, see Ashcraft, 2008). For many years, researchers have posited the relationship between jobs and the bodies who typically fill them as an outcome of economic, institutional, or cultural-political (e.g., patriarchal) forces. Scholars have especially deliberated whether tasks have inherent properties that, in light of cultural norms, summon particular bodies to perform them; or whether the initial sex and race composition of a job, more a product of other forces, leads to the gender and race coding of its tasks. Even as discursive and critical perspectives have begun to influence the debate, symbolic activity is rarely considered as a viable answer to this debate. At best, discourse is taken as a maintenance mechanism (or "inertial force"; see Charles & Grusky, 2004) that helps to preserve already existing gender and race labor divisions, rather than as a generative force that activates divisions in the first place.

Following Ashcraft, Kuhn, and Cooren (2009), I am coming to think that a communicative explanation departs from all of these accounts, that it treats the work-body relation as an indeterminate symbolic-material object constituted in communication. In other words, which bodies "logically" or "naturally" align with tasks is never self-evident; neither is it a matter of economic, institutional, or even cultural destiny. Instead, the work-body relation is always up for grabs to some extent and, thus, requires claims to be staked—a social construction contest of sorts (Ashcraft, 2008). Communication is the dynamic mechanism of that struggle; it is how individual and institutional voices vie for the particular combinations of materiality and symbolism in which they are invested.

Thus far, I have attempted to illustrate such a communicative explanation with the historical case of U.S. commercial airline pilots (Ashcraft, 2007; Ashcraft & Mumby, 2004). Today, we might assume that flying labor was readily aligned with white men due mostly to task properties, cultural norms, and institutional links with the military, but such is not the case. By the late 1920s, both men and women were flying in the public eye. Dominant images of male pilots up to that point (e.g., the "intrepid birdman" of air shows, the rugged airmail pilot, the daredevil "barnstormer," the dashing Hollywood flier, the WWI "ace") put the pilot's body front and center, provoking adoration for his physical and sexual prowess but also epidemic fear of flight as the hazardous task of supermen (Corn, 1979). Constituents in the general aviation industry countered this fear with the emerging "ladybird" or "ladyflier" image (personified by Amelia Earhart and a sizeable cohort of female pilots). Promoters overtly employed ladyfliers to act in a hyper-feminine fashion, even primping in the public eye, because the point was to shame men into flying with the message: "'Flying must be easy and safe if *she* can do it" (Corn, 1979). But the mid-1920s saw the public in the throes of a love affair with the ladybird, and her intense popularity launched unanticipated turns. Commentators began to muse about whether flying was women's work; and constructions of the pilot's task began to range wildly, from physically and technically taxing, high-risk labor to a graceful, artful, sensitive, intuitive pastime.

It was into this tangle of images—none of which inspired public faith in flight as a viable mode of transportation—that the commercial aviation industry intervened. Responding to faltering ticket sales and widespread anxiety about airline safety, airlines and the budding pilot union collaborated in the late 1920s to transform the pilot into a dependable professional (Hopkins, 1998). The transformation involved a full-body makeover to minimize physicality with the cloak of professional regalia, such as that of a ship's captain—an officer's uniform complete with symbols of rank, a navigation kit housing technical manuals and resembling a briefcase, an intercom system broadcasting the invisible voice of authority, and so on. Ironically, this careful overhaul of the pilot's body was designed to erase it. Against the hyperfeminized body of the ladybird, the commercial airline pilot was reborn as a reliable professional. The communicative dust had mostly settled by the mid- to late-1930s, well before WWII brought a significant influx of military-trained pilots.

As this research suggests, neither initial demographics nor intrinsic task content adequately explain the case of airline pilots. Neither did status closure processes nor institutional strategies of occupational closure precede the social construction contest over the pilot's body and the work of flight. Indeed, the discursive struggle that activated the ladyflier and professional airline pilot *enabled* such processes and strategies. In other words, as communication constitutes the work-body relationship, it facilitates representational and material conditions in which certain economic, institutional, and physical realities are more likely to find footing.

The airline pilot case supplies one tangible example of a communicative explanation of occupational segregation and its (common yet understudied) intersection with professionalization (Ashcraft, 2008). But by asking *as a field* how communication wields difference to organize work, we could begin to develop a recognizable collective voice that contributes useful alternative theories and allied intervention tactics to a major interdisciplinary concern. In short, we could make a difference on a larger scale, both theoretically and practically.

3: Challenge current conceptions of gender and develop innovative vocabularies of difference (i.e., no more gender alone!)

Already, organizational communication scholars have contributed significantly to interdisciplinary literatures on gender and organization. For instance, we have joined CMS and other scholars in calling out the tendency, among mainstream and critical analyses, to treat gender as a special interest in otherwise gender-neutral organizational systems and relations. We have also taken vital steps toward questioning binary models of gender and cultivating intersectional consciousness—that is, awareness of how embodied formations of difference such as gender, race, and class are entwined. Thus far, however, these steps have blazed more conceptual than empirical ground (Ashcraft, 2009).

I suggest that it is time for organizational communication scholars to systematically *conduct* (not only call for) analyses of difference that balance, on the one hand, sensitivity to intersections of difference as they unfold in work contexts and, on the other, commitment to theorizing formations of difference beyond gender in their own right. Stated bluntly, at this moment in the discipline, we need no more analyses of gender alone; in fact, the persistence of gender-only approaches in our field hinders its potential for broader contributions.

My call for a moratorium on analyses of gender alone takes two forms. First, difference scholarship can begin to genuinely exemplify the claim that gender identities in practice vary widely precisely because they are simultaneously about race, class, sexuality, and so forth. In this sense, difference scholars (myself included) can usefully apply our criticism of gender-neutral organization studies to our own work: Just as relations of power are never experienced in the abstract (i.e., we all inhabit gendered bodies), so gender is never lived in the generic (i.e., we all inhabit bodies that are simultaneously marked by factors other than gender). A major obstacle to making good on this claim is the fact that scholars, too, are trapped in an obstinately binary gender vocabulary (Alvesson & Billing, in press). A decent start, therefore, is relentless accountability to the following questions: *Which* women, *which* men? How, when, and why are references to *women and men* and *masculine and feminine* (counter)productive, and what alternative terms might usefully refuse or reframe the binary, activating sensitivity to difference in situ? I am skeptical about the adequacy of referring to "multiple masculinities" (e.g., Collinson & Hearn, 1996) and femininities, because this habit continues to imply gender as a primary difference a priori and to situate plurality within a dualistic frame, risking the impression that the masculine-feminine divide is better understood as a continuum of options (Ashcraft, 2009). To fully realize the claim that gender is never lived in the generic, our notions of masculine and feminine need far more than plurality. Among other radical encounters with difference, they need, for example, the heteronormativity supporting them utterly upended (Rich, 2006).

Calling for the suspension of gender-only analyses is *not* to say that we should stop theorizing the operation of other difference formations in their own right. It *is* to say, rather, that we have overdeveloped our understanding of gender as an organizing principle relative to other forms of difference. As such, there is actually ample danger in theorizing difference off of gender—in assuming that race, sexuality, and other dimensions are parallel organizing mechanisms that function similarly (Collins et al., 1995). Put simply, it is premature to cluster all forms of difference as organizing principles, even in the name of intersectionality. Instead, we can temporarily prioritize the examination of difference formations beyond gender—not in isolation (e.g., race alone), but in their own right (e.g., race as a specific organizing mechanism, entangled yet also distinct in comparison with gender).

The second form of my case against analyses of gender alone also requires balance; it involves recognizing that, as much as gender is an ever-pressing factor, organizing is always about more than gender and other forms of difference. Gender and organization scholars have pressed the former point of omni-relevance, as noted earlier, but have shown understandable reticence to affirm the latter claim. I would argue, however, that admitting (and even foregrounding) the salience of other organizing factors does not relegate difference to the backseat. On the contrary, it acknowledges, and engages difference with, the complexity of pressures people face. Such a stance opens new possibilities for dialogue across organization studies, and I see this as a shared responsibility. In other words, the so-called ghettoization of difference research does not simply reflect mainstream unwillingness to listen; it also reflects the tendency of difference scholarship not to frame problems in widely shared terms. I wish more organization scholars would ask: How is this problem *also* about difference? But I also wish difference scholars would ask more often: What *else* is this problem about?

In sum, my plea for "no more gender alone" is an argument against analyses of gender as (a) detached from other differences (or as the primary difference a priori) and (b) detached from other organizing phenomena. Phrased in more affirmative terms, it is an argument for engaging intersectionality in its most common usage (i.e., the meeting of gender, race, class, and so on), as well as enhanced intersectionality between difference scholarship and other research areas in work and organization studies. I do not mean to claim that gender and organizational communication studies is (or even has been) more prone to gender-only perspectives than other difference disciplines. On the contrary, it is my sense that these struggles—to substantively integrate multiple differences into our analyses, to let go of lingering gender binaries, to engage difference scholarship with wider audiences—are shared among gender and organization scholars in many fields. However, if we could collectively prioritize these struggles and make substantial progress toward helpful alternatives, we would be developing contributions of great value to the interdisciplinary conversation on difference, work, and organization.

Returning to the occupational segregation literature affords a provocative interdisciplinary example of the consequences of treating gender in isolation from (a) other forms of difference and (b) other organizing phenomena. As previously reviewed, the gender and race segregation of labor have been treated mostly as separate phenomena and measured independently, while many scholars maintain that gender segregation is more pervasive than racial segregation (Charles & Grusky, 2004). But to what extent might this claim and the imposing statistics supporting it stem from the fact that gender is still operationalized around a binary variable, whereas the same is not tenable with racial and ethnic identities? And is a binary gender variable defensible, particularly in light of overwhelming empirical evidence of immense variation within so called women's and men's work? Such variation—for example, between the sorts of women who welcome guests to a fine hotel and those who clean their messy rooms, or between the kinds of men who fly commercial planes and those who serve the passengers in the cabin—hinge on intersections with other formations of difference, especially race, sexuality, class, age, ability, and nation. If we took such variation seriously and theorized from the lived reality that there is no gender in the generic, what would be the sense, meaning, or utility of claims about the binary division of labor? At the very least, it seems that occupational segregation research is helping to bolster, through the discourse of scientific methods, the cultural "fact" of two, and only two, sexes. In so doing, it compresses a wealth of evidence indicating otherwise and ignores its immersion in the very cultural patterns it seeks to challenge. In short, precisely because gender is one of many organizing principles, it is increasingly unacceptable to theorize it as an entirely discrete phenomenon.

Most of the occupational segregation literature could also be said to illustrate the second form of gender-only analysis: detachment from other organizing phenomena—in this case, mainstream theories of the organization of work. As I argued earlier and demonstrate elsewhere (Ashcraft, 2008), this detachment is the result of omissions on all sides. For example, scholars "returning to work" in studies of management and the professions continue to neglect the bodies performing labor, as if they are (co)incidental to the organization of work. Meanwhile, occupational segregation scholars tend to address one another rather than confront mainstream theories—of professionalization or knowledge-intensive work, for example—with the role of difference in the cultural and economic evaluation of labor (for examples of exceptions, see Weeden, 2002; Witz, 1992). Consequently, we know little about how occupational segregation enables professionalization, much less how taking difference seriously would disrupt other traditional models of work.

If organizational communication difference scholars prioritized battling both fronts of gender detachment (i.e., from other differences and organizing phenomena), the resulting contributions could even exceed those of communicational explanations because they would introduce new tools and models (e.g., difference vocabularies) desperately needed across disciplinary lenses. As illustrated by the earlier example of occupational segregation in the professionalization of airline pilots, studying the work-body relation as an evolving historical formation provides one promising path forward. Not only would such studies address the meeting of discourse and materiality, they would also ask how embodied formations of difference become relevant in specific work contexts, rather than presume gender or any other difference as primary in the abstract. In this way, alternative difference vocabularies might arise from the diverse ways in which bodies are invoked to organize work. But this is only one possibility, and it will take concentrated collective effort to generate others.

4: Expand the methodological preferences and capacities of difference scholarship (i.e., adding to the toolbox, fostering new talents)

This section began by emphasizing how the revised conceptions of difference and organizational communication embedded in the alternative question induce ontological and epistemological change. Here, I stress the latter—specifically, methodological aspects of the challenge. Like most organizational communication scholarship that is both critical and empirical, difference research reflects a nearly totalizing preference for qualitative research methods. Most often, these involve participant observation and interviewing; and textually based forms of (rhetorical and discourse) analysis are increasingly included in the favored toolbox (e.g., Ashcraft & Flores, 2003; Bell & Forbes, 1994; Holmer Nadesan & Trethewey, 2000). To examine the organization of work across space and time, these qualitative techniques need stretching.

First, the notion of multiple work*places* induces site and boundary dilemmas for participant observation and interview methods. Whereas conventional organizational ethnography entails immersion in an organization site to study people and activities that members deem within their borders, a dis- or re-located conception of work raises the question: Where (and how far) do we go to know work? There are no easy answers to the associated dilemmas of research design, but it is clear that difference scholars cannot effectively theorize the spatially dispersed organization of work without developing skills in multi-site qualitative methods. Moreover, the relevant sites may not all be organizational in the usual sense. We might need methodological lessons from our colleagues in interpersonal and family communication studies, or archival techniques from our rhetorical and media studies colleagues. Second, while recent difference scholarship employs textually based analytic methods, our collective training in this area—as a subfield—is currently insufficient to capture the temporally diffuse organization of work. Organizational communication difference scholars need greater agility with historical, archival research to address the alternate question posed above. As with studying multiple sites, we may initially turn to collaboration with other disciplinary colleagues (e.g., rhetoricians) who are more familiar with such methods. Ultimately, however, methodological training specific to organizational communication studies will need to be enhanced accordingly.

Finally, we cannot continue to treat quantitative methods as necessarily antithetical to critical difference inquiry. I do not mean to minimize vital critical and feminist critiques of positivist social science (e.g., Hawkins, 1989); my point is that such critiques no longer warrant (if they ever did) the near-categorical exclusion of quantitative methods that they are still invoked to support. In the wake of the linguistic (or interpretive) turn, post-positivist research methods are not inevitably incompatible with social constructionist ontology (Miller, 2000). If for no other reason than the quantitative bent of the interdisciplinary literature on occupational segregation, we cannot afford to dismiss the potential of quantitative critical analyses and innovative quantitative-qualitative fusions. Doing so diminishes our capacity to participate in interdisciplinary conversation and curtails our ability to make a difference beyond academic communities. Instead, we can grow our collective dexterity with methodological vocabularies and techniques, mindful rather than fearful of the tensions and politics incurred.

5: Cultivate interdisciplinary and international affiliations (i.e., practice disciplinary outreach)

As noted earlier, the division and hierarchy of labor by gender and race is a global, interdisciplinary concern. Although individual organizational communication scholars are regularly cited by scholars in other disciplines (especially when the former publish in the disciplinary outlets of the latter), the collective field and its difference scholarship continue to struggle for broader disciplinary recognition. In other words, scholars of work and organization in other fields rarely seem to seek out communication perspectives (say, in *Communication Monographs* or even *Management Communication Quarterly*) unless particular names or works cross their path. (For more on this, see Ashcraft et al., 2009; Mumby & Ashcraft, 2006.)

However we may mourn this condition, the upshot is that the initial work of outreach falls to organizational communication scholars. This can entail many loosely connected individual and collaborative activities. At the very least, it involves purposeful reading and publishing beyond communication circles. To engage the interdisciplinary study of occupational segregation, for example, difference scholars must develop not only methodological dexterity, but also a capacity to seek, read, and respond to work from other disciplines, as well as deftness in translating communicational accounts for external audiences. Redressing the U.S.-centric tendencies of organizational communication scholarship, difference researchers would also do well to learn more about the international organization of work and to frame our research problems and contributions with a sharp eye toward concerns and literatures beyond North American borders. Admittedly, these are not simple tasks for those simultaneously trying for tenure in their home discipline. Hence, the greater share of this work may initially fall to senior scholars who can encourage a more interdisciplinary, international consciousness in students of difference by integrating broader literatures and research problems into graduate seminars.

Of equal importance, and stemming in part from reading and publishing widely, effective outreach necessitates strategic and supportive network-building. Speaking practically, organizational communication scholars will have to find creative ways to reach out beyond our discipline—to specific scholars; research projects, consortia, and centers; interdisciplinary and international conferences; grant opportunities and funding agencies; and other people and institutions concerned with the organization of work via difference—in order to nourish the four developments mentioned here with rich outside influences and then share them beyond our own disciplinary silo. As I have been learning recently (Ashcraft, 2006b), it may actually be through participating in wider conversations—fostering relationships across disciplinary and continental divides—that we best begin to appreciate what organizational communication can offer.

❖ CONCLUSION

This chapter has made two broad moves: first, to challenge and change the underlying question motivating difference inquiry and, second, to propose specific implementation strategies that reflect sensitivity to the significant challenges—ontological and epistemological as well as practical and political—sparked by such a change. To make both moves, I have drawn on struggles encountered in my work and explored some ways in which those are not so much idiosyncratic as indicative of larger patterns in the field. My intent is not to generalize from my own case (after all, that would be suspect auto/ethnographic practice!) but, rather, to share my experience in the hopes of hearing yours and, ultimately, of stimulating collective contemplation. Applying critical insights about the politics of identity closer to home, it becomes clear that our individual efforts to manage the identity of a research program not only reflect our own participation in systems of race, class, gender, and other axes of difference, but also interact with our collective sense of self, shaping our potential for being and acting as a field. In a twist on the chapter's title, then, we can better know— and do—our work through the communication of difference as well.

❖ NOTE

1. For diverse samples of acclaimed reviews that illustrate, elaborate, and complicate the characterization and terms provided here, see Blackburn, Browne, Brooks, & Jarman, (2002), Bradley (1989), Charles and Grusky (2004), Hakim (1992), Reskin (1993), and Tomaskovic-Devey (1993).

❖ REFERENCES

Adib, A., & Guerrier, Y. (2003). The interlocking of gender with nationality, race, ethnicity and class: The narratives of women in hotel work. *Gender, Work and Organization, 10*(4), 413–432.

Alvesson, M., Ashcraft, K. L., & Thomas, R. (2008). Identity matters: Reflections on the construction of identity scholarship in organization studies. *Organization, 15*(1), 5–28.

Alvesson, M., & Billing, Y. D. (in press). *Understanding gender and organizations* (2nd ed.). London: Sage.

Alvesson, M., & Willmott, H. (1992). On the idea of emancipation in management and organization studies. *Academy of Management Review, 17,* 432–464.

Ashcraft, K. L. (2002). Practical ambivalence and troubles in translation. *Management Communication Quarterly, 16*, 113–117.

Ashcraft, K. L. (2004). Gender, discourse, and organizations: Framing a shifting relationship. In D. Grant, C. Hardy, C. Oswick, N. Phillips, & L. L. Putnam (Eds.), *Handbook of organizational discourse* (pp. 275–298). Thousand Oaks, CA: Sage.

Ashcraft, K. L. (2005). Feminist organizational communication studies: Engaging gender in public and private. In S. May & D. K. Mumby (Eds.), *Engaging organizational communication theory* (pp. 141–169). Thousand Oaks, CA: Sage.

Ashcraft, K. L. (2006a). Back to work: Sights/sites of difference in gender and organizational communication studies. In B. Dow & J. T. Wood (Eds.), *The SAGE handbook of gender and communication* (pp. 97–122). Thousand Oaks, CA: Sage.

Ashcraft, K. L. (2006b). Falling from a humble perch: Re-reading organizational communication with an attitude of alliance. *Management Communication Quarterly, 19*(4), 645–652.

Ashcraft, K. L. (2007). Appreciating the "work" of discourse: Occupational identity and difference as organizing mechanisms in the case of commercial airline pilots. *Discourse and Communication, 1*, 9–36.

Ashcraft, K. L. (2008). *Bringing the body back to work, whatever and wherever that is: Occupational evolution, segregation, and identity.* Paper presented at the National Communication Association.

Ashcraft, K. L. (2009). Gender and diversity: Other ways to 'make a difference.' In H. Willmott, M. Alvesson, & T. Bridgman (Eds.), *Handbook of critical management studies* (pp. 304–327). Oxford: Oxford University Press.

Ashcraft, K. L., & Allen, B. J. (2003). The racial foundation of organizational communication. *Communication Theory, 13*, 5–38.

Ashcraft, K. L., & Flores, L. A. (2003). "Slaves with white collars": Decoding a contemporary crisis of masculinity. *Text and Performance Quarterly, 23*, 1–29.

Ashcraft, K. L., & Kedrowicz, A. (2002). Self-direction or social support? Nonprofit empowerment and the tacit employment contract of organizational communication studies. *Communication Monographs, 69*, 88–110.

Ashcraft, K. L., Kuhn, T., & Cooren, F. (2009). Constitutional amendments: "Materializing" organizational communication. In J. P. Walsh & A. P. Brief (Eds.), *The Academy of Management Annals, 3*, 1–64.

Ashcraft, K. L., & Mumby, D. K. (2004). *Reworking gender: A feminist communicology of organization.* Thousand Oaks, CA: Sage.

Barley, S. R., & Kunda, G. (2001). Bringing work back in. *Organization Science, 12*(1), 76–95.

Bell, E. L., & Forbes, L. C. (1994). Office folklore in the academic paperwork empire: The interstitial space of gendered (con)texts. *Text and Performance Quarterly, 14*, 181–196.

Benschop, Y., Halsema, L., & Schreurs, P. (2001). The division of labour and inequalities between the sexes: An ideological dilemma. *Gender, Work and Organization, 8*(1), 1–18.

Blackburn, R. M., Browne, J., Brooks, B., & Jarman, J. (2002). Explaining gender segregation. *The British Journal of Sociology, 53*(4), 513–536.

Bradley, H. (1989). *Men's work, women's work: A sociological history of the sexual division of labour in employment.* Minneapolis: University of Minnesota Press.

Buzzanell, P. M. (Ed.). (2000). *Rethinking organizational and managerial communication from feminist perspectives.* Thousand Oaks, CA: Sage.

Calás, M. B. (1992). An/other silent voice? Representing "Hispanic woman" in organizational texts. In A. J. Mills & P. Tancred (Eds.), *Gendering organizational analysis* (pp. 201–221). Newbury Park, CA: Sage.

Calás, M. B., & Smircich, L. (1991). Voicing seduction to silence leadership. *Organization Studies, 12,* 567–602.

Carlone, D., & Taylor, B. (1998). Organizational communication and cultural studies. *Communication Theory, 8,* 337–367.

Charles, M., & Grusky, D. B. (2004). *Occupational ghettos: The worldwide segregation of women and men.* Stanford, CA: Stanford University Press.

Cheney, G. (2000). Thinking differently about organizational communication: Why, how, and where? *Management Communication Quarterly, 14,* 132–141.

Cheney, G., & Ashcraft, K. L. (2007). Considering "the professional" in communication studies: Implications for theory and research within and beyond the boundaries of organizational communication. *Communication Theory, 17,* 146–175.

Cloud, D. L. (2005). Fighting words: Labor and the limits of communication at Staley, 1993 to 1996. *Management Communication Quarterly, 18*(4), 509–542.

Collins, P. H., Maldonado, L. A., Takagi, D. Y., Thorne, B., Weber, L., & Winant, H. (1995). Symposium: On West & Fenstermaker's "Doing Difference." *Gender and Society, 9*(491–513).

Collinson, D., & Hearn, J. (1996). "Men" at "work": Multiple masculinities/multiple workplaces. In M. Mac an Ghaill (Ed.), *Understanding masculinities: Social relations and cultural arenas* (pp. 61–76). Buckingham, UK: Open University Press.

Collinson, D., & Knights, D. (1986). 'Men only': Theories and practices of job segregation. In D. Knights & H. Willmott (Eds.), *Gender and the labour process* (pp. 141–178). Aldershot: Gower.

Cooren, F. (2000). *The organizing property of communication.* Amsterdam: John Benjamins.

Corn, J. J. (1979). Making flying "unthinkable": Women pilots and the selling of aviation, 1927–1940. *American Quarterly, 31,* 556–571.

Cotter, D. A., Hermsen, J. M., & Vanneman, R. (2001). Women's work and working women: The demand for female labor. *Gender and Society, 15,* 429–452.

Craig, R. T. (1999). Communication theory as a field. *Communication Theory, 9*(2), 119–161.

Cross, S., & Bagilhole, B. (2002). Girls' jobs for the boys? Men, masculinity and non-traditional occupations. *Gender, Work and Organization, 9*(2), 204–226.

Davies, C. (1996). The sociology of the professions and the profession of gender. *Sociology, 30*(4), 661–678.

Deetz, S. (1994). Representational practices and the political analysis of corporations: Building a communication perspective in organizational studies. In B. Kovacic (Ed.), *New approaches to organizational communication* (pp. 211–244). Albany: State University of New York Press.

Ganesh, S. (2007). Grassroots agendas and global discourses: Tracking a planning process on children's issues. *International and Intercultural Communication Annual, 30,* 289–316.

Gibson, M. K., & Papa, M. J. (2000). The mud, the blood, and the beer guys: Organizational osmosis in blue-collar work groups. *Journal of Applied Communication Research, 28,* 68–88.

Hakim, C. (1992). Explaining trends in occupational segregation: The measurement, causes, and consequences of the sexual division of labour. *European Sociological Review, 8,* 127–152.

Hawkins, K. (1989). Exposing masculine science: An alternative feminist approach to the study of women's communication. In K. Carter & C. Spitzack (Eds.), *Doing research on women's communication: Perspectives on theory and method* (pp. 40–64). Norwood, NJ: Ablex.

Hinze, S. W. (1999). Gender and the body of medicine or at least some body parts: (Re)constructing the prestige hierarchy of medical specialties. *The Sociological Quarterly, 40*(2), 217–239.

Holmer Nadesan, M. (1996). Organizational identity and space of action. *Organization Studies, 17,* 49–81.

Holmer Nadesan, M., & Trethewey, A. (2000). Performing the enterprising subject: Gendered strategies for success(?). *Text and Performance Quarterly, 20,* 223–250.

Hopkins, G. E. (1998). *The airline pilots: A study in elite unionization.* Cambridge, MA: Harvard University Press.

Hossfeld, K. J. (1993). "Their logic against them": Contradictions in sex, race, and class in Silicon Valley. In P. S. Rothenberg (Ed.), *Feminist frameworks: Alternative theoretical accounts of the relations between women and men* (pp. 346–358). New York: McGraw-Hill.

Kirkham, L. M., & Loft, A. (1993). Gender and the construction of the professional accountant. *Accounting, Organizations and Society, 18*(6), 507–558.

Lewis, L. K. (2005). The civil society sector: A review of critical issues and research agenda for organizational communication scholars. *Management Communication Quarterly, 19*(2), 238–267.

Medved, C. E. (in press). Crossing and transforming occupational and household gendered divisions of labor: Reviewing literatures and deconstructing divisions. *Communication Yearbook, 33.*

Miller, K. (2000). Common ground from the post-positivist perspective: From "straw person" argument to collaborative co-existence. In S. R. Corman & M. S. Poole (Eds.), *Perspectives on organizational communication: Finding common ground* (pp. 46–67). New York: Guilford.

Mills, A. J. (1998). Cockpits, hangars, boys and galleys: Corporate masculinities and the development of British Airways. *Gender, Work and Organization, 5,* 172–188.

Monaghan, L. F. (2002). Hard men, shop boys and others: Embodying competence in a masculinist occupation. *The Sociological Review, 50,* 334–355.

Mumby, D. K., & Ashcraft, K. L. (2006). Striking out from the backwater: Organizational communication studies and gendered organization (A response to Martin and Collinson). *Gender, Work, and Organization, 13,* 68–90.

Phillips, A., & Taylor, B. (1980). Sex and skill: Notes toward a feminist economics. *Feminist Review, 6*(7), 79–88.

Putnam, L. L., Phillips, N., & Chapman, P. (1996). Metaphors of communication and organization. In S. R. Clegg, C. Hardy, & W. R. Nord (Eds.), *Handbook of organization studies* (pp. 375–408). London: Sage.

Redding, W. C., & Tompkins, P. K. (1988). Organizational communication: Past and present tenses. In G. Goldhaber & G. Barnett (Eds.), *Handbook of organizational communication* (pp. 5–33). Norwood, NJ: Ablex.

Reskin, B. F. (1993). Sex segregation in the workplace. *Annual Review of Sociology, 19,* 241–270.

Rich, C. O. (2006). *(Un)binding binaries in feminist organizational communication: Toward a queer theoretical approach to sex/gender/sexuality/ities in organization.* Paper presented at the National Communication Association.

Smith, R. C. (1993). *Images of organizational communication: Root-metaphors of the organization-communication relation.* Paper presented at the International Communication Association.

Sokoloff, N. J. (1992). *Black women and white women in the professions: Occupational segregation by race and gender, 1960–1980.* New York: Routledge.

Spencer, A., & Podmore, D. (Eds.). (1987). *In a man's world: Essays on women in male-dominated professions.* London: Tavistock.

Taylor, J. R., & Van Every, E. J. (2000). *The emergent organization: Communication as its site and surface.* Mahwah, NJ: Lawrence Erlbaum.

Tomaskovic-Devey, D. (1993). *Gender & racial inequality at work: The sources & consequences of job segregation.* Ithaca, NY: ILR Press.

Van Maanen, J., & Barley, S. R. (1984). Occupational communities: Culture and control in organizations. *Research in Organizational Behavior, 6,* 287–365.

Weeden, K. A. (2002). Why do some occupations pay more than others? Social closure and earnings inequality in the United States. *American Journal of Sociology, 108*(1), 55–101.

Williams, C. L. (Ed.). (1993). *Doing "women's work": Men in non-traditional occupations.* London: Sage.

Witz, A. (1992). *Professions and patriarchy.* London: Routledge.

Wright, R., & Jacobs, J. A. (1994). Male flight from computer work: A new look at occupational resegregation and ghettoization. *American Sociological Review, 59,* 511–536.

2

Intersecting Difference

A Dialectical Perspective

Linda L. Putnam, Jody Jahn, and Jane Stuart Baker

Research on gender and diversity is rooted in conceptions of difference. Drawn from lay definitions of this concept, *difference* typically refers to dispersions among categories or distinctions among members of reference groups. In its Latin roots, *different* means "to differ *from*" or "*to move away from*" a central point of reference (Reeder, 1996). Thus, to be different implies a comparison to a focal point. In the gender literature, the focal point is typically the dominant group; thus, the comparison group becomes the *other* or the *outlier*.

Conceptions of difference in the diversity literature also draw on this broad-based definition. Even while valuing heterogeneity, the diversity literature continues to treat difference as movement away from a focal point, which leads to such designations as the *majority*, the *minority*, or the *underrepresented* (Cox, 1994). Moreover, treating difference as movement in relation to a focal group inadvertently hides or ignores political, historical, and contextual reasons for differences, especially among such categories as gender, race, ethnicity, sexual orientation, age, and disability.

This definition of difference treats it as a universal concept and fails to problematize its variety of meanings, assumptions, and types

of relationships. Subtle nuances emerge in how the concept of difference surfaces in the extant organizational literature. We begin this
chapter with a brief review of three approaches to the study of difference
that are prevalent in the literature: difference as deficient, difference
as value added, and difference as discursive practices. Then, we advocate a dialectical perspective to examine how difference is constructed through language and power relationships. Finally, we
provide exemplars for applying dialectical analysis to the study of
difference: a set of examples rooted in intersectionality and another
one that centers on employee diversity networks.

❖ DIFFERENCE AS DEFICIENT

Early work on gender in the workplace typically focused on sex differences or a comparison of men and women in leadership roles, performance, evaluation, pay, and promotions (Eagly & Johnson, 1990).
Difference, defined by biological identification or sex-role socialization,
emerges as relatively stable over time, is typically centered on women
(especially White, middle-class women), and is oriented toward male-
dominated patterns of success in corporate life (Ashcraft & Mumby
2004). From this view, difference is cast in terms of what is privileged,
while everything else is considered deficient. Three broad themes highlight ways that this deficiency emerges: (1) difference as deviations
from an ideal or *valued* model, (2) difference as devalued categories,
and (3) difference as unsuitable fit.

Difference as Deviations

Consistent with lay definitions of difference, research on sex-role stereotypes in the workplace focuses on dispersions or deviations from an
ideal type. This work emphasizes binaries (e.g., man/woman), differen-
tiates feminine qualities (e.g., communal, nurturing) from masculine
traits and behaviors (e.g., competitive, agentic), and compares global
evaluations of women and men, both empirically and prescriptively,
regarding the nature of these traits and the values placed on them
(Wajcman, 1996). At the empirical level, scholars report inconsistent findings between and within groups of men and women and continue to
struggle with the amount of variance that holds across situations
(Harrison & Klein, 2007; Yoder & Kahn, 2003). Researchers have developed terms such as *alpha biases* to designate gross differences and *beta
biases* to signify minimal differences (Hare-Mustin & Marecek, 1988).

Yet even though scholars find minimal differences between men and women and often considerable similarities in the management styles of top leaders (Wajcman, 1996), the research typically aligns privilege with traits deemed successful, namely drive, motivation, and authoritative styles typified by men and deemed deficient for women (Peterson, 2007). Thus, difference becomes linked to deviations from a valued masculine ideal. These deviations are reinforced through social sanctioning in which women enact masculine behaviors to gain legitimacy in the workplace but are ironically punished for acting too masculine (Diekman & Goodfriend, 2006).

Difference as Devalued Categories

An alternative to sex-role stereotypes casts difference as a typology or a set of schemas that recognizes multiple categories rather than binary comparisons between men and women. Nested in patterns of thought, gender schemas are mental models based on functional, evaluative, and relational notions of differences: for example, a *career* woman as a particular type of woman (Foldy, 2006). Typologies, however, typically align with the ways that men gain and legitimate power through relationships with women. For example, drawing on organizational culture, Kanter (1977) developed a typology of women's informal organizational relationships (e.g., as mother, seductress, pet, iron maiden) and Parker (2005) identified typologies of Black women relative to both White men and women (Sapphire/Jezzabel), Mammy, Black Matriarch, Superwoman, Castrator, welfare queen, and over-achieving Black lady). These derogatory categories, however, continue to devalue women and minorities. In a similar way, women in the workplace develop their own categories to dis-identify with other women. For example, women who are farmers distance themselves from farmer's wives (Pilgeram, 2007) and female executives differentiate themselves from "dolly birds," "chit chatty women," and "ditzy girls" (Olsson & Walker, 2004). Research that explores difference as typologies of gender schemas neglects the processes and practices by which these categories are constituted and how they become imbued with power relationships.

Difference as Unsuitable Fit

Difference as unsuitable fit locates gender in jobs, division of labor, and organizational levels. This approach, also rooted in gender as a variable and in comparisons between men and women, focuses on differences in assignments, expertise, and career paths based on the presumed fit and the relative value of the job. For example, while men play central production roles, women are often placed in the periphery of organizations in low paying and less prestigious customer service jobs or in boundary spanning positions with partnering firms (Skuratowicz & Hunter, 2004). This notion of difference as fit becomes particularly salient when organizations enact gender images by placing women in care work and men in technical positions, particularly during organizational changes (Lindsay, 2008) or when self-managing teams play out the family metaphor of men as breadwinners and women as emotional supporters (Kugelberg, 2006; Ollilainen & Calasanti, 2007). Difference as fit is closely related to deviations from the ideal type when managerial elites hold firm views of the "ideal worker" as masculine and enact these views in organizational ideologies and placement practices (Ozbilgin & Woodward, 2004).

In summary, difference as deficient treats men and women as binary categories, compares the groups, and assesses deviations from an ideal type—that is, a masculine model of success. Originating in the 1970s when women were entering managerial positions (Henning & Jardim, 1977), difference as deficiency is clearly prevalent in the current literature. Whether it stems from sex-role stereotypes or division of labor, scholars, including many psychologists, critique this work as "empirically unknowable," unable to sort causal relationships, often splintering similarities, and devoid of social and cultural context factors (Yoder & Kahn, 2003). This perspective continues to perpetuate double binds in which women are damned if they adopt masculine traits and damned if they don't (Ashcraft & Mumby, 2004). Hence, whether the research findings bolster or challenge the status quo, they cannot change it (Yoder & Kahn, 2003). Finally, this approach treats organizations as sites in which gender differences occur rather than as social constructions of gendered practices. Thus, the difference as deficient approach rests on "a tired logic" (Ashcraft & Mumby, 2004)—one grounded in gender uniformity, static categories, and self-perpetuating notions of ideal types.

❖ DIFFERENCE AS ADDED VALUE

The flip side of the deficiency coin treats difference as added value, or as an asset rather than a weakness. Drawn from studies of women's experiences, scholars who work within this tradition celebrate difference and believe it enhances creativity and innovation. This perspective crosses two dissimilar strands of work: (1) difference as feminine advantage and (2) difference as diversity. Drawn from women's ways of knowing, the first strand contends that women's experiences in family and communities give them a competitive edge, particularly in employing intuition, emotional support, and connectedness in leadership positions (Helgesen, 1990) or in enhancing self-worth and encouraging followers through using interactive styles (Rosener, 1990). Known as *difference theories* or *difference feminism,* scholars examine how women use these differences to inspire followers, create emotional bonds, and transform social situations (Dow, 1995), especially outside the corporate environment.

The diversity literature also adopts a view of difference as added value. Extending beyond binary categories, diversity refers to employees who differ in race, ethnicity, sexual preference, age, nationality, and background. This perspective focuses on the economic benefits of a diverse workforce through tapping into a flexible labor pool (Zanoni & Janssens, 2004). In addition, diversity adds value through enhancing innovation and quality problem solving (Cox 1994; Harrison & Klein, 2007) and reaffirming meritocracy (Liff & Wajcman, 1996). Thus, in the diversity literature, difference as added value becomes a means to an organizational end through implementing best practices to improve the bottom line.

Both approaches, however, treat difference as universal and objective. Similar to sex-role stereotypes and divisions of labor, difference as added value assumes that individuals who reside in designated categories are essentially the same. As Dow (1995) noted, "a feminism of difference tends to be a feminism of uniformity" (p. 108). Specifically, celebrating gender differences may provide a moral critique that is absent in difference as deficiency, but both approaches homogenize women. Moreover, gynocentric or separatist approaches tend to ignore power relationships and the costs of treating women as special; hence, they inadvertently sustain rather than challenge patriarchy. The diversity literature, rooted in managerial and economic rationality, also hides bureaucratic power by casting organizations as neutral arenas in which competences are equally valued and opportunities are readily available (Zanoni & Janssens, 2004).

❖ DIFFERENCE AS DISCURSIVE PRACTICES

The third approach, *difference as discursive practices,* treats difference as a process that is socially constructed. Thus, difference is enacted through language, texts, and actions that are fluid, evolving, and contested

(Mumby, 2006). Through an ongoing, interactive process, difference becomes an accomplishment rather than a set of traits, schemas, or categories that reside in individuals or reference groups (West & Fenstermaker, 1995). This definition departs from a view of difference as dispersion and focuses on the doing of difference in relation to multiple focal points.

Doing difference is also meaning-centered in that language and texts are rooted symbolically in societal systems that represent gender and race. Hence, the issue in working through difference is determining "what are the differences that make a difference in this production process" (Mumby, 2006, p. 93). Moreover, in this perspective, power relationships stem from the ways that subject positions are constituted rather than through a comparison with a privileged or marginalized category. Thus, the doing of difference can be both enabling and constraining and can simultaneously challenge and reproduce power relationships.

The research on doing difference typically downplays biological categories and focuses on processes through which individuals discursively construct their identities relative to other organizational members. In particular, studies reveal ways that women executives "do gender" to align themselves with others in powerful positions and to differentiate themselves from marginalized groups (Olsson & Walker, 2004). Nentwich (2006) analyzed discourses of sameness and difference as enactments of behavioral repertoires that blur gendered divisions of labor, while Linstead and Pullen (2006) proposed conceptions of doing difference that incorporate ontologies of desire and social motivation.

❖ DIFFERENCE AS MANAGING DIALECTICAL TENSIONS

For this chapter, we propose a dialectical approach to the study of differences, one that draws on difference as a discursive practice. Dialectics centers on the simultaneous push-pull that emanates from the unity of opposites; thus, it focuses on the interplay of tensions between contradictions (Baxter & Montgomery, 1996). In the differences as deficit and the added value approaches, opposites exist as binary, static poles in which individuals function in *either* one *or* the other category (Poole & van de Ven, 1989). Specifically, terms such as *feminine* or *masculine* are not simply bipolar opposites; rather, they are intrinsically interrelated concepts such that adjustments in one directly effect changes in the other. Thus, dialectics is a form of resistance to traditional static categories through questioning the nature of presumed opposites and challenging the position of fixed binary poles.

The dialectical perspective has a rich history that dates back to dis- agreements between Plato and Aristotle about the value of debate and persuasion (dialectic and rhetoric) as ways of knowing. It evolved into an ontological framework with pragmatic implications when theorists treated it as a social phenomenon inherent to and embedded in the eco- nomic relationships of human history (Marx, 1977; Hegel, 1969). More recently, communication scholars have adopted Giddens' notion of dialectics of control, in which primary contradictions arise in the enact- ment of rules and resources that, in turn, set up secondary contradic- tions or unintended consequences in organizational life (Papa, Auwal, & Singhal, 1997). For this chapter, we draw on Mikhail Bakhtin's (1981) notion of dialectics, in which human relationships are derived from and constituted within oppositional forces. Bakhtin's dialogic view of dialectics conceives of the tensions between opposites as managing ongoing social forces rather than as problems that need solutions.

In communication studies, research on dialectics is typically aligned with interpersonal relationships (Baxter, 1993). Related studies of dialectics in organizational communication also center on identities and role conflicts (Tracy, 2004; Vaughn & Stamp, 2003). Yet in organi- zational scholarship, research has moved beyond dyadic relationships to focus on teams and self-governance in workplace democracy (Carroll & Arneson, 2003), paradoxes of participation (Stohl & Cheney, 2001), leadership processes (Collinson, 2005), organizational change (Kellett, 1999), work-family balance (Medved & Graham, 2006), and organizational resistance (Fleming & Spicer, 2002). As these studies reveal, dialectic tensions pervade all aspects of organizational life, not just identity negotiations and interpersonal relationships. They cross organizational units and boundaries, form sites of cultural struggles, and enact processes of change (Trethewey & Ashcraft, 2004).

The work on dialectics is particularly suited to studying how gender differences create fundamental tensions in organizational relationships and how individuals manage these tensions in ways that constrain or enable them (Ashcraft, 2001; Martin, 2004; Trethewey, 1997). Drawn from second wave feminism, contemporary feminists often examine relational tensions as inherent contradictions that separate and privilege gender in groups and organizations (Johnson & Long, 2002). Feminist scholars embrace a dialectical lens rooted in women's struggle to find a sense of self and a voice amid tensions between domination and subordination, privilege and marginalization, and control and resistance to both patri- archy and bureaucracy (Ferguson, 1993).

In dialectics, difference resides in the tensions between opposites as well as in the medium and the outcome of managing contradictions.

That is, differences are embedded in the way that actors socially construct opposites: namely, how they enact both poles as contradictions. As a medium, difference also surfaces through the interplay of trying to hold *both* poles together. In effect, organizations discursively construct bipolar opposites as forces that gain significance and meaning through managing their interdependent relationships. Difference surfaces in dialectics through unfolding contradictions that shift, evolve, and change through the interplay between the tensions.

Gherardi's (1995) work on doing gender illustrated how difference emanates from constructing opposites, calling them into play, and holding them in tension with each other. Her example of a woman engineer who is slapped on the back for a job well done shows how difference emerges dialectically through aligning appreciation for her work (symbolic male praise) with deprecation as a woman (not "one of the boys"). Difference surfaces dialectically as a medium through the interplay between these opposites: For example, should the woman acknowledge or ignore the gendered nature of the symbolic act? Should she overtly resist or accept the honorary male membership? Difference then emerges in the social construction of the opposites through discursive actions and in the tensions that surface from trying to hold them together.

Difference is also a product or output of making decisions and moving forward amid these opposite pulls. Specifically, individuals and organizational units enact choices to manage or cope with dialectical tensions. These choices lead to negotiating the meaning of difference as a product of coping with and working through interwoven tensions. Theorists identify five ways that dialectical tensions are managed: selection, separation, integration, transcendence, and connection (Baxter & Montgomery, 1996; Seo, Putnam, & Bartunek, 2004). Selection occurs when individuals and units select one side of the pole and ignore the other. For example, organizational members might choose rationality over emotionality and, thus, reify difference as a dualism or binary opposite. Both poles may be acknowledged (e.g., emotions in organizations exist), but one is deemed more desirable than the other (e.g., emotion is treated as off-limits or as only to be expressed behind closed doors). This approach, however, produces a notion of difference that segments it from the essential elements that define its existence (i.e., rationality can only be known or understood through its tensions with emotionality).

Separation, the second approach, involves vacillating between the poles or addressing only one of them at a given time or in a given situation; thus, the poles may become separated by temporal periods, topics, or spatial location. For example, tensions might be managed through locating rationality spatially at the organizational level and emotionality at the individual level or by relegating rationality to a topical area of decision making and dealing with emotional expression as social support or cultural displays. A variation of selection is source splitting, which occurs when members or units split their attentions between the two poles: for example, the leader of a group focuses on rationality and the members emphasize emotionality (Tracy, 2004). Similar to selection, this choice ignores the mutual influence between the poles and blocks ways to capitalize on difference as a source of creative energy and new understandings.

The next approach, *integration,* results from interactions that merge both poles simultaneously through compromising each pole or creating a forced merger between them. Difference is minimized in this option through finding a middle ground, diluting the two poles, or canceling the effects of both of them. This approach reverts back to selection when parties cancel or wash out differences. For example, rationality and emotionality merge into a different mode of expression or become emotional labor that positions emotions in the service of rationality.

The fourth type of response, *transcendence,* refers to transforming the dichotomies into a reformulated whole so that the original tensions no longer exist. This process involves reframing or working toward a new definition of the situation. This approach transcends difference through casting it in a new light; thus, tensions are used as energy to create a new form or a space that lies outside of the opposite poles. For instance, Mumby and Putnam (1992) used this approach to identify a construct known as *bounded emotionality,* which reframes the traditional dualism between rationality and emotionality. Transcendence, then, recognizes opposites, provides a creative and useful way to manage them, and recasts differences in a new form that incorporates tensions from both poles.

Because these choices separate, dismiss, or transcend differences, Baxter and Montgomery (1996) proposed a fifth approach, *connection.* Through connection, parties find ways to link differences together; that is, they intertwine the opposites in ways that generate insights from respecting, preserving, and interrelating them. In a postmodern way, connection favors indeterminacy through being open to multiple interpretations and rejecting the tendency to use difference to produce teleological change (Seo et al., 2004). To illustrate, organizational members might embrace emotionality to understand rationality, and vice versa. In this way, both are respected, valued, and mutually informing in generating action. In connection, the medium and product of difference are one and the same. Thus, the continual process of aligning tensions from opposites produces the differences that make a difference.

Overall, in dialectics, difference surfaces in multiple ways: namely, as the social construction of opposites, as a medium in the interplay among tensions, and as a product that results from coping with, acting on, or moving forward amid the tensions. As a product, differences can be denied or ignored (selection), recognized but split in specialized ways (source splitting), alternated between opposites (separation), diluted or merged (integration), transformed or recast (transcendence), and embraced and preserved (connection). Of note, the choice to connect or hold opposites together casts the medium and the product of managing differences as one and the same rather than as separate processes.

Hopson and Orbe's (2007) study illustrated how difference emerged as a medium and product of managing dialectical tensions. They examined the tendency for Black organizational members to rationalize the discriminatory practices of Whites, especially when subtle prejudicial comments were made. Differences emanated from the tensions between inclusion and exclusion in a White, male-dominated workforce and from socially constructing derogatory comments in particular ways. Because the remarks differed from blatant forms of racism, Black employees vacillated between judging them as acceptable or unacceptable and treating them as rational or irrational. To interpret the comments as rational at face value was irrational because it caused pain; to excuse the comments as irrational denied the existence of the discriminatory remarks. Thus, Black employees typically brushed off such comments as insignificant and enacted difference as a product that constrained workplace relationships but enabled organizational inclusion.

Difference as a medium surfaced through making sense of the comments and responding to the remarks. Basically, the dialectical patterns were nested in each other such that the choices between inclusion and exclusion were intertwined with managing the tensions between rationality-irrationality and acceptable-unacceptable behaviors. Thus, differences as a product surfaced through the vacillation between the rationality issues and the selection of acceptable behaviors (as opposed to unacceptable), which, in turn, fostered the selection of inclusion. Difference, then, emerged from discursively managing the dialectical tensions in ways that favored one pole—the one privileged by White, middle-class patriarchal culture.

Dialectical Tensions and Intersectionality

As this study suggests, a dialectical approach is particularly robust for examining the intersection of multiple forms of identity, namely race, gender, class, ethnicity, and sexuality (Ashcraft, 2004; Ashcraft &

Mumby, 2004). Intersection refers to the ways that multiple systems of power come together in everyday interactions to advantage and disadvantage organizational members simultaneously (Collins, 1998; Steinbugler, Press, & Dias, 2006). A dialectical approach rejects the notion that difference emanates from discrete categories or that it functions in an additive way to place some individuals in "double jeopardy" (Ward, 2004). Instead, difference involves an interweaving of multiple systems in which one area is emphasized (or deemphasized) relative to the marginalization of others (Adib & Guerrier, 2003; Bowleg, 2008). The nature of difference comes into consideration when interactions challenge presumptions within one system of power, alter points of comparison, and shift the nature of privilege. Thus, a dialectical approach aids in understanding how organizational members negotiate identities through drawing on different texts as systems of power and resistance. Texts refer to organizational forms (e.g., bureaucracy) and larger societal narratives (e.g., occupations) that individuals call into consideration in working out their identities.

In applying dialectics to the study of intersectionality, two processes seem critical for understanding difference: centering and de-centering and masking and unmasking. *Centering* refers to how a system of power or resistance is emphasized, accented, or treated as salient in discursive interactions. It involves the ways that discursive practices bring texts and historic meanings to the forefront or center stage, making one or more of the systems figure and the others ground. The tensions between centering and de-centering focus on the ways that difference emerges from the discursive practices that draw on texts of dominant systems.

Masking refers to the process of hiding that keeps difference invisible. Juxtaposed with unmasking, it examines how exposing, unearthing, and making the absent present enters into discursive processes and the production of meanings. A fundamental concern in unmasking is developing a name for the invisible or labeling it so it can enter into the interplay among the tensions that characterize systems of domination, namely, privilege and marginalization, equity and inequity, and control and resistance. In a similar way, unmasking aims for a process of claiming in which an actor recognizes and acknowledges problems of inequity and privilege.

To illustrate how difference emerges from dialectical tensions, we employ three extended examples of intersectionality from several published articles. Using these scenarios, we show how actors draw on social and organizational texts to negotiate the meanings of difference that emerge from the interplay of dialectical tensions. In these situations, we highlight the discursive practices of centering and masking as critical features in managing oppositional pulls.

Exclusion versus Inclusion. The first example centers on an HIV prevention organization that targets primarily gay Hispanic males and, to a lesser extent, lesbian Hispanic females. In the past, the male staff members conducted a larger number of support group meetings than did the females and, therefore, laid claim to an attractive meeting space while the women rotated among makeshift locations. A situation arose in which Fatima (a Hispanic lesbian) asked her male supervisor if she could share the space that the male support groups typically used. She summarizes this incident as follows:

> He was telling me . . ."I've been facilitating this group with the same men for about two years, and we worked hard to get this . . . nice group discussion room. I feel, for lack of a better word, offended that you are even asking me to share the room." [And Fatima said], "It's not like I am taking something away from you. I'm asking you to share what we have together within the agency." And he said that he had to think about it! (Ward, 2004, p. 93)

In this excerpt, Fatima enacts a dialectical tension between inclusion and exclusion of female staff members by centering on male privilege and highlighting the presumption that women lack access to the room. Her request draws on the text of organizational mission that presumes gender while it foregrounds race and sexual orientation. Fatima raises the tensions between privileged and not privileged and shared versus owned by invoking organizational membership (i.e., "together within the agency"). Both sets of tensions draw on a system of domination that masks gender and de-couples it from race and sexual orientation.

When her first effort fails to unmask gender, she decides to transcend the oppositional pairs (for example, exclusion vs. inclusion; owned vs. shared) by reframing the situation through drawing on Whiteness as a parallel system of domination that both of them understand. Fatima remarks, "How would you feel if a group of White people were using that nice discussion room all the time, while the people of color are having to [use the makeshift space] . . ." and he [is] like, "No, I'm sorry, you can't be using that . . . No, I don't want you to use that example!" Fatima responds: "It's a perfect example" (Ward, 2004, p. 94). Renaming the problem as race-based exclusion unmasks gender and makes it central to the discussion of inclusion and equity. It draws from historically-rooted social texts in which people of color were often relegated to the back rooms or back of the bus. Thus, it negotiates difference through de-centering the invisible male privilege and comparing it to the ways that White people treat people of color. Fatima's comparison and renaming make it possible for her supervisor to recognize the problem because he indirectly admits that her example of racial discrimination hits home. His statement, "you can't be using that," implies that she caught him and exposes his unequal treatment in a way that makes gender similar to aligning race with marginal space.

Normal versus Abnormal. A second example explores the intersection of gender, sexual orientation, and heteronormative behaviors. In a study of gay men's close relationships in a healthcare organization, Rumens (2008) observed that homosexuality is often invisible in a heteronormative workplace. In this setting, organizational members often hold preconceived ideas about appropriate behaviors between male colleagues and view a close friendship between two men, particularly when one of them is gay, as being possibly homosexual in nature. To support this claim, he provided an example of how Morgan, a gay employee, negotiated difference as a right to have close friendships among straight men at work. Morgan mentioned an instance in which his heterosexual colleagues "raised their eyebrows" in disapproval when he "unwittingly touched John" (a straight coworker friend) in a tender manner. These raised eyebrows, in Morgan's view, stemmed from his use of nonverbal cues that appeared to be tender or intimate rather than rough horseplay that typically characterizes male touching at work.

His account also showed how he negotiated difference by foregrounding gender and aligning the dialectical tensions of soft versus rough and unwitting versus purposeful actions with masculine and feminine behaviors. By aligning horseplay with the dominant system of masculinity, he de-centered homosexuality and called normalcy into question. Morgan described the pressures that he felt: "I did not want to be press-ganged by staff into explaining my friendship with John as though it was some kind of peculiar object of fascination" (Rumens, 2008, p. 21). This remark reflected a presumption that friendships between men at work were normal and acceptable; thus, Morgan unmasked homosexuality by connecting normative and nonnormative behaviors (e.g., "treating it as a peculiar object"), holding them in tension with each other, and situating them as a right for homosexuals to have close male friendships at work.

Insider versus Outsider. A third illustration of how difference is negotiated through dialectical tensions examines the intersection of gender, sexual orientation, and the firefighter occupation. In this instance, the firefighter cadet negotiated difference through naming a situation as humor and engaging in repartee to pass a membership test. As she remarked,

> They actually ran a book, a betting book, to see who the first guy would be who could get off with me and change me, or my orientation. I only found out about it a year after it had been running and they were like, 'We've given up now!' And I was like, "I wish you'd have told me if there was any money involved: I might have just done it. We could have shared, come on!" They also bet on when my period was due. They never could tell. (Ward & Winstanley, 2006, p. 214)

The female cadet in this example de-centered sexual orientation and gender by naming the situation as an occupational membership rite. The presumption of masculine heterosexuality is evident in terms like "first guy" and "change my orientation." Hence, she drew on occupational social texts, accepted masculine hegemony, and negotiated difference through the interplay of tensions between being an insider and an outsider. She vacillated between the poles—as an outsider who is lesbian and female and as the insider who uses humor and repartee to pass the test ("I wish you would have told me!"), but in the end, as her male colleagues took bets on when her period was due, she reframed her situation as just "the guys" engaging in initiation rituals. In this way, she decentered sexuality and gender, defined the situation as an organizational initiation, and masked it as a game in which she wins. ("They could never tell.")

Crossing the three examples illustrates how difference emerges from the social construction of opposites that are cast in tension with each other. These forces draw on organizational and occupational texts as well as systems of domination embodied in negotiating identities and taking actions on issues. All three call presumptions into question through de-centering privilege, normalcy, and exclusion and either masking or unmasking the invisible. Fatima de-centers gender and unmasks male privilege and female exclusion; Morgan de-centers heteronormativity and unmasks homosexuality; and the firefighter cadet de-centers sexual orientation and gender and masks the initiation rite as a game.

Difference emerges as a medium and product of managing dialectical tensions through drawing on organizational texts and systems of power and control. Specifically, Fatima and her supervisor drew from the text of togetherness in the agency to vacillate between inclusion and exclusion and the sharing and owning of the meeting space.

When Fatima used Whiteness to transcend gender, she centered the issue in a different system of power relationships, renamed the invisible, and shifted the ownership of the inequity. Morgan drew on societal texts of masculine and feminine behaviors to enact tensions between rough and soft touch between men. Morgan de-centered and unmasked the heteronormativity of the workplace by highlighting the conflicting meanings of horseplay (as masculine and friendly) versus tenderness (as feminine and romantic). He unmasked the tension between what was considered normal versus abnormal in order to argue for gay men's rights to workplace friendships. Finally, in the firefighter example, difference became marginalized through the way that the female cadet vacillated between being an outsider and an insider, naming the membership rite as a game, and tolerating the practices of testing her sexual orientation and gender as a rite of passage. By drawing on occupational texts, she privileged the masculine hegemony of the firefighters and masked the gender and sexuality biases embedded in the initiation ritual.

Dialectical Tensions and Intergroup Practices

Research on the role of difference in mundane talk, however, places undue faith on micro interactions while it typically overlooks the strategic and institutional factors that underlie difference (Ashcraft, 2004). Even though analyses of routine interactions draw on organizational and societal texts, they often fail to problematize institutional factors in the social construction of difference. The diversity literature provides insights into how difference emerges at the intergroup level in a way that constructs diversity at the margins of an organization.

Diversity discourses in organizations align individuals in categories linked to multiple, yet interconnected groups. Markers of difference, such as dress, dialect, and rituals, separate and reinforce diversity groups as being in opposition to the mainstream culture. Human resource (HR) managers often treat these multiple categories as univocal and as in tension with the mainstream culture (Tomlinson, 2008). Thus, reference groups, such as gender, race, disability, and sexual orientation share difference as a unifying feature. Although HR managers often view diversity as adding value, they simultaneously place reference groups at the margins of an organization (Zanoni & Janssens, 2004), a process that has widespread implications for these "culturally-defined, bounded communities" of difference (Tomlinson, 2008, p. 16).

To examine the role of difference at the intergroup level, we provide an exemplar of two employee network groups in a Global 100 energy corporation, Summit International, a company recognized in the industry for its diversity practices. The company initially established and funded five employee network groups—a Black, a Hispanic, an Asian Pacific, a Women's, and a GLBT group—to help with recruitment, retention, and advancement of minority employees. This exemplar draws from a study of 30 interviews with Black and Hispanic network members, conversations with diversity officers, observations of board meetings, and field notes from annual conferences (Baker, 2009).

Dialectical tensions revealed how discourse socially constructed difference at strategic and structural levels in ways that enabled and constrained the groups. The overarching tension that grew out of the relationship between the network groups and the Diversity Office was autonomy versus control. Basically, the groups saw themselves as autonomous; that is, they elected their own officers, ran their own finances, selected diversity goals to pursue, and had only a modicum of input from the Diversity Office. On the control end of the pole, the organization mandated that network membership be open to anyone who wanted to join their groups, and the Diversity Office evaluated the groups on a scorecard based on achieving strategic initiatives, such as developing innovations to recruit and retain minorities, forming bonds with minority suppliers, increasing membership in the networks, and providing educational programs for employees. Hence, the groups felt autonomous in their routine operations, yet they also felt controlled by management. As one employee in the Black network stated, "The diversity police could do more to help us."

In managing the tensions, network members vacillated between autonomy and control through two related dialectics—distinctive versus universal and cooperation versus competition. On the one hand, groups struggled to keep their identities and mission unique to their racial interests: for example, connecting Blacks with Blacks, developing a specialized mentorship programs for Blacks, and offering professional development for Black employees. On the other hand, difference was enacted as universal since network membership was open, the groups engaged in similar recruitment activities, and network functions drew attendance through casting a wide net and focusing on general topics. For the most part, the groups employed source splitting to manage the tensions with some members favoring distinctiveness and others fostering universality. This approach led to controversy because some members preferred activities that made their groups distinctive while others pursued topics and events that had wide appeal.

The source splitting among members fueled the tensions between cooperation and competition that also enabled and constrained the groups. To enhance efficiency and avoid reinventing the wheel, the networks collaborated with each other to host social events, training seminars, and board meetings. These collaborations led to increased universality and reduced distinctiveness through replicating high visibility programs across groups and through looking to each other for best practices. Yet they competed with each other for recognition and for attaining a premier status on the annual scorecard evaluation. To manage these tensions, group members separated cooperation and competition into functional areas and vacillated between them. For example, during new employee orientation, the networks participated in collective rather than targeted membership drives while they competed for new employees to join their particular group.

Overall, the management of these tensions created a system of difference in which network groups were distinct yet universal. They walked a fine line between feeling respected and being ignored. The groups had distinctive interests, but they resembled each other in overall mission and objectives. They boasted about having hundreds of members, but had few active participants; and they competed with each other for recognition while cooperating with each other to reduce costs.

In many ways, this system of dialectics led to a form of intergroup concertive control in which the networks promoted diversity interests through encouraging conformity while simultaneously precluding radical change. For example, the Black network began a series of Fireside Chats to promote candid interactions among minorities, but in their efforts to be recognized for this innovation, they included minority corporate leaders. Opening the group's boundary to executives, however, closed off the safe haven that employees needed to discuss the challenges that they faced and precluded efforts to pursue radical change.

The enactment of dialectical tensions at the intergroup level highlighted the ways that diversity networks constructed the structural and institutional factors that imposed on them. It showed how they engaged in discursive practices that privileged universality while struggling to develop group distinctiveness. In effect, dialectical tensions revealed how the organization produced a system that instantiated a particular meaning of diversity, one that homogenized and marginalized difference.

❖ SUMMARY AND CONCLUSION

This chapter challenges how the extant literature on gender and diversity conceives of difference as a deviation from an ideal model, as a devalued category, and as an unsuitable fit. These approaches locate difference in binary categories that privilege masculine options for organizational success. When difference surfaces as adding value in the feminine advantage and diversity literatures, scholars reverse the moral claim on deficiency but continue to treat categories of difference as universals. In contrast, difference as a discursive practice shifts the focus from binary categories to socially constructing identities; thus, difference becomes a process developed through language, texts, and ongoing interactions.

Dialectics is a particular approach to the study of difference as a process. Focusing on the tensions enacted through the unity of opposites, it challenges binary categories by demonstrating how opposites function in interdependent ways. Difference emerges as a medium for and product of the choices made in managing the interplay of these tensions. Doing difference, then, is not simply identity work or using language and texts to unearth the meanings constructed in organizational life. Rather, doing difference through a dialectical lens requires understanding how individuals and groups enact interrelated sets of tensions, draw on organizational and social texts, and make choices to deal with these tensions in particular ways.

What dialectical theory offers that is not present in many other forms of doing difference is theoretical guidance as to how to embrace differences and alter the course of discriminatory practices. Specifically, transcendence and connection as options for managing the interplay of tensions offer the potential to de-center or shift the figure-ground relationships that can unmask particular practices. In this case, transcendence is not a synthesis of opposites but a reframing in which organizational members rename or label situations differently. The practice of connection holds the tensions together to shift both the naming and claiming of practices through a continual interplay between the poles. Also important, a number of projects that focus on dialectical tensions fail to examine which differences make a difference and how inequitable situations can be changed (Medved & Graham, 2006).

The fundamental area for continued research on differences as dialectics is how to engage in de-centering and unmasking organizational practices, what to name particular situations, and how organizations can use naming and claiming to create texts that alter privileged positions. Studies of intersectionality and group-organizational relationships provide opportunities to unearth these patterns. Specifically, studies need to show how organizational members draw on texts from a variety of power-based systems, how the naming of issues and problems shifts through altering texts, and how structural and institutional factors interface with these routine interactions.

It is particularly important that scholars focus on materiality and the economic aspects of these constructions. For example, in our example of employee network groups, resource allocations were a critical area of autonomy versus control. In general, formal allocations of corporate funds were insufficient to meet network needs, and the Diversity Office rarely granted requests for additional resources. Thus, network officers often supplemented their meager budgets with funds and supplies obtained through their organizational positions. In this way, they reframed control, reallocated corporate funds for diversity efforts, and integrated diversity as part of their job functions. This example reveals how managing dialectical tensions functions not only as a mode of covert resistance but also as an avenue for challenging economic issues in the management of difference. The study of dialectical tensions, however, typically falls into the symbolic sphere of social construction through relying on language, texts, and discursive practices rather than material constructions, such as objects, sites, and bodies (Cooren, 2004). Applying dialectics to the material-idealist dualism provides a way to understand how nonhuman elements in organizational life contribute to constructing difference as a capacity for action.

Organizational communication scholars have made great strides in studying difference as discursive processes. These studies have moved beyond binary categories to examine how difference is negotiated in mundane interactions by drawing on organizational and social texts and through examining institutional arrangements. Difference, then, is not simply the movement away from a central reference point or even movement across boundaries. Rather, difference emerges as a negotiation that resembles Derrida's (1976) notion of *différance*. That is, the constitution of and interplay between oppositional poles challenge what it means to differ and how to defer or avoid fixing the meaning of any performance or organizational text. Moreover, through dialectical tensions actors can resist fixed meanings, open up space for a middle voice, and create opportunities to reframe or transform their organizational lives.

❖ REFERENCES

Adib, A., & Guerrier, Y. (2003). The interlocking of gender with nationality, race, ethnicity and class: The narratives of women in hotel work. *Gender, Work and Organization, 10,* 413–432.

Ashcraft, K. L. (2001). Organized dissonance: Feminist bureaucracy as hybrid form. *Academy of Management Journal, 44,* 1301–1322.

Ashcraft, K. L. (2004). Gender, discourse, and organization: Framing a shifting relationship. In D. Grant, C. Hardy, C. Oswick, & L. L. Putnam (Eds.), *The Sage handbook of organizational discourse* (pp. 275–298). London: Sage.

Ashcraft, K. L., & Mumby, D. K. (2004). *Reworking gender: A feminist communicology of organization*. Thousand Oaks, CA: Sage.

Baker, J. S. (2009). *Buying into the business case: A bona fide group study of dialectical tensions in employee network groups*. Unpublished Dissertation, Texas A&M University, College Station, TX.

Bakhtin, M. M. (1981). *The dialogic imagination: Four essays by M. M. Bakhtin* (C. Emerson & M. Holquist, Trans.). Austin: University of Texas Press.

Baxter, L. A. (1993). The social side of personal relationships: A dialectical analysis. In S. Duck (Ed.), *Social context and relationships* (pp. 139–165). Newbury Park, CA: Sage.

Baxter, L. A., & Montgomery, B. M. (1996). *Relating: Dialogues and dialectics*. New York: Guilford.

Bowleg, L. (2008). When Black + lesbian + woman ≠ Black lesbian woman: The methodological challenges of qualitative and quantitative intersectionality research. *Sex Roles, 59*, 312–325.

Carroll, L. A., & Arneson, P. (2003). Communication in a shared governance hospital: Managing emergent paradoxes. *Communication Studies, 54*, 35–55.

Collins, P. H. (1998). *Fighting words: Black women and the search for justice*. University of Minnesota Press.

Collinson, D. (2005). Dialectics of leadership. *Human Relations, 58*, 1419–1442.

Cooren, F. (2004). Textual agency: How texts do things in organizational settings. *Organization, 11*, 373–393.

Cox, T. (1994). A comment on the language of diversity. *Organization, 1*, 51–58.

Derrida, J. (1976). *Of grammatology* (G. Spivak, Trans.). Baltimore, MD: Johns Hopkins University Press.

Diekman, A. B., & Goodfriend, W. (2006). Rolling with the changes: A role congruity perspective on gender norms. *Psychology of Women Quarterly, 30*, 369.

Dow, B. J. (1995). Feminism, difference(s), and rhetorical studies. *Communication Studies, 46*, 106–117.

Eagly, A. H., & Johnson, B. T. (1990). Gender and leadership style—A meta-analysis. *Psychological Bulletin, 108*, 233–256.

Ferguson, M. (1993). *Colonialism and gender from Mary Wollstonecraft to Jamaica Kincaid*. New York: Columbia University Press.

Fleming, P., & Spicer, A. (2002). Workers' playtime? Unraveling the paradox of covert resistance in organizations. In S. Clegg (Ed.), *Management and organizational paradoxes* (pp. 65–85). Amsterdam: John Benjamins.

Foldy, E. G. (2006). Dueling schemata: Dialectical sensemaking about gender. *Journal of Applied Behavioral Science, 42*, 350–372.

Gherardi, S. (1995). *Gender, symbolism, and organizational cultures*. London: Sage.

Hare-Mustin, R. T., & Marecek, J. (1988). The meaning of difference: Gender theory, postmodernism, and psychology. *American Psychologist, 43*, 355–464.

Harrison, D. A., & Klein, K. J. (2007). What's the difference? Diversity constructs as separation, variety, or disparity in organizations. *Academy of Management Review, 32*, 1199–1228.

Hegel, G. W. F. (1969). *The science of logic.* London: George Allen & Unwin. (Original work published in 1807.)

Helgesen, S. (1990). *The female advantage: Women's ways of leadership.* New York: Doubleday.

Henning, M., & Jardim, A. (1977). *The managerial woman.* New York: Anchor.

Hopson, M. C., & Orbe, M. P. (2007). Playing the game: Recalling dialectical tensions for black men in oppressive organizational structures. *The Harvard Journal of Communication, 18*, 69–86.

Johnson, S. D., & Long, L. M. (2002). Being a part and being apart: Dialectics and group communication. In L. R. Frey (Ed.), *New directions in group communication.* Thousand Oaks, CA: Sage.

Kanter, R. M. (1977). *Men and women of the corporation.* New York: Basic Books.

Kellett, P. M. (1999). Dialogue and dialectics in managing organizational change: The case of a mission-based transformation. *Southern Communication Journal, 64*, 211–231.

Kugelberg, C. (2006). Constructing the deviant other: Mothering and fathering at the workplace. *Gender, Work and Organization, 13*, 152–173.

Liff, S., & Wajcman, J. (1996). "Sameness" and "difference" revisited: Which way forward for equal opportunity initiatives? *Journal of Management Studies, 33*, 79–94.

Lindsay, S. (2008). The care-tech link: An examination of gender, care and technical work in healthcare labour. *Gender, Work and Organization, 15*, 333–351.

Linstead, S., & Pullen, A. (2006). Gender as multiplicity: Desire, displacement, difference and dispersion. *Human Relations, 59*, 1287–1310.

Martin, D. M. (2004). Humor in middle management: Women negotiating the paradoxes of organizational life. *Journal of Applied Communication Research, 32*, 147–170.

Marx, K. (1977). *Capital* (Vol. 1). (B. Fowkes, Trans.). New York: Vintage. (Original work published in 1867.)

Medved, C. E., & Graham, E. E. (2006). Communicating contradictions: (Re)Producing dialectical tensions through work, family, and balance in socialization messages. In L. Turner & R. West (Eds.), *The family communication sourcebook* (pp. 353–372). Thousand Oaks, CA: Sage.

Mumby, D. K. (2006). Gender and communication in organizational contexts: Introduction. In B. J. Dow & J. T. Woods (Eds.), *The SAGE handbook of gender and communication* (pp. 89–95). Thousand Oaks, CA: Sage.

Mumby, D. K., & Putnam, L. L. (1992). The politics of emotion: A feminist reading of bounded rationality. *Academy of Management Review, 17*, 465–486.

Nentwich, J. C. (2006). Changing gender: The discursive construction of equal opportunities. *Gender, Work and Organization, 13*, 499–521.

Ollilainen, M., & Calasanti, T. (2007). Metaphors at work: Maintaining the salience of gender in self-managing teams. *Gender and Society, 21*, 5–27.

Olsson, S., & Walker, R. (2004). The wo-men and the boys: Patterns of identification and differentiation in senior women executives. *Women in Management Review, 19,* 244–251.

Ozbilgin, M. F., & Woodward, D. (2004). "Belonging" and "otherness": Sex equality in banking in Turkey and Britain. *Gender, Work and Organization, 11,* 668–688.

Papa, M. J., Auwal, M. A., & Singhal, A. (1997). Organizing for social change within concertive control systems: Membership identification, empowerment, and the masking of discipline. *Communication Monographs, 64,* 219–249.

Parker, P. S. (2005). *Race, gender and leadership.* Mahwah, NJ: Lawrence Earlbaum Associates.

Peterson, H. (2007). Gendered work ideals in Swedish IT firms: Valued and not valued workers. *Gender, Work and Organization, 14,* 333–348.

Pilgeram, R. (2007). "Ass-kicking" women: Doing and undoing gender in a US livestock auction. *Gender, Work and Organization, 14,* 572–595.

Poole, M. S., & van de Ven, A. H. (1989). Using paradox to build management and organizational theories. *The Academy of Management Review, 14,* 562–578.

Reeder, H. M. (1996). A critical look at gender difference in communication research. *Communication Studies, 47,* 318–330.

Rosener, J. B. (1990). Ways women lead. *Harvard Business Review, 68,* 119-125.

Rumens, N. (2008). Working at intimacy: Gay men's workplace friendships. *Gender, Work and Organization, 15,* 9–30.

Seo, M., Putnam, L. L., & Bartunek, J. M. (2004). Dualities and tensions of planned organizational change. In M. S. Poole & A. H. van de Ven (Eds.), *Handbook of organizational change and innovation* (pp. 73–107). New York: Oxford University Press.

Skuratowicz, E., & Hunter, L. W. (2004). Where do women's jobs come from? *Work and Occupations, 31,* 73–110.

Steinbugler, A. C., Press, J. E., & Dias, J. J. (2006). Gender, race, and affirmative action: Operationalizing intersectionality in survey research. *Gender and Society, 20,* 805–825.

Stohl, C., & Cheney, G. (2001). Participatory processes/paradoxical practices. *Management Communication Quarterly, 14,* 349–407.

Tomlinson, F. (2008). Marking difference and negotiating belonging: Refugee women, volunteering and employment. *Gender, Work and Organization.* doi:10.1111/j.1468-0432.2008.00399.x

Tracy, S. J. (2004). Dialectic, contradiction, or double bind? Analyzing and theorizing employee reactions to organizational tension. *Journal of Applied Communication Research, 32,* 119–146.

Trethewey, A. (1997). Resistance, identity, and empowerment: A postmodern feminist analysis of clients in a human service organization. *Communication Monographs, 64,* 281–301.

Trethewey, A., & Ashcraft, K. L. (2004). Introduction. *Journal of Applied Communication Research, 32,* 81–88.

Vaughn, M., & Stamp, G. H. (2003). The empowerment dilemma: The dialectic of emancipation and control in staff/client interaction at shelters for battered women. *Communication Studies, 54,* 154–168.

Wajcman, J. (1996). Desperately seeking differences: Is management style gendered? *British Journal of Industrial Relations, 34,* 333–349.

Ward, J. (2004). "Not all differences are created equal": Multiple jeopardy in a gendered organization. *Gender and Society, 18,* 82–123.

Ward, J., & Winstanley, D. (2006). Watching the watch: The UK fire service and its impact on sexual minorities in the workplace. *Gender, Work and Organization, 13,* 193–219.

West, C., & Fenstermaker, S. (1995). Doing difference. *Gender and Society, 9,* 8–37.

Yoder, J. D., & Kahn, A. S. (2003). Making gender comparisons more meaningful: A call for more attention to social context. *Psychology of Women Quarterly, 27,* 281–290.

Zanoni, P., & Janssens, M. (2004). Deconstructing difference: The rhetoric of human resource managers' diversity discourses. *Organization Studies, 25,* 55–74.

3

Theorizing Difference From Transnational Feminisms

Sarah E. Dempsey

Over ten years ago, Hegde (1998) issued a powerful call for feminist communication research to become more "transnationally responsive and politically engaged with issues of difference" (p. 271). Against the backdrop of global economic integration and fragmentation, scholars increasingly recognize that difference is an inescapable part of contemporary organizational life (Allen, 2004; Buzzanell, 2000; Ganesh, Zoller, & Cheney, 2005; Townsley, 2006). At the same time, there remains an ongoing need to situate current discussions of difference in the context of global capitalist relations and their gendered dimensions, including the lingering effects of colonialism and imperialism (Broadfoot & Munshi, 2007; Hegde, 1998; Prasad, 2003). As Stohl (2005) observed, globalization is the "widening, deepening, and speeding up of worldwide interconnectedness in all aspects of contemporary social life" (p. 231). The recognition of increasing multiplicity prompts the need to challenge the fiction of homogeneous workplaces and organizational forms.

In these respects, Hegde's (1998) call has ongoing relevance for organizational communication research. While organizational communication scholarship reflects its rich engagement with feminist and postmodern theories, it is less likely to move beyond the nation-state or to adopt transnational and postcolonial perspectives (for exceptions, see Broadfoot & Munshi, 2007; Dempsey, 2007, 2009; Flanagin, Stohl, & Bimber, 2006; Ganesh, Zoller, & Cheney, 2005; Prasad, 2003). For organizational scholars, transnational feminist perspectives provide a valuable vantage point from which to develop critical accounts of difference within the contemporary global moment.

At its broadest, transnational feminism refers to multiple practices and theories emerging from women's mobilizations at the global level. However, there has been considerable debate and ambiguity surrounding the term *transnational feminism*. This debate concerns the extent to which the term obscures the multiplicity and heterogeneity of the practices and theories to which it refers, as well as the contested nature of feminism across diverse cultural contexts. In what follows, I detail several key turning points in the development of transnational feminism to show how contemporary articulations differ from a unified conception of global sisterhood. Then, rather than attempting a comprehensive account of transnational feminisms in all of their diversity and richness, I highlight three key insights that a transnational feminist perspective brings to scholars interested in the intersections of difference and organizing. First, transnational feminism contributes an understanding of difference as intersectional, relational, and as a basis for identification and collective action. Second, transnational feminism encourages a broader understanding of the gendered aspects of globalization as they relate to the study of organizational difference. Third, transnational feminists have been at the forefront in wrestling with the complexities of balancing multiple forms of difference with a unifying agenda or set of common concerns (Pettman, 2004). As such, transnational feminist praxis provides illuminating models of organizing difference within a transnational context.

❖ THE EMERGENCE OF TRANSNATIONAL FEMINISMS

Transnational feminism refers to a highly self-reflexive body of theory and practice that has developed over time. The history of transnational feminism involves diverse women organizing across local and global scales to bring forth political, economic, and cultural empowerment (Desai, 2007). Throughout their development, these mobilizations have actively incorporated self-critique and analysis of their internal power relations. In this way, current articulations of transnational feminism have grown out of the sustained efforts by feminists to address the problem of difference within their organized efforts.

Described as the first wave of international women's activism, the period between 1880 and 1930 included mobilizations around issues of women's suffrage, temperance, and equal access to education, work, and labor legislation (Keck & Sikkink, 1998). During this time, relationships of colonialism and parochialism complicated women's international collaboration. For example, the efforts of Western women in Asia and Africa during colonial rule risked mirroring the project of modernization, including attempts by missionaries to promote Christian beliefs and values (Tripp, 2006).

After World War II, the United Nations (UN) Commission on the Status of Women became a focal point for advocacy, marking the beginning of a second wave of women's international activism. The UN International Women's Decade laid important groundwork for contemporary configurations of transnational feminism. Spanning from 1975 to 1985, the Decade for Women marked the convergence of the international women's rights movement, the human rights movement, and ongoing movements against colonialism (Antrobus, 2004). The Decade for Women not only drew attention to the status of women globally, but also provided forums for diverse women to gain knowledge about one another, share strategies, and build organizational capacity (Pettman, 2004). The UN context gave birth to issue-based networks at local, regional, and global levels, bringing together practitioners in the field of women and development, policymakers, academics, representatives of women's and feminist organizations, and women who identified themselves with the women's movement (see Antrobus, 2004, especially p. 61). During the 1970s, a series of conferences related to the Women in Development and Gender in Development movement brought together second wave feminists and women involved in anticolonial and economic justice struggles within the Global South (Pettman, 2004). Together, these international meetings facilitated the growth of a globalized women's movement characterized by interlinked research, activism, and networking across local and global scales.

While the Decade for Women and its associated international conferences and meetings allowed women to exchange information and forge new alliances, these alliances introduced their own power dynamics. In the period after 1975, women from the Global South increasingly challenged what they saw as the ideological dominance of Western groups in defining women's needs globally. This included contesting the promotion of universalizing models of liberation centered on Western values. In addition to highlighting the politics of representation at work within global women's organizations, they questioned the dominance of White, middle-class women from the North in leadership positions (Antrobus, 2004; Tripp, 2006). This included highlighting the privileging of White, heterosexual, middle-class women's standpoints on issues (Collins, 1990; Davis, 1981; hooks, 1984; Zinn, 1996). Thus, the so-called third wave of international women's activism is characterized by a critique of representational politics and a challenge to the construction of global sisterhood, in which all women are seen as occupying shared conditions of oppression.

Contemporary versions of transnational feminism depart from "one voice" feminism and a romantic conception of global sisterhood. The critique of global sisterhood reflects the understanding that "sisterhood cannot be assumed on the basis of gender," but is instead "forged in concrete historical and political practice and analysis" (Mohanty, 2003, p. 24). Such a realization has spurred a number of shifts within transnational feminist theory and practice. For example, women from the Global South are increasingly initiating and leading global feminist networks and organizations (Tripp, 2006). However, transnational feminism prompts ongoing questions about participation, voice, and representation, particularly in terms of how transnational feminist practice inadvertently reproduces existing inequalities among women (McLaughlin, 2007). Ultimately, the critique of universalizing conceptions of "woman" has prompted the development of robust perspectives on difference, including theories of feminist solidarity.

Transnational feminist perspectives are varied, and they contribute rich insight into ongoing interdisciplinary discussions surrounding the complexities of contemporary globalizations. Because a comprehensive account of their contributions is outside the bounds of this chapter, I focus on three areas of particular relevance to organizational scholars interested in the intersections between difference and organizing within the broader global context: theories of difference, gendered analyses of globalization, and models of organizing difference.

❖ THEORIZING DIFFERENCE

Differences as Intersectional and Relational

An ongoing debate within feminist theory includes the extent to which women are understood as experiencing a set of commonalities and shared concerns (Hegde, 1998; hooks, 1984; Lorde, 1984; Zinn, 1996). This has included sustained critique of the problematic assumptions reproduced within feminist theory itself. From a post-structuralist perspective, the instability of the category "woman" creates an episte-mological problem, whereby any account of "women's experience risks naturalizing one group of women's experience as normative and thereby marginalizing that of another group's" (Moya, 2000, p. 3). The ferment within feminist theory has been highly productive, prompt-ing new insights into the ways gender intersects with other categories of social identity, like race and class.

A transnational feminist perspective on difference departs from additive approaches, which treat various differences as discrete cate-gories. Such a perspective builds upon the work of scholars like Patricia Hill Collins, bell hooks, Audre Lorde, and Elizabeth Spelman, who highlight the ways in which women experience themselves as simultaneously gendered, raced, classed, and sexualized. As Mohanty (2003) noted, categories of social identity function as relational terms, in which they foreground a relationship among, for example, race, gen-der, and nation. Thus, people's experience of difference depends upon their particular social location within hierarchical structures of race, class, gender, sexuality, nation, and ethnicity (Zinn, 1996).

Patricia Hill Collins (1990) argued that categories of difference function as interlocking systems of domination and emancipation. Women experience these intertwined systems differently, including at the level of their personal biography, at the group or community level, and at the institutional level. Transnational feminist theories have been instrumental in outlining how unequal global relations continually articulate the politics of race, class, and gender within local contexts (Shome, 2006). A transnational feminist perspective extends discus-sions of intersectionality by situating categories like race, class, gender, and sexuality within the relationships of particular nation-states, including histories of capitalism, colonialism, and military conflict. Combined with postcolonial critique, these theories emphasize the need to situate aspects of identity within their shifting geopolitical arrangements and the relations of nations and inter/national histories.

Informed by postcolonial critique, transnational feminist perspec-tives draw attention to the ongoing economic, physical, and social influence of colonialism and neocolonialist ways of being. In particular, the analysis of the colonizer-colonized relationship prompts new insights into power, control, and resistance within organizations (Prasad, 2003). Mendez and Wolf's (2001) study illustrated how neo-colonial relations may be reproduced unwittingly within the organiz-ing process. Reflecting on their involvement with a feminist exchange program that brought "Third World" women to their U.S. campus, they noted the ease with which the program put into play patron-client relationships. Within such a paternalistic and unequal relationship, the "patron" uses his or her power to protect or support the "client," with the expectation that the "client" will defer to the patron. This creates systems of dependency, and it reinforces relations of domination. Members of the program unwittingly reproduced such relationships through their administration of, and participation in, the stipend program. Here, the program helped constitute the U.S. scholars and graduate students as "rich patrons willingly bestowing some of their resources on 'worthy' women of the South" (p. 732). Such examples reveal how unequal power relations originating from the history of colonialism and ongoing global, regional, and local economic relations play out within core organizing processes.

Postcolonial theories are useful to organizational scholars in that they invite defamiliarization, prompting new insights into organizational practices and discourses (Prasad, 2003). For example, concepts such as cultural hybridity and the border-lands provoke questions about how organizational scholarship conceptualizes the very idea of difference (Bhabha, 1994; Cooks, 2001; Kraidy, 2002). While a contested term, the concept of *hybridity* challenges the notion of a "pure" culture or identity. As Kraidy (2002) explained, an intercontextual theory of hybridity highlights "the mutually constitutive interplay and overlap of cultural, economic, and political forces in international communication processes" (p. 333). Drawing upon the work of Gloria Anzaldúa, Leda Cooks (2001) suggested that the concept of borderlands is a generative one for scholars interested in theorizing difference. She made two points: (1) that the social construction of borders . . . "involve[s] a range of (inter)actions [that are] . . . enacted with a particular consequentiality," and (2) that "we encounter the borders of culture and discipline, of history and identity, not as an immutable scientific fact, but as a dynamic discursive force that both constrains and enables mobility and social relations" (p. 346). While Cooks (2001) applied the concept of borderlands to critique the contours of intercultural communication research, her description is also useful in thinking about how differences are produced and maintained within the organizing process itself.

Finally, a transnational feminist approach problematizes a privileged view of communication rooted in the West; a perspective largely influenced by modernist intellectual practices (Broadfoot & Munshi, 2007; Prasad, 2003; Shome, 2006; Shome & Hegde, 2002). As Broadfoot and Munshi (2007) warned, when we "unthinkingly adopt the discourse and knowledge of mainstream Euro-American organizational communication scholarship, we potentially absorb . . . a particular way of understanding the world" (p. 264). Organizational scholarship benefits from increased reflexivity in that our key theories and concepts reflect a particular set of narrow cultural values and perspectives. For example, the GLOBE project includes a number of large-scale studies conducted by the Global Leadership and Organizational Behavior Effectiveness research program. After surveying 17,300 managers in 62 countries, the study classified their leadership according to Western-defined cultural dimensions (House, Hanges, Mansour, Dorfman, & Gupta, 2004). In this way, theories and concepts developed to explain organizational practices within Western contexts become the implicit yardstick to evaluate organizations in non-Western contexts.

Representing Difference

Ongoing debates within transnational feminism also draw needed attention to the highly politicized nature of academic knowledge production, including how scholarly representations contribute to essentialism. Chandra Mohanty (2003) discussed the ways in which Western feminist academic discourses contain problematic treatments of difference. Drawing upon textual analysis, she argued that many feminist authors construct Third World Women as a homogenous group:

> Automatically and necessarily defined as religious (read: not progressive), family-oriented (read: traditional), legally unsophisticated (read: they are still not conscious of their rights), illiterate (read: ignorant), domestic (read: backward), and sometimes revolutionary (read: their country is in a state of war, they must fight). (p. 40)

Mohanty (2003) argued that feminist writing functions as a form of discursive colonization, in which the authors rely on analytical categories shaped by a somewhat arbitrary set of Western-centric feminist interests. Particularly problematic is the way in which such representations assume an "ahistorical, universal unity between women" drawing heavily upon a generalized notion of their common subordination (p. 31).

In addition to politicizing academic knowledge practices, a transnational feminist perspective locates the need to attend to the ways in which problematic treatments of difference, such as essentialism, play out within transnational forms of organizing. For example, Booth's (1998) study of the World Health Organization's Global Program on AIDS (GPA) provided a valuable glimpse into the daily practices of feminist bureaucrats. She described how organizational members constructed women living with AIDS as either "national mothers" or "global whores." Each implied a particular response to the problem of AIDS. A discourse of women as national mothers constructed AIDS as an individualized and localized problem best addressed by strengthening national governments. A second discourse constructed women as global whores, thereby politicizing the problem of AIDS in terms of the persistence of sexual inequality within the broader global context. Booth argued that, although each discourse implies the need for intervention, they both reflect a particular set of Western values and help naturalize the ongoing representation of Third World women as passive victims. While departing from a focus on organizational communication, Booth's study serves as a rich example of dilemmas related to representation that arise within transnational forms of organizing—particularly those characterized by the intersections of multiple forms of difference.

Feminist Models of Solidarity

Transnational feminism itself embodies the struggle over the theoretical and practical complexities involved in balancing multiple forms of difference with a desire to pursue joint action (Grewal & Kaplan, 1994). As Mendez and Wolf (2001) noted, transnational feminist practice involves purposive attempts by people from different backgrounds and social locations to work together around common goals while attending to their differences. Building upon feminist, critical race, and postcolonial traditions, transnational feminism develops a vision of coordinated action built around the simultaneous engagement of both difference and commonality. (See Shome, 2006, for a review.) Within the U.S. context, conceptions of solidarity have been historically linked to Karl Marx's call for revolutionary class-consciousness based on the shared interests of the working class. However, several iterations of feminist theorizing challenge the presumed universality (and fixity) of class and other social identities, such as gender, ethnicity, and race.

Transnational feminist perspectives conceptualize solidarity as based on shared social location rather than on fixed or ahistorical notions of class, culture, or experience. Mohanty (2003) proposed a model of feminist solidarity in which the idea of common difference forms the basis for coordinated action. Such an approach reflects Audre Lorde's (1984) observations that while "the need for unity is often misnamed as a need for homogeneity . . . difference can serve as a basis of identification." Mohanty (2003) developed this further, arguing for an understanding of solidarity in terms of a relationship among diverse communities characterized by mutuality, accountability, and common interests. From this perspective, difference is a foundational force within the organizing process. She wrote,

> In knowing differences and particularities, we can better see the connections and commonalities because no border or boundary is ever complete or rigidly determining. The challenge is to see how differences allow us to explain the connections and border crossings better and more accurately, how specifying difference allows us to theorize universal concerns more fully. It is this intellectual move that allows for my concern for women of different communities and identities to build coalitions and solidarities across borders. (p. 226)

Feminist models of solidarity intentionally confront and plan for issues of difference, in part by valuing the boundaries between diverse participants. Such an approach differs from traditional melting pot discourses of diversity aimed at minimizing or managing individual differences (Prasad, Mills, Elmes, & Prasad, 1997). At the same time, the metaphor of solidarity provides a suggestive way to conceive of how difference can function as a productive or generative force within cross-sector partnerships and other organizational forms characterized by diverse members.

Nagar's (2006) recent study, *Playing with Fire,* provides a rich example of the need to understand how forms of solidarity are shaped and enacted within specific locales. Set primarily in Uttar Pradash, India, a target of multiple "development" efforts, the study tells the multilayered story of the Sangtin Collective, an alliance formed between Richa Nagar, a University of Minnesota professor, seven village-level NGO activists, and a district-level NGO activist. Together, these diverse women developed a model of mutual empowerment and solidarity based upon an accounting of their multiple and differential experiences of oppression and empowerment. They draw upon discussions of their own autobiographical writing as tools for analysis and critique of how their unique standpoints bear upon their partnership. The writers collectively determined the topics of these writings, with each iterative discussion phase marked by shared decision making. In the interest of accounting for their relatively privileged positions, Nagar and the district-level NGO employee withdrew from the process of collective writing.

One of the key lessons that *Playing with Fire* offers for an understanding of organizing in the context of difference is that solidarity remains deeply situated within place and culture. Claims of a universal solidarity, like many attempts to "think globally," inevitably express only the specific vision, interests, and cultural values of small groups of people (Esteva & Prakash, 1998). Thus, the model of solidarity enacted by members of the Sangtin Collective emerged from their collective analysis of the concrete power relations governing their organizing practices. As opposed to offering grand maxims, then, a transnational feminist perspective provokes new insights into the ongoing interplay between commonality and difference within the organizing process. In particular, feminist conceptions of solidarity draw attention to the fact that, in many cases, difference functions as a primary impetus for organizing.

❖ GENDERED ANALYSES OF GLOBALIZATION

Transnational feminism also refers to a diverse and highly self-reflexive body of First and Third World feminist theorizations on globalization. This body of scholarship enables a critique of the gendered impacts of globalization, including how global capitalist relations perpetuate gender difference. In this way, it equips organizational scholars with an understanding of how global economic and political processes shape existing patterns of economic, racial, and gender inequalities. This includes the recognition that the practices and effects of globalization are contradictory. As Hegde (2006) observed, while globalization processes "enable women to escape some social regulations, [they] also subject them to other types and patterns of global subordination" (p. 445). Transnational feminist perspectives and theories take a multifaceted approach to explore these gendered contradictions.

While feminist perspectives on economic globalization take different tacks and contain much disagreement, they converge around the critique of popular accounts of globalization. Popular accounts typically adopt a proglobalization stance, which sees the spread of capitalist markets, increased competition, new technologies, and free trade as overwhelmingly positive trends (Murray, 2006), wherein individuals benefit depending upon the extent of their participation within the global market. This perspective was well illustrated in *New York Times* columnist Thomas Friedman's (2005) oft-cited, best selling observation that "the world is flat." Friedman argued that, through a series of globalizing technological innovations such as the Netscape Internet browser, an increasing number of groups benefitted from globalization. In its strongest versions, proglobalization perspectives conceive of globalization as an unstoppable force, and as an inevitable continuation of modernist progress.

Most notably, many of the proglobalization perspectives tend to ignore or downplay the role of gender and race within global processes (Acker, 2004). Feminist perspectives challenge popular accounts, in part by questioning the assumption that global capital is all-determining in its practices and effects (Freeman, 2001; Gibson-Graham, 2006). Specifically, feminist perspectives draw attention to the ways in which global economic processes depend upon, and actively produce, the stratification of difference. In doing so, they respond to the need for insight into how globalized and gendered processes play themselves out within particular locales (Hegde, 2006). In addition, feminist critiques have also begun outlining a more nuanced account of globalization that is better able to speak to the duality of power and resistance within the global context (Mumby, 2005). In the section that follows, I illustrate how feminist research contributes rich insight into gendered organizing processes in the context of increasing economic and social integration.

Gender Difference and the Global Assembly Line

Feminists have made important contributions to understanding the social implications of transnational labor flows, including developing critical perspectives on the feminization of the global labor force. This work demonstrates that global assembly lines have as much to do with the production of gender and racial difference as they do with the restructuring of labor and capital (Fernández-Kelly, 2007; Freeman, 2000). Current configurations of global commodity chains and transnational labor flows have emerged from a series of important historical shifts. Beginning in the 1970s, many domestic companies in the United States and other rich countries began moving portions of their production overseas in a search for cheaper labor. Moving production activities offshore allowed corporations to benefit from the lax labor laws, anti-union policies, and minimal oversight in developing countries (Sassen, 2000). In doing so, companies benefitted from the increasing popularity of neoliberal policies, which involved the removal of barriers to trade between various nation-states. These policies led to the creation of free trade zones designed to enhance the flow of capital across nation-state borders (Eisenstein, 2005). Each of these factors has contributed to the now commonplace use of global assembly lines organized across multiple nation-state borders.

Female labor plays a critical role in the global assembly line because women make up the vast majority of the workforce within electronics, textiles, and telework industries (Collins, 2002; Eisenstein, 2005;

Freeman, 2000). The incorporation of female labor into the global assembly line is accompanied by a consistent discourse of women workers within developing contexts as naturally suited to this work. This discourse depends upon, and reproduces, two gendered and raced assumptions: (1) that female bodies in the developing world are much more docile and easily controlled when compared to their male or female counterparts in the developed world, and (2) that female bodies in the developing world are uniquely and naturally equipped with the skills needed to labor on the global assembly line. Thus, rather than simply tapping into available labor forces, multinational corporations engage in the complex and active construction of workers' subjectivities along deeply gendered and racial lines. These constructions depend upon and reproduce development ideologies and nation-state hierarchies.

A number of feminist studies have demonstrated how notions of skill reflect gendered ideologies of the body. The apparel industry provides a particularly poignant example of how these discourses of skill depend upon deeply held cultural assumptions about femininity and the female body. Research describes the reproduction of the "fairy fingers" or "nimble fingers" conception of women's labor. This conception assumes that young female workers are uniquely prepared for the global apparel industry given girls' involvement in the domestic sphere. Here, girls are assumed to already possess relevant sewing skills. The naturalization of female skill includes the conviction that women are innately better at using needle and thread. The comparatively smaller size of their hands functions as a marker of natural skill. Together, these discourses tie women's skill to the private sphere of bodies and domesticity. In the global apparel industry, the naturalization of women's skill denies that their labor derives from "learned and practiced competencies, knowledge, and creativity involved in sewing," instead locating these capacities "in the realm of the private body rather than the public sphere of the market and waged work" (Collins, 2002, p. 926). In this way, gendered discourses of skill function as a double-edged sword. While they provide women with access to the labor market and a means of livelihood, they contribute to the devaluing of this labor, thereby perpetuating the payment of survival wages.

In addition to naturalizing the skills of the female body, companies use gendered discourses of skill to justify moving higher wage, unionized jobs to countries with lower wages and non-unionized workforces. In this way, gendered discourses of skill intersect with development discourses. In her qualitative study of the globalizing garment industry, Collins (2002) showed how managers of an apparel company headquartered in Virginia, USA, employed gendered ideologies of skill to justify their search for inexperienced workers in low-wage nations. Drawing upon open-ended interviews with corporate officers and midlevel managers, she argued that gendered discourses of skill allowed manufacturers to defend their use of off-shore, low-wage labor. Managers claimed that because women's sewing skills in the United States were disappearing, they needed to seek out this skill in parts of the world in which this skill was more plentiful. Here, the portrayal of low wage female labor as a naturally occurring resource within the Global South not only justifies the movement of capital in search of new markets, but does so by drawing upon intersecting ideologies of gender, race, class, and national difference.

In another example of how the global assembly line depends upon the production of difference, Wright (2003) discussed how male Hong Kong managers within a U.S.-based corporation control the turnover rate of their female migrant labor force in China. Drawing on interviews and observations, Wright highlighted how managers constructed their managerial role along paternal lines. They employed intersecting discourses of gender and cultural identity to justify their ability to enforce and police Confucian cultural expectations about "good" Chinese daughters. Adopting the role of concerned fathers tasked with governing unruly daughters, they employed extensive disciplinary measures. These measures included invasive procedures for monitoring female worker's mobility and sexuality. Wright saw this case as symptomatic of an emergent form of corporate management seen within the global context of increasing economic and intercultural interdependence. In the reconfigured corporate landscape that crosses nation-state, race, and regional borders, modern managers draw upon deeply embedded cultural assumptions about gender and age to perfect their ability to assert managerial control.

While feminist researchers detail how gendered and raced notions of skill justify forms of managerial control, they have also challenged the image of the docile female body subject to global capitalism. Ngai's (2005) *Made in China: Women Factory Workers in a Global Workplace* focuses on the emergence of a new global identity: the *dagonmei* (working girls). The dagonmei are an itinerant workforce of young girls from rural areas working in China's Shenzen district. Ngai lived and worked alongside factory workers, joining them in their weekend activities. She drew upon her ethnographic observations to argue that girls' participation in assembly line work reflects their choice to adopt new modern selves. At the same time, she argued that global capitalism exploits their labor. This exploitation occurs through three overlapping systems of oppression: (1) patriarchal familial expectations, (2) the

Chinese *hukou* system of residence restrictions, and (3) the broader cultural discrimination and contempt for rural identities. Ngai resisted the temptation to privilege the workers' oppression over their resistance, detailing how they use their bodies to assert some control over the work process. She argued that the global factory system and its associated discursive, spatial, and institutional controls conspires with existing ideologies of race, class, gender, and regional identity to create a docile female body. At the same time, the dagonmei use their bodies to survive and transgress. In this, they adopt "tactical bodies" that scream, feel pain, faint, and slow the pace of the assembly line. Faced with little means to constitute themselves as a political force, the workers draw upon the afflictions of their bodies to exert control. Here, although modern disciplinary power regulates the factory body through micropractices of control, such as spacing and timing, the tactical body resists. In reading bodily afflictions as forms of transgression, Ngai challenged conventional portrayals of female factory labor as comprised of passive, docile workers.

Gender, Race, Class, and Reproductive Labor

Feminist perspectives have been instrumental in highlighting the multiple forms of labor and production that exist globally. This includes expanding beyond paid labor in the formal sector to highlight reproductive labor. The development of the idea of "reproductive labor" has emerged alongside the critique of gendered and racial divisions of labor. Conceived broadly, reproductive labor refers to the various forms of "caring" work involved with maintaining existing life as well as ensuring social reproduction (Duffy, 2007). For example, reproductive labor includes paid and unpaid housework, childcare and eldercare, and household and agricultural labor. As Acker (2004) detailed, the reproductive labor essential to maintaining human life is typically not included in analyses of globalization. Along with many others, she argued that this division between commodity production in the capitalist economy and the reproduction of human beings and their ability to labor is fundamental to the production of difference and inequality in the global context (e.g., Barker & Feiner, 2004; Gibson-Graham, 2006). These perspectives advocate for increased attention to the restructuring of reproductive labor by globalization and, in particular, to the ways that it assumes and depends upon the production of gender and racial differences.

The global division of reproductive labor is a result of a restructuring of the global workforce and capitalism's demand for cheaper and more plentiful labor. Within post-industrialized countries, this is supported by market-based rationalities that privilege the pursuit of paid labor over other aspects of social life (Hoffman & Cowan, 2008; Kirby & Krone, 2002) and counsel workers to reorganize family life around capital's demands for labor (Sotirin, Buzzanell, & Turner, 2007). These forces contribute to overwork and the neglect of reproductive labor by a particular set of high-wage workers. For example, Blair-Loy and Jacobs (2003) drew on interviews with 61 stockbrokers and their managers to document their lengthening work hours. Such developments reinforce gender and racial inequality at the workplace, at home, and abroad through the displacement and reassignment of reproductive labor. As they put it, "global capital depends on the concentration of well-paid financial services professionals alongside low-paid, less-skilled service workers who are often immigrants and minorities" (p. 231). Here, the reproductive labor needed to sustain a particular subsection of the workforce within post-industrial countries (such as household chores, eldercare, and childcare) prompts the "international transfer of caretaking." This international transfer maintains a gendered, racialized division of reproductive labor in which, for example, White, middle-class women purchase the low-wage services of immigrant women and women of color (Parrenas, 2000).

❖ ORGANIZING DIFFERENCE

The term *transnational feminism* not only refers to feminist analyses of globalization, but also points to the increasing importance of the transnational context for feminist praxis. Diverse groups of women are responding to the inequities of global capitalism by organizing for transformative social change across nation-state borders. As articulated by the feminist network Women in Development Europe (WIDE), the shift to transnational alliance-building reflects the recognition that "feminism in one country is not sustainable . . . [and that] feminism [is needed] at a global scale" (quoted in Hawkesworth, 2006, p. 1). These efforts provide organizational scholars with rich insight into the intersections of multiple differences within the context of organizing.

Transnational feminist networks (TFNs) provide a particularly illuminating example of the purposive attempt to organize across multiple differences. TFNs involve groups of women from at least three countries organizing around issues such as women's human rights, reproductive health, peace, and economic justice. Members provide each other with mutual support and education and engage in a combination of lobbying, advocacy, and direct action toward greater equality and empowerment within the context of globalization (Moghadam, 2005). When compared to more formalized organizations, TFN membership tends to be ad hoc, temporary, and fluid, and it may change depending upon shifting interests or needs within the broader political arena. TFNs adopt feminist principles and goals within their organizing process, including the use of decentralized leadership, collective decision making, and the distribution of power. They vary in professionalization and centralization. While a handful of well-resourced, Western TFNs include paid staff members at a central office, many TFNs depend upon their own volunteer labor (see Dempsey, Parker, & Krone, 2007).

One of the primary characteristics of TFNs includes the intentional engagement with multiple forms of difference, including nation, region, race, class, caste, ethnicity, sexuality, and religion (Dempsey et al., 2007). As such, they bring together diverse participants with conflicting goals, ethical values, and experiences. Peggy Antrobus, a founding member of both the Caribbean Association for Feminist Research and Action (CAFRA) and the Development Alternatives with Women for a New Era (DAWN) networks outlines what she sees as six key, overlapping strategies employed by women organizing for social change at the global scale. Taken together, these strategies provide a glimpse into the daily organizing practices of TFNs, including how members plan for and negotiate their multiple differences.

A first strategy includes consciousness-raising, or a process in which women reflect on their personal experiences of gender-based oppression in order to gain a "deeper understanding of the experience of other forms of oppression based on class, race, ethnicity, culture, and international relations" (Antrobus, 2004, p. 110). This strategy indicates a particular responsiveness to the intersections among multiple forms of difference, including how they are experienced at both the individual and group levels. Another strategy includes employing women's circles, or small groups of trusted friends or colleagues. These groups provide safe spaces for participants to engage in analysis, mutual support, and information and skill sharing. Caucuses comprise a third strategy, and their use has emerged within the framework of women's activism within the UN context. Caucuses are public forums or conferences in which diverse participants engage in detailed analysis, negotiation, and debate about particular political strategies, policies, and agendas. This strategy is particularly revealing of a commitment to dialogue and debate within the organizing process. A fourth strategy includes coalition and alliance building. This includes multistakeholder participation, or the networking of networks. For example, during the 1990s, women's networks concerned with environmental issues began forming alliances and partnerships with networks focused on reproductive rights and development. Such alliance building emerges from a particular under-standing in difference, including the acknowledgment of "the linkages between the social, political, and economic and cultural concerns of women, along with an analysis that links women's experiences at the personal and micro level of the community to the common policy framework of neo-liberalism" (Antrobus, 2004, p. 112).

A fifth strategy includes global conferencing, which provides critical places for networking, the sharing of news and strategies, and the strengthening of relationships among diverse participants. A final strategy includes campaigns, which describe loosely orga-nized efforts around a particular political goal or outcome. Examples include the Global Campaign for Women's Human Rights (GCWHR), which brought together diverse stakeholders to address women's human rights.

According to Antrobus (2004), participants employ these six strate-gies across interpersonal, group, and organizational levels:

> Like a pebble dropped in water, the individual experience extends to progressively larger circles, incorporating, or being incorporated by, increasing diversity, until in the campaign the individual may find herself part of a mass movement of people who often have conflicting interests. (p. 110)

Such a statement is particularly revealing of a purposive commit-ment to engaging difference. However, as they organize across multi-ple, intersecting differences, TFNs face several characteristic challenges (Dempsey et al., 2007). A first challenge involves negotiating participa-tive dilemmas. For example, participatory and consensus-based deci-sion making is particularly time-consuming (Mansbridge, 1973). Depending on socioeconomic factors, participants may be unable to travel to global conferences or spend time attending long meetings. A second challenge includes navigating the politics of representation. TFNs often engage in the highly problematic task of advocating on the behalf of groups with little access to the public sphere. TFNs must negotiate the politics of their communicative labor, including mem-bers' differing abilities to advocate on the behalf of themselves and oth-ers (Dempsey, 2009). Even when well-meaning, this may reproduce existing inequalities, such as when relatively well-resourced or English-speaking groups play a disproportionate role in designing public statements. While the efforts of TFNs provide organizational scholars with a glimpse into purposive attempts to organize across multiple differences, they also indicate the need to understand how these efforts introduce their own complex dilemmas.

❖ CONCLUSION

As developed in this chapter, a transnational feminist perspective brings three key insights to current discussions of organizing as it relates to difference. First, it contributes to the conceptualization of difference in terms of intersectionality and to an understanding of difference as relational. In forwarding a critique of additive approaches to difference, transnational feminist theorists propose new forms of solidarity and alliance-building among diverse women. Taken together, these new forms illuminate how difference serves as a foundational resource for organizing. Second, transnational feminism contributes new understandings of the gendered effects of global economic processes. Through critical analysis of the global assembly line and the inequalities of reproductive labor, this work highlights how global capitalism depends upon the reproduction of gender, race, and class difference. Third, transnational feminism has emerged from the concrete activities and strategies of heterogeneous feminist actors who have pioneered new forms of participative practice aimed at bringing together diverse groups. This includes, for example, the networking, lobbying, and information-sharing activities of social movement participants, community-based activists, NGOs, and transnational feminist networks, as well as feminists' involvement within the UN system and other international forums. In these ways, transnational feminism provides rich insight into the dilemmas involved with organizing across multiple differences, including how these dilemmas gain additional complexity within a transnational context.

❖ REFERENCES

Acker, J. (2004). Gender, capitalism and globalization. *Critical Sociology, 30*, 17–41.
Allen, B. J. (2004). *Difference matters: Communicating social identity.* Long Grove, IL: Waveland Press.
Antrobus, P. (2004). *The global women's movement: Origins, issues and strategies.* London: Zed Books.
Barker, D. K., & Feiner, S. F. (2004). *Liberating economics: Feminist perspectives on families, work, and globalization.* Ann Arbor: The University of Michigan Press.

Bhabha, H. K. (1994). *The location of culture*. New York: Routledge.

Blair-Loy, M., & Jacobs, J. A. (2003). Globalization, work hours, and the care deficit among stockbrokers. *Gender & Society, 17*, 230–249.

Booth, K. M. (1998). National mother, global whore, and transnational femocrats: The politics of AIDS and the construction of women at the World Health Organization. *Feminist Studies, 24*, 115–139.

Broadfoot, K. J., & Munshi, D. (2007). Diverse voices and alternative rationalities: Imagining forms of postcolonial organizational communication. *Management Communication Quarterly, 21*, 249–267.

Buzzanell, P. (Ed.). (2000). *Rethinking organizational and managerial communication from feminist perspectives*. Thousand Oaks, CA: Sage.

Collins, J. (2002). Mapping a global labor market: Gender and skill in the globalizing garment industry. *Gender & Society, 16*, 921–940.

Collins, P. H. (1990). *Black feminist thought: Knowledge, consciousness, and the politics of empowerment*. New York: Routledge.

Cooks, L. (2001). From distance and uncertainty to research and pedagogy in the borderlands: Implications for the future of intercultural research. *Communication Theory, 11*(3), 339-351.

Davis, A. Y. (1981). *Women, race, and class*. New York: Random House.

Dempsey, S. E. (2007). Negotiating accountability within international contexts: The role of bounded voice. *Communication Monographs, 34*, 311–322.

Dempsey, S. E. (2009). NGOs, communicative labor, and the work of grassroots representation. *Communication and Critical/Cultural Studies, 6*, 328–345.

Dempsey, S. E., Parker, P. S., & Krone, K. (2007, May). *Organizing tensions within transnational collective action spaces: An analysis of feminist transnational networks*. Paper presented at the International Communication Association meeting, San Francisco, CA.

Desai, M. (2007). The messy relationship between feminism and globalizations. *Gender & Society, 21*, 797–803.

Duffy, M. (2007). Doing the dirty work: Gender, race, and reproductive labor in historical perspective. *Gender & Society, 21*, 313–336.

Eisenstein, H. (2005). A dangerous liaison? Feminism and corporate globalization. *Science & Society, 69*, 487–518.

Esteva, G., & Prakash, M. S. (1998). *Grassroots post-modernism: Remaking the soil of cultures*. London: Zed Books.

Fernández-Kelly, P. (2007). The global assembly line in the new millennium: A review essay. *Signs, 32*, 509–521.

Flanagin, A., Stohl, C., & Bimber, B. (2006). Modeling the structure of collective action. *Communication Monographs, 73*, 29–54.

Freeman, C. (2000). *High tech and high heels in the global economy: Women, work, and pink-collar identities in the Caribbean*. Durham, NC: Duke University Press.

Freeman, C. (2001). Is local:global as feminine:masculine? Rethinking the gender of globalization. *Signs, 26*, 1007–1037.

Friedman, T. (2005). *The world is flat: A brief history of the twenty-first century*. New York: Farrar, Straus, and Giroux.

Ganesh, S., Zoller, H. M., & Cheney, G. (2005). Transforming resistance, broadening our boundaries: Critical organizational communication meets globalization from below. *Communication Monographs, 72,* 169–191.

Gibson-Graham, J. K. (2006). *A postcapitalist politics.* Minneapolis: University of Minnesota Press.

Grewal, I., & Kaplan, C. (Eds.). (1994). *Scattered hegemonies: Postmodernity and transnational feminist practices.* Minneapolis: University of Minnesota Press.

Hawkesworth, M. E. (2006). *Globalization and feminist activism.* Lanham, MD: The Rowman & Littlefield Publishers.

Hegde, R. S. (1998). A view from elsewhere: Locating difference and the politics of representation from a transnational feminist perspective. *Communication Theory, 8,* 271–297.

Hegde, R. S. (2006). Globalizing gender studies in communication. In B. J. Dow & J. T. Wood (Eds.), *Sage handbook of gender and communication* (pp. 433–450). Thousand Oaks, CA: Sage.

Hoffman, M. F., & Cowan, R. L. (2008). The meaning of work/life: A corporate ideology of work/life balance. *Communication Quarterly, 56,* 227–246.

hooks, b. (1984). *Feminist theory: From margin to center.* Boston, MA: South End Press.

House, R. J., Hanges, P. J., Mansour, J., Dorfman, P. W., & Gupta, V. (Eds.). (2004). *Culture, leadership, and organizations: The GLOBE study of 62 studies.* Thousand Oaks, CA: Sage.

Keck, M. E., & Sikkink, K. (1998). *Activists beyond borders: Advocacy networks in international politics.* Ithaca, NY: Cornell University Press.

Kirby, E., & Krone, K. J. (2002). "The policy exists but you can't really use it": Communication and the structuration of work-family policies. *Journal of Applied Communication Research, 30,* 50–77.

Kraidy, M. M. (2002). Hybridity in cultural globalization. *Communication Theory, 12,* 316–339.

Lorde, A. (1984). *Sister outsider.* Freedom, CA: The Crossing Press.

Mansbridge, J. (1973). Time, emotion, and inequality: Three problems of participatory groups. *Journal of Applied Behavioral Science, 9,* 351–368.

McLaughlin, L. (2007). Transnational feminism and the Revolutionary Association of the Women of Afghanistan. In D. K. Thussa (Ed.), *Media on the move: Global flow and contra-flow* (pp. 221–236). London: Routledge.

Mendez, J. B., & Wolf, D. L. (2001). Where feminist theory meets feminist practice: Border-crossing in a transnational academic feminist organization. *Organization, 8,* 723–750.

Moghadam, V. M. (2005). *Globalizing women: Transnational feminist networks.* Baltimore, MD: The Johns Hopkins Press.

Mohanty, C. T. (2003). "Under western eyes" revisited: Feminist solidarity through anticapitalist struggles. *Signs, 28,* 499–539.

Moya, P. M. L. (2000). Reclaiming identity. In P. M. L. Moya & M. R. Hames-Garcia (Eds.), *Reclaiming identity: Realist theory and the predicament of postmodernism* (pp. 1–26). Berkeley, CA: University of California Press.

Mumby, D. (2005). Theorizing resistance in organization studies. *Management Communication Quarterly, 19,* 19–44.

Murray, W. (2006). *Geographies of globalization.* London: Routledge.

Nagar, R. (2006). *Playing with fire: Feminist thought and activism through seven lives in India.* Minneapolis: University of Minnesota Press.

Ngai, P. (2005). *Made in China.* Durham, NC: Duke University Press.

Parrenas, R. S. (2000). Migrant Filipina domestic workers and the international division of reproductive labor. *Gender and Society, 14,* 560–580.

Pettman, J. J. (2004). Global politics and transnational feminisms. In L. Ricciutelli, A. Miles, & M. H. McFadden (Eds.), *Feminist activism and vision: Local and global challenges* (pp. 49–63). London: Zed Books.

Prasad, A. (Ed.). (2003). *Postcolonial theory and organizational analysis.* New York: Palgrave MacMillan.

Prasad, A., Mills, A., Elmes, M. B., & Prasad, P. (Eds.). (1997). *Managing the organizational melting pot: Dilemmas of workplace diversity.* Thousand Oaks, CA: Sage.

Sassen, S. (2000). Women's burden: Counter-geographies of globalization and the feminization of survival. *Journal of International Affairs, 53*(2), 503–524.

Shome, R. (2006). Transnational feminism and communication studies. *The Communication Review, 9,* 255–267.

Shome, R., & Hegde, R. (2002). Culture, communication and the challenge of globalization. *Critical Studies in Media Communication, 19,* 72–189.

Sotirin, P., Buzzanell, P. M., & Turner, L. H. (2007). Colonizing family: A feminist critique of family management texts. *Journal of Family Communication, 7,* 245–263.

Stohl, C. (2005). Globalization theory. In S. May & D. K. Mumby (Eds.), *Engaging organizational communication theory and research: Multiple perspectives* (pp. 223–261). Thousand Oaks, CA: Sage.

Townsley, N. C. (2006). Love, sex, and tech in the global workplace. In B. J. Dow & J. T. Wood (Eds.), *The Sage handbook of gender and communication* (pp. 143–160). Thousand Oaks, CA: Sage.

Tripp, A. M. (2006). The evolution of transnational feminisms: Consensus, conflict, and new dynamics. In M. M. Ferree & A. M. Tripp (Eds.), *Global feminism: Transnational women's activism, organizing, and human rights* (pp. 51–75). New York: New York University Press.

Wright, M. W. (2003). Factory daughters and Chinese modernity: A case from Dongguan. *Geoforum, 34,* 291–301.

Zinn, M. B. (1996). Theorizing difference from multiracial feminism. *Feminist Studies, 22,* 321–331.

4

Leadership Discourses of Difference

Executive Coaching and the Alpha Male Syndrome

Gail T. Fairhurst, Marthe L. Church,
Danielle E. Hagen, and Joseph T. Levi

I hold two parallel images of the culture in organizations. In a traditional model, as people rise through the ranks, they are recognized for their skills and achievements. They are rewarded through promotion and increased status. However, there is also the shadow-side in organizations, where promotion is based on "corridor politics" and informal communication systems. Somewhere between these two polarities lies the reality for many people. However, there is increasing evidence that access to promotion is still not equally available to women, or to people from different backgrounds than the white, middle class, educated elite. This is a remarkable statement to make in the twenty-first century, but the evidence is there.

—Angela Eden, Executive Coach

Source: Material from Ludeman, K., & Erlandson, E. (2006). *Alpha male syndrome*. Boston: Harvard Business School. Used with permission.

Recently, Eden (2006) wrote about why—after so much evidence of women leaders' effectiveness, government steering, and industry initiatives—women are still not seen as natural leaders. Her solution is to recommend senior-level women for executive coaching. Indeed, executive coaching has become a mainstay for executives whose companies can afford the private sessions that coaching requires. It is perhaps a sign of the maturity of this leadership development technology that the publishing industry has responded in full force. There are a host of books (Brunning, 2006; Downs, 2002; Goldsmith, Lyons, & Freas, 2000; O'Neil, 2000; Underhill, McAnally, & Koriath, 2007; Valerio & Lee, 2005) and articles (Berglas, 2002; Gray, 2006; Kampa-Kokesch & Anderson, 2001; Kets de Vries, 2005; Levinson, 1966; Ludeman & Erlandson, 2004, 2007; Sherman & Freas, 2004) on executive coaching, and it has become the subject of parody in the likes of *Business Week* (Brady, 2006) and *Fortune* (David, 2003).

However, as Eden's recommendation suggests, of particular interest is the executive coaching literature's treatment of gender. *Alpha Male Syndrome* and its accompanying *Harvard Business Review* article, "Coaching the Alpha Male," written by executive coaches Kate Ludeman and Eddie Erlandson (2004, 2006), are the most prominent reads on gender.[1] The authors make the case that (a) 75% of all senior-level executives are alpha males; (b) alpha males are high achievers whose value to their organizations erodes when they become overly competitive, belligerent, or impatient; (c) *alpha male syndrome* is the label given to such dysfunction; and (d) female alphas are few in number and generally not prone to the alpha syndrome.

On the surface, such an argument appears foundational to a counter-masculinity management discourse, a discourse of difference between men and women that women leaders and concerned coaches like Angela Eden should laud. After all, consider the dedication in *Alpha Male Syndrome:*

> We dedicate this book to the indomitable women executives we have been privileged to work with and learn from. We admire your wisdom, your curiosity, your perseverance, and your commitment to stand your ground and get the best from your alpha male colleagues. We salute your courage and tenacity. (p. iii)

With such positive regard, what, if anything, is the problem? Unfortunately, there is also a strong gender subtext running through the work of Ludeman and Erlandson that unwittingly naturalizes masculinity and males as the leadership norm, disavows the feminization of executive coaching, "others" the female leader, and reinforces a binary gender system that contributes to its reinscription in organizational leadership discourse. We begin by setting the context—examining executive coaching as a powerful disciplinary technology. We then examine the gender text in *Alpha Male Syndrome* (hereafter, *AMS)* followed by gender as subtext and its implications for the study and practice of leadership in Western societies.

❖ EXECUTIVE COACHING AS A DISCIPLINARY TECHNOLOGY

Fairhurst (2007) first wrote about the power implications of executive coaching discourses, working from Foucault's (1980, 1983, 1990, 1995) view of discourse as a historically and culturally situated way of thinking, talking, and acting toward a subject. Power and knowledge are inextricably linked in this view because once a subject is known in particular ways, he or she can be acted upon. Foucault's view of power thus becomes both diffuse and relational as varying power technologies in institutional environments weave together knowledge, competence, and qualification in rather specific ways. Executive coaching is one such technology.

Executive coaching, performance appraisal, and 360-degree feedback are all performance management technologies. The latter two strive to make the employee visible through examination; that is, through assessment techniques that normalize judgment—especially around those who underperform (Newton & Findlay, 1996; Townley, 1993). Emblematic of Foucault's panoptic power, 360-degree feedback garners the evaluations of all members of a person's role set and thus has the power to discipline the individual even beyond that which is in management's reach through the performance appraisal. As Fairhurst (2007) observed, "With an unobstructed 360-degree view, the individual is permanently on show and open to examination—or at least he or she presumes as much as the individual ultimately disciplines him- or herself in response to the collective gaze of the role set" (p. 85).

Executive coaching adds a confessional technology to the examination techniques of appraisal and 360-degree feedback, and it should come as no surprise that all three are used in tandem. Typically, the coach enters into a three-party contractual relationship (client, coach, coachee) with the organizational client who pays the costly fees but accedes to the coach's demand that the coach-leader relationship remain confidential. That is, there should be no further reporting by the coach to the organization because the latter should be able to witness firsthand the leader's transformation. The hope is that the leader will self-disclose to the coach without fear that such disclosures will be used against him or her.

If trust forms, executive coaching is extraordinary for its "ability to gaze on the subjectivity of the worker, to know their feelings, anxieties, their identity and their consciousness" (Newton & Findlay, 1996, p. 48)—a characterization of performance management technologies generally, but one that is especially apt for the coaching relationship. The confessional aspect of executive coaching derives from a quasi-therapeutic model and is designed to get to the "truth" of the leader's putative dysfunctional behavior. However, as Foucault suggested, the truth is not *revealed* as much as it *co-constructed*—a joint formulation of a confessor's avowal (in this case, the leader's self disclosures) and the expert's uptake (that is, the coach's interpretations). Executive coaching succeeds when the leader's behaviors become incorporated into a coaching discourse of inferences, descriptions, and judgments, which discipline and drive the leader to act differently with or without the coach's presence.

Enter the alpha male as the prime target of executive coaching. The term *alpha male* is metaphorical, deriving from the male animal in charge of all others in a social group. In organizations, they become coaching targets because of their overriding need for control; the acting out of such a need in bursts of anger, unreasonable demands, or extreme competitiveness; and reliance on masculinity discourses, which maintain an instrumentalism and emotional distance in social relationships. The power dynamics behind coaching the alpha male begin with one of the first jobs of an executive coach, which is to get the alpha male's attention by calibrating the feedback from the 360 to "hit him hard enough to hurt" (Ludeman & Erlandson, 2004, p. 63). Because alphas routinely use hard-hitting language with others, "We regulate the level of pain, keeping it high enough to get their full attention but also presenting the changes as attainable" (Ludeman & Erlandson, p. 63). According to Fairhurst (2007), whether it is deserved or not, whether it is effective or not,

> One can't help but be reminded of Foucault's (1995) discussion of the art of torture, where a corpus of knowledge was developed to precisely measure and control the application of pain to the body so the person being tortured does not die too quickly. While pain is calibrated and applied to the body in the case of torture, it comes in

calibrated emotional wallops to the psyche of the leader. Not unlike the forced confession at the end of a public torture, it is only after receiving these comments that the alpha is properly situated to realize or 'avow' the consequences of his behavior. The modus operandi of the torturer and the executive coach are clearly different, but the confessional technology is the same. (p. 89)

Other coaching techniques involve getting the alpha male to use a defensiveness scale to discipline himself to avoid defensive routines, creating alter egos to strike down as targets in coaching sessions, and more (Fairhurst, 2007; Ludeman & Erlandson, 2004, 2007). But what of alpha females, and more to the point, why question the restricted categorization of the alpha term if various technologies of power are specifically deployed to eradicate the worst of male leadership behavior?

❖ THE GENDER TEXT IN ALPHA MALE SYNDROME

In order to answer the previous questions, Ludeman and Erlandson's (2006) explicit treatment of gender requires a serious look. Consider some of their claims around male and female alpha behavior in their book:

1. Because of the popular image of the alpha male, with his powerful physical presence and tough-guy demeanor, we seldom hear the term *alpha female.* But a great many women in leadership positions do possess the fundamental traits that define alphas. One of them is the author of this book. We decided to focus on alpha *males* . . . because there are more of them . . . [and because] a great deal of wreckage is caused by boys behaving badly. (p. 4, emphasis original)

2. Our coaching experience, our own research data, and a large body of scientific research all suggest that women in general display their leadership traits somewhat differently than men . . . Like their male counterparts, female alphas are ambitious and drawn to positions of authority, but as a rule, they are less inclined to dominate. Better attuned to the emotional climate, they are more likely . . . to look for ways to collaborate and to find win-win solutions to conflicts. . . . In other words, alpha women want to lead, but they don't necessarily need to rule (p. 21).

3. Alpha males are more likely . . . to see themselves as exceptionally competent—so much so, in fact, that they relish visible,

high-risk competitions in which they expect to stand out . . .
Women . . . are more likely to shy away from competition even
when they stand a good chance of winning . . . women thrive on
the calming influence of endorphin-producing activities, such as
conversation and relationship building. (p. 22)

4. It must be emphasized that neither style is better than the other.
   What's important is for individuals to become adept at using
   both under the appropriate circumstances, and to draw upon
   the natural strengths in the brains of the other sex . . . Whatever
   its origin, the style we think of as "feminine" certainly seems to
   soften the edges of female alpha tendencies. (p. 23)

5. Are female alphas the perfect antidote to the alpha male downside? In many ways they are. But they have challenges of their
   own . . . If, for example, you're overly concerned about people's
   feelings, your communication might be so indirect that no one
   can figure out what you want and what you think . . . Another
   reason sensitivity can turn from asset to liability is that women
   are often seen as *too* emotional . . . an enraged man is considered tough and strong, but an irate woman is hysterical and
   irrational. And if they lean in the opposite direction, female
   alphas run the risk of being too soft. (p. 25, emphasis original)

These generalized sentiments are distilled in the chapter organization of *AMS* around four styles of dysfunctional alpha male behavior—
"commander," "visionary," "strategist," and "executor." The authors
reported on male and female versions of each style based upon survey
research of 1,523 readers of *Harvard Business Review*, laced with their
own consulting examples. For example, in a table marked "Hard data
on types," Ludeman and Erlandson (2006) noted:

- Men scored higher than women on commander risks and strategist strengths and risks, but not on the executor or visionary
  scales.

- While not large, the differences as a whole tell a consistent story:
  men display more of the cold, domineering, calculating alpha
  behaviors. (p. 47)

In Chapter 3, commanders were "natural leaders who inspire
trust, respect, and sometimes even awe, they are take-charge
types . . ." (p. 66), but they can become ruthlessly competitive, expect

too much, and manifest explosive rage. On female alpha commanders, the authors observed that they are few in number and "tend to soften their aggressive commander traits with maternal nurturance." (p. 78).

The visionaries in Chapter 4 think big and are wide open to other's ideas, but might lack follow-through. Conflict is also an issue as "Women visionaries tend to handle opposition differently than men . . . (they) tend to respond to disagreement in a more collaborative way" (p. 111). The authors also noted, "needless to say, this is a generalization; individual women can be as volatile and impatient as any man" (p. 111).

The alpha strategist in Chapter 5 of *AMS* is an analytical genius who, unfortunately, can morph into a stubborn know-it-all. "Female strategists can in general match the analytic skills of their male counterparts but don't carry the same interpersonal risks. They are less likely to be seen as arrogant know-it-alls because they tend to welcome different perspectives and validate the ideas of others" (p. 130). For example, Louise O'Brien, Dell's former vice president of strategy, "lacked the go-for-the-jugular quality that many alpha male strategies bring to the job—either to their advantage or to their detriment" (p. 131).

Finally, Chapter 6's alpha executors believe strongly in the bottom line; they are extraordinarily productive and efficient, but their insatiable drive for success can become unbearable to those around them. While women can be as results-oriented as men, "alpha males issue detailed directives, [and] women are more likely to drop hints and to give people license to create their own processes. Women might micromanage, but they generally try to cajole or persuade rather than to harass or threaten" (p. 161). As a result of their tendency to soften their messages, alpha women's directives often come off as "mere suggestion."

Certainly, there are both encouraging words and familiar refrains in the preceding profile. Encouragingly, there appears to be no "alpha female syndrome"; thus, women's ways of leading seemingly register much less on the dysfunctional side—accounting perhaps for far fewer pages devoted to women leaders. If not in the title, at least in the book's dedication and in the chapters, the authors position male and female leaders as equals; for example, there are male and female alphas for all four alpha styles. Moreover, the authors position themselves as gender neutral on the suitability of men and women for organizational leadership.

Familiar refrains are the essentializing terms in which the sexes are depicted; for example, women are hard-wired to be more inclusive, attuned to other's emotions, and soothe conflict—qualities that may or may not assist them in leading others. Men are depicted as naturally strong, competitive, and dominating, qualities—so says the book cover—that produce "astonishing results" but may inadvertently leave "a path of destruction." As stated below, one consequence of reinscribing gender differences in leadership discourse is that it also unwittingly casts leadership in male terms.

❖ GENDER AS SUBTEXT IN *AMS*

Recently, Bendl (2008) joined the list of researchers who have revisited organizational texts for their gendered assumptions (Acker & van Houten, 1974; Calas, 1993; Fondas, 1997; Mumby & Putnam, 1992; Roper, 2001). This body of work asserts that organizations and organizational theory are not gender-neutral and that gender is constitutive of organizing (Ashcraft, 2001, 2004; Buzzanell, 1994, 2000; Calas & Smircich, 1999, 2006; Martin, 1990; Mumby, 1996, 2001). As Ashcraft and Mumby (2004) observed, gender "is an omnipresent, defining feature of collective human activity, regardless of whether such activity appears to be about gender" (p. xv). Although the dominant texts of organizational discourse may appear to be gender neutral, Bendl (2005) drew from Smith (1988) to suggest that underlying texts often unwittingly (re)produce latent gender distinctions. Bendl thus defined *gender subtext* as

> a set of hidden, latent, and subtly power-based gendered, gendering, as well as en-gendering processes that systematically reproduce gender distinctions, (and) categorize between sex/gender (normally in terms of men and women) based on objectified forms, rational procedures and the abstracted conceptual organization, which (should) create an appearance of neutrality and impersonality in organizations, organizational empirical research and theorizing, and the discipline of Organizational Studies itself. (p. 34)

Bendl (2008) analyzed 24 organizational texts, mostly postmodern/post-structural, to derive a list of gendered subtexts.[2] Each text reflected Lacan's (1977) "law of the father," in which meaning is either implicitly or explicitly configured in patriarchal terms. For Lacan, meaning and the symbolic order form through a primary transcendental signifier, or "phallus," that inevitably produces patriarchy. The central organizing principle is the linguistic opposition between *masculine phallic presence* (term A: norm, reason, culture, presence, etc.) and *feminine lack* (term not-A: difference, emotion, nature, absence, etc.). Bendl's (2008) study thus consisted of looking for the various ways in which the binary opposition of gender (either as duality or hierarchy) emerge in language patterns with term "A," or traditional male-oriented representations, as the norm and term "not-A," or female-oriented representations, as "other." (p. 52)

Does *AMS* also reflect Lacan's (1977) law of the father? Drawing from Bendl's (2008) analysis of gendered subtexts, the answer appears to be "yes." We begin with the first subtext, which attributes masculinity and males as the leadership norm.

❖ SUBTEXT OF ATTRIBUTED MASCULINITY AND MALES AS THE LEADERSHIP NORM

Throughout the book, Ludeman and Erlandson (2006) alternate use of the terms *alphas* and *alpha males*. Frequently, the surrounding text positions alpha as shorthand for alpha males, without the authors' explicit statement of such, thus leaving open to question the status of alpha females—especially as segregated discussions of their status appear elsewhere in the chapters (a point taken up later). This appears to be part of an overall gender subtext that attributes masculinity and males as the leadership norm (Bendl, 2008). For example, compare the passages in the introductory pages of the book that are strategically ambiguous with respect to alpha (and where *male* is inserted parenthetically) with those that specify alpha male directly:

1. Human history is the story of alphas (males), those indispensable powerhouses who take charge, conquer new worlds, and move heaven and earth to make things happen. Whether heading a band of warriors, bringing a vital new product to market, guiding a team to glory, or steering a giant conglomerate, alphas (males) are hardwired for achievement and eager to tackle challenges that others find intimidating . . . The business world swarms with alpha males . . . The healthy ones—well balanced human beings in full command of their alpha (male) strengths—are natural leaders . . . (p. 1)

2. An alpha (male) is defined as "a person tending to assume a dominant role in social or professional situations, or thought to possess the qualities and confidence for leadership." . . . Often charismatic figures who command attention, they exert influence even when they're low-key and inconspicuous. (p. 3)

3. Make no mistake: the world needs alpha males. We could not do without their courageous leadership, their goal-driven focus, their unwavering sense of responsibility, and all the other qualities they bring to bear when they roll up their sleeves and take charge. (p. 7)

4. Overall, alpha traits correlate with being male, with increasing levels of education, with low anxiety, with supervisory positions, and with type A personality traits . . . (pp. 14–15)

5. We all know that factors such as knowledge, skill, and experience are vital for effective leadership, and high-ranking alpha males have all those in spades. (p. 29)

6. Make no mistake, the magnificent strengths of alphas (males) make them the most likely—and the most appropriate—people to assume positions of leadership. Yet, for many alpha males, the skills that today's leaders require—motivating, inspiring, teaching, communicating, modeling integrity and personal growth—do not come naturally . . . (p. 33)

As the excerpts demonstrate, the galvanizing strengths of the alpha are the same galvanizing strengths of the alpha male. Note how in the first quote, "Human history is the story of alphas," but the story lines read masculine as strength, sports, and war metaphors get invoked. To wit, alphas are those "indispensable powerhouses," (who) "conquer new worlds," (by) "heading a band of warriors" (or) "guiding a team to glory" and so on. Note how the swarm metaphor, as in "the business world swarms with alpha males," naturalizes the gendered structuring of leadership in the work context. These linguistically direct and indirect statements become the context for the authors' subsequent observation that "The healthy ones—well balanced human beings in full command of their alpha (male) strengths—are natural leaders." Collectively, these statements suggest a transitive relationship of the order: alpha = male = natural leader.[3] Leadership is conceptualized in male terms that evoke strength, competitiveness, and dominance, a norm-producing pattern repeated in one way or another in the remaining quotes. Thus, in the second quote alpha (male) = leader = charismatic; in the third and fourth quotes, alpha = male = leader; in the fifth quote, high ranking alpha = male = effective leader; and in the sixth quote, alpha (male) = most appropriate leader. Collectively, they create a subtext of attributed masculinity and males as the leadership norm.

❖ SUBTEXT OF FEMINIZATION

With one exception, the previous excerpts also simultaneously exclude alternative ways of leading that might favor women (or alternative ways of being masculine) and reproduce their relative absence in high-level leadership positions. That exception involves the last quote, in which "for many alpha males, the skills that today's leaders require—motivating, inspiring, teaching, communicating, modeling integrity and personal growth—do not come naturally . . ." (Ludeman & Erlandson, 2006, p. 33). Using the authors' own rubric for gender differences—and, it must be said, many others (Ashcraft, 2004)—it is ironic that executive coaching, so therapy-like, targets extreme alpha-ness through a more feminized "cure," but it is not labeled as such by the authors. Earlier in the book, they hint that women may be responsible for changes in today's leadership requirements, but they leave open to question any forward progress on this score and ignore research that suggests that female leaders are readily adopting masculinity discourses already (Ashcraft, 2004; Ashcraft & Mumby, 2004). Ludeman and Erlandson (2006) wrote the following:

> Overall, the attributes we associate with masculinity, such as rationality, toughness, and physical strength, have historically made alpha males the natural leaders of human groups. But today's job description is different, and the slow emergence of women at higher levels of management is both a result of that change and a leading cause of it. It remains to be seen whether alpha women will transform the face of management entirely or become more like alpha males (p. 26).

In addition, this brief mention is eclipsed by other instances of disavowing the feminization of leadership wrought by executive coaching. The following example offers some clues, perhaps, as to why:

> We've found that most alpha males who resist coaching are afraid that changing their behavior will limit their ability to drive high-level performance. It's a perfectly understandable concern, coming from people who value results above all else. They think that becoming more empathic, listening better, and easing off on the whip will make them weak. They fear that acting nicer would be both inauthentic and ineffective, and they haul out stories about sweet, kind executives who are loved but not productive. We assure you—as we do our clients—that it's simply not in your nature to become too soft. As Eddie (one of the authors) told one tough-as-nails-leader with the

steely bearing of a marine, who bluntly accused us of trying to turn him into a wimp, "You become a wimp? I'm not that good a coach." (Ludeman & Erlandson, 2006, pp. 229–230)

In an earlier quote, Ludeman and Erlandson (2006) posed their own rhetorical question, "Are female alphas the perfect antidote to the alpha male downside?" They only partly answer in the affirmative because, as mentioned, they essentialize women as more empathic, better listeners, and less controlling than men. However, the authors also hedge because the "feminine cure" begets the "wimp factor" for leaders of the nice-sweet-kind-soft variety whose performance is always suspect by the alpha males in their midst.

Bendl (2008) asserted that texts of this nature "construct term not-A-oriented values, such as care and emotion, as being superior to term A-oriented ones, yet do not show explicitly the 'overturning' . . . of masculine values" (p. 57). Moreover, Fondas (1997) proffered two reasons why the feminine is not labeled. First, as can be seen from the "wimp" charge in the extract, feminization would signal that management is no longer a masculine pursuit. Second, assigning superiority to the feminine would subordinate the masculine in most management discourses. It would thus call into question "the entire system of gender relation that underpins most organization and management theory, that is, the assumption that traits associated with masculinity are 'given' and essential to organizational life, whereas those associated with femininity constitute the 'other,' marginalized and unessential associated with peripheral organizational functions" (p. 273).

There is perhaps a third reason, clues to which can be found in the statement made by Ludeman and Erlandson (2006) that I quoted on the previous page: "They (alpha males) fear that acting nicer would be both inauthentic and ineffective," (p. 230). As Alice Eagly (2005) argued, "Finding . . . authenticity by knowing and being oneself is a luxury enjoyed by people from groups that have traditionally inhabited high-level leadership roles—in most contexts, White men from relatively privileged backgrounds" (p. 471). Precisely because authenticity is a privilege of the powerful, Eagly urged the female leader to aim for a kind of "relational authenticity" by toning down the extremes of her femininity or masculinity (to avoid labels like "battle axe," "dragon lady," "bitch," and so on) so her male colleagues would not be made uncomfortable or withhold identification. In a critique of relational authenticity, Fairhurst (2007) asked, "Is there no authenticity for women leaders unless it conforms to male expectations?" (p. 107). At risk in a feminized executive coaching discourse, therefore, would be a soft masculinity, one that would be made to conform to feminine leadership norms rather than the other way around. It is noteworthy that the authors suggest to the rather paranoid alpha male in the above quote that he has little to fear.

❖ SUBTEXT OF THE FEMALE LEADER AS OTHER

According to Bendl (2008), instead of focusing on males as the norm, this subtext focuses on the discursive (re)production of the woman as other. Bendl drew from Martin (1990) to suggest that women are "othered" when they become associated with a gender model at work (i.e., female = emotional, nurturing, the private sphere, etc.) that is deemed to have less value than a job model (i.e., male = rational, the public sphere, etc.).

As mentioned earlier, there are segregated sections of most chapters in *AMS* that address alpha females or how women can hold their own with alpha males. Thus, women are not excluded by any means, but they are described in terms of a gender model that typically fails to measure up, thus heightening the need for executive coaching. Indeed, in virtually *all* of the examples in *AMS*, females require coaching in masculinity discourses because they are not alpha enough (recalling that alpha = leader). Consider the following three examples along with the extrapolated advice the authors give:

1. Kathy . . . was a middle manager at . . . a large financial services company. Strong, assertive, and highly competent, her managerial style was so motherly that she was known around the office as Mom . . . People questioned whether she had the authoritative presence required of a high level executive. When employees didn't get their work done . . . she chided them with guilt-inducing remarks that lacked the punch of real consequences . . . To her credit, when Kathy's career stalled, she . . . learned to be more of a director and an orchestrator, and less of a rescuer and nurturer . . . (p. 78)

2. Advice: Not every female alpha commander learns those lessons, however, and perceived softness . . . can stall their careers. This is especially true of women who take it personally when colleagues push back. Getting emotional or judgmental when someone disagrees with you plays right into the stereotype that women aren't tough enough to lead at the highest

levels. Similarly, expecting your instincts to be followed without backing them up with facts and data . . . can also work against you. (p. 79)

3. Linda . . . was finally handed the purse strings of an enormous organization at the heart of U.S. military operations . . . Because of her quiet demeanor, Linda's insights often got lost in the shuffle despite her obvious qualifications. In a room filled with male alpha commanders, her soft voice would literally go unheard . . . Linda knew her soft-spoken style was a significant risk . . . She knew she had to be seen as a strong leader . . . When Admiral Lippert asked us to help her, we started by asking her to identify the personas that diminished her authority. One she called Truth Broker; the other Peacemaker . . . As the first persona, she facilitated truth-telling by others but was not forthcoming herself. As Peacemaker she was so focused on keeping the peace that she did not stand her ground or deliver needed feedback . . . We showed her how to speak forcefully and to assert herself into the circle of conversation. Before long . . . she conveyed a powerful, convincing, and inspiring presence . . . she took a page from their (alpha males) book by tapping into her own dormant leadership traits. (pp. 91–92)

4. Advice: Watch out for the tendency to call forth personas that actually reinforce the alpha commander's worst tendencies. Chief among these are three cousins—the Accommodator, the Pleaser, and the Complainer. Accommodators and pleasers dislike conflict so much they pretend to be in agreement when they don't mean it. They need to learn that it's usually more important to make things happen than to make things nice. (p. 89)

5. Louise O'Brien, Dell's former vice president of strategy . . . is more typical of female alpha strategists . . . Before moving to Dell, Louise was a partner at Bain & Company, where, she says, "I always migrated toward the more quantitative cases and the more masculine industries . . . I knew I could easily get labeled as a powder puff. I tried to hit home runs with dazzling analysis that no one else had thought of." Those home runs earned her a partnership . . . a rarity for women even now . . . As a leader, Louise lacked the go-for-the-jugular quality that many alpha male strategies bring to the job—either to their benefit or their detriment . . . As Dell's VP of strategy, "I was powerful because my bosses, Michael Dell and Kevin

Rollins, were powerful. To be honest, I liked having the benefits of referred power without having to fight the battles."
Alpha male strategists who need to sit atop the pyramid would
have trouble working in the shadow of two such influential figures. But it worked beautifully for Louise . . . (pp. 131–132)

6. Advice: If you're overly concerned about hurting people's feelings . . . you won't stand up for your views or oppose a wrong-
headed idea. You might also let your heart overrule the tough
decisions of your analytic mind . . . women may find it more
wrenching to make those difficult choices, while men run
the . . . risk of being too cut off from the human consequences.
Healthy alpha strategists—male and female alike—balance the
traits of heart and head . . . (p. 132)

A gender model of women leaders is fully entrenched in the above
quotes. Note the stereotyped role of mother accorded to Kathy in the first
quote. In the advice that follows in the second quote, women suffer the
career consequences not only due to their perceived softness, but their
apparent emotionality, judgmental nature, or overreliance on intuition.
In the third quote, Linda is too soft, inclusive, and attentive to other's
needs, but recognizes the need to rid herself of these qualities and thus
creates feminine personas to be erased in coaching. Subsequent advice in
the fourth quote appears to blame-the-victim, that is, the alpha male is
not responsible for his untoward behavior, but those (presumably,
women) who provoke it are doing so by being too accommodating, trying to please too much, or worse yet, complaining. In the fifth quote,
Louise is a senior level Dell manager for whom the private sphere
"worked beautifully," while her male bosses enjoyed the limelight in the
public sphere. In the final quote, women are likely to be rendered inca-
pable of making the tough decisions because their weakness as women
is in matters of the heart. Ironically, for Ludeman and Erlandson, it isn't
women leaders' overly aggressive alpha qualities that require executive
coaching—hence the alpha *syndrome*. Rather, it is their feminine qualities
that must be erased—a "not-A, female syndrome" perhaps?

❖ GENDER SUBTEXT OF BIOGRAPHY AND PRETENDED EQUALITY BETWEEN MALES AND FEMALES

The gender subtext of biography focuses on the link between aspects of
the author's biography and the ideas proffered in her research and

publication (Bendl, 2008). In this respect, *AMS* is especially interesting because one of the authors, Kate Ludeman, is female and a self-described alpha. She wrote the following of herself:

> Even as a child, Kate exhibited the ambition and drive of an alpha female. She was also fascinated by the alpha males she encountered growing up in South Texas. In the first grade, she figured out how to beat the strongest boys in the game of red rover, using direct eye contact and a smile to break through their supercharged strength as she approached the line. Later she found a way to entice alpha boys to attend a summer school she organized in her small town, and in the fourth grade she bit the wrist of a bully to get him to quit bothering her friends. In college, she was one of only eight girls among 4,000 engineering students, and she was the one to organize lab teams that consistently came in first.
>
> When she turned to organizational development work in her 30s, Kate focused on coaching alpha males, often joking that she was an expert in transforming jerks into nice guys . . . Kate's business succeeded because she found a way to get through to these tough guys and help them become better leaders. There were two keys. First, her training as an engineer gave her a knack for turning soft information about human relationships into the metrics-oriented language that alpha males understand best. Using hard data, she spelled out the risks of their current behavior and the bottom-line benefits of changing, then gave them a way to measure their progress. The other key was that she used her skills as a psychologist and her alpha female tenacity to stand up to alpha bullies—not an easy thing for women to do. The combination of straight talk and data earned the respect of hard-headed alpha males, and has since helped more than a thousand executives accelerate the progress of their career and their companies (p. 5).

Kate Ludeman modeled a putative equality between male and females. She appears to have succeeded in an alpha male world from an early age due to her willingness to confront and outsmart alpha males, most recently by deploying discourses of science and engineering alongside masculinity discourses. The impression that is left is that individual skills, strategy, and a steely determination are all that women leaders need in order to succeed, and executive coaching is the answer for those who may be lacking.

However, as Eden (2006) argued, executive coaching can help a person to develop confidence, clarity, and focus, but it is unlikely to have any direct influence on inherent sexism—either systemic (e.g., recruitment practices) or attitudinal (e.g., myths about women's skills and abilities). On the contrary, executive coaching may lead a woman leader—and those to whom she reports—to falsely expect that individual action alone, not system-level interventions, can overcome institutional bias. These expectations may be heightened if she comes to believe that women's ways of leading are superior to men's—as Helgesen (1990) demonstrated in her book, *The Female Advantage: Women's Ways of Leading.* Bendl (2008) thus observed

> In a context which privileges individualism and evaluates term not-A orientation (female) in management positions higher than the A orientation (male), structures of male domination and female suppression are considered to have lost their relevance ("they aren't in charge of your careers—and by extensions our *lives*—anymore. We are. It is up to us to fashion ourselves," [Peters, 2001, p. 12]). (p. 60)

When no less a source than management guru Tom Peters (2001) suggests that individuals have the power to take full control of their careers, it becomes increasingly difficult to see how women leaders *as a group* might be systemically discriminated against.

❖ DISCUSSION

To summarize, *AMS* targets the worst of alpha male leadership behavior for extinction. The *AMS* authors believe that alpha females' behavior does not rise to the level of syndrome, but that their stylistic softness creates the opposite problem of not being alpha-enough to be seen as natural leaders. Paradoxically, female leaders are urged to emulate their male colleagues because *alpha* is tantamount to *leader*, but when executive coaching advances the so-called feminine cure of empathy, listening, and shared control for extreme alpha-ness, such labeling is largely bereft of any feminine association. As a consequence, the women in *AMS* have no chance to be "natural leaders" because gender differences are inscribed in such a way that they naturalize masculinity and males as the leadership norm and other the female leader.

How representative is *AMS* of executive coaching literature? We examined the business press literature and reviewed 12 of the most current books on executive coaching. There were volumes that barely mentioned gender differences (Hunt & Weintrub, 2007; Kilburg, 2000; O'Neil, 2000; Underhill et al., 2007; Valerio & Lee, 2005). There were just a few that were either alpha male oriented (Downs, 2002; Flaherty, 2005) or stressed adoption of masculinity discourses for female leaders

(Brunning, 2006) in the relatively few executive coaching examples provided. Finally, several offered a mix of generic and gender-based examples, including alpha male syndrome and recommended masculinity discourses for female leaders (Anderson & Anderson, 2005; Doyle, 1999; Goldsmith et al., 2000; Stephenson, 2000). Thus, *AMS* certainly did not introduce anything new to the literature, yet it most certainly reinforced a gendered model of leadership more strongly that any of these volumes.

With this state of affairs, how do we move forward in thinking about leadership? Interestingly, there is a changing perception of alpha-ness among primatologists like Robert Sapolsky, who finds that the most successful alphas are being out-produced by lower-ranking beta males who have taken up "alternative strategies" to tribe life (David, 2003, p. 1). The stress on alpha males apparently takes its toll, and their drama appears to have distracted early primatologists in what Sapolsky calls the "idiot, caveman, chest-thumping era of primatology" (David, 2003, p. 1).

Today, primatologists are focusing not just on the alpha males, but also on beta males—those highly affiliated nice guys; (vastly underestimated) female choice; and the latter's apparent preference for affiliation over aggression in this complex, hierarchical system. To anyone who is a fan of the U.S. television show *The Office,* this lesson rings true because the beta male in the show, Jim, appears to be one of the few sane characters among the parodied alphas in his midst. The Jim character signals the need for alternative leadership models, which indeed can be found in follower-centered leadership (Haslam & Platow, 2001; Meindl, 1995), servant or spiritual leadership (Bellingham & Meek, 2001; Dent, Higgins, & Wharff, 2005; Graham, 1991; Patzer, 2003), and distributed or shared leadership in teams (Day, Gronn, & Salas, 2004, 2006; Manz & Sims, 1987; Mehra, Smith, Dixon, & Robertson, 2006; Uhl-Bien & Graen, 1992). All have ample precedent in the leadership literature, especially as we have seen the growing democratization of the workplace.

Given this increasing democratization, alternative leadership models such as those mentioned in the previous paragraph, and technologies like executive coaching that are aimed at eliminating the worst alpha male behavior, is it just a matter of time before the number of women leaders rising to executive ranks becomes proportional to that of men? The more pessimistic answer is "no" because hierarchy endures, even if only at the topmost levels of democratized organizations (Kanter, 1983; Stohl & Cheney, 2001)—levels that have proved the most difficult for women leaders to crack (Ashcraft, 2004; Buzzanell, 1995). Such pessimism is rooted in work on the sex structuring of organizations (Acker & van Houten, 1974), in which feminist critiques of bureaucratic forms (such as hierarchical authority) amply demonstrate how they privilege masculinities, marginalize femininities, shape interaction, and (continue to) institutionalize gender inequities (Acker, 1990; Britton, 1997; Maier, 1999; Morgan, 1996; Mumby, 1998). The glass ceiling for women leaders is the most obvious example of institutionalized gender inequity.

The more optimistic answer is rooted in those who demonstrate how gendered systems of control are navigable, oftentimes by opening up the processes of social construction to promote more feminist organizing (Ashcraft & Mumby, 2004; Buzzanell, 1995; Buzzanell et al., 1997; Mumby & Putnam, 1992). Somewhat consistent with this view is the recent emergence of the "gamma woman" in the popular press and marketing circles. Based on observations of middle school girls reported on by a *Washington Post* writer (Stepp, 2002), of high school girls reported on by a *Newsweek* writer (Meadows, 2002), and of women leaders by the business press (Helgesen, 1990), market researchers Finn and Johnson (2008) of the Meredith Corporation argued that teenage girls and twenty- and thirty-something young women—aided by new technologies—are redefining power in ways that challenge the alpha-beta dualism. Gammas are neither alpha leaders nor beta followers:

> By definition, Alphas operate within a clearly defined top-down hierarchy ... influence flows from the top downward ... Gammas' influence ... spreads outward in all directions. They position themselves in the center of a web of equals and their connections ... are interactive ... Because of this structure, Gammas tend to have stronger bonds with ... the people in their networks ... Collaboration creates value; sharing is currency ... (Gammas) thrive in democracy. (pp. 12–13)

> In the gamma model of technology-mediated interaction, the management style of women leaders is rooted in her placement at the center of a democratic, interconnected group; an emphasis on inclusion and accessibility rather than exclusivity and hierarchy; and the promotion of a free exchange of ideas and information (p. 14).

Of course, the gamma nomenclature reported on by the popular press writers is a marketer's dream; appealingly essentialized market segments, especially new ones, are sine qua non to commercial success. However, such essentialism flies in the face of the social constructionist project (Gergen, 2001; Hacking, 1999) and, certainly, those wishing to promote more feminist forms of organizing (Ashcraft & Mumby, 2004; Buzzanell, 1995; Buzzanell et al., 1997; Mumby & Putnam, 1992).

But following Spivak (1987, 1988; Spivak & Grosz, 1990), it might be valuable to ask if some essentializing is worth hanging onto, if only temporarily, because gamma women putatively redefine power relations not only unencumbered by the alpha-beta dualism, but with a self-conscious rejection of alpha-ness. To wit, new technologies enable ways of living and organizing that suit work-family interests, in which women are unapologetic about value commitments to relationships, family, work, or community, as the case may be. Thus, to be *strategically essentialist* is not to look upon the world "as descriptions of the way things are," but as a momentary stance in order to label, discern, and critique such a world (Spivak & Adamson, 1990, p. 51). Such analyses might build on Bennis and Thomas's (2002) archeological analysis of leadership differences between the historical eras of the "geeks" versus the "geezers." With emerging evidence linking the treatment of women executives to firm profitability (Adler, 2009), the stakes remain high for long overdue alternatives to alpha leadership in today's organizations.

❖ NOTES

1. The subject of gender has been addressed by other business press writers, but usually in a single book chapter.

2. Bendl defines *text* in postmodern/post-structural terms, which "incorporates written words and speech, as well as other symbolic phenomena through which the social production of meaning occurs" (p. 52).

3. The word *transitive* is meant in a mathematical sense, in which one element's relation to a second element and the second in relation to a third element implies the first element is in relation to the third element, as in the relation "less than or equal to."

❖ REFERENCES

Acker, J. (1990). Hierarchies, jobs, bodies: A theory of gendered organizations. *Gender and Society, 4,* 139–158.

Acker, J., & van Houten, D. (1974). Differential recruitment and control: The sex structuring of organizations. *Administrative Science Quarterly, 19,* 152–163.

Adler, R. D. (2009). Profit, thy name is . . . woman? *Miller-McCune, 2*(2), 32–35.

Anderson, D., & Anderson, M. (2005). Coaching that counts: Harnessing the power of leadership coaching to deliver strategic value. Oxford, UK: Elsevier Butterworth-Heinemann.

Ashcraft, K. L. (2001). Organized dissonance: Feminist bureaucracy in hybrid form. *Academy of Management Journal, 44,* 1301–1322.

Ashcraft, K. L. (2004). Gender, discourse, and organization: Framing a shifting relationship. In C. H. D. Grant, C. Oswick, & L. Putnam (Eds.). *The Sage handbook of organizational discourse* (pp. 275–291). London: Sage.

Ashcraft, K. L., & Mumby, D. K. (2004). *Reworking gender: A feminist communicology of organization.* Thousand Oaks, CA: Sage.

Bellingham, R., & Meek, J. (2001). *The manager's pocket guide to spiritual leadership.* Amherst, MA: HRD Press.

Bendl, R. (2005). *Revisiting organizational theory—From the integration and deconstruction of gender to the transformation of organizational discourse.* Frankfurt am Main, Germany: Peter Lang.

Bendl, R. (2008). Gender subtexts—Reproduction of exclusion in organizational discourse. *British Journal of Management, 19,* S50–S64.

Bennis, W. G., & Thomas, R. J. (2002). *Geeks and geezers: How era, values, and defining moments shape leadership.* Boston: Harvard Business School Press.

Berglas, S. (2002, June). The very real dangers of executive coaching. *Harvard Business Review, 80*(6), 86–92.

Brady, D. (2006, June, 26). Charm offensive: Why America's CEOs are suddenly so eager to be loved. *Business Week,* 76–80.

Britton, D. M. (1997). Gendered organizational logic: Policy and practice in men's and women's prisons. *Gender and Society, 11,* 796–818.

Brunning, H. (2006). *Executive coaching: Systems-psychodynamic perspective.* New York: Karnac.

Buzzanell, P. M. (1994). Gaining a voice: Feminist organizational communication theorizing. *Management Communication Quarterly, 7,* 339–383.

Buzzanell, P. M. (1995). Reframing the glass ceiling as a socially constructed process: Implications for understanding and change. *Communication Monographs, 62,* 327–354.

Buzzanell, P. M. (2000). *Rethinking organizational and managerial communication from feminist perspectives.* Thousand Oaks, CA: Sage.

Buzzanell, P. M., Ellingson, L., Silvio, C., Pasch, V., Dale, B., Mauro, G. et al. (1997). Leadership processes in alternative organizations: Invitational and dramaturgical leadership. *Communication Studies, 48,* 285–310.

Calas, M. (1993). Deconstructing charismatic leadership: Rereading Weber from the darker side. *Leadership Quarterly, 4,* 305–328.

Calas, M., & Smircich, L. (1999). From "the woman's" point of view: Feminist approaches to organization studies. In S. Clegg & C. Hardy (Eds.), *Studying organizations: Theory and method* (pp. 212–251). London: Sage.

Calas, M., & Smircich, L. (2006). From "the woman's" point of view ten years later: Toward a feminist organization studies. In S. Clegg, C. Hardy, W. Nord, & T. B. Lawrence (Eds.), *Handbook of organization studies* (2nd ed., pp. 285–346). London: Sage.

David, G. (2003, August 11). Alpha romeos. *CNNMoney.com.* Retrieved April 24, 2008, from http://money.cnn.com/magazines/fortune/fortune_archive/2003/08/11/346799/index.htm

Day, D. V., Gronn, P., & Salas, E. (2004). Leadership capacity in teams. *Leadership Quarterly, 15,* 857–880.

Day, D. V., Gronn, P., & Salas, E. (2006). Leadership in team-based organizations: On the threshold of a new era. *Leadership Quarterly, 17,* 211–216.

Dent, E. B., Higgins, M. E., & Wharff, D. M. (2005). Spirituality and leadership: An empirical review of definitions, distinctions, and embedded assumptions. *Leadership Quarterly, 15,* 625–654.

Downs, A. (2002). *Secrets of an executive coach.* New York: Amacom.

Doyle, J. S. (1999). *The business coach: A game plan for the new work environment.* Toronto, Ontario, Canada: John Wiley & Sons.

Eagly, A. H. (2005). Achieving relational authenticity in leadership: Does gender matter? *Leadership Quarterly, 16,* 459–474.

Eden, A. (2006). Coaching women for senior executive roles: A societal perspective on power and exclusion. In H. Brunning (Ed.), *Executive coaching: Systems-psychodynamic perspective* (pp. 79–93). New York: Karnac.

Fairhurst, G. T. (2007). *Discursive leadership: In conversation with leadership psychology.* Thousand Oaks, CA: Sage.

Finn, L., & Johnson, L. (2008). The gamma factor: Women and the new social currency. *Meredith Corporation,* 1–33.

Flaherty, J. (2005). *Coaching: Evoking excellence in others.* Boston: Burlington.

Fondas, N. (1997). Feminization unveiled: Management qualities in contemporary writings. *Academy of Management Review, 22,* 257–282.

Foucault, M. (1980). *Power/knowledge: Selected interviews and other writings 1972–1977.* New York: Pantheon.

Foucault, M. (1983). The subject and power. In H. L. Dreyfus & P. Rabinow (Eds.), *Michel Foucault: Beyond structuralism and hermeneutics* (pp. 208–226). Chicago: Chicago University Press.

Foucault, M. (1990). *The history of sexuality: Volume 1.* New York: Vintage/Random House.

Foucault, M. (1995). *Discipline and punish.* New York: Vintage/Random House.

Gergen, K. (2001). *Social construction in context.* London: Sage.

Goldsmith, M., Lyons, L., & Freas, A. (Eds.). (2000). *Coaching for leadership: How the world's greatest coaches help leaders learn.* San Francisco, CA: Jossey-Bass/Pfeiffer.

Graham, J. W. (1991). Servant-leadership in organizations: Inspirational and moral. *Leadership Quarterly, 2,* 105–119.

Gray, D. E. (2006). Executive coaching: Towards a dynamic alliance of psychotherapy and transformative learning processes. *Management Learning, 37,* 475–497.

Hacking, I. (1999). *The social construction of what?* Cambridge, MA: Harvard University Press.

Haslam, S. A., & Platow, M. J. (2001). Your wish is our command: The role of shared social identity in translating a leader's vision into followers' action. In M. A. Hogg & D. J. Terry (Eds.), *Social identity processes in organizational contexts* (pp. 213–228). Philadelphia, PA: Psychology Press.

Helgesen, S. (1990). *The female advantage: Women's ways of leadership.* New York: Doubleday-Currency.

Hunt, J. M., & Weintrub, J. R. (2007). *The coaching organization: A strategy for developing leaders.* Thousand Oaks, CA: Sage.

Kampa-Kokesch, S., & Anderson, M. Z. (2001). Executive coaching: A comprehensive review of the literature. *Consulting Psychology Journal: Practice and Research, 53,* 205–228.

Kanter, R. M. (1983). *The changemasters.* New York: Simon and Schuster.

Kets de Vries, M. F. R. (2005). Leadership group coaching in action: The Zen of creating high performance teams. *Academy of Management Executive, 19,* 61–76.

Kilburg, R. R. (2000). *Executive coaching: Developing managerial wisdom in a world of chaos.* Washington, DC: American Psychological Association.

Lacan, J. (1977). *Écrits. A selection.* London: Tavistock.

Levinson, H. (1966). Executive coaching. *Consulting Psychology Journal: Practice and Research, 48,* 115–123.

Ludeman, K., & Erlandson, E. (2004, May). Coaching the alpha male. *Harvard Business Review,* 58–67.

Ludeman, K., & Erlandson, E. (2006). *Alpha male syndrome.* Boston: Harvard Business School Press.

Ludeman, K., & Erlandson, E. (2007, Spring). Channeling alpha male leaders. *Leader to Leader,* 38–44.

Maier, M. (1999). On the gendered substructure of organization: Dimension and dilemmas of corporate masculinity. In G. N. Powell (Ed.), *Handbook of gender and work* (pp. 69–94). Thousand Oaks, CA: Sage.

Manz, C. C., & Sims, H. P., Jr. (1987). Leading workers to lead themselves: The external leadership of self-managing work teams. *Administrative Science Quarterly, 32,* 106–128.

Martin, J. (1990). Deconstructing organizational taboos: The suppression of gender conflict in organizations. *Organization Science, 1,* 339–359.

Meadows, S. (2002, June 3). Meet the gamma girls. *Newsweek.*

Mehra, A., Smith, B. R., Dixon, A. L., & Robertson, B. (2006). Distributed leadership in teams: The network of leadership perceptions and team performance. *Leadership Quarterly, 17,* 232–245.

Meindl, J. R. (1995). The romance of leadership as a follower-centric theory: A social constructionist approach. *Leadership Quarterly, 6,* 329–341.

Morgan, D. (1996). The gender of bureaucracy. In D. L. Collinson & J. Hearn (Eds.), *Men as managers, managers as men* (pp. 61–77). Thousand Oaks, CA: Sage.

Mumby, D. K. (1996). Feminism, postmodernism, and organizational communication: A critical reading. *Management Communication Quarterly, 9,* 259–295.

Mumby, D. K. (1998). Organizing men: Power, discourse and the social construction of masculinity(s) in the workplace. *Communication Theory, 8,* 164–183.

Mumby, D. K. (2001). Power and politics. In F. M. Jablin & L. L. Putnam (Eds.), *The new handbook of organizational communication* (pp. 585–623). Thousand Oaks, CA: Sage.

Mumby, D. K., & Putnam, L. L. (1992). The politics of emotion: A feminist reading of bounded rationality. *Academy of Management Review, 17,* 465–486.

Newton, T., & Findlay, P. (1996). Playing God? The performance appraisal. *Human Resource Management Journal, 6,* 42–58.

O'Neil, M. B. (2000). *Executive coaching with backbone and heart: A systems approach to engaging leaders with their challenges.* San Francisco: Jossey-Bass.

Patzer, J. (2003). *The road ahead: A vision for spiritual leadership in the 21st century.* Nampa, ID: Pacific Press.

Peters, T. (2001). *The brand you 50.* New York: Alfred A. Knopf.

Roper, M. (2001). Masculinity and the biographical meanings of management theory: Lyndall Urwick and the making of scientific management in interwar Britain. *Gender, Work and Organization, 8,* 182–204.

Sherman, S., & Freas, A. (2004). The wild west of executive coaching. *Harvard Business Review, 82,* 82–93.

Smith, D. M. (1988). *The everyday world as problematic: A feminist sociology.* Milton Keynes: Open University Press.

Spivak, G. C. (1987). *In other worlds: Essays in cultural politics.* New York: Methuen.

Spivak, G. C. (1988). Can the subaltern speak? In C. Nelson & L. Grossberg (Eds.), *Marxism and the interpretation of culture* (pp. 271–313). Urbana: University of Illinois Press.

Spivak, G. C., & Adamson, W. (1990). The problem of cultural self-representation. In S. Harasym (Ed.), *The post-colonial critic: Interviews, strategies, dialogues* (pp. 50–58). New York: Routledge.

Spivak, G. C., & Grosz, E. (1990). Criticism, feminism, and the institution. In S. Harasym (Ed.), *The postcolonial critic: Interviews, strategies, dialogues* (pp. 1–16). New York: Routledge.

Stephenson, P. (2000). *Executive coaching.* Australia: Griffin Press.

Stepp, L. S. (2002, February 23). Alpha girl: In middle school, learning to handle the ABCs of power. *Washington Post,* C01.

Stohl, C., & Cheney, G. (2001). Participatory processes/paradoxical practices. *Management Communication Quarterly, 14,* 349–407.

Townley, B. (1993). Foucault, power/knowledge, and its relevance for human resource management. *Academy of Management Review, 18,* 518–545.

Uhl-Bien, M., & Graen, G. B. (1992). Self-management and team-making in cross-functional work teams: Discovering the keys to becoming an integrated team. *Journal of High Technology Management, 3,* 225–241.

Underhill, B. O., McAnally, K., & Koriath, J. J. (2007). *Executive coaching for results: The definitive guide to developing organizational leaders.* San Francisco: Berrett-Koeler Publishers.

Valerio, A. M., & Lee, R. J. (2005). *Executive coaching: A guide for the HR professional.* San Francisco: Pfeiffer.

Part II

Teaching Difference and Organizing

5

Critical Communication Pedagogy as a Framework for Teaching Difference and Organizing

Brenda J. Allen

As organizational communication scholars increasingly respond to calls to investigate difference and organizing, I urge them to heed a parallel and equally pressing need to incorporate difference into their teaching. Scholars and teachers should strive to help students understand how varying dimensions of social identity articulate with one another, with a focus on the consequences of those articulations for organizing (Simpson & Allen, 2006). While difference is a focus of study in several fields, communication scholars can offer students a uniquely communicative understanding of these issues and how humans (re)produce them. Such an approach can provide pivotal insight and understanding to prepare students to interact effectively and humanely in contemporary organizational contexts, where matters of difference are ever more apparent and important. However, because teaching difference and organizing can be particularly daunting and complex, faculty can benefit greatly from resources that can guide their efforts.

One potential framework for teaching difference and organizing is critical communication pedagogy, a relatively new perspective that studies relationships between power and communication in educational contexts. In this chapter, I present critical communication pedagogy as a useful approach for teaching organizing and difference. I begin by describing critical pedagogy—the theoretical and philosophical foundation upon which critical communication pedagogy rests. Then, I lay out the critical approach to communication pedagogy. Next, I suggest ways to apply critical communication pedagogy to teaching organizing and difference, including an overview of an organizational communication course about difference. Finally, I discuss challenges and benefits of using this approach.

❖ CRITICAL PEDAGOGY

Critical pedagogy is an approach to teaching and learning that seeks to analyze and transform educational contexts by applying principles of critical theory (Giroux, 1997). Like critical theory and critical organization studies (e.g., Deetz & Mumby, 1990; Mumby, 1993, 2001), critical pedagogy strives to critique and change power relations in society. However, critical pedagogy concentrates on educational contexts and related structures in society. More specifically, critical pedagogy advocates a social justice orientation for transforming oppressive educational institutions into sites of emancipation and equality. Marking education as a crucial site of power dynamics, proponents of critical pedagogy examine impacts of dominant ideologies on teaching and learning, and they seek to create more democratic and socially responsible arrangements (McLaren, 2003). For example, they encourage educators to become social activists, and they invite us to interrogate and revise our teaching perspectives and practices. As Henri Giroux (1994) explained, critical pedagogy "signals how questions of audience, voice, power, and evaluation actively work to construct particular relations between teachers and students, institutions and society, and classrooms and communities" (p. 30).

Critical pedagogy relies heavily on the work of scholar-activist Paolo Freire (1970), who conceptualized liberatory education as a process where learners come to consciousness (*conscientization*) through praxis, which integrates critical theory with reflection and practice. According to Freire, educational processes are not neutral; they can either domesticate or liberate. That is, they can indoctrinate students to accept dominant ideologies and go along with the status quo, or they can raise students' consciousness by identifying and challenging those ideologies. Thus, a primary goal of liberatory education is to develop students' (and teachers') critical consciousness of how power tends to serve some groups more favorably than others. The hope is that after students become more aware of these dynamics, they will be empowered and inspired to construct and enact alternate, more equitable social realities. To accomplish this goal, Freire recommended moving away from a traditional, passive "banking model" of education, in which educators deposit knowledge into students and reward those who regurgitate that knowledge, to a problem-solving approach that regards all subject matter as sociohistorical constructs to be questioned and encourages students to challenge authority. As one scholar explained: "In this democratic pedagogy, the teacher is not filling empty minds with official or unofficial knowledge but is posing knowledge in any form as a problem for mutual inquiry" (Shor, 1992 p. 33). Freire also endorsed engaging students in dialogue—for instance, by inviting them to name and narrate their own experiences and to relate those experiences to what they are learning.

Critical pedagogy enjoys an enduring tradition in the United States, and its proponents have developed numerous variations that retain the central aim of applying critical theory to transform education (Giroux & Giroux, 2006). Contemporary advocates of critical pedagogy have extended Freire's work to encompass issues that are especially relevant for teaching difference and organizing. Whereas Freire took a Marxist perspective that tended to focus on essentialist, class categories, some critical pedagogy scholars have developed postmodern, constructionist conceptions of identity and difference (e.g., Giroux, 1994, 1997; hooks, 1994; McLaren, 2003). They acknowledge the importance of difference and identity politics by adopting critical perspectives that draw on feminist, performative, queer, and critical Whiteness studies (see Fassett & Warren, 2007). They also emphasize complexities of identities, asserting that most people simultaneously embody identities associated with privilege *and* oppression (e.g., Alexander, 1999; Allen, 2004; Cooks, 2003; Johnson & Bhatt, 2003; Orbe, 1998). As critical pedagogy infuses various disciplines, communication scholars have begun to provide substantive insight and direction about the crucial role of communication in critical pedagogy.

❖ CRITICAL COMMUNICATION PEDAGOGY

Communication scholars Deanna L. Fassett and John T. Warren (2007) developed critical communication pedagogy as a framework for studying relationships between power and communication in educational contexts. In this perspective, they position communication as central to the processes through which humans reproduce or resist power relations. Critical communication pedagogy encompasses "critical theory's dedication to social change as a goal of research as well as communication studies' analytical focus on mundane practices" (Warren, 2009, p. 214). Fassett and Warren (2007) based critical communication pedagogy on elements of critical theory, critical pedagogy, and two areas of study in communication: (1) communication education, which focuses on how best to teach communication, and (2) instructional communication, which strives to improve classroom communication processes in any discipline. Fassett and Warren began their efforts after communication scholars in the early 1990s invoked critical pedagogy to interrogate conventional studies of communication education and communication instruction that typically focus on helping teachers to be more effective (Fassett & Warren, 2007; Rodriguez & Cai, 1994; Sprague, 1992, 1993, 2002). Along with other scholars, they critiqued functionalist tendencies of communication education and communication instruction, as well as assumptions about communication pedagogy related to knowledge and curriculum construction, teacher-student relationships, and functions of language and power in the classroom. (See, for example, Sprague, 1990, 1992.) To guide their efforts, Fassett and Warren (2007) relied on critical paradigms as well as related scholarship in education. Thus, critical communication pedagogy emerges at the intersection of critical theory/pedagogy and communication.

Critical communication pedagogy incorporates tenets of critical pedagogy while focusing explicitly on how everyday communication helps to (re)produce and (de)construct dominant ideologies. Similar to critical pedagogy, critical communication pedagogy depicts teachers as "transformative intellectuals who are located in a position to radically transform culture" (Sprague, 1992, p. 17), and it portrays the classroom as a significant site of social influence where actors engage in the social construction of their and other's identities. However, critical communication pedagogy operates through the basic premise that humans communicatively constitute power relations through social interaction, and therefore, we can use social interaction to change those relations. (See, for example, Deetz & Mumby, 1990.)

A communication approach to critical pedagogy provides methods, discourses, and perspectives that might be particularly useful for accomplishing the goals of critical pedagogy. For example, critical communication pedagogy studies how humans use communication to constitute identity(ies), power, and culture. As Fassett and Warren (2007) explained:

> Critical communication educators look to postmodern and post-structural understandings of human identity, to senses of students and teachers as relational selves produced in collusion and collision, to theories and methodologies that help them account for identities as produced in cultural—and therefore inherently ideological—contexts. (p. 40)

Fassett and Warren (2007) detailed ten fundamental, interconnected commitments of their vision for critical communication pedagogy that can guide processes for teaching organizing and difference. The first commitment asserts that humans produce identity in and through communication. Critical communication pedagogy characterizes identity as performative: Gender, race, class, sexuality, and so forth are not fixed, inherent qualities that we *have;* rather, they are contingent features of our identities that we *perform* in everyday social contexts (Butler, 1993; Warren, 2001). Thus, critical communication pedagogy moves away from essentialist, static notions of social identities that pervade instructional communication studies and toward a social constructionist perspective of identities as fluid, emergent, contextual, relational, and therefore, changeable (e.g., Allen, 2004; Burr, 1995).

The second commitment portrays power as dynamic and complex, in contrast to the traditional notion of power as something that only persons in authority (e.g., teachers) possess and wield. The latter viewpoint frames power as a tool or skill for gaining student compliance and discouraging student resistance, and it seeks to give teachers strategies for using communication to manage their classroom and to maintain order (Sprague, 1992). In contrast, critical communication pedagogy sees power as a processual, shared, and reciprocal element of classroom interactions. Thus, for example, this commitment invites teachers to be self-reflexive regarding the power dynamics of how they "manage" their classrooms. Combined with the first commitment, this perspective encourages educators to monitor how they might interact with students based on dominant ideologies about identities (e.g., teacher, student, as well as other social categories such as gender, race, and class).

The third commitment stresses the centrality of culture in the classroom. It debunks the idea that classrooms and education are neutral and apolitical by acknowledging and valuing diverse ways of knowing and being among students and teachers. Therefore, it encourages educators to acknowledge that culture matters, to incorporate culturally-diverse reading materials and classroom activities, and to invite multiple cultural perspectives on course concepts. This approach can illustrate and validate course concepts while also helping students who are members of nondominant groups to feel more included.

The fourth commitment highlights a "focus on concrete, mundane communication practices as constitutive of larger social structural systems" (Fassett & Warren, 2007, p. 43). This commitment signifies how a critical communication approach can contribute to critical pedagogy by acknowledging how everyday interactions help to (re)produce knowledge, (re)construct identities, and (re)iterate ideologies.

The fifth commitment extends the fourth by situating mundane communication practices in institutional and social contexts, and by conceptualizing them as co-constructive. Therefore, as we critique everyday interactions in the classroom and how they help to (re)construct institutional norms, we should also consider the contexts in which these interactions occur. For example, our behaviors in the classroom can interrelate with our academic department, the university, the surrounding community, our discipline, and society at large. My choices for course materials and assignments are subject to my sense of what seems appropriate in my department, on my campus, and within my discipline. When I teach organizing and difference, I often invoke my department's mission statement—which refers to helping students become more humane and civil communicators—as a rationale for delving into difference matters and as a goal for students to work toward as they process what they are learning. Also, I often refer to current events and concerns in my local community or society as topics for teaching. Moreover, as a full professor, I feel freer to engage in more radical ways of teaching than I did as an assistant professor seeking tenure and promotion because I am not as concerned about potential sanctions from students or my colleagues.

The sixth commitment extends the constitutive role of communication by asserting the centrality of language. Fassett and Warren (2007) underscore language as a system we use to objectify subjective meanings and to internalize socially constructed meanings. They also note that language holds major ramifications for identity development. For instance, when I teach difference matters, I provide an historical overview of labels and their meanings for members of the racial group with which I identify. These labels include *nigger, Negro, colored, Black, African American,* and *Afro-American*. I tell students that I prefer Black because it represents pride in my racial identity, a perspective that activist groups in the 1960s constructed in resistance to earlier labels whose meanings were more derogatory. I also ask students if they have preferences for social identity labels for groups to which they belong, and to explain why.

Commitment seven centers on radical reflexivity as essential to critical communication pedagogy, encouraging us to be aware of ourselves and how we enact our identities as scholars, teachers, learners, researchers, and so forth, as well as the ideologies that drive us. This commitment also requires us to reflect on how we as critical scholars simultaneously challenge and reinforce dominant ideologies through everyday discourse.

Commitment eight harkens back to Paulo Freire's (1970) notion of praxis by urging teachers and students to reflexively bridge knowledge with action to transform the conditions that they critique. When I teach difference matters, I usually ask students to develop and begin to employ strategies for applying what they have learned to their everyday interactions. The final project in a class I taught on difference and communication in the ivory tower required students to develop their research for a specific stakeholder group (or groups) and to develop actionable items to submit to that group based on their research. I encouraged them to share their ideas with those groups, and I was committed to facilitating that process. In addition, I modeled this commitment after two students came out to our class as having learning disabilities. As I reflected on these students' compelling narratives about their struggles with navigating university systems for students with disabilities, as well as their recurring challenge of deciding when and if to inform professors of their disabilities due to fear of being stigmatized, I decided to take action. As chair of my college's diversity council, I enlisted that group's buy-in to reform our campus policy and procedures related to students with learning disabilities, and they agreed. I also told my class what I had done and why, and I thanked the two students for being courageous enough to share their stories. Each of them was gratified to know that their stories may lead to better experiences for other students with learning disabilities.

Commitment nine enjoins faculty to see our identities and our agency as individuals in complicated and nuanced ways. Warren (2009, p. 215) explained: "What counts is how one engages—the effort to see the self and other as complex beings, each striving for meaning and purpose, is to engage them with a kind of care that embraces the ethics of a critically compassionate communication pedagogy."

The last of the ten commitments emerges from and elaborates the other nine commitments. It cites dialogue as a key principle of critical communication pedagogy that offers a means for deconstructing power and constructing new, more socially just realities. In my classes on organizing and difference, I describe Buber's (1958) perspective on dialogue, and I frequently refer to this perspective during classroom interactions. I invite willingness to create something new through being open-minded and by avoiding the tendency to debate one another, or to defend our side of a discussion.

In sum, critical communication pedagogy advocates a dialogic, reflexive approach to teaching and learning, in which participants collaborate with one another to critique and transform educational practices and to consider how language and forms of interaction proactively (re)construct teaching and learning environments. Classroom interactions conscientiously refer to knowledge about power dynamics as they unfold within the classroom, rather than referring to external, more abstract examples of power. The goal is to facilitate classrooms that are sites of resistance and empowerment, where students acquire (and faculty hone) critical perspectives and skills that can not only reform the classroom and higher education, but also translate into other contexts.

Critical communication pedagogy provides a viable, valuable framework for teaching organizing and difference because it speaks to the constitutive role of communication in a specific context of organizing (education), and it emphasizes relationships among power, identity, and culture. It invites instructors to specify higher education and the classroom as crucial sites of power dynamics rather than referring to external examples and examining politics in the "real" world. Thus, the common ground of education among participants can serve as a pivotal source for collaboration and learning as they observe and analyze how relations of power develop contextually. It also can help respond to students' recurrent refrain of "What's in it for me?" by "highlighting the immediate power of communication, power that may be both oppressive and liberating depending on local contexts" (Nainby, Warren, & Bollinger, 2003, p. 207). Therefore, a critical communication pedagogy framework may engender learning that leads to raising students' consciousness and empowering them to be change agents.

In addition to being valuable for teaching organizing and power dynamics, critical communication pedagogy can facilitate teaching difference because it focuses on how humans use communication to produce identity. This approach permits a type of experiential learning that can punctuate the focus of critical organizational communication studies on organizations as key sites of identity (re)construction where we learn much of what we know about ourselves and others (Alvesson, Ashcraft, & Thomas, 2008). For example, Sprague (1992) asserted that classroom interaction "cannot be considered as the result of conscious cognitive choices without regard for the interplay of factors like class, race, gender, sexual orientation, and able-bodiedness that shape each encounter" (p. 17).

Therefore, critical communication pedagogy corresponds well with contemporary critical organizational communication studies that increasingly treat power relations in terms of complex intersections of salient social identities (e.g., gender, race, class, ability, age, and sexuality, as well as professional roles and disciplinary identities) that induce varying degrees of privilege and oppression (Allen, 2004; Ashcraft & Allen, 2009). Consequently, this approach can help prepare students for a multicultural world by helping them understand and negotiate identity politics. Basically, a critical communication approach to pedagogy can equip and empower students to understand and resist power dynamics related to social identity politics while they are students and, in the future, as they participate in other organized settings.

❖ IMPLEMENTING CRITICAL COMMUNICATION PEDAGOGY IN TEACHING DIFFERENCE AND ORGANIZING

Numerous challenges can impede achieving the benefits of applying critical communication pedagogy to teaching organizing and difference. Preparing to teach in this way can be time-consuming because it entails creating a nontraditional course design that casts the teacher in the role of facilitator instead of the traditional "sage on the stage," while also anticipating various learning styles and incorporating a variety of course activities and materials. Furthermore, as they implement their courses, faculty should be ready to respond to emergent developments and to incorporate new resources that students provide.

In addition, critical communication pedagogy reconfigures student-teacher relationships, which can be difficult for students and teachers, and which makes everyone vulnerable. If faculty members wish to adhere to Fassett and Warren's (2007) commitments, they will have to relinquish some of their authority in the classroom. They will have to decide not only how much power to share but also how to do so. Faculty will need to be self-reflexive and willing to acknowledge and disclose to themselves and their students how they may be enacting and experiencing domination and oppression in the classroom and at related sites. They will need to "find ways to teach critically while also actively searching for ways to call privileged perspectives—including [their] own teacherly perspectives—into question with students" (Nainby, Warren, & Bollinger, 2003, p. 199). They will also have to balance seeming to propagandize and providing information to allow students to choose to be engaged with critical communication pedagogy.

In addition, faculty will need to be attentive and responsive to all students, who will vary in learning capacity and style, cultural background, receptivity, communication skill and style, and social identity composite. As instructors strive to teach course content, they will also need to be acutely aware of, and responsive to, socio-emotional issues in the classroom. I once neglected to observe that a student was distressed during a class discussion about race as I pressed her to explain her perspective, which seemed to reflect a position of White privilege. Fortunately, she was comfortable enough with me to write an e-mail that explained her feelings and stated that she wasn't sure if she would feel safe again in class. As I read her message, I initially felt defensive, and I thought that she may have been overreacting. However, as I replayed the conversation and tried to put myself in her shoes, I began to empathize with her. Although I had engaged in the discussion as a sort of intellectual exchange, I could see that I had failed to recognize complex power dynamics related to my role as professor and hers as student, combined with my identity as a Black person and hers as a White person as we enacted those roles in the public space of the classroom. After apologizing to her privately, I also apologized to her during the class (with her permission), and I deconstructed the experience with students as an example of the complexities of identity politics in a classroom. I am pleased to report that she resumed her active engagement with the class, and that I became more vigilant about my behaviors and feelings, as well as about picking up on nonverbal cues.

As another example, I once taught a class where a White male student tried, at the beginning of two class sessions, to sit outside the circle of seats in the classroom. Both times, I gently invited him to join us. In subsequent classes, he began to sit in the circle without prompting, and I was conscientious about responding to any nonverbal cues implying that he had something to share. During a discussion about power and social identity, he offered compelling comments about religious discrimination on campus, and I affirmed the importance of his perspective. He later told me in an e-mail that he had felt alienated by some of his peers during the first session of the class because of his religious affiliation. I think that he became more comfortable as the class continued because of how I responded to him. Perhaps the other students also became more receptive to him because of my behaviors.

As these examples imply, although critical communication pedagogy will bring challenges for faculty, it probably will be even more taxing for students, whom faculty will ask to engage in nontraditional ways of learning while also contesting their beliefs about a variety of issues, including identity (theirs and others), power, and equality. Faculty will tell students to think for themselves, to challenge authority, to ask questions. Faculty will also expect students to learn and understand complex concepts such as *hegemony, ideology, privilege, praxis,* and *social construction.* Students may struggle to understand content while also processing their responses and reactions, as well as their peers' and professor's. If we do our job well, students will feel various emotions about what they are learning, and they may not know how to process those emotions. Faculty may need to respond to painful consequences of raising students' consciousness. When I taught a course on difference for undergraduates, two middle class White males disclosed in reflection papers that they were having headaches from thinking about the issues we were exploring as they began to understand the concept of unearned privileges. I reminded them to view privilege as a means for effecting social change, rather than as something about which to feel guilty.

As students process their learning, they may respond by complaining to other faculty members or administrators, by resisting course activities, by accusing the instructor of proselytizing, and by evaluating the course and instructor negatively. As a result, faculty may experience disciplinary consequences from colleagues, students, and others. Basically, to apply critical communication pedagogy to teach organizing and difference, faculty will need to ask a lot of students and themselves, and everyone may experience varying types of discomfort and pain. To put it mildly, taking this on is much, much easier said than done. However, I believe that the potential benefits are well worth the effort.

I also think that faculty can be proactive to try to optimize success and minimize obstacles. For example, they can alert students that the learning process probably will be different than they have experienced and that it probably will challenge them in new ways. I often tell students that we will consciously think *and* feel as we explore course content. I explain that although college classrooms and higher education tend to devalue emotionality in favor of rationality, we will honor and value both. I also highlight rationality as an example of hegemony and ideology.

Faculty should plan to ease students and themselves into the experience of critical communication pedagogy to teach organizing and difference. Rather than attempt to implement major overhauls of courses or create brand new ones, they could select aspects of existing courses to experiment with some of the commitments of critical communication pedagogy. For example, they could denote higher education as one type of organizational context where we enact power and difference, and they could assign readings about difference and higher education to exemplify course concepts such as socialization. They could also develop assignments that invite students to critically analyze power dynamics in their roles and relationships in higher education or to conduct critical case studies of difference in their educational contexts and to propose ways to transform those contexts. As they teach students about organizing and difference, faculty could disclose their own struggles with power in the academy, especially those related to their own social identity intersections. These are just a few examples of how faculty might take steps toward developing and implementing courses about difference and organizing that employ critical communication pedagogy.

Another more ambitious and challenging option for incorporating critical communication pedagogy into teaching organizing and difference is to treat organizational communication education as a distinct, representative site of politics, as a living case through which to teach and learn how social identities and other relations of power become organized. To illustrate this approach, I offer next an overview of a master's course in communication that I taught, titled "Difference Matters in Organizational Communication: Power in the Ivory Tower." This course could be adapted for senior level undergraduates or doctoral students in communication studies. I created and began to teach this course as I wrote this chapter because I wanted to provide specific examples of how to use critical communication pedagogy for teaching organizing and difference. In addition, I wanted to respond to the recurring call for critical theorists to engage in praxis.

I also decided to take advantage of my circumstances, which demonstrates the significance of socio-cultural context for the type of power dynamics in higher education that the course covers. As I mentioned earlier, I am a full professor who probably doesn't feel as much pressure as non-tenured faculty regarding student or faculty evaluations of my teaching. Please understand that I'm not saying that I don't value feedback, because I do. What I mean is that I don't have to be concerned that those evaluations will affect my job security. In addition, I have the authority to create the course as I wish because I developed the original seminar ("Difference Matters in Organizational Communication"), and I have the leeway to frame it as I wish (i.e., by focusing on power in the ivory tower). I also have extensive experience teaching, writing, and talking about difference matters for a wide variety of audiences, and I have received positive feedback about my endeavors. In addition, I teach in a department that values diversity and that strives to prepare students to be advocates for social justice. Therefore, I suspected that my class wouldn't be too out of line with others that students had taken in my department. Finally, as a social justice activist, I am committed to increasing my efforts to make a positive difference in the world, and I would be remiss if I didn't try to optimize this opportunity to (1) take my own teaching and learning to another level, (2) model processes of developing and implementing courses based on critical communication pedagogy for others, and (3) disseminate practical knowledge that might effect change in the discipline.

In the next section, I provide excerpts from the overview of the course, after which I discuss a few aspects of how it was implemented. My goal is to offer insight that might inform anyone interested in applying critical communication pedagogy to teach organizing and difference.

❖ COURSE OVERVIEW

Difference Matters in Organizational Communication: Power in the Ivory Tower

This course will apply perspectives on power to investigate higher education-as-organization. We will engage in a variety of activities to explore the ideas that we are all located in intersectional systems and relations of work and power, and our routine organizational communication in higher education contexts (re)produces those systems and relations. Rather than view communication as one factor of modern organizational life, we will approach our study from the perspective that communication constitutes organizations. Moreover, we will emphasize the idea that power pervades all communication. However, we will not view *power* as a four-letter word! Instead, we will actively explore the positive consequences of power, as well as ways that we can empower ourselves and others to accomplish our personal and professional goals. Therefore, a primary premise of the course will be as follows: Those who constitute an organization are responsible for creating and changing communication systems associated with an organization. Although members of an organization have different levels of power for socially constructing its communication systems, everyone has at least some capacity to change those systems.

(Continued)

(Continued)

This course will review concepts, theories, and research about power in organizational communication studies and other disciplines to develop a comprehensive framework for understanding power dynamics by studying higher education. We will consider these dynamics as related to various micro-, meso-, and macro-level contexts, from our specific course and classroom to the department, the college, the university, the community, the discipline of communication, and beyond. To investigate these and other issues, the course will draw on the expertise and experiences of all class members to conceptualize, design, implement, and evaluate course activities.

During the course, we will study higher education as political process and product and consider how relations of power develop contextually rather than universally. All members will engage in open, collective self-analysis (as teachers, students, or as a classroom community). We will focus on theoretical and practical issues regarding relationships between communication processes in higher education contexts and socially constructed aspects of identity, including gender, race, sexual identity, social class, ability, and age—and their intersections. Intersections of these social identities matter because most individuals simultaneously occupy privileged and nonprivileged social identity groups. Therefore, I will stress the ideas that social identities are complex and multifaceted and that intersections of social identity matter. The course will focus on how systems of power and privilege help shape perceptions of salient social identity groups within the United States and on how individuals and groups resist and transform those systems. We will also investigate the role of discourse in constructing social identity throughout the history of the United States. To study these issues, we will rely on social constructionism, a theoretical perspective which basically contends that humans create reality through communication and interaction. . . .

Throughout the course, we will explore ways that discourse produces, maintains, or resists systems of power and inequality, especially as related to social identity and higher education. The course will also delve into communication issues relevant to ways that we learn about social identities from such sources as our families, education, the media, and organizations.

To explore these matters, we will take a critical approach, which means looking for power dynamics, including ways that people comply with dominant ways or resist power to change conditions in society. We also will self-consciously delve into our personal perceptions, perspectives, and experiences as related to course materials. In addition, we will discuss implications of our studies for social change, especially in higher education. . . .

I e-mailed this overview to students before the first session to give them an idea of what to expect. I also e-mailed them the following message:

> *I am so excited that you have signed up for our course. We are going to have a learning good time! I am pleased to tell you that we will take a different approach to the course than you may ever have experienced. Specifically, we will reflect upon our experiences in the classroom and the course to learn and enact the concepts that we will study. This means, for one thing, that I am going to offer to share my power with you by inviting you to co-construct and co-conduct the learning experience. Also, we all will engage in self-reflexivity as we study issues such as social identity, power, resistance, and reform. To do so, we will refer to a wide variety of resources, including traditional academic sources as well as popular press, the Internet, film, television, and so forth. We also will engage in lots of interactive activities in the classroom. Please see the attached overview for more information about the goals and the framework of the course. (Allen, personal correspondence, January 14, 2009)*

During my first class session with students, I talked about my vision and rationale for the course. I hoped to give anyone who might not be interested in the course an opportunity to opt out, even as I understood that some of them may not have had other options due to limited course offerings, scheduling constraints, and so forth. As I frequently do in courses on difference and communication, I shared a list of guidelines for interaction (see Appendix). We discussed each of the guidelines and agreed to follow them throughout the course. The goal of this exercise was to help establish and maintain a safe classroom, where everyone feels empowered, included, and invited to express her or his thoughts and feelings. Although this exercise usually takes almost an hour to complete, the time spent is worth it. I think it was especially important for this class because it helped to set the stage for constructing a classroom community by providing an implicit framework and foundation on difference and power dynamics. I realized while writing this essay that this exercise corresponds with several of Fasset and Warren's (2007) commitments because the guidelines elicit self-reflexivity, value cultural differences, and foster agency and dialogue.

During that first class, I shared my philosophy of teaching, which, briefly, is to provide a teaching-learning experience where everyone in the class has an opportunity to grow during the course of our time together. I also always hope to provide class members with experiences that bolster their sense of agency. And I view myself as the lead learner who has primary responsibility for facilitating learning, but who also actively seeks to learn from everyone else. I explained further that I wanted to share my power with them, and I asked them to reflect on my invitation during the following week. I asked them to be prepared to talk about why they should or should not agree. I also asked them to put themselves in my shoes and to discuss why I should or should not be willing to share my power.

Then, I asked them to write their thoughts (for their eyes only) about their philosophy of learning. I was pleased with their responses. They said that no one had ever asked them such a question, and they appreciated the challenge. This exercise seemed to help form the foundation for the class by reminding students about their responsibility for learning and by encouraging them to remind themselves of what they hoped to accomplish as students. It also began the process of self-reflexivity, a pivotal aspect of critical communication pedagogy.

Among notable experiences with the course is that students eventually agreed to accept my invitation to share the power with them. Although I had asked them to be responsible for 50% of the grading schema (I had developed the other 50% as follows: attendance and participation—15%, three reflection papers—20%, and a final project—15%), we struggled, primarily because they ended up with a lengthy list of possible assignments, and they couldn't come to consensus. The only items everyone agreed on were (1) to assemble final projects as a resource for future classes, and (2) for groups of students to be responsible for developing and implementing class sessions during the last month of the semester (to which we ended up assigning 25% of the final grade). As we discussed other possibilities, an international student who hadn't spoken much said that she needed more points for written assignments because she believed that it took her much longer because English is not her native language. Her comment was pivotal for my response, which was to offer each student an opportunity to develop an individualized plan for 25% of her or his final grade. I also told them that they could add any of those points to existing assignments. Everyone agreed to this approach, and I marked our discussion as a great example of dialogue because, through listening and thoughtful sharing of perspectives, we had created something we couldn't have predicted prior to engaging in the decision-making process.

I also couldn't have predicted the consequences of this plan. Most exciting is that many students generated ideas that I wouldn't have imagined, including a slam poetry performance about difference matters; a down-to-earth guide for working-class parents and families whose children will be first generation college students; a website on inclusive teaching; and a report of experiences volunteering at an agency devoted to members of a non-dominant group. As part of her 25%, the international student who expressed concern about the time she needed to write proposed to produce three short video recorded commentaries on current events related to our course, and to add 10% to her written assignments. Two students who had established a routine of meeting for lengthy talks about the class immediately following each session asked for credit to continue those conversations, and to generate a letter to each other about what they had learned because of those conversations, as well as to refer to those sessions in their final projects. Their request was noteworthy because although they are similar to one another in terms of race, gender, and age, they realized that they are also very different in terms of other aspects of social identity, including sexual orientation.

Because I met with each student individually, this process took a lot of (well-spent) time. Scheduling also proved challenging because a few students worked full-time jobs and could only meet after 5 P.M. Many of them seemed reticent to share their ideas, possibly due to skepticism that they really could do whatever they wanted. I decided to accept whatever they proposed, as long as they could tie their projects explicitly to course objectives and give me criteria for how to evaluate their assignments. Most students seemed to gain respect for faculty because they hadn't thought previously about the challenge of creating a grading rubric.

In addition to spending time figuring out students' 25% of their grade, I took more time than usual with students who came to see me during office hours or asked to schedule appointments. I think their visits reflected their excitement and enthusiasm about the course as well as their need for reassurance and guidance on individual and group projects. I needed extra time for grading because each student had a different grading schema. I also spent a lot of time finding current materials that related to the course and that responded to that group of students' interests. Consequently, I definitely plan to teach the course again so that the time feels well invested!

I did not anticipate that I would sacrifice time that I usually apply during the course to cover certain information and to engage in certain activities that have been productive during previous courses. Because I needed to ensure that students fully understood course concepts and that they were comfortable as a learning community before I relinquished the final month of the class to them, I focused more on accomplishing those goals during the first couple of months than usual. For instance, we didn't view and discuss films that I usually show.

I feel quite good about what we accomplished. Although the group was diverse in terms of visible aspects of identity, such as race and gender, students disclosed invisible aspects of identity, such as social class backgrounds, sexuality, ability, nationality, educational experiences, and religion, in ways that punctuated (1) the significance of intersectionality and (2) the idea that most individuals simultaneously embody positions of privilege and disadvantage according to dominant ideologies in the United States. These points have become increasingly important as I teach this course and conduct other work on difference because they diminish the likelihood of polarized groups within a class while optimizing a sense of shared responsibility and agency among students for effecting social change. Students also embraced the notion that identity is performative, and they often offered or highlighted examples to substantiate it.

I already learned many lessons, especially since I was looking for them (self-reflexivity elicits lessons galore). For instance, I struggled more with sharing my power than I expected. I can justify some of the tension with a logical concern for providing adequate resources and information to accomplish course goals. However, I also discerned reluctance based on my need to be in control, period. And although I believe that students will rise to the occasion when you ask and empower them to be creative, I often was surprised when students fulfilled that premise. So I probably am more jaded and judgmental about students than I realized.

On a more pragmatic note, when I teach the course again, I will need to be more directive about student-led sessions by providing resources and grading criteria related to issues such as generating learning objectives, facilitating discussions, managing time during class, and performing as a team. The good news is that even if I never teach this course again, I am so glad that I undertook this project. My interest in pedagogy has been heightened, and I definitely grew as an educator. More important, most of the students seem to have gotten the material, as based on their reflection papers, in-class discussions, blog posts, one-on-one conversations with me, and final projects, which included substantive, specific, action plans related to difference and power in the ivory tower for various stakeholder groups, including Hispanic families, African American male high school students, the Office of Disability Services, faculty members of dominant groups who teach subject matter about non-dominant groups, graduate students who are mothers, international students, the university's Board of Regents, and the Human Resources Department at our university.

In conclusion, I encourage those who teach organizing and difference to consider applying critical communication pedagogy because it can facilitate our efforts to teach organizing and difference and allow us to accomplish the important goal of preparing students to be "critically-reflexive citizens" (Warren, 2009, p. 216) in our increasingly multicultural world. Fortunately, a wealth of resources exists to direct and support applying critical communication pedagogy. Faculty can refer to the growing body of publications by scholars describing their experiences with critical communication pedagogy, teaching difference, and related topics. (See, for example, Alexander, 1999; Allen, Orbe, & Olivas, 1999; Ashcraft & Allen, 2003; Ashcraft & Mumby, 2004; Cooks, 2003, Hendrix, Jackson, & Warren, 2003; Lewis & Hayward, 2003; Nainby et al., 2003; Shor, 1992.) Faculty also can study relevant literature on pedagogy, organizational communication, and difference, while using Fassett and Warren's ten commitments as a primary framework to develop and implement course content, policies, and practices.

Benefits of employing critical communication pedagogy to teach (and learn!) organizing and difference may be incremental, especially if we are proactive. We should form alliances with others who teach similar topics, and we should share our experiences with one another. We also can parlay teaching experiences into websites, textbooks, and other resources. And our teaching experiences can inform other aspects of our scholarship, including research, service, and consulting. Furthermore, as educators deal explicitly with organizing and difference, we will imply to students that those topics matter to organizational communication studies, which might attract, orient, and socialize future scholars. Ultimately, we can help grow organizing and difference into a substantive, transformative area of study in communication.

❖ REFERENCES

Alexander, B. (1999). Performing culture in the classroom: An instructional (auto) ethnography. *Text and Performance Quarterly, 19*, 307–331.

Allen, B. J. (2004). *Difference matters: Communicating social identity.* Long Grove, IL: Waveland Press.

Allen, B. J., Orbe, M., & Olivas, M. O. (1999). The complexity of our tears: Dis/enchantment and (in)difference in the academy. *Communication Theory 9*, 402–430.

Alvesson, M., Ashcraft, K. L., & Thomas, R. (2008). Identity matters: Reflections on the construction of identity scholarship in organization studies. *Organization, 15*(1), 5–28.

Ashcraft, K. L., & Allen, B. J. (2003). The racial foundation of organizational communication. *Communication Theory, 13,* 5–38.

Ashcraft, K. L., & Allen, B. J. (2009). Politics even closer to home: Repositioning CME from the standpoint of communication studies. *Management Learning, 40,* 11–30.

Ashcraft, K. L., & Mumby, D. K. (2004). *Reworking gender: A feminist communicology of organization.* Thousand Oaks, CA: Sage.

Buber, M. (1958). *I and thou.* (R. G. Smith, Trans.). New York: Scribner's.

Burr, V. (1995). *An introduction to social constructionism.* London: Routledge.

Butler, J. (1993). *Bodies that matter: On the discursive limits of "sex."* New York: Routledge.

Cooks, L. (2003). Pedagogy, performance, and positionality: Teaching about whiteness in interracial communication. *Communication Education, 52,* 245–257.

Deetz, S., & Mumby, D. K. (1990). Power, discourse, and the workplace: Reclaiming the critical tradition. In J. Anderson (Ed.), *Communication yearbook* (Vol. 13, pp. 18–47). Newbury Park, CA: Sage.

Fassett, D., & Warren, J. (2007). *Critical communication pedagogy.* Thousand Oaks, CA: Sage.

Freire, P. (1970). *The pedagogy of the oppressed.* New York: Continuum.

Giroux, H. A. (1994). *Disturbing pleasures: Learning popular culture.* New York: Routledge.

Giroux, H. A. (1997). *Pedagogy and the politics of hope: Theory, culture, and schooling.* Boulder, CO: Westview Press.

Giroux, H. A., & Giroux, S. S. (2006). Challenging neoliberalism's new world order: The promise of critical pedagogy. *Cultural Studies/Critical Methodologies, 6(1),* 21–32.

Hendrix, K., Jackson, R., II, & Warren, J. (2003). Shifting academic landscapes: Exploring co-identities, identity negotiation, and critical progressive pedagogy. *Communication Education, 52(3/4),* 177–190.

hooks, b. (1994). *Teaching to transgress: Education as the practice of freedom.* New York: Routledge.

Johnson, J., & Bhatt, A. (2003). Gendered and racialized identities and alliances in the classroom: Formations in/of resistive space. *Communication Education, 52(3–4),* 230–244.

Lewis, L., & Hayward, P. (2003). Choice-based learning: Student reactions in an undergraduate organizational communication course. *Communication Education, 52(2),* 148–156.

McLaren, P. (2003). *Life in schools: An introduction to critical pedagogy in the foundation of education.* Boston: Allyn & Bacon.

Mumby, D. K. (1993). Critical organizational communication studies: The next ten years. *Communication Monographs, 60,* 18–25.

Mumby, D. (2001). Power and politics. In F. M. Jablin & L. L. Putnam (Eds.), *The new handbook of organizational communication: Advances in theory, research, and methods* (pp. 585–623). Thousand Oaks, CA: Sage.

Nainby, K., Warren, J., & Bollinger, C. (2003). Articulating contact in the classroom: Towards a constitutive focus in critical pedagogy. *Language & Intercultural Communication, 3*(3), 198–212.

Orbe, M. (1998). *Constructing co-cultural theory.* Thousand Oaks, CA: Sage.

Rodriguez, J., & Cai, D. (1994). When your epistemology gets in the way: A response to Sprague. *Communication Education, 43*(4), 263–272.

Shor, I. (1992). *Empowering education: Critical teaching for social change.* Chicago: University of Chicago Press.

Simpson, J., & Allen, B. J. (2006). Engaging difference matters in the classroom. In J. Simpson & P. Shockley (Eds.), *Engaging communication, transforming organizations: Scholarship of engagement in action* (pp. 147–170). Cresskill, NJ: Hampton Press.

Sprague, J. (1990, February). Problematizing power in the classroom. Applying the critical perspective to a significant issue in instructional communication. Paper presented at the meeting of the Western States Communication Association, Sacramento, CA.

Sprague, J. (1992). Expanding the research agenda for instructional communication: Raising some unasked questions. *Communication Education, 41*(1), 1–25.

Sprague, J. (1993). Retrieving the research agenda for communication education: Asking the pedagogical questions that are "embarrassments" to theory. *Communication Education, 42*(2), 106.

Sprague, J. (2002). Communication education: The spiral continues. *Communication Education, 51*(4), 337.

Warren, J. T. (2001). Doing whiteness: On the performative dimensions of race in the classroom. *Communication Education, 50,* 91–108.

Warren, J. T. (2009). Critical communication pedagogy. In S. W. Littlejohn & K. A. Foss (Eds.). *Encyclopedia of Communication Theory* (pp. 213–216). Thousand Oaks, CA: Sage.

❖ APPENDIX

Working Assumptions for Class Interaction

These will be discussed in class and agreed upon by the whole group in order that respect for diversity permeates all aspects of class interaction and learning.

1. Acknowledge that sexism, racism, ageism, heterosexism, and other types of discrimination have most often been systematically taught and learned.

2. We cannot be blamed for information we have learned, but we will be held responsible for repeating misinformation after we have learned otherwise.

3. We do not blame others if they do not have the advantages and opportunities that we may have.

4. We will assume that people are always doing the best they can.

5. We will actively pursue information about our own groups and those of others. We are each assumed to be the experts on our own reality and very much involved in researching that reality with each other.

6. We will share information about our own groups with other members of the class and we will NEVER demean, devalue, or in any way put down people for their experiences.

7. We each have an obligation to actively combat the myths and stereotypes about our own groups and other groups so that we can break down walls, which prohibit group cooperation and group gain.

8. In every way, we will work to create a safe atmosphere for open discussion.

9. We will recognize the uniqueness of each student.

10. The process of learning is an ongoing process for all involved in this class and requires constant critique, reflection, and action. Learning is seen to be a collective process, where participants share and analyze experiences together in order to address concerns, relying on each other's strengths and resources rather than either addressing problems individually or relying on outside experts to solve them.

11. Content in this process is emergent. Each of us has to be involved not only in determining content but in explicitly reflecting on what counts as knowledge, how learning takes place, and our own roles in this process. The "bank" from which content is drawn is the social reality of our lives: It may range from the very immediate context of the classroom itself to family and community content to broader political issues.

12. The teacher's role in this is to act as a problem-poser, facilitating the process of uncovering important issues and reflecting on them, rather than as a transmitter of knowledge and skills. Because students are the experts on their own reality, the teacher is a co-learner.

13. We will become lifelong learners, continually accepting differences among diverse populations, including ethnicity, disabilities, social class, culture, gender, religion, sexual orientation, and race.

Source: Adapted from: http://www.d.umn.edu/~hrallis/courses/1100sp04/index.html

6

"But Society is Beyond ___ism" (?)

Teaching How Differences are "Organized" via Institutional Privilege↔Oppression

Erika Kirby

> Systems, structures, institutions are in place throughout society that maintain inequality. Their greatest force may lie in their "everydayness," their normal taken-for-granted place . . . Rather than enacting visible oppression, they operate for the most part by continuing to define, produce, study, and adjudicate, over and over, groups of people targeted for "one-down-ness." (Creighton, 2003a, p. 4)

My chapter explores the ways I encourage students to recognize how differences based on social identity (social identity differences: SIDs) are often organized in ways that are oppressive to some and to be reflective about their privilege in order to transform the ways they think about and act upon difference. I have found such teaching and learning to be hard work as I try to get students "to question their underlying assumptions, to capture their attention without alienating them, *to compel students who are privileged to understand the benefits of privilege without blaming those who are disadvantaged* ... to inspire not offend, and to interest not anger" (Johnson & Bhatt, 2003, p. 107).

I have been (literally) frowned at by my students when talking about issues of privilege↔oppression, such as when I explain the following: how I refuse to open mail to "Mrs. Robert Kirby" because no such person exists in my mind; how I change *God as father* to *God as creator* in my prayers; and how I have eliminated (and want them to eliminate) phrases like *that's lame, that's so gay* or *that's so retarded* from their speech. I have been told that U.S. society is beyond sexism and racism. I was asked by a student if I was "stretching it a bit to find another form of oppression" when I introduced the notion of socioeconomic classism. Underlying much of this resistance is the fact that students from privileged backgrounds "are frequently hostile, or at best neutral" to discussing stratification based on differences in social identity (Bohmer & Briggs, 1991, p. 154).

In Chapter 5 of this volume, Allen defines the utility of critical communication pedagogy for increasing students' understanding of difference and organizations. My contribution follows suit, weaving together (a) writings in communication, education, sociology, and psychology; (b) my experiences; and (c) outside teaching resources to explain both how I have applied critical communication pedagogy in my senior undergraduate capstone class on *Communication and Community* (see Kirby, 2009 for syllabus) and what modifications I would make if concentrating more centrally on organizing difference.

I encourage students to examine the multiplicity of ways in which all SIDs entwine with degrees of privilege↔oppression, as well as how these differences function in intersection since we are all comprised of multiple SIDs (Ashcraft & Mumby, 2004). The analogy I utilize (following Audre Lorde's 1984 metaphor of "ingredients") is to have students think of the multiple facets of their social identity as colored pencils. Imagine they (stereotypically) start by coloring their sex as pink or blue, then color over that with their gender (perhaps in purple), then color over that with a shade near their skin tone, then color yellow over that to illustrate their social class, and so forth. Then, if they "want to just concentrate on showing the purple-ness of . . . gender . . . purple has been combined with pink/blue, a shade of brown, and yellow— and so ..[they] cannot just take it back without erasing everything . . . the ingredients intersect and are inextricably linked" (Kirby & McBride, 2009, p. xix).

But in practice, it is not quite so straightforward to teach about the ways that difference (including privilege↔oppression) is (re)constructed in everyday life. Numerous theorists (e.g., Bohmer & Briggs,

1991; Johnson & Bhatt, 2003; Millstein, 1997) have illustrated that students are often resistant to having their worldviews challenged. Davis (1992) identified three typical student responses to teaching about difference and inequality—resistance, paralysis, and rage. Resistant students often deny that inequality exists or "argue that conditions are improving so rapidly that no intervention is needed" (p. 232) and insist that discussions of inequality remain on an abstract, intellectual level (see also Griffin, 1997b). Students may also become "paralyzed" to the point where they no longer want to talk about inequality. Finally, discussing difference can make students on both sides angry: students from oppressed groups feel anger from injustice, while students from privileged groups may get angry when they are made aware of their privilege because many are unaware of how their greater resources increase their life chances (Johnson & Bhatt, 2003; Misra, 1997). The challenge thus becomes how to artfully frame dialogue about difference in organizations so that students are receptive to conceptualizing difference as both privilege and oppression.

❖ PREPARING TO DIALOGUE ABOUT DIFFERENCE AND PRIVILEGE↔OPPRESSION IN ORGANIZATIONS

Allen (Chapter 5 of this volume) suggests that instructors should ease into teaching with critical communication pedagogy. I second this advice; the first time I taught racial privilege↔oppression, I (naively) assumed students would possess the basic vocabulary and, therefore, we could just jump right in to talking about difference and breaking down stereotypes—which proved to be a colossal mistake. Without common language/vocabulary to frame students' experiences, class discussion seemed to reify individual stereotypes rather than question organizational practices and institutional isms. I immediately revised my course prep, rooting subsequent discussions of difference in a "systems of oppression" approach (a relational way to think about difference in terms of privilege↔oppression, see Adams, Bell, & Griffin, 1997; Hill Collins, 1990; Lucal, 1996). And now, after teaching this course four times—the first time feeling some regret, three times feeling mostly success—I have gathered numerous strategies for teaching about SIDs and privilege↔oppression in organizations.

Griffin (1997a) asserted that instructors should determine "personal readiness" for critical pedagogy in five areas: (a) the availability of professional and personal support for teaching about inequality; (b) passion for educating about oppression; (c) self-awareness; (d) knowledge

about different manifestations of social oppression; and (e) having multiple teaching strategies to help create a learning environment in which
students can productively engage with each other and the instructor
(pp. 279–281). For me, self-awareness has been crucial because "we
struggle alongside our students with our own social identities, biases,
fears, and prejudices. We, too, need to be willing to examine and deal
honestly with our values, assumptions, and emotional reactions to
oppression issues" (Bell, Washington, Weinstein, & Love, 1997, p. 299).
My (gradually emerging) confidence in teaching about difference as a
largely privileged person—female, White, upper-middle class, heterosexual, able-bodied, and thirty-something—comes from reflecting often
on this positionality.

There is debate as to whether or not instructors should reveal
aspects of their own social identity that may not be readily apparent
(e.g., sexuality, ability). I have chosen disclosure, offering my experiences with dominant and targeted identities as a text for my students.
For example, when discussing classism, students are asked to speculate
as to my social class background given that this identity can be invisible. Since I am now a highly educated college professor, they almost
always assume an upper-middle class background and are somewhat
shocked to hear that I was raised in a single parent home hovering
around the poverty line and, consequently, have had consistent paid
employment since I was 14 (holding three jobs in college).

I have also benefited from Simpson, Causey, and Williams's (2007)
multiple instructional strategies for having discussions that tackle SIDs
and privilege↔oppression. After researching student and teacher attitudes and practices in addressing race in the classroom, they found
that students appreciate instructors who provide them with clear
guidelines for class content and discussion, including using existing
pedagogical structures (e.g., the syllabus, comments about what is to
come) to communicate that the class will offer attention to difference,
the possible difficulties that may emerge, and what instructors hope for
related to these discussions. (See Allen, this volume, for more ideas.)
Students want instructors to clearly guide discussion using a variety of
formats and pedagogical strategies and to encourage a range of opinions on issues—even if that invites disagreement. Concomitantly, when
uninformed perspectives about issues of difference are articulated, students want instructors to challenge those ideas by asking where the
student got her or his information or by countering them with a more
informed perspective (Simpson et al., 2007).

Grading is also a concern for students when they are talking about
potentially volatile issues such as SIDs, and so Simpson et al. (2007)

suggested that instructors link grades to learning objectives, "which might include the ability to apply course concepts to issues of [difference] in and outside of the classroom" (p. 46). My adaptation of this is that when I grade student activities (typically in the form of exploratory writing), the *grade* is based on the completeness of and the amount of reflection in the activity—but in my *comments,* I tackle any ideas that are misinformed or prejudiced. This leads to perhaps the most important lesson I have learned when teaching about privilege↔oppression: to worry less about learner approval and to not be afraid to make students frustrated, frightened, or angry (Bell et al., 1997). I recently had a student say he felt like "an angry tiger" because he had so much cognitive dissonance related to my class—and I took that as evidence of accomplishing my objectives.

Of course, students also need to be prepared for this type of learning; trust needs to be established to productively discuss elements of difference and privilege↔oppression in the classroom. To encourage useful instructor-student interaction, I try to get to know students by having them write a note after the first class that shares whatever they want me to know about them, and of course I learn a lot about them though reading their exploratory writing (discussed later in this chapter). To encourage productive student-student interaction, my class shares a meal together on the first night of class in order to build trust. Because of the tension and emotion surrounding aspects of difference (Simpson et al., 2007), it is also beneficial to establish ground rules for class discussion to provide a cooperative atmosphere and encourage equal status for all class members (see also Harris, 2003; Neville Miller & Harris, 2005). While our ground rules evolve during the class, I do take along a set of assumptions for class interaction (Mongan-Rallis & Higgins, 2004—included in this volume as Allen's appendix; see also Creighton, 2003a).

Hubbard and DeWelde (2003) illustrated that a danger of a trusting and "candid classroom environment was that students with oppressive and prejudiced views assumed that they could freely indulge those views," and they "found it difficult, yet absolutely imperative, not to reject or punish students who asserted their [prejudices]"; instead, they "pointed out to them how potentially destructive or debilitating such emotions could be to themselves as well as to others" (p. 82). Yet it is also possible that privileged students may stay silent and feel vulnerable about expressing their beliefs in class because they think their experiences are not as well received or legitimate as those of traditionally marginalized groups (Johnson & Bhatt, 2003; Neville Miller & Harris, 2005). This is where introducing a systems of oppression framework becomes important for students. Since no one person is entirely privileged, nor entirely disadvantaged (Lucal, 1996), "examining intersections of identity provides a way to address how [people] can experience both privilege and oppression simultaneously" (Johnson & Bhatt, 2003, p. 234).

❖ SYSTEMS OF PRIVILEGE↔OPPRESSION: A FRAMEWORK FOR EXAMINING DIFFERENCE

A systems of oppression framework embraces the dialectics of privilege/advantage and penalty/disadvantage (Johnson & Bhatt, 2003; Martin & Nakayama, 1999). As articulated by Hill Collins (1990), the social world can be conceptualized as a matrix containing multiple, interlocking oppressions—every SID has both opportunity and oppression associated with it—and individuals derive varying amounts of penalty or privilege from these systems of oppression (also see Moremen, 1997). Thus, while we *study* forms of social identity in isolation in order to understand each, to understand the system of oppression we must also study how each and all of these intersect and inform each other. To help elucidate the systems of oppression framework, I assign students "Difference matters" (Allen, 2004, Chapter 1), "Power matters" (Allen, 2004, Chapter 2), and Lorde's (1984) "There is no hierarchy of oppressions."[1]

Students should be familiarized with *oppression*, or "those attitudes, behaviors, and pervasive and systematic social arrangements by which members of one group [nondominant/target groups] are exploited and subordinated while members of another group [dominant/agent] are granted privileges" (Bohmer & Briggs, 1991, p. 155). Oppression implies a relationship of unequal power between at least two groups (see also Lucal, 1996). *Individual oppression* includes individual beliefs, attitudes, and actions that reflect prejudice against a social group; this can occur at both an unconscious and conscious level, and it can be both active and passive. Many students equate isms with prejudice and discrimination on this individual level, and so oppression serves as a less familiar construct that also includes *societal/cultural* (sociocultural) *dimensions*—the multiplicity of ways in which social norms, roles, rituals, language, music, and art reflect and reinforce the belief that one social group is superior to another—and *institutional dimensions* (Bohmer & Briggs, 1991; Goldsmith, 2006).

Institutional oppression is structured into organizations as well as political and social institutions; since "organizations are rooted in the same systematic inequalities as the rest of U.S. societal institutions . . .

organizations, often unintentionally, function as tools of oppression" (Griffith, Childs, Eng, & Jeffries, 2008, p. 288). Examples of institutions include (a) family, (b) school/education system, (c) religion, (d) real estate/housing, (e) business/jobs/corporations, (f) criminal justice/prison system, (g) organized sports, (h) military, (i) banks/financial institutions, (j) health care/medical, (k) media (TV/cable, Internet, music, books, video games, newspapers, magazines, etc.), (l) government/laws, and (m) history books (Creighton, 2003a).

Institutional oppression encapsulates the policies, laws, rules, norms, and customs enacted by organizations and social institutions that organize difference—creating differential access to goods, services, and opportunities—by disadvantaging some social groups and advantaging others, whether or not such discrimination is intentional. Such differential access eventually becomes common practice—"the way things are"—and so the people in power in institutions may oppress simply as part of carrying out their jobs. Consequently, disparities are often tolerated as normal rather than investigated and challenged. Adams and Balfour (2004) referred to such practices of organizing difference that contribute to institutional oppression as *administrative evil*. They asserted that because of the diffuse and hierarchical nature of organizational systems, people can act in ways that are harmful (and oppressive) to others without being aware of their negative effect: "it is entirely possible to adhere to the tenets of public service and professional ethics and participate in even a great evil and not be aware of it until it is too late (or perhaps not at all)" (p. 11).

Oppression can occur based on a multiplicity of SIDs in each of these institutions, and organizational communication constructs are relevant to many (all?) of these institutions. Discussing institutional racism, Griffith et al. (2008) explained how oppression can permeate different organizational characteristics and dimensions:

> At the individual level, [rac]ism operates through staff members' attitudes, beliefs, and behaviors. At the intraorganizational level, institutional [rac]ism operates through an organization's internal climate, policies, and procedures. These include the relationships among staff, which are rooted in formal and informal hierarchies and power relationships. At the extraorganizational level, institutional [rac]ism explains how organizations influence communities, public policies, and institutions. Also, institutional [rac]ism describes how organizations are affected by larger institutions (i.e., regulatory, economic, political, professional) and are shaped by the sociopolitical and economic contexts that frame an organization's policies, procedures, and functioning. (p. 289)

Thus, to understand how difference is organized, students need to understand oppression *and* privilege, which is an advantaged status based on social identity that tends to "make life easier" to get around, to get what one wants, and to be treated in an acceptable manner (Griffin, 1997b; McIntosh, 1993). Disadvantages faced by members of oppressed groups are often linked directly to advantages enjoyed by the privileged (Bohmer & Briggs, 1991). Frankenberg (1993) illustrated that "the self, where it is part of a dominant cultural group, does not have to name itself" (p. 196); race does not automatically infer Whiteness, gender issues are thought of as women's issues, class is invisible for middle-class people, and so forth. Thus, privilege is typically invisible for those who have it—an "invisible knapsack" of sorts (McIntosh, 1993).

My goal is to enable students of privilege to recognize the "invisible knapsacks" (McIntosh, 1993) of privilege they carry into organizational life so they can more readily recognize institutional oppression. I find that students often resist admitting privilege and instead fall back on scripts of reverse oppression, arguing that "other racial groups sometimes exclude Whites" or policies such as affirmative action discriminate against them. In the remainder of this chapter, I concentrate on ways to dialogue about *institutional* (and organizational) *oppression,* and in order to explore a few SIDs in depth, I include privilege↔oppression based on sex, race, and social class.[2]

❖ TEACHING ABOUT INSTITUTIONAL PRIVILEGE↔OPPRESSION

In teaching about privilege↔oppression in organizational and institutional life, I want students to explore if and how people are discriminated against or marginalized institutionally based on an aspect of their social identity—and conversely, how those of privilege escape (and sometimes perpetuate) such treatment. A pedagogical strategy I continually utilize in pushing students to recognize privilege↔oppression is reflective writing because the act of writing about such issues (in and of itself) is thought to create learning (see Goldsmith, 2006). Thus, prior to discussing any given SID in class, I have students write about their thoughts. Allen (2004) created an "ID Check" of 12 questions at the end of each chapter in her book, *Difference Matters,* for students to reflect upon in discerning their social identities, and I utilize these as one form of journaling/exploratory writing. Many of these questions begin at the (intra)individual level, such as the following: How important is your [SID] to you? What advantages (privilege) do you enjoy based upon your [SID]? Are you ever aware of stereotypes about your [SID] as you interact with others? Following Allen, I have asked students to respond to sources of pride in their SIDs, when they have been discriminated against because of their SIDs, and when/if they have discriminated against others because of their SIDs.

I then try to get students to think beyond the individual level through organizational/institutional questions such as, "What structures, norms, and practices contribute to [SID] oppression on campus (in the local community, etc.)?" (see Moremen, 1997). At the individual reflection stage, I have also found it useful to assign students different Implicit Association Tests (IATs) on the Harvard websites (https://implicit.harvard.edu/) to test their invisible biases and stereotypes about social groups that may translate to their organizational behaviors (e.g., for sexism: gender↔career; for racism: light skin↔dark skin, African American↔White, Native American↔White, and Asian American↔White; see Morgan, 2008, for a related *Communication Teacher* activity).

Then, once we are together in the classroom, the (even) harder work begins. In discussing how institutional oppression operates, I have found two websites to be invaluable resources. First, the Southern Poverty Law Center has multiple classroom activities as part of its Teaching Tolerance Project (see http://www.tolerance.org/index.jsp), and I utilize their volume, *Speak Up! Responding to Everyday Bigotry*, as one of my course texts. Second, Allan Creighton (2003) has an entire curriculum for social justice (i.e., a facilitator guide, 2003a; a foundational unit, 2003b; and multiple curricula for individual SIDs—classism, 2003c; racism, 2003d; and sexism, 2003e) that can be accessed online (http://www.socialjusticeeducation.org/social_justice/creighton/curriculum).

Based on advice I have taken from these curricula, when we gather as a class for discussion, I encourage students to "just suppose that it's true" that institutional oppression *does exist* for the SID we are studying (i.e., institutional sexism, racism, classism, etc.; the same can be done for individual oppression and sociocultural oppression). The point of "just supposing that" is to enable dialogue about what the form of institutional oppression might look like, rather than preemptively denying the possibility of its existence. For any given SID, I have found it useful to explore organizing difference by separating students into groups that are given different institutions and organizations in order to explore questions related to institutional privilege↔oppression, such as the following:

1. How is difference based on sex, race, class, and so on organized in this institution? What group(s) is privileged and what group(s) is oppressed?

2. What are examples of advantages the privileged group receives in this institution, even if they do not realize it, and even if they do not want inequality to exist?

3. What are examples of disadvantages the oppressed group receives in this social institution, even if they do not realize it, and even if they do not want it to exist?

4. What (if any) costs does the system of institutionalized oppression have for the privileged group?

5. How does the institution work to hide or cover up SIDs or distract people from seeing differences in how people are treated based on sex, race, class, and so on? (For example, to cover class differences, management urges workers to "work for the company team.")

6. What are possible ways this institution could (and sometimes does) work *against* oppression to promote equality? (See Creighton, 2003, for more information.)

Given this overall frame for how I approach reflecting and discussing organizing difference via SIDs, I now offer some specified definitions and areas of discussion for three SIDs: sex, race, and class.

❖ DIALOGUING ABOUT INSTITUTIONAL PRIVILEGE↔OPPRESSION RELATED TO SEX/GENDER[3]

As a form of oppression, *sexism* is a set of beliefs and practices that privileges one sex and subordinates another; *institutional sexism* includes the policies, laws, rules, norms, and customs enacted by organizations and social institutions that disadvantage one sex and advantage another. This system is partially upheld by patriarchy and *male privilege*, which is the unearned, (typically) unacknowledged entitlement men receive simply because of being a male in a sexist society. The challenge I have found in teaching about institutional sexism is that both male and female students would like to believe that sexism in U.S. society is a thing of the past—that women no longer face discrimination in organized institutions and that women can be and do anything. (Students also argue that men are readily willing to take on what is traditionally "women's work," such as staying home with children full time.)

To move toward "just supposing it does exist" in institutional sexism, I begin with pregnancy discrimination. Obviously, there *is* legislation to (ostensibly) prevent the advantaging of men and disadvantaging of women based on the Pregnancy Discrimination Act of 1978, which was enacted more than 30 years ago to make clear that employers could not use pregnancy as an excuse to deny women job opportunities. Yet as the 2008 Pregnancy Discrimination Report (National Partnership for Women and Families, 2008) noted and the movie *The Right Focus on: Pregnancy and Discrimination* showed (Minnesota Department of Human Rights, 2008), pregnancy discrimination remains a real barrier to women's employment. Such discrimination includes women being fired, forced to take leave, and denied a promotion or even a job opportunity due to pregnancy or *a fear that she might become pregnant*—a barrier (privileged) men never face. After these examples, students may be more willing to grant that institutional sexism exists; a suggested reading is Buzzanell (1995) who advocates rethinking the glass ceiling from a lens of language and everyday practices to see how sex inequality is (re)constructed in daily organizational life.

Of course, multiple institutions organize difference in ways that are sexist. In the family, the organization of domestic labor based on sex and the amount of domestic work that women perform even when both partners work can be discussed. There are numerous conversations that can be held surrounding sexism in religion and who is allowed to lead; certainly, my own religion (Roman Catholicism) provides an interesting exemplar of institutional sexism. In government and politics, Hilary Clinton's 2008 presidential campaign, where sexist norms and roles were consistently reiterated—including signs of "Iron my shirt!" at a town hall meeting—clearly suggested a woman's place is not as President. In education, students could research the ratio of male to female faculty members at different levels on campus (and if possible, find corresponding salaries), and then compare those numbers to the local K-12 system. In the media, both Norander (2008) and Shuler (2003) examined how the glass ceiling is perpetuated through imagery and news surrounding the feminized representation of (high-powered) women executives, particularly former Hewlett-Packard CEO Carly Fiorina. And in thinking about health care as an institution, practices that make reproductive health mainly the woman's responsibility (e.g., Gardisil vaccination) could be discussed.

Then, to introduce the role of male privilege in institutional sexism, I address some of the questions previously introduced. For example, some of the benefits to men of an institutionally sexist system are as follows: earning more money; having better jobs; receiving more power and recognition; getting taken care of by women and having their children taken care of; participating in better-funded sports; being able to expect better, more respectful, treatment from salespeople, car mechanics, bank officials, and so on; and of course, that history is mostly about men. At the same time, there are costs to men that can be discussed, such as working in high-pressure jobs, increased feelings of isolation and stress, and increased chance of injuries on the job or in the military. Students often introduce that (of course) men can be hurt and oppressed by women; I remind them that institutional oppression is "not about individual mistreatment, but much larger inequality—how on a society-wide scale women earn less, have fewer jobs, have fewer leadership positions, and suffer more extreme violence from men" (Creighton, 2003e, p. 14).

❖ DIALOGUING ABOUT INSTITUTIONAL PRIVILEGE↔OPPRESSION RELATED TO RACE[4]

Discussions of racism are difficult and distressing for most college students, so the challenges to teaching racism are numerous. (For longer explanations, see Neville Miller & Harris, 2005; Simpson et al., 2007.) White (privileged) students may perceive discussions of racism as personal attacks on themselves or their family members and may feel they cannot honestly discuss issues of race oppression without being labeled as racist (Neville Miller & Harris, 2005). Conversely, students of targeted racial groups may feel uncomfortable and self-conscious during these discussions due to concerns that their White classmates are looking for their reactions (Neville Miller & Harris). In these discussions, students may proffer a color-blind approach to race (Goldsmith, 2006; Simpson et al., 2007).

Racism is the systematic subordination of members of targeted racial groups who have relatively little power (in the United States, African Americans/Blacks, Hispanic Americans/Latino/Latinas, Native Americans, Arab Americans, and Asian Americans) by the members of the agent racial group who have relatively more power (in the United States, Euro-Americans/Whites). *Institutional racism* includes the policies, laws, rules, norms, and customs enacted by organizations and social institutions that disadvantage targeted racial groups and advantage others. In the United States, this system is partially upheld by *White privilege*, which is the unearned, (typically) unacknowledged entitlement Euro-Americans receive simply because of having white skin in a racist society (see McIntosh, 1993). The recognition of White privilege is a challenge in and of itself; it is easier for White students to know about the characterizations of other racial and ethnic groups, yet to know only what Whites are not (Frankenberg, 1993). Simply put, "Racially speaking, White is not a color" (Neville Miller & Harris, 2005, p. 224).

Consequently, this discussion of organizing difference needs to concentrate on the invisibility (and simultaneous ubiquity) of Whiteness as a racialized position in society. This can be instigated by having students read Ashcraft and Allen's (2003) analysis of the field of organizational communication's institutional racism as they articulate the multiple ways that our texts and scholarship are centered in Whiteness. A dialogue of institutional racism can be further facilitated by asking students to generate and discuss examples of institutional racism within their everyday lives: In what ways are organizations, the media, the healthcare system, the government, the educational system, and so forth, racist?

I have used the lack of adequate health care across racial and ethnic groups—that has been attributed to bias, cultural ignorance, and/or the limited language capacity of health care providers—as an extended example of institutionalized racism. (I avoid beginning the discussion with employment discrimination to increase the likelihood of students being able to just suppose that institutional racism exists before the inevitable questions about affirmative action and reverse discrimination are introduced.) The recent emphasis on health care reform in the Obama administration has created many such conversations in the media; a recent segment with Dr. Elizabeth Cohen on CNN argued that there are disparities in health care between Whites and African Americans—beyond just not having similar insurance. (The webpage http://blog.case.edu/ccrhd/2009/06/23/racial_disparities_in_health_care_cnn_video is a good source for in-class viewing). In 2003, the U.S. Institute of Medicine published *Unequal Treatment: Confronting Racial and Ethnic Disparities in Healthcare* that could be highlighted. Sack (2008) summarized a study in *The Archives of Internal Medicine* (Sequist et al., 2008) that attributed differences in health outcomes in White and African American diabetic patients who had the same doctors to a systemic failure to tailor treatments to patients' cultural norms. The researchers "recommended that doctors and other members of the health care system learn more about minority communities" and found "the problem of racial disparities is not characterized by only a few physicians providing markedly unequal care, but that such differences in care are spread across the entire system, requiring the implementation of system-wide solutions (¶ 10–11)." Finally, Griffith et al. (2008) described the efforts of one county public health department in the rural South to examine how racism was manifested in its organizational practices and in the services it provided—and then how it took steps to correct institutional racism.

There are numerous contexts of institutionalized racism that can be explored with students. (And these differ across racial groups; see Kivel, 1995.) In finance and banking, an example of institutional racism is the redlining of communities, resulting in differential development based on their racial composition. In the criminal justice system, students can discuss racial profiling (and sometimes police brutality) by security and law enforcement workers. In organized sports, discussion can address the use of stereotyped racial caricatures by institutions (e.g., "Indian" mascots) and how this is increasingly coming under fire. In the media, all targeted racial groups have examples of underrepresentation and misrepresentation. Other areas for discussion might include job, educational, and housing discrimination and barriers to employment or professional advancement based on race. Institutional racism emerges in unequal pay for equal work; unequal funding for education; anti-immigrant legislation and law-enforcement; "English-only" language legislation; forced abandonment of Native-based spiritual practices; and a lack of "minority" representation in social, political, economic, and legal institutions. And the recent movement by several states to abolish affirmative action can start a dialogue as to whether this policy is still needed—or if White privilege is a thing of the past.

Dialogue should ultimately address how White privilege accompanies institutional racism. The "knapsack of (White) privilege" (McIntosh, 1993) ensures most Whites the security of not being pulled over by the police as a suspicious person and the ability to have a job hire or promotion attributed to skills and background rather than affirmative action. Some of the benefits to Whites in a system of institutionalized racism are that in comparison to other racial groups, they have better, safer, and securer housing; better jobs and education; and that candidates for public office typically look like them. In these discussions, White students may raise concerns about how they feel discriminated against when people of oppressed racial groups "stick to their own," as well as express anger at what they perceive as "reverse discrimination" with affirmative action. When such perspectives are expressed, it is important to again direct discussion back to the bigger picture—that institutionalized racism is not about individual mistreatment but much larger (and patterned) inequalities in U.S. society.

❖ DIALOGUING ABOUT INSTITUTIONAL PRIVILEGE↔OPPRESSION RELATED TO SOCIAL CLASS[5]

A challenge in teaching classism is that it is a newer form of privilege to be confronted in the United States; as noted, a student recently asked me if classism as a construct was "stretching it a bit" to find something to talk about. As Hattery (2003) asserted, few college students grew up on welfare; so the lessons of social inequality need to be somehow made more real. Because of the individualistic belief in meritocracy in U.S. society and the myth of a classless society, social class is a sensitive topic—those who are privileged want to believe they have *earned* all the privileges they enjoy. Further, people have not been questioned on epithets such as *trailer trash* or *poor White trash* in the same ways that other SIDs have had language issues called to question. Consequently, I have come to expect student resistance in dialoguing about how social class organizes difference.

Social class is a relative social ranking of individuals or families by power based on economic capital (financial), cultural capital, and social capital (esteem or social status). It is a system of stratification that is associated with a systematically unequal allocation of resources and constraints (e.g., money, savoir-faire or know how, social skills, authority, experience, clout). *Classism* is the set of practices and beliefs that assign differential value to people according to their social class and an economic system that creates excessive inequality and causes basic human needs to go unmet. *Institutional classism* includes the policies, laws, rules, norms, and customs enacted by organizations and social institutions that disadvantage people of "lower" class and advantage people of "higher" class.

Class-based privilege is one of the many tangible or intangible unearned advantages of higher-class status, such as personal contacts with employers, good childhood health care, inherited money, and speaking the same dialect and accent as people with institutional power (see http://www.classism.org/home_definition.html). Social class is typically conceptualized on a continuum where targets are the lower class/poor (i.e., poor, unemployed, imprisoned, welfare recipients, homeless, elderly/fixed-income), the working class is mostly a target group, the middle class is mostly an agent group, and the owning or ruling class is always an agent group.

To begin a dialogue about institutional classism, I facilitate the "10 chairs" exercise with students (taken from United for a Fair Economy, 2004). The activity starts with 10 chairs and 10 volunteers, where each person represents one-tenth of the U.S. population and each chair represents one-tenth of all the private material wealth in the United States (and thus one person is the top 10%). Instructors should note to students that if wealth were evenly distributed, this is what society would look like—one person, one chair—but then reiterate that this picture of equal wealth distribution has never existed in the United States. Next, the volunteer representing the top 10% should be asked to take over seven chairs, evicting the current occupants because, as of 2004, the top 10% owned 71% of all private wealth. The rest of the volunteers (representing 90% of the U.S. population) must then share three chairs (or about 30% of the wealth). Instructors should emphasize that while one person has seven chairs, even within the top 10% there is actually great disparity; the top one percent owns 34% of all wealth (or three and a half chairs)—as much wealth as the bottom 90% have combined. Yet while perhaps we "should" be angry about one person having all that wealth, in reality this group remains largely invisible, while the divisiveness emerges between people in the bottom 90% based on differences in social identity as we all vie for space on the few remaining chairs.

Institutional classism organizes difference in a multitude of ways. Related to government, students can plan a budget for a family whose only sources of income are Aid to Families with Dependent Children (AFDC) and food stamps. Working with actual figures provided by the local welfare office, students realize that these families have very little money, even for basic necessities, and that the reality of "living off welfare" does not match its discursive construction. In healthcare, there is little doubt that the system is stratified and that those who are uninsured receive lower quality health care than those who can afford insurance. In education, exploring how the local public school system in many areas is districted based on social class (and race), with schools receiving more (or less) money based on the property taxes paid by those in the district, can facilitate productive discussion about oppression in our educational system. In the media, imagery of who is portrayed as doing certain types of work and resulting ways of organizing illustrates class-based privilege. The series *Dirty Jobs* is illustrative of what work is considered dirty in U.S. society, and the NBC sitcom *My Name is Earl* centers in a lower-class set of characters and plays on trailer park stereotypes; the only work Earl is shown doing is stealing. At my institution, I have actually heard of students having "trailer trash parties"—certainly such events are worthy of discussion as to how students are (re)producing classism.

Institutional classism cannot be confronted without dealing with its accompanying myth of meritocracy, which suggests that if a person has a lower social class than they would like, they can "pull themselves up by their bootstraps," because "anybody can get ahead if they try." This mentality leads to faulty assumptions that people who have a lot earned it and people who don't have a lot haven't tried enough. Debunking this myth presents a challenging dialogue in that it intersects with class privilege, and so those who do have wealth may get defensive that they deserve what they have and have "earned it."

I typically discuss institutional classism after sex and race because "classism works through and backs up all the other 'isms'" (Creighton, 2003e, p. 17). Consequently, readings about social class in organizational communication also seem to emphasize intersectionality with other SIDs (rather than being centered on social class); some sources for students to read include Parker's (2003) exploration of African American women in "raced, gendered, and classed" work contexts, and Cheney and Ashcraft's (2007) (re)consideration of the ways that *professional* is utilized in communication studies.

❖ FINAL REFLECTIONS ON DIFFERENCE AND INSTITUTIONAL PRIVILEGE↔OPPRESSION

Allen (2004) illustrated how difference makes a difference when humans perceive and treat one another differently based on the social identity categories they embody—when difference becomes organized in ways that are oppressive. I therefore conclude each unit of organizing difference by trying to empower students to be allies and take action or speak up when treatment based on SIDs becomes oppressive. This helps to bring them full circle in reflecting on institutional privilege↔oppression. In their exploratory writing, students always answer the same final two questions: (a) After your readings and reflections, what are three to five things you learned about your own privilege↔oppression based on SID? (b) What are three ways you can interrupt ___ism in your daily life?

Notably, in my capstone class as I currently teach it (across individual, institutional, and sociocultural oppressions), students almost never suggest ways to interrupt forms of oppression at the institutional level. While this is likely a product of having the individual level to fall back on, writing this chapter has motivated me to push them to think of ways to interrupt oppression at *all* levels and to ask, "What is one way you can interrupt institutional ___ism on campus?" to push them toward considering how they might have an effect on organizational and institutional practices that are oppressive. Of course, being an ally in terms of individual behaviors (such as listening to targeted groups and taking action when you hear oppressive language) is easier to comprehend than at the institutional level where being an ally against institutional oppression means dismantling oppressive structures and transforming them into institutions that work to benefit all people. It involves "re-structuring a system that is based on privilege for some into one that provides opportunities for all members of the society to participate to the extent of their desire, need, and potential" (Creighton, 2003a, p. 4).

Yet social movements start with individuals who engage in grassroots organizing, and history has many examples of what this can look like. Sexism as a form of oppression has been resisted through the various waves of feminism—from the first wave of suffrage to the second wave of civil rights to the emerging third wave of feminism. Racism as a form of oppression has been resisted throughout history, in civil rights movements (for multiple racial groups), anti-slavery movements, anti-apartheid movements, ongoing organizing to prevent hate crimes and against the racial profiling of multiple racial groups, immigrant cultures organizing to preserve their cultural practices, immigrants' rights and legal advocacy movements, and over 150 years of legal contest for land rights and the upholding of U.S. treaties by Native Americans. Classism as a form of oppression has been resisted through the formation of unions; public organizing to make corporations more responsible to their local communities; informal and formal work slowdowns, stoppages, and strikes to secure better working conditions; worker organizing at shareholder meetings; and public campaigns against corporate chain domination (see Creighton, 2003c). Organizing and resistance efforts have resulted in the Living Wage Movement.

Sharing with students examples of how grassroots organizing (started by individual action) ultimately had collective impact can help them understand how their participation in organizations can (re)produce or challenge institutional forms of oppression. *Organizations* are collectives of individuals, so while institutional racism appears in policies and practices, such policies and practices cannot be changed without individual action. In moving toward transformative change, the National Association of Social Workers (2008) asserted that the following steps are necessary in organizations: (a) recognizing and creating awareness of institutional oppression (including how it is ignored through denial); (b) developing educational and training opportunities for individuals to learn more about the multiple forms of institutionalized oppression; (c) creating opportunities for members of privileged and target status to dialogue in groups; and (d) "developing official goals, policies, and procedures that will enable the organization to evolve" and analyzing how such oppression "can be ameliorated or reversed through programming, hiring, training, supervision, and other forms of institutional processes" (NASW, 2008, p. 18).

For me, the goal of studying institutional oppression is for students who are targeted based on a given SID to become *empowered* and for students who are privileged/agents to recognize their privilege and become *allies* against oppression. I aspire to Harris's (2003) vision: "Instead of perceiving themselves as victims or innocent bystanders, students [will] self-identify as 'activists'" (p. 316). Thus, for all SIDs, I ask students about their various forms of privilege and how to interrupt ___ism in daily life. As a final motivation toward alliance, I ask this question: "How is remaining passive when you observe institutional ___ism a form of collusion in its (re)production?" Closing class in this way sets up an expectation for action among the students. Certainly, I am not so naïve as to think that all students are forever changed by these discussions, but I take comfort in knowing they have at least been exposed to dialoguing about how difference is organized based on SIDs in ways that create privilege↔oppression and in knowing that I have encouraged them to combat institutional oppression.

❖ NOTES

1. As an instructor, resources I have found valuable include Bohmer and Briggs's (1991) "Teaching privileged students about gender, race, and class oppression," Kimmel and Ferber's (2004) *Privilege: A reader*, and Griffin's (1997a) "Introductory module for the single issue courses" (Adams, Bell, & Griffin, 1997, Chapter 5).

2. In my class, I also discuss (individual, sociocultural, and institutional) heterosexism, ableism, and ageism.

3. When examining the SID of "sex/gender," student reading might include Allen's (2004, Chapter 3) "Gender matters," while instructors can utilize Goodman and Schapiro's (1997) "Sexism curriculum design" (Adams et al., 1997, Chapter 7; unless otherwise noted, all definitions of sexism are derived from this chapter).

4. When examining the SID of "race," student reading might include Allen's (2004, Chapter 4) "Race matters," while instructors can utilize Wijeyesinghe, Griffin, and Love's (1997) "Racism curriculum design" (Adams

et al., 1997, Chapter 6; unless otherwise noted, all definitions surrounding racism come from this chapter).

5. When examining the SID of "social class," student reading might include Allen's (2004, Chapter 5) "Social class matters," while instructors can utilize Yeskel and Leondar-Wright's (1997) "Classism curriculum design" (Adams et al., 1997, Chapter 11; unless otherwise noted, all definitions surrounding classism come from this chapter).

❖ REFERENCES

Adams, G. B., & Balfour, D. L. (2004). *Unmasking administrative evil* (rev. ed.). Armonk, NY: M. E. Sharpe.

Adams, M., Bell, L. A., & Griffin, P. (1997). *Teaching diversity and social justice: A sourcebook.* New York: Routledge.

Allen, B. J. (2004). *Difference matters: Communicating social identity.* Long Grove, IL: Waveland Press.

Ashcraft, K. L., & Allen, B. J. (2003). The racial foundation of organizational communication. *Communication Theory, 13,* 3–39.

Ashcraft, K. L., & Mumby, D. K. (2004). *Reworking gender: A feminist communicology of organization.* Thousand Oaks, CA: Sage.

Bell, L. A., Washington, S., Weinstein, G., & Love, B. (1997). Knowing ourselves as instructors. In M. Adams, L. A. Bell, & P. Griffin (Eds.), *Teaching for diversity and social justice* (pp. 299–310). New York: Routledge.

Bohmer, S., & Briggs, J. L. (1991). Teaching privileged students about gender, race, and class oppression. *Teaching Sociology, 19,* 154–163.

Buzzanell, P. M. (1995). Reframing the glass ceiling as a socially constructed process: Implications for understanding and change. *Communication Monographs, 62,* 327–354.

Cheney, G., & Ashcraft, K. L. (2007). Considering "the professional" in communication studies: Implications for theory and research within and beyond the boundaries of organizational communication. *Communication Theory, 17,* 146–175.

Creighton, A. (2003a). *Tools for building justice: Facilitator guide.* Retrieved June 15, 2009, from http://www.socialjusticeeducation.org/social_justice/creighton/downloads/crieghton_PDF/facilitatorguide.pdf

Creighton, A. (2003b). *Tools for building justice: Foundation unit.* Available from http://www.socialjusticeeducation.org/social_justice/creighton/downloads/crieghton_PDF/foundationsessions.pdf

Creighton, A. (2003c). *Tools for building justice: Unit on classism.* Available from http://www.socialjusticeeducation.org/social_justice/creighton/downloads/crieghton_PDF/classism.pdf

Creighton, A. (2003d). *Tools for building justice: Unit on racism.* Available from http://www.socialjusticeeducation.org/social_justice/creighton/downloads/crieghton_PDF/racism,finaldraft,12,18,02.pdf

Creighton, A. (2003e). *Tools for building justice: Unit on sexism.* Available from http://www.socialjusticeeducation.org/social_justice/creighton/downloads/creighton_PDF/sexism,final,12,20,02.pdf

Davis, N. (1992). Teaching about inequality: Student resistance, paralysis, and rage. *Teaching Sociology, 20,* 232–238.

Frankenberg, R. (1993). *White women, race matters: The social construction of whiteness.* Minneapolis: University of Minnesota Press.

Goldsmith, A. (2006). Learning to understand inequality and diversity: Getting students past ideologies. *Teaching Sociology, 34,* 263–277.

Goodman, D., & Schapiro, S. (1997). Sexism curriculum design. In M. Adams, L. A. Bell, & P. Griffin (Eds.), *Teaching diversity and social justice: A sourcebook* (pp. 110–140). New York: Routledge.

Griffin, P. (1997a). Facilitating social justice education courses. In M. Adams, L. A. Bell, & P. Griffin (Eds.), *Teaching for diversity and social justice* (pp. 279–298). New York: Routledge.

Griffin, P. (1997b). Introductory module for single-issues courses. In M. Adams, L. A. Bell, & P. Griffin (Eds.), *Teaching for diversity and social justice* (pp. 61–81). New York: Routledge.

Griffith, D. M., Childs, E. L., Eng, E., & Jeffries, V. (2008). Racism in organizations: The case of a public county health department. *Journal of Community Psychology, 35,* 287–302.

Harris, T. M. (2003). Impacting student perceptions of and attitudes toward race in the interracial communication course. *Communication Education, 52,* 311–317.

Hattery, H. J. (2003). Sleeping in the box, thinking outside the box: Student reflections on innovative pedagogical tools for teaching about and promoting a greater understanding of social class inequality among undergraduates. *Teaching Sociology, 31,* 412–427.

Hill Collins, P. (1990). *Black feminist thought: Knowledge, consciousness, and the politics of empowerment.* Boston: Unwin Hyman.

Hubbard, E. A., & De Welde, K. (2003). "I'm glad I'm not gay!": Heterosexual students' emotional experience in the college classroom with a "coming out" assignment. *Teaching Sociology, 31,* 73–84.

Institute of Medicine (U.S.). (2003). *Unequal treatment: Confronting racial and ethnic disparities in healthcare.* Washington, DC: The National Academies Press.

Johnson, J. R., & Bhatt, A. J. (2003). Gendered and racialized identities and alliances in the classroom: Formations in/of resistive space. *Communication Education, 52,* 230–244.

Kimmel, M. S., & Ferber, A. L. (Eds.). (2004). *Privilege: A reader.* Boulder, CO: Westview Press.

Kirby, E. L. (2009). Communication and community syllabus. Available from http://www.creighton.edu/ccas/communicationstudies/facultystaff/fulltime/kirby/index

Kirby, E. L., & McBride, M. C. (2009). *Gender actualized: Cases in communicatively constructing realities.* Dubuque, IA: Kendall Hunt.

Kivel, P. (1995). *Uprooting racism: How white people can work for racial justice.* Gabriola Island, British Columbia, Canada: New Society Publishers.

Lorde, A. (1984). *Sister outsider.* Trumansberg, NY: The Crossing Press.

Lucal, B. (1996). Oppression and privilege: Toward a relational conceptualization of race. *Teaching Sociology, 24,* 245–255.

Martin, J. N., & Nakayama, T. K. (1999). Thinking dialectically about culture and communication. *Communication Theory, 9,* 1–25.

McIntosh, P. (1993). White privilege and male privilege: A personal account of coming to see correspondence through work in women's studies. In A. Minas (Ed.), *Gender basics* (pp. 30–38). Belmont, CA: Wadsworth.

Millstein, K. H. (1997). The taping project: A method for self-evaluation and information consciousness in racism courses. *Journal of Social Work Education, 33,* 491–506.

Minnesota Department of Human Rights. (2008). *The right focus on: Pregnancy and discrimination.* Retrieved July, 6, 2009, from http://www.humanrights .state.mn.us/quicktimeDec08/qt_pregnancy.html

Misra, J. (1997). Teaching stratification: Stimulating interest and critical thinking through research projects. *Teaching Sociology, 25,* 278–291.

Mongan-Rallis, H., & Higgins, H. (2004). Working assumptions for class interaction. Syllabus for Education 1100: Human Diversity. Retrieved March 15, 2009, from http://www.d.umn.edu/~hrallis/courses/1100sp04/index.html

Moremen, R. D. (1997). A multicultural framework: Transforming curriculum, transforming students. *Teaching Sociology, 25,* 107–119.

Morgan, M. (2008). Explicit versus implicit stereotypes: "What biases do I really hold?" *Communication Teacher, 22*(3), 84–88.

National Association of Social Workers. (2008). *Institutional racism and the social work profession: A call to action.* Washington, DC: Author. Available online at http://www.socialworkers.org/diversity/InstitutionalRacism.pdf

National Partnership for Women and Families. (2008). *2008 Pregnancy Discrimination Report.* Washington, DC: Author. Available online at http://www .nationalpartnership.org/site/DocServer/Pregnancy_Discrimination_ Act_-_Where_We_Stand_30_Years_L.pdf?docID=4281

Neville Miller, A., & Harris, T. M. (2005). Communicating to develop white racial identity in an interracial communication class. *Communication Education, 54,* 223–242.

Norander, S. (2008). Surveillance/discipline/resistance: Carly Fiorina under the gaze of *The Wall Street Journal. Communication Studies, 59,* 99–113.

Parker, P. S. (2003). Control, resistance, and empowerment in raced, gendered, and classed work contexts: The case of African American women. *Communication Yearbook, 27,* 257–291.

Sack, K. (2008, June 10). Doctors miss cultural needs, study says. *The New York Times* [online]. Retrieved July 9, 2009, from http://www.nytimes.com/ 2008/06/10/health/10study.html

Sequist, T. D., Fitzmaurice, G. M., Marshall, R., Shaykevich, S., Safran, D. G., & Ayanian, J. Z. (2008). Physician performance and racial disparities in diabetes mellitus care. *The Archives of Internal Medicine, 168*(11), 1145–1151.

Shuler, S. (2003). Breaking through the glass ceiling without breaking a nail: Women executives in *Fortune* Magazine's "Power 50" List. *American Communication Journal, 6*(2).

Simpson, J. S., Causey, A., & Williams, L. (2007). "I would want you to understand it": Students' perspectives on addressing race in the classroom. *Journal of Intercultural Communication Research, 36,* 33–50.

Southern Poverty Law Center. (n.d.). *Speak up! Responding to everyday bigotry.* Retrieved March 30, 2007, from http://www.tolerance.org/speakup/pdf/speak_up_full_document.pdf

United for a Fair Economy (2004). 10 Chairs activity. Available from http://www.faireconomy.org/files/GD_10_Chairs_and_Charts.pdf

Wijeyesinghe, C. L., Griffin, P., & Love, B. (1997). Racism curriculum design. In M. Adams, L. A. Bell, & P. Griffin (Eds.), *Teaching diversity and social justice: A sourcebook* (pp. 82–109). New York: Routledge.

Yeskel, F., & Leondar-Wright, B. (1997). Classism curriculum design. In M. Adams, L. A. Bell, and P. Griffin (Eds.), *Teaching diversity and social justice: A sourcebook* (pp. 231–260). New York: Routledge.

7

Teaching Difference as Institutional and Making it Personal

Moving Among Personal, Interpersonal, and Institutional Constructions of Difference

Jennifer Mease

H uman differences aren't just interpersonal—they're institutional. As organizational scholars, we accept this as a significant truth. Differences are built into the very structures of organizations (Acker, 1990; Allen, 2004; Ashcraft & Mumby, 2004; Parker, 2002, 2003). We dedicate our time, thought, and many journal pages to exploring how this truth—and its corollary power imbalances—is created, maintained, and resisted through the daily practices and policies that construct organizations. We examine how texts, professions, leadership, interpersonal interaction, reward structures, and organizational norms can manifest a bias toward one group over another. And if that challenge is not enough, we are then met with the task of bringing this truth and its many explorations to our students. Guiding students to see difference as institutional as well as interpersonal is a theoretical, pedagogical, and interpersonal task.

The United States is a country that emphasizes individuality, and colleges are often the training ground for individualism. Many of our students have been practicing the art of the "enterprising subject" (du Gay, 1996) since they were young teenagers, building their resumes with memberships and leadership positions in order to simply be admitted to college. Once at the university, we train students to enter a knowledge economy where their individual intellectual and social capital will mark them as unique and valuable. I suspect this emphasis on individualism is one reason that students have difficulty turning their attention to difference as an institutional phenomenon. Many stumble when analyzing difference as constructed and imposed through systems, institutions, and organizations, getting caught up on individual intentions and interpersonal interactions. Perhaps the following situation might be familiar to you: You give your students case studies and ask them to discuss how the organization might respond to the social bias discussed in the scenario. Their responses sound something like "It seems like he just didn't feel confident about his sexuality, he should have been more honest"; "I guess that *could* be gender discrimination, but she was probably just overreacting"; "If that happened to me, I wouldn't think anything of it"; "Some people are just ignorant, and you can't let those people get in your way." Many students gravitate toward individual choices and interpersonal behaviors as both the source of and the solution to problems associated with human difference. While it is not my intention to dismiss these individually-based realms of difference as both problematic and ameliorative, I suggest that as organizational scholars we must rise to the task of helping students to make a leap toward a more institutional understanding of human differences.

The challenge, I have learned, is not to get students to think institutionally *rather* than individually, but to help students understand that the personal is never separate from the institutional. In this chapter, I reflect on my own strategies for navigating this challenge as I present the theoretical structure of the social human as a possible foundation for any class that emphasizes difference and social action. The goal of this chapter is to explore one possibility for drawing students away from understanding difference as a property of the modern individual whose good intentions are what matter most. Instead, I hope to engage what it means to be a person shaped by social identities laden with power dynamics that are often beyond the realm of our choices. What I convey is the paradoxical potential of making difference less individual, but more personal.

By *more personal*, I mean that I want students to, in the colloquial sense, "take it personally." I want them to develop a critically engaged consciousness that allows them to analyze and respond to social constructions of difference and associated power dynamics as personally relevant. In setting this goal, I acknowledge that students' life experiences have varying levels of privilege that influence the extent to which social bias based on human difference is already salient and personal. Admittedly, this call to take it more personally increases in relevance and necessity in relationship to the extent of privilege one's subject position offers. For those who experience institutional oppression on a daily basis, taking it personally is not a choice. I have no doubt that this pedagogical task is potentially, though not exclusively, more relevant and necessary when teaching students who occupy privileged positions, and my focus on it is influenced by my own relatively privileged life experience as a White, upper-middle class, heterosexual woman. By acknowledging this focus, my intention is not to recenter (Grimes, 2002) those privileged subject positions, but to deconstruct them.

Regardless of one's relative level of privilege, guiding students to see, feel, and respond to difference as institutional yet personally relevant cannot be accomplished by an explanation of theory alone. Letting go of the notion that social inequalities can be chalked up to intentional discrimination practiced by bigoted individuals or a lack of self-confidence and self-motivation can be scary, relieving, frustrating, or despairing. Guiding students through this process requires careful attention to the subject positions from which they learn, including the experiences, emotions, and possibilities for action that those positions may or may not involve. As teachers, we must incorporate students' experiences into explanations of the theory if we expect them to, in turn, use theory to interrogate their own lives.

What you'll find in this chapter is a pedagogical and theoretical approach that emphasizes post-structural and institutional forms of difference. I begin by laying out a theory of the social human that both connects and distinguishes concepts of the self, identity, and subjectivity. I then turn my attention to organizational processes as they produce discourses and experiences of difference that shape and influence the social human. The goal is not only to present a theoretical underpinning but to demonstrate how this foundation has enabled me and my students to explore institutional constructions of difference in our own lives. In order to do this, I've chosen to share some of the practical strategies that foster conversations about the social conditions that influence students' personal choices and experiences: that is, activities that acknowledge difference as both personal and

institutional. By sharing these strategies for addressing the organizational and institutional conditions that surround personal choices, I
offer one path (a path that I am still exploring) for transforming
reliance on individual behaviors as the explanation and panacea for
conflict based on human difference into an understanding that
acknowledges institutional influences and identifies possibilities for
personal responses to those systems. This does not mean that we
ignore or avoid discussions about individual behavior, but rather that
we examine them in context. My attention to difference as an organizational and institutional phenomenon should not frame discussion of
individual behaviors as the door that allows students to escape the
discussion of organizational constructions of difference. Instead, these
discussions are the door that allows us to enter into the conversation.
In the end, my hope is that students will have their own principled
response to this question: "How do I personally respond to social bias
based on human differences, given the possibilities and constraints of
subject position I find myself occupying?"

❖ THE SOCIAL HUMAN

I begin with the social human as a way of meeting students where they
are. I mean this in two ways. First, discussions that center around oneself provide the possibility for students to find their own voice in discussions of difference and the chance to explore one's subject position
before focusing on the power-laden labels that can evoke feelings of
fear, anger, guilt, or defensiveness. While this sets the interpersonal
ground for students to take difference more personally, a more theoretical mandate suggests that in order to interrogate systems that construct differences, we must begin with students where they are by
deconstructing the places from which they speak. In order to critique
institutional and organizational constructions of difference, we must
first locate the positions from which each of us speak and understand
how those positions condition what we experience, how we interpret
experiences, and how others interpret us.

  Self, identity, and *subjectivity* are all words scholars use to describe
the human condition. They are not terms that should be used inter-
changeably. Each of these terms describes a different aspect of the
process by which we all become social beings marked by various forms
of human difference. Each one emphasizes different nuances of the relationship between individual and society. While a more detailed description of these follows, it is helpful to begin with the basic notions that

questions of the self focus on the personal process of self-contemplation; that questions of identity focus on the social construction of the lenses we use to contemplate our selves; and that questions of subjectivity focus on the possibilities and constraints of human interaction, based on social positions established at the intersections of various socially constructed identities. Exploring these three aspects of the social human allows students to identify and analyze the social and institutional processes that affect them personally and to make more critically engaged choices about how they respond to those influences.

The Self: Theoretical Framing

For our purposes, Mead's (1934) notion of the self as a social construction is a useful starting point. Mead argued that humans are unique in their ability to simultaneously occupy the place of *subject* who contemplates oneself as an *object*. It is through this process that human beings shape and create themselves as individuals and coordinate human interaction, transforming human biological entities into socially relevant human beings. By considering myself as an object, I can shape myself, evaluate myself according to norms and values, change my behaviors, change my appearance, and so forth. In other words, it is through this process that I create myself as a socially recognizable entity. This emphasis on self-contemplation and the ability to shape oneself through such contemplation can be seen in the work of Foucault (1990a, 1997), who, while most concerned with issues of subjectivity (and despite his differences with Mead), referred to technologies and the care of the self when he spoke of the process of contemplating and acting upon one's own human being.

But even when focusing on this process of self-contemplation, the self is not wholly determined by the individual. This split of the self into a mutually implicated subject and object, the contemplating and contemplated self, or what Mead (1934) called the "I" and the "me," emphasizes the psychological, but implies the social. When I think about me, I do so from the imagined perspective of the other: What would my mother, my friend, or a potential romantic partner think of me? Through many social interactions, we develop a conglomerate perspective of the *generalized other* that we use to evaluate our own behaviors and construct our selves. Using this perspective, we create our *self* according to social discourses and norms, norms that are informed by various ideas of human difference.

This point, that the very process of self-understanding and self-determination is inherently social, is critical to understanding human differences as both personal and institutional. Self-contemplation and self-creation always imply a socially constructed lens that we use to view ourselves. This lens is shaped and colored by society, including our institutional and organizational interactions. This construction of self is not a fully individualized process because we understand our selves through the lens of a social context that is not within our realm of control. Forms of human difference that shape and color that lens, such as gender, race, or sexuality, are not inherent properties of individuals. Rather, they become meaningful to the self as we integrate them into our process of self-creation. We cannot take the self for granted; we always have to understand it as socially conditioned.

The Self: Taking it Personally

To help students really engage the social influence on their self-understanding, I provide them with a list of various forms of social difference, including race, gender, sexuality, physical ability, class, and nationality, and ask them to rank them, 1 being the thing they feel or think about most on a day to day basis, and 6 being the thing that they barely think about or feel at all. I then post signs around the perimeter of the room for each of these categories and ask students to stand by the category that they ranked as most significant. Once the students have taken their positions, I ask them to make observations about what the room looks like. I do the same for the second most significant, then least significant and the second least significant. The point is not to look at each individual's position, but to look at patterns that we demonstrate as a collective, giving us a concrete and personal illustration upon which to base our discussion of why we use or think about a particular lens to view ourselves and the world.

This activity allows us to use individuals' experiences and the positions they take in the room to focus on how social systems personally affect us. It demonstrates that how we understand and consequently construct ourselves is not always a matter of personal control or even intention. For example, if the two foreign exchange students are alone in ranking nationality first, this helps us to understand that processes of self-contemplation are contextually contingent because U.S. born students would probably do the same if they were in a foreign country. We can see that personal histories, often beyond our control, also influence forms of difference that we feel and contemplate, as when the woman who appears fully able-bodied explains that she thinks about physical ability most because her mother is blind.

It also allows us to see that we don't necessarily have to be conscious of the way forms of difference influence how we understand ourselves. When only 1 of 14 White students stands by race as one of his or her two most significant, and 11 of 14 stand by race as one of their two least significant constructs, a paradox emerges. If we take individual perceptions as the "truth," that would lead us to believe race is generally not significant to White students. However, the pattern tells us that being White often leads one to be relatively unconscious of the ways race affects our lives and interactions. 1 of 14 stating race as significant and 11 of 14 stating little significance is by no means a normal or random distribution. We can begin to discern that the more privileged or "normal" a category of difference is, the less likely we are to think about it. Yet we can look around the room and literally see how it is influencing our process of self-contemplation. Similarly, when 90% of the students stand by sexuality as the category they think about least and no one puts it in their top two, what does that tell us? Perhaps more important, what might be the consequences that one has to consider if they claim sexuality as one of their top two? Of course, questions about the meanings associated with each form of difference and the consequences for claiming them lead us to identity and subjectivity respectively.

Identities: Theoretical Framing

While the I-me split of the self helps to illustrate that the self is inherently social, the concept of identity allows us to examine specific categories or lenses that influence this process. If the concept of the self emphasizes a relationship between the I and the me, the concept of identity allows us to examine the lenses that mediate that relationship. There are many identities that one uses to make sense of oneself: social identities, personal identities, institutional identities, and so forth. Categories of human difference, such as race, class, gender, and sexual identity, fall into the category of social identities, which Brenda Allen (2004) defined as "aspects of a person's self-image derived from the social categories to which an individual perceives himself/herself as belonging" (p. 10). Using the language of the social human, social identities constitute parts of the self that are created when we contemplate ourselves using the lens of a social group we claim membership in. These social identities intersect with personal identities, such as sister, daughter, and friend, and organizational identities, such as student and teacher.

While a conventional modern definition of identity emphasizes the ability to incorporate all of these lenses into one coherent individual identity—one consistently and constantly applied to the self—a post-modern perspective leaves these in play (Holland & Lachicotte, 2007). For example, I have varying identities as woman, White person, teacher, friend, and daughter. My romantic partner would not be very happy if I approached him from the identity of a teacher. In student-teacher meetings, I find myself drawing on identities of both teacher and friend to understand and help students with their academic difficulties. Depending on the identity I draw on at a particular moment, I perceive and display my *self* and my actions differently.

Yet identities are never wholly separate or discrete; rather, they intersect. As West and Fenstermaker (1995) argued, this intersectionality is not simply an additive model of universal experiences. They argue that each aspect of one's identity conditions other aspects of one's identity, such that the experience of being a woman who is White is different from the experience of being a woman who is Latina. Likewise, the experience of being a Latina woman who is college educated in the United States and the experience of being a Latina woman who speaks little English are also different. It follows that we cannot make generalizations about what it means to be a woman in the United States, or even a Latina woman in the United States. Yet, these categories still remain relevant to our perceptions of self and others. During the activity I explained previously, a great illustration of intersectionality emerged when a non-traditional student claimed gender as her most felt identity. When others asked her to reflect on that, she explained that she was 35, married, and didn't have children. The intersection of her age and gender combined with the decision of whether or not to have children shaped her identity in ways different from younger women who share her gender or from her husband who shares her age and interest in children.

As intersectionality attests, there is no universal experience for any social identity group. This points to the fact that there is nothing natural or essential about the social identity groups; rather, they are socially constructed (Hall, 1996). While individuals might have biological and genetic differences, the meanings that we assign these differences and the way we treat those differences is socially constructed. The changing categories of race listed on the census illustrate how even the categories themselves are constantly changing. Foucault's (1988, 1990a, 1990b) work on sexuality also demonstrates how even though physically intimate same-sex relationships have existed historically, they didn't amount to an identity category in Ancient Roman and Greek culture.

Once we have destabilized these identity categories, we must ask this question: How is the meaning of any identity group created and sustained? In addition to the more personal process of synthesizing and patching these various identities into a cohesive—though not necessarily coherent—sense of self (Holstein & Gubrium, 2000), communication scholars examine the role of communication in broad social processes that create these identity categories as objects of shared social knowledge, in spite of their instability. These seemingly natural categories that we integrate into our self-understanding are not only socially constructed, they require constant maintenance! Foucault (1990a, 1995) explained that social discourse, manifested in organizations, media, and interpersonal interactions, lends meaning to these categories. While these discourses of gender, race, and so forth, may not reflect some external or natural truth, they become real aspects of identities when they inform an individual's generalized other perspective. Watching TV, listening to music, watching my parents, maintaining my friendships, and role models at work all contribute to my idea of what it means to be a good, or normal, woman, professor, White person, girlfriend, and so forth.

One of the ways categories are maintained is through juxtaposition with an *other*. As Hall (1996) explained, "It is only through the relation to the Other, the relation to what it is not, to precisely what it lacks, to what has been called its *constitutive outside* that the 'positive' meaning of any term—and thus its 'identity'—can be constructed" (pp. 4–5). Thus, the widely varied forms of femininity are held together, not by some essential unity, but by their binary opposition to masculinity. As Foucault (1990a, 1995) explained, we garner an understanding of normal by creating categories of deviance. These categories of deviance may not define a core characteristic of normal, but they mark the boundaries beyond which one has ventured into deviance. Thus, when we shape and form our selves, we do so by avoiding certain identities as much as we take up others.

Butler's (2007) theory of performativity also lends insight to the maintenance of categories of difference that constitute identities. Following our deconstruction of any kind of essential category, Butler suggested that there are no preexisting "truthful" genders to be "expressed." She explained, "As performance, which is performative, gender is an 'act,' broadly construed, which constructs the social fiction of its own psychological interiority" (p. 195). Much like Mead's (1934) self-construction, Butler claimed that one's self *becomes* gendered by taking gender up in social performances. While this might appear natural, the gendered self is accomplished through performance or action. In this sense, it is more social or relational rather than internally psychological.

By suggesting that gender is performative, Butler (2007) also suggested that neither gendered bodies nor categories exist prior to them being performed. In other words, both our gendered bodies and the corollary categories of gender are constituted through "a stylized repetition of acts" (p. 187) that occur in our everyday interactions (i.e., our style of walk, modes of speech, our dress and accessories). To argue for a performative theory of difference more broadly is to suggest that we become part of social groups not because we belong to them naturally, but through our identification with social groups and our compliance with social norms (Hall, 1996). We *become* (as opposed to express) raced, gendered, classed selves through our appropriate performance of these categories. At the same time, these categories are maintained by our compliance with them.

But identities, and their consequent values, meanings, and expectations are not socially over-determined either. Through both verbal and nonverbal communicative acts, individuals signal compliance and resistance to various identities or demonstrate which identity role they are playing at the moment. These lenses we use to view ourselves and shape our actions are both *offered to* us by social discourses and the histories that inform them and *shaped by* us as they run up against our own personal histories (Holland, Lachicotte, Skinner, & Cain, 1998). This constrained agency suggests that critically engaged students cannot ignore how the institutional and historical inequalities associated with race, gender, sexuality or other forms of difference affect all of us; nor can they render themselves as helpless victims of that history who have no ability to respond to those influences.

Thus, identity and self are mutually implicated. Identity necessarily emerges from the processes self-contemplation (which has gained historical and social continuity) and the self requires identities in its framing and making sense of oneself. Thus, identities are sense-making apparatuses existing at the intersection of the self and the social. For example, I draw from discourses of femininity, Whiteness, physical ability, education, friendship, and family to make sense of myself and to position myself in larger society. At the same time, through my daily practices I adapt these discourses to fit together in my own unique identity—what Holland et al. (1998) called "accenting" discourses offered to me as a means of self-authoring. Through this practice of merging and accenting, I author my own identity at the intersection of all the identities imposed on me by social discourse and interaction.

Identity: Making it Personal

I usually lead a discussion of identity with students naming all of the groups they are a part of as well as the labels that apply to them. After brainstorming in groups we put all of these on the board and begin by parsing out the personal, social, and organizational identities. Building on the already established concept of self, our first discussion is based on the question, Do you ever think about your self apart from all of these categories? This often demands some probing on my part: How about when you are alone in your house? What if you moved to a completely new location where you didn't know anyone? What if the world experienced a catastrophic natural disaster and as far as you could tell, you were the last remaining survivor? I believe the best answer one student came up with involves waking up one day with complete amnesia. But she followed up her own comment with the observation that the first thing you would be told is that you were an amnesia patient and that identity would immediately take over. The point here is for students to grasp that they always act with social categories in mind (often not of their own choosing), even if they act in rebellion. Of course, the next question is this: "Well, if you are always acting in accordance with categories that are socially established for you, then are you ever thinking on your own?" This eventually leads us to a discussion of intersectionality as a source for creativity in the processes of self-authoring.

Another activity that students really enjoy is one where I ask students to choose two songs and bring them to class on some kind of player (CD, computer, iPod). One song should be a song that they feel they really identify with, the other should be a song that they really like, but they don't think is good or appropriate for them to listen to. I divide the class in half and ask the students to form two concentric circles, with the inner circle facing the outer circle, so that each person lines up with a partner in the outer circle. (This seems relatively easy, but it always ends up being a challenge!) Each student should have their own pair of headphones that they plug into their partner's player. The partner chooses one of the two songs for the other person to listen to (they don't tell which one it is, but often share after listening). I let them listen for two minutes, then rotate one of the circles so that they line up with a new partner. Usually they listen to three songs total.

After listening to the songs we discuss whether anyone's music tastes really surprised others in the class, or for the most part did our taste in music comply with the identities we've taken up? When there are no surprises, we discuss how easily we take up and perform identities that are expected of us. When there are surprises, we discuss where our expectations come from and why one might violate those expectations. We also talk about the construction of deviance using the songs we feel like we're not supposed to listen to, helping to illustrate the notion of the "constitutive outside" (Hall, 1996, p. 4). We talk about how easy or difficult it is to discern whether the song heard was one of identification or the one considered inappropriate for one's identity. Would you assess deviance and identification differently for a nontraditional 42 year old White woman student than for a 21 year old male of mixed race identity? Again, the point here is not to suggest that students' musical preferences aren't real, but that their experience of music, including their preferences, are constructed and influenced by identity categories that are often loaded with meanings associated with various forms of human difference.

Subjectivity: Theoretical Framing

Putting self and identity in relationship with subjectivity is a way of treating both within constellations of power. When considering subjectivity, we emphasize neither the process of self-contemplation nor the application of various lenses, but the way these processes position people in power-laden relationships with others—hence the often-used term *subject position*. To consider subjectivity is to acknowledge that not all identities are created equal. Categories of difference are not simply created through opposition; that opposition involves a hierarchy. A given identity in a specific context offers particular capacities to exercise power. Depending on the context, some identities offer more useful and pervasive forms of power than others. To become a subject is to take up identities that offer a place in this constellation of categories and power dynamics. But as already discussed, taking up identities that place us in these constellations or systems and integrating them into our concept of self is not always a matter of our own choosing. We are pushed to take on some identities and discouraged from taking up others.

In addition, the identities from which these power-laden constellations are constructed are both historically and socially contingent. When we use the term *subjectivity* rather than *identity* we put that contingency in context by attending to the discourses, language games, and power/knowledge constraints that a particular historical formation imposes on subjects (by shaping possibilities of identities, which are integrated into the self). Rather than simply examining how we fall into and perform identities according to constructed norms, subjectivity turns our attention to the power implications of challenging or acquiescing to those norms; for example, the consequences of claiming a gay identity vs. a straight identity during a classroom activity. This includes how any given position both enables and constrains possibilities for agency.

Chapter 7:   Teaching Difference as Institutional and Making it Personal   163

Butler (2007) again proves useful in illustrating this point. As she demonstrated, rejecting the subject positions that are deemed appropriate for a person in a given system risks completely losing voice in that system. As in the case of the men who fail to perform masculinity, the result is often harassment, rejection, or even violence. The implications for this are both personal and systemic. People are disciplined into maintaining identities and taking up subject positions deemed appropriate for them. As a result, the system and the limited array of subject positions are maintained along with the sense that they are natural. When Foucault (1990a, 1995) spoke of power/knowledge he was referring to this capacity to maintain categories and strategies of knowing people that binds them to acceptable subject positions within a given culture, constraining their agency and limiting their ability to challenge systems of power. This is why Foucault was so heavily concerned with the self as a site of power negotiations. If individuals can find the capacity to deconstruct their own subject positions, therein lies the capacity to deconstruct the system.

Subject positions produce and are produced by identities, and they consequently mediate one's ability to contemplate and constitute the self. This is particularly problematic when a society ties physical appearance to social identities and, in turn, ties those identities to unbalanced power dynamics. When the categories themselves and the sorting of who gets to or has to take up the identity associated with a category are constructed and accepted as natural, we are just a short step from the naturalization of power hierarchies as well. As discussed in the section on identities, there is still a capacity for self-authoring, but that capacity is constrained and enabled by one's subject position and the power potentials of the identities that are imposed on a person. It is only through an awareness of those constraints and possibilities that one can respond to and challenge the construction of one's own position and that of others.

Subjectivity: Taking it Personally

In my gender and communication course, one of the optional assignments is for students to choose to violate a gendered communication norm for a short period of time.* They choose their gender norm based on verbal or nonverbal behaviors. Generally, students

---

*I cannot take credit for conceiving of this assignment. I learned this activity from Dr. Julia Wood and my graduate student colleagues at the University of North Carolina.

experience how they are disciplined into maintaining their subject positions, and occasionally, they experience how freeing and helpful it is to break those norms. Men have tried carrying purses, increasing eye contact and smiling, or even wearing makeup. Women have tried using more direct language, taking up more space, or initiating romantic interaction. Of course, results always vary by person, but my students and I are always astounded by how common it is for men who break gender norms to be verbally harassed or even threatened with physical violence by other men. Although women also report various forms of correction, including correction from friends, they are also more likely to report advantages for taking on more masculine behaviors, including more respect in organizational contexts or people being more deferential to them. One thing that almost always comes up is that breaking gender norms seems to be more acceptable for women than men, which we consider in sociohistorical context where men are the more privileged group. Another point that I try to draw out is how breaking norms of gender can sometimes make it difficult for people to interact with you. Men carrying a feminine purse or wearing makeup often note that people were conspicuously uncomfortable with them in everyday interactions. In short, we examine how failure to comply with social categories affects people's capacity to hear and respond to us.

Another useful illustration has been to begin discussion about the subject position of college student, a position that the students hold in common. We discuss what kinds of power are granted by occupying this position, or even the subject position of a student or graduate of a particular university. At the same time, we talk about the subject position of student in relation to college professor. We talk about the system of the university that positions students such that their agency is limited, especially in the face of requests made by their teachers. Most students can think of an example with a teacher who they thought was unethical, unfair, disrespectful of students, or a waste of their time, and yet in most of these cases students acquiesce to the teacher by virtue of their subject position as students and the teacher's subject position as teacher. In addition, we talk about how that subject position is experienced differently by virtue of its intersection with other identities. How is being a first generation college student different from having a family where three generations have graduated from the same university? How is the subject position of student different if only 10% of the class shares your gender or racial identity? If you've never been in that position, why not, and what does that tell you about your own subject position?

The point of these exercises and discussions is not to disempower students by illustrating how they have little power over their own positioning, but to offer them a tool they can use to examine their own choices and the constraints and possibilities that lead to those choices. In doing so, I hope that students also become more aware of how others experience different limitations and possibilities based on their subject position. The next step is to examine some of the specific processes where these constraints and possibilities play out and to examine the possible responses and consequences that different people might experience in those situations.

❖ THE SOCIAL HUMAN AND ORGANIZING

As organizational communication scholars, our job is only half done when we have provided our students with the theoretical tools to critique their own and other's experiences as social humans who are constantly constructing selves, taking up identities, and navigating constraints and possibilities of the subject positions we find ourselves in. Having acknowledged that human differences are personal, but not a natural property of the individual, we must explore how organizations are constructed in ways that affect people's self-construction by maintaining notions of human difference and creating power-laden conditions that privilege some positions over others. I posit here several ways that human differences are organizational, and I emphasize how we can approach these constructions using the concept of the social human.

Jobs are Not Neutral

Acker's (1990) work has strongly influenced research that illustrates how organizations are not simply containers into which human differences are inserted, but that human differences help to constitute organizations. Acker argued that the conceptual "job" is not gender neutral, but that gender is built into the concept of the job itself. Ashcraft and Mumby's (2004) analysis of airline pilots complicates this claim even further because they demonstrate how historically the airline industry has appropriated gender as a way to construct understandings of flying as a safe form of travel. Namely, women pilots were used by the commercial airline industry to demonstrate how tame and safe air travel could be. In contrast to more commonly known hyper masculine pilot daredevils who flew stunt planes, commercial planes were so safe that even a woman could fly them! Moreover, the male pilot was remade as the rational, professional, and trustworthy father figure, while the feminine role was later pushed out of the cockpit and relegated to attending to passengers' needs.

To make this complicated concept simpler, I ask the class as a group to respond to a list of occupations by stating either "male" or "female" out loud. The list includes occupations like pilot, high school principal, administrative assistant, nurse, hair stylist, surgeon, day care provider, police officer, flight attendant, school teacher, and CEO. While not all students will agree on every one of these, there is usually enough agreement that we identify a significant trend. The more challenging question is, Which came first? Do these professions draw on existing gender values to create the meaning of the profession, or does the profession create the meaning of gender? We also discuss the power dynamics involved: pilot/flight attendant, surgeon/nurse, CEO/administrative assistant, and principal/school teacher are neither gender neutral, nor power neutral. Traditionally, masculine positions tend to be the more powerful of these gendered pairs.

The social conception of gendered, raced, and classed jobs influences the kinds of jobs we pursue and deem appropriate. The implication here is that our identities constrain our self-understanding and what we consider to be realistic job options for our selves. As a case in point, how many college students seriously considered being a hairdresser, a plumber, or a carpenter? Why or why not? In terms of subjectivity, we begin to see how challenging these gendered, raced, and classed expectations can create consequences for those who engage in jobs outside of their norms. What would their parents say if they decided to quit school and become a telemarketer? There are also tensions one experiences when taking up a job that isn't typically expected for one's identity. For example, Martin (1999) explained that women police officers find themselves in a double bind: If they are too feminine they aren't fit for the job; if they are too masculine they are not appropriate for their gender. This bind requires balancing behaviors that are appropriate to the job and behaviors that are appropriate to one's identity and evokes a tension that is easily avoided by those whose identities coincide with the institutionalized social identity associated with the job. But the perception of police work as masculine is a construction. As Martin pointed out, *police officer* is not a naturally masculine job. Much of the work associated with it could be considered feminine: comforting victims of crime, assisting people who have been in a car accident. Rather, it is discursively constructed as masculine and maintained as such through the enforcement of masculine behaviors.

Organizational Entry Is Easier When You Fit the Norm

When an organization is constituted by a majority of members who share a common identity, it is often easier for members of that group to enter into the organization. Part of this comes from the fact that they come prepared to engage in communication norms that might be specific to the identity group in the majority. In her description of classrooms, Lisa Delpit (1995) described this as "the culture of power" (p. 24). In order to make the argument that her description applies to organizations more broadly, I have substituted the word organizations where she uses classrooms:

1. Issues of power are enacted in [organizations].

2. There are codes or rules for participating in power; that is, there is a "culture of power."

3. The rules of the culture of power are a reflection of the rules of the culture of those who have power.

4. If you are not already a participant in the culture of power, being told explicitly the rules of that culture makes acquiring power easier.

5. Those with power are frequently least aware of—or least willing to acknowledge—its existence. Those with less power are often most aware of its existence. (p. 24)

When those who know the rules of power best are not even aware of the rules they concede to—such as direct or indirect language, appropriate means for addressing conflict, appropriate strategies for self-promotion or self-advocating—it is difficult for them to explicitly share them. This concept helps to explain research findings that suggest that people who do not share a dominant identity may spend more time getting up to speed or emerging as high potential employees (Thomas & Gabarro, 1999).

This situation might be further complicated by informal networking and mentoring. Principles of homophily suggest that we tend to develop relationships with those whom we perceive to be similar to us (Hallinan & Williams, 1987, 1989). Informal norms that are unique to the organization and not associated with any cultural group can often be learned through these kinds of relationships. In addition, anxiety over communication across differences, avoidance due to a fear of being accused of racism or sexism, or fear of developing relationships that might threaten one's heterosexual life partner are all concerns that could cause a person to feel more comfortable developing informal mentoring relationships with people who are similar to them.

Any of these cases demonstrates institutional bias that is not necessarily born out of intentional discrimination, but is a product of perceived likeness based on social identities. Furthermore, the ways that identity norms are integrated into the self might also smooth social interaction if both parties have learned the same rules and norms for establishing and maintaining relationships. For some, entering into an organization may require taking up a lens or identity that complements their existing lenses or identities for self construction, while for others it may require an entire renegotiation of identity. This demonstrates how the dominance of one group and the privileged subject positions that derive from it are not always an intentional act of domination, but rather emerge from implicitly learned skills associated with specific identities that allow one to navigate and perform in an organizational context with greater ease.

Dealing With Potential Bias Requires More of Some Subject Positions Than Others

Brenda Allen (1998) summarized this point best when she spoke of those who question her interpretation of interactions that are racist:

> Some White persons discount my interpretations of these types of encounters by observing that they have had similar experiences. However, I do not think they understand how I feel as someone who repeatedly deals with these types of exchanges across numerous contexts, and who finds herself spending valuable mental and emotional energy trying to process them. (p. 579)

Hence, regardless of whether a person intends bias or not, those who identify with traditionally nondominant or oppressed groups have to spend time and energy discerning whether or not an incident involves bias, how to respond to the incident, the personal consequences for various responses, and the implications of various responses (or lack of response) for one's cultural group as a whole. The key here is that a minimal possibility or threat of bias is all that is needed to maintain this emotional and intellectual burden.

Such a situation can put a double bind on one's subject position. If one chooses not to respond, then one risks persistent racism, sexism, homophobia, or other forms of xenophobia, that constrain possibilities for success in organizations. On the other hand, if one chooses to respond, one risks being stereotyped as militant, aggressive or in your face about differences. As Allen (1998) and Ashcraft (1998) indicated, the result is often self-censorship that results in pent up anger and frustration. These risks and costs are greatly mitigated for a person who is of a privileged position and speaks out against incidents that provide that privilege at a cost to others. For example, as a White person I can question potentially racist acts against people of color without being perceived as self-interested.

This is precisely why it is so important for people in privileged subject positions to take it more personally and join in the process of questioning social bias in organizational structure. Framing discussions of this form of bias using the social human helps to focus on the social and relational. By shifting the focus from the individual's intention, and trying to parse out whether an incident really was racist, sexist, or homophobic using the theoretical frame of the social human allows us to focus on the identity constructions from which such tensions might emerge, the uniquely personal possibilities and constraints for responding to the situation, and the effects that it might have on a person's self-construction.

❖ TEACHING PERSONALLY

Encouraging students to think about differences as institutional is not about denying students their uniqueness or sense of agency. Rather, it is about locating their uniqueness and agency within a constrained context. I have found the concept of the social human particularly useful because it allows me to shift classroom conversations from individual intention to institutional forces that require personal responses. In doing so, I am able to push students to ground hypothetical conversations about various isms in personal experience by locating their own subject positions within institutional constructions of difference. Whether privileged or oppressed, the systems we critique are personal. And whether privileged or oppressed, we have to make choices about how we will respond to those systems.

I often describe institutional bias and social privilege as a series of conveyor belts. Those who occupy positions of privilege are standing on belts that move forward with little effort. Some have no belt at all; they are left to walk forward on their own. Others are on belts that pull them back, even as they try to move forward. The concept of the social human illustrates how we take these places on conveyor belts not through intentional prejudice or discrimination, but through processes of self, identity, and subjectivity that are constructed through everyday practices, such as those outlined as part of organizing processes. Without a critical consciousness about ourselves as social human beings, we fail to look down and see the belts that move us forward and hold us back, or move others forward and hold them back. Without seeing these belts, we have little choice about how to respond. We perceive the speed at which we move along to be the product of our own volition. But once we have learned about the belt, how processes of self, identity, and subjectivity are built into our very sense of self and our relationships with power structures in society, we are faced with a choice. To do nothing is to participate in social bias. It allows us to move along with the belts, to take part in the processes of the social human that naturalize institutional forms of human difference. By examining organizational processes using the frame of the social human, teachers can encourage students to develop a critical and principled response to these belts at work in students' daily lives. We can help students to analyze the powers their position offers and to challenge the limitations that constructions of human difference impose on themselves and others. In short, we must teach and learn to respond to institutional bias personally.

❖ REFERENCES

Acker, J. (1990). Hierarchies, jobs, bodies: A theory of gendered organizations. *Gender and Society, 4,* 139–158.

Allen, B. J. (1998). Black womanhood and feminist standpoints. *Management Communication Quarterly, 11,* 575–586.

Allen, B. J. (2004). *Difference matters: Communicating social identity.* Long Grove, IL: Waveland Press.

Ashcraft, K. L. (1998). "I wouldn't say I'm a feminist but . . .": Organizational micropractice and gender identity. *Management Communication Quarterly, 11,* 587–597.

Ashcraft, K. L., & Mumby, D. K. (2004). *Reworking gender: A feminist communicology of organization.* Thousand Oaks, CA: Sage.

Butler, J. (2007). Performative acts and gender constitution: An essay in phenomenology and feminist theory. In H. Bial (Ed.), *The performance studies reader* (2nd ed., pp. 187–199). New York: Routledge.

Delpit, L. (1995). *Other people's children: Culture conflict in the classroom.* New York: The New Press.

du Gay, P. (1996). *Consumption and identity at work.* Thousand Oaks, CA: Sage.

Foucault, M. (1988). *The care of the self: The history of sexuality* (R. Hurley, Trans.). New York: Vintage Books.

Foucault, M. (1990a). *The history of sexuality: An introduction* (R. Hurley, Trans.). New York: Vintage Books.

Foucault, M. (1990b). *The use of pleasure: The history of sexuality* (R. Hurley, Trans., Vol. 3). New York: Vintage Books.

Foucault, M. (1995). *Discipline and punish: The birth of the prison* (A. Sheridan, Trans.). New York: Vintage Books.

Foucault, M. (1997). Technologies of the self. In P. Rabinow (Ed.), *Ethics: Subjectivity and truth* (Vol. 1, pp. 223–252). New York: The New Press.

Grimes, D. S. (2002). Challenging the status quo?: Whiteness in the diversity management literature. *Management Communication Quarterly, 15,* 381–409.

Hall, S. (1996). Introduction: Who needs "identity"? In S. Hall & P. du Gay (Eds.), *Questions of cultural identity* (pp. 1–17). London: Sage.

Hallinan, M. T., & Williams, R. A. (1987). The stability of students' interracial friendships. *American Sociological Review, 52,* 653–664.

Hallinan, M. T., & Williams, R. A. (1989). Interracial friendship choices in secondary schools. *American Sociological Review, 54*(1), 67–78.

Holland, D., & Lachicotte, W. S. (2007). Vygotsky, Mead, and the new sociocultural studies of identity. In H. Daniels, M. Cole, & J. Wertsch (Eds.), *The Cambridge companion to Vygotsky* (pp. 101–135). New York: Cambridge University Press.

Holland, D., Lachicotte, W. S., Skinner, D., & Cain, C. (1998). *Identity and agency in cultural worlds.* Cambridge, MA: Harvard University Press.

Holstein, J. A., & Gubrium, J. F. (2000). *The self we live by: Narrative identity in a postmodern world.* New York: Oxford University Press.

Martin, S. E. (1999). Police force or police service? Gender and emotional labor. *Annals of the American Academy of Social Sciences, 561,* 111–125.

Mead, G. H. (1934). *Mind, self, and society: From the standpoint of a social behaviorist.* Chicago: The University of Chicago Press.

Parker, P. (2002). Negotiating identity in raced and gendered workplace interactions: The use of strategic communication by African American women senior executives within dominant culture organizations. *Communication Quarterly, 50,* 251–268.

Parker, P. (2003). Control, resistance, and empowerment in raced, gendered, and classed work contexts: The case of African American women. *Communication Yearbook, 27,* 257–301.

Thomas, D. A., & Gabarro, J. J. (1999). *Breaking through: The making of minority executives in corporate America.* Boston: Harvard Business School Press.

West, C., & Fenstermaker, S. (1995). Doing difference. *Gender and Society, 9,* 8–37.

8

Difference and Cultural Identities in Aotearoa New Zealand

Pedagogical, Theoretical, and Pragmatic Implications of the Josie Bullock Case

Shiv Ganesh

y objective is to situate pedagogical issues in organizing difference with reference to contemporary cultural and political tensions in Aotearoa New Zealand. Broadly speaking, I aspire to demonstrate the intricacies of strategizing or theorizing pedagogy on difference, and more specifically, I hope to engage the reader with a series of issues surrounding difference with which I have engaged in the five years that I have taught in this country. To achieve this, I draw upon a range of theories to explore a teaching exemplar and narrate both my personal and pedagogical engagement with issues of difference in Aotearoa New Zealand.

I spend the first portion of the chapter acquainting the reader with what came to be known in the media as the "Josie Bullock case," and I contextualize it with reference to bicultural politics in contemporary

Aotearoa New Zealand. I then trace how students engaged with the issue in class, uncovering key issues in their engagement by employing three lenses that also serve as a pedagogical strategy: *organizing, reorganizing*, and *disorganizing*. I unpack these processes by uncovering how discussions of the case can turn students toward understanding how identities are intersectionally organized. I then discuss how some students are able to begin a process of reflexive reorganization of their own cultural identities as a result of the case by drawing upon Spivak's (1993) notion of strategic essentialism. In the last portion of the essay, I employ Levinasian notions of responsibility and dialogue to trace three moves whereby we might push ourselves and our students to understand difference in terms of a protoethics of disorganizing rather than an ontology of organizing.

❖ THE JOSIE BULLOCK CASE

In December 2004, corrections officers in a Maori-focused antiviolence program in Auckland filed into a room for a *poroporoaki*, a farewell ceremony conducted for Maori offenders. Poroporoaki in Aotearoa New Zealand[1] are said to signify the restoration of *mana*, or authority and respect, and are considered opportunities for *manuhiri* (guests) and *tangata whenua* (hosts/people of the land) to express their thoughts and feelings about their time together. Poroporoaki are a historically important part of Maori *tikanga*, or customary practices that are passed on from generation to generation, including *powhiri* (welcome ceremonies) and *hui* (formal extended communal discussions and deliberations). Poroporoaki are performed on *marae*, which are spaces sacred to Maori, and in modern Aotearoa New Zealand many organizations have marae on their premises to facilitate tikanga and honour the Treaty of Waitangi, upon which the country rests a significant part of its cultural identity. Maori tikanga themselves form an important part of rehabilitation practices in correctional facilities across Aotearoa New Zealand, where Maori constitute a disproportionately high percentage of inmates (Durie, 2003).

On this day, as any other, as they prepared to hear the *kaumatua* (Maori elders) speak, male correctional officers followed tikanga and moved toward the front of the room while female correctional officers moved toward the back. One female officer, however, did not go to the back but rather went to the front row and sat there along with the men. Her name was Josie Bullock. She was later given an oral warning by her supervisor for unprofessional conduct because she refused to respond to requests to move to the back with the other women. A few months later, she contacted print and television media about what she saw as a gender discrimination issue. As she said in a 2006 opinion piece in the conservative NZCPR (New Zealand Centre for Political Research) Forum, "Being given an oral warning for sticking up for women's rights stuck in my craw, so I went to the media, and in October 2005, got the sack for doing so" (p. 2).

The Josie Bullock case quickly became a prominent news story in 2005. As Bullock (2006) talked to the media that year, her complaints rested significantly upon the issue of gender equity in Maori tikanga. She said the following:

> . . . whatever sugar coating people want to put on it, the women are definitely subordinate. Clearly, lots of aspects of Maori culture aren't good and should be done away with. Just as cannibalism has gone, so too should the sexism inherent in these ceremonies. Cultures aren't set in concrete. They change as time goes by. Otherwise we'd still be living in caves and women would be the chattels of men. (p.1)

The Josie Bullock case continued to cause a furor in the country at regular intervals over the next few years. The initial coverage of Bullock's refusal to go to the back saw people in the country both support and criticize her. Supporters tended to compare her to Rosa Parks, the African American woman whose famous refusal to go to the back of the bus made her a civil rights pioneer. Others saw her as a feminist. Critics, in the context of the country's colonial history, questioned her place as a Pakeha (European/White) woman to criticize Maori tikanga. Further, her rhetoric, while couched in the language of gender equity, was significantly and clearly racist, especially in her startling equation of poroporoaki with cannibalism.

Bullock was fired by the Corrections department for procedural violations which included approaching the media to publicize an internal organizational dispute. In 2006, even as it refused to reinstate Bullock, the Corrections department made changes to its tikanga-related protocol, saying that *whakatau*—informal practices that do not require specific spatial codes—would be used instead of formal powhiri-related practices, of which poroporoaki are a part. This move was immediately criticized in parliament by the Maori Party, which said that Corrections had no place in redefining Maori cultural practices. In 2007, Bullock launched a simultaneous critique of and appeal to the Human Rights Commission's Review Tribunal, which has adjudicatory power over human-rights related issues. On one hand, she criticized the tribunal's Office of Proceedings, which sponsors cases that it believes should be heard by the tribunal, for being politically correct and declining to support her case while supporting many other "piffling" issues (Bullock, 2006, p. 1). On the other, she went ahead and filed a direct complaint to the Human Rights Commission herself, said, "I will have to take the case to the Tribunal myself. I've wasted a lot of time running up blind alleys, trying to get the help I believe I'm entitled to." She asked the Commission to award her more than $100,000 in compensation. In March 2008, the Human Rights Commission ruled that Corrections' oral warning against Bullock for violating protocol had been discriminatory, but upheld the department's decision to dismiss her for going to the media with her grievance. Predictably, Bullock hailed the discrimination verdict and denounced the lack of compensation.

Background and Context

I first heard about the Josie Bullock Case even before I arrived in Aotearoa New Zealand in July 2005; I had been avidly following the New Zealand media since December 2004, just before the case broke. For me, it became a way of learning about the intricacies of cultural politics, ethnicity, and gender in contemporary Aotearoa New Zealand. As the case unfolded, so did my experience of the multiculturalism of the society that I was encountering as a new immigrant. It appeared to me that some of the controversy over the Bullock case was embedded in larger cultural politics of contention in Aotearoa New Zealand, most evident in the huge controversy over the passage of the Foreshore and Seabed Act in 2004, which led to the formation of the Maori Party in the run-up to the November 2005 election. That the Foreshore and Seabed Act was a discursive background for the Josie Bullock case was evident in a series of interviews I conducted with global social justice activists all over the country. One of them, prominent in the peace movement, said: "Labour has systematically screwed Maoridom, and the passage of the act was the last straw because it demonstrated that they didn't give a fuck about Tangata Whenua. It's that ability to disregard and denigrate basic rights of Maori that allow people like, say, Josie Bullock to stand up [and] insult tikanga in the name of gender equality." (personal communication, May 8, 2007)

The Foreshore and Seabed Act was passed by the Labour government in late 2004, after Maori *iwi* (communities) registered claims with the Waitangi Tribunal for historical ownership of the country's foreshore and seabed. The Tribunal itself had been set up as an attempt by the government to set right the many violations of the Treaty of Waitangi (Te tiriti e Waitangi) that was signed on February 6, 1840 between the British Crown and many Maori iwi. The treaty was originally signed both in English and Te Reo Maori, and multiple interpretations of it exist. From the British point of view, the treaty gave the Crown sovereignty and the right to govern New Zealand and gave Maori "exclusive and undisturbed possession of their Lands and Estates, Forests, Fisheries and other properties." This, from the Crown's point of view, was the foundation of New Zealand's biculturalism (Jones, Pringle, & Shepherd, 2000).

From Maori points of view, te tiriti granted Maori *rangatiratanga*, or sovereign control, while according the governor the status of *kawanatanga*, a Te Reo word that drew etymologically from *governor*, a concept that itself was alien to Maori understandings of order and control. Further, while the British assumed that they had given Maori rights to property, Maori understandings of the word *taonga* diverged significantly from the Pakeha term *property*—while the latter signifies concrete and material assets, taonga refers to all objects and ideas that have special spiritual value. Thus, Maori interpretations of the treaty highlighted their self-determination and independence from colonial authority: their right to manage their own world without interference from the Crown (Orange, 1990). For the Crown, the most immediate effect of the treaty was to ensure that Maori land was sold purely to the Crown and no other private entity. And even within the British interpretation of the treaty, there were significant violations of the treaty over the years, with land seized from Maori through misrepresentation, deception, and war.

After the Waitangi Tribunal was set up in 1975 in order to redress colonial injustices, and with the Maori renaissance in the 1980s, violations of the original treaty were increasingly made visible. As Maori groups gained political influence, they were able to bring several cases to court for redress. One of them, which claimed ownership of the foreshore and seabed of Ninety-mile Beach in Northland, was made by the Ngati Apa iwi; it went to the court of appeals, which ruled on it in mid 2003 and granted that iwi were allowed to seek customary title over foreshore and seabed from New Zealand's Land Court. There was a political storm over the issue, which polarized public opinion, and the Labour government passed the act on November 14, 2004, thereby declaring that the foreshore and seabed belonged to the Crown.

I do not describe the Foreshore and Seabed Act in detail as an attempt to define or represent Maori cultural politics. Indeed, the problems associated with outsiders representing Maori histories and cultures have been extensively documented by scholars such as Linda Tuhowhai Smith (1997, 1999). Rather, my discussion of it is designed to provide the reader with a context for how I, as a cultural outsider, found myself changing ideas and perspectives about the society into which I was transitioning. Having observed both the Josie Bullock case and its larger context, the Foreshore and Seabed debate, from afar, I found myself initially opining that: (a) it was unjust to engage in gender discrimination in order to preserve cultural traditions and (b) land ought to be managed publicly, through government, rather than privately, through iwi. Both these opinions changed dramatically in the first year that I spent in Aotearoa New Zealand.

As someone who had a westernized, educated, and privileged upbringing in India and elsewhere, I had been brought up to value secularism, which in my childhood was set up against the idea of communalism. As children, we were told over and over again that India had a secular identity because we needed to combat the clash of communal identities, mostly in the form of conflict between Hindus and Muslims. "Unity in Diversity" our teachers told us, was the backbone of Indian polity, culture, and civic life, and if multiple cultures in India could not coexist, it would not survive. So when I arrived in New Zealand as a thirty-something adult, I reverted back to those childhood messages about multiculturalism almost instinctively as I heard debates about Maori cultural practice, the treaty of Waitangi, and the Foreshore and Seabed Act.

As I attempted to make sense of the cultural-political drama that was unfolding in front of me, I also found myself raising critical questions about my own position and the position of other minorities in the cultural life of New Zealand. Several people have argued that Aotearoa New Zealand is a multicultural society grappling with a bicultural history, and I empathized with that view—especially after a range of conversations with many members of Chinese and Indian communities, both inside and outside of the University of Waikato, that highlighted their sense of exclusion from debates about cultural identity, mostly because they felt that the idea of a bicultural New Zealand explicitly left out the possibility that other cultures could coexist in the country.

After a few months in the country, I found myself arriving at different conclusions about the Josie Bullock case, prompted first by a question: Why was sitting in the back row considered to be inferior? Couldn't sitting in the outside ring emphasize other cultural roles, such as protection? After all, women had significant roles in many aspects of tikanga that men didn't have. Was it really the place of Pakeha to make decisions about what was culturally appropriate for Maori? And didn't cultural accommodation have a part to play here? After all, I took my shoes off at the doorstep of many homes for cultural reasons, even though I might not do the same in my own house. As my position on the Bullock issue changed, so did my broader position on the Foreshore and Seabed Act; I began to reflect upon whether the Crown would really be able to hold the foreshore and seabed as a valuable public resource or whether they would open it up for privatization, corporate control, and mining, as they had done so many times in the past. The environmentalist in me began to feel that Maori iwi would do a much better job of preserving the ecological integrity of the country's foreshore and seabed, precisely because they had a deeply ecological and historical stake in its maintenance. This position was reinforced by arguments made by many activists I interviewed over the next few years. And thus, the increasing complexity of my positions on these two issues, along with my engagement with the case in class, marked my transition into the perplexities of cultural life in Aotearoa New Zealand.

Pedagogical Problems

As mentioned earlier, I spent a significant amount of time interviewing activists across the country about how they organized around global social justice issues, and the Josie Bullock case, along with the Foreshore and Seabed Act, cropped up in the extended discussions I had with them. They were also brought up both by students in my large undergraduate classes and students in my postgraduate seminar on organizational communication. We first started talking about the Josie Bullock case during a guest lecture I delivered in an undergraduate class on organizational communication in October 2005, at the height of its controversy. When I tentatively brought up the subject, students responded vigorously to the issue, and they have continued to do so ever since. The first time the case came up, some students questioned why it was OK for men to sit in the front while women sat in the back, at which point the discussion turned to how students sitting in the front of the class felt as compared to students sitting at the back. Wasn't it a sign of being cool, said other students, to be sitting at the back of the class? Several Maori and Pasifika students, like the activists I interviewed, put the Josie Bullock issue in the context of the Foreshore and Seabed Act, expressing their chagrin at the feeling that decisions about culturally appropriate Maori customs were being made by non-Maori, even as the government appeared to be eroding and curtailing the historical property rights of Maori.

As an instructor, a new migrant, and a researcher, I felt that I needed to hear my students' points of view, that I could learn something from people who had lived in the country for much longer than I, and that my own scholarship and reflexivity would benefit as a result. And I was also nervous about my own discursive position as a relative outsider who did not have a clearly defined standing to discuss the issue. So I was pleased when many students felt free to articulate their points of view to each other, and to me, in relatively free-ranging discussions where we were able to gain important insights into colonial practices and postcolonial politics as they operated in public, corporate, and nonprofit organizations in Aotearoa New Zealand. And critically, it allowed students to move beyond understanding organizations as reified systems of collective coordinated activity and to appreciate organizations as sites of cultural identity formation. More broadly, it allowed students to understand multiple connections between identity and organizing and to interpret Josie Bullock's actions as the result of the intersections between discourses of gender, Euro-American notions of civil rights, and contemporary Pakeha identity.

As they unpacked the issue, however, students themselves tended to speak from very particular identity positions, often discussing both issues in terms of men versus women, Pakeha versus Maori, and Natives versus Migrants. In mid 2006, a student came in to see me during office hours, fired up about a discussion on the subject we had had during one of my lectures on negotiation and persuasion. She had felt that because her parents immigrated to New Zealand from China, she had no space to contribute to the discussion, despite having been born in the country. I e-mailed her recently to obtain permission to use her example for this essay, and in replying, she said: "Thank you for remembering [me]. I felt hurt but in hindsight it was a very useful discussion because it made me realize that sometimes there are places where you simply can't say anything."

Her original concern drove me to be more attentive to voice, silence, and student identity when discussing the Josie Bullock case in class, and the next semester, as I structured a reflective exercise on the case, I aimed to be more thorough and particular about asking students to be more reflexive about their own identities as they discussed the case. Thus, I asked students how they would think through the Josie Bullock issue from a variety of subject positions, including new migrants and Pasifika communities. Yet as the student's comments and e-mail indicate, the tactic needed to be thought through in terms of more comprehensive questions about how pedagogical exercises might inevitably construct subject positions for students from which they are unable to speak. In addition, I needed to ask the question as to how I, as an instructor who identified with multicultural spaces, was to think through the politics and ethics of my own still nervous cultural positioning and voice in postcolonial classrooms in Aotearoa New Zealand. Put another way, I needed to understand differences among students, my own differences from students when considered as a whole, as well as the entire project of understanding issues of difference *with* students.

In what follows, I theorize and strategize about how I attempted to increase both students' and my own reflexivity about the Josie Bullock case by drawing upon some insights from Gayatri Chakrabarty Spivak's (1993) notion of strategic essentialism as a means of engaging with silent subaltern identities. The concept, grounded as it is in postcolonial scholarship's concern with theorizing voice and silence in the context of historical cultural politics, is useful in enabling us to trace how discussions of the Josie Bullock case sometimes resulted in processes of reflexive reorganizing of student identities. Thus, I provide the reader with an overview of Spivak's arguments on the subject, and I discuss how it helped identify key reflexive moments in classroom discussions of the Josie Bullock case. Following this, I discuss some limitations of the notion and discuss ways in which I have tried to push such reflexive reorganizing even further, by way of drawing upon Levinasian protoethics of responsibility and dialogue in order to trace a protoethics of disorganizing.

❖ POSTCOLONIAL POLITICS: QUESTIONING REPRESENTATION

Spivak's work on the subaltern marked an important turning point in postcolonial historiography in general. The object of her critique was the idea of a subaltern consciousness as it had developed in subaltern studies. In an early essay, she indicated two pervasive problems in the work of the South Asian subaltern studies collective (Spivak, 1988a). First, she said that the group was united in their unqualified assumption about the existence of a pure form of peasant subaltern consciousness that could be easily understood and represented by critics and scholars. Their attempt to identify and excavate such voice-consciousness was, she insisted, a simplistic, essentializing, and somewhat positivistic project (Spivak, 1988a). Instead, she said, critics needed to situate ethical concerns surrounding pedagogy with reference to contemporary international divisions of labour and demarcations of identity, considering how they are rooted in nineteenth-century territorial imperialism, and treating the question of whether subaltern identities can speak, as a problem rather than an assumption (Papastergiadis, 1998).

Second, Spivak (1988a) also critiqued the idea that one can address the absent subaltern by "reserving a space on the international table" (p. 296) for her as nostalgic rhetoric that is ultimately grounded in tokenism. Such nostalgic rhetoric, she said, is as unproductive as the attempt to recover some sort of pure, essential subaltern consciousness, as it attempts to address the absence of the subaltern without any fundamental structural or perceptual adjustment on the part of the critic, scholar, or teacher. Both nostalgia and attempts to incorporate and excavate subaltern identity occur, in Husserl's (1962) terms, within an immanent structure of meaning: within a system of signifiers that are produced by none other than oneself. Pedagogical transcendence in the face of such self-orientation is thus impossible because students and instructors are caught in performing or assuming pre-assigned identities, in terms of how they approach both themselves and understand other people.

From this point of view, it would be problematic to treat a student who, through accident of birth, was positioned as a Chinese immigrant as someone who could readily speak as an uncomplicated and direct voice for Chinese students or as someone in need of a quick multicultural remedy in the context of the discursive history of biculturalism in Aotearoa New Zealand. It is imperative, said Spivak (1988b) for scholars to develop more heterogeneous, polysemous images of the other that do not rest on one's own *a priori* conceptions of what a cultural other should look like and, in doing so, achieve transcendence in the classroom. In other words, it is necessary to move outside the structure of immanence, within which cultural identities are constructed, and engage with the other in terms of *exteriority*.

❖ STRATEGIC ESSENTIALISM: OPENING AND COLLAPSING CATEGORIES

A prominent ambiguity in Spivak's (1988b) deconstruction of the subaltern is that while she makes a radical critique of subaltern consciousness as it was understood by the subaltern studies collective, she simultaneously endorses the project of excavating a subaltern consciousness itself. At the heart of such ambiguity lies her advocacy of a "strategic essentialism" on the part of the scholar. She said

> I am suggesting, rather, that although the [Subaltern Studies] group does not wittingly engage with the post-structuralist understanding of consciousness, our own transactional reading of them is enhanced if we see them as strategically adhering to the essentialist notion of consciousness, that would fall prey to an anti-humanist critique, within a historiographic practice that draws many of its strengths from that very critique. (p. 15)

Critics were quick to point out the dissonance between Spivak's endorsement of strategic essentialism on one hand, and her strong advocacy of deconstruction as a practice on the other (Eagleton, 1995; Eagleton, Jameson, & Said, 1990). Spivak's rejoinder on the subject was to complain that her critics read her idea of *essentialism* without regard to her ideas about *strategy* (Spivak, 1993). A strategy, for Spivak (1993), necessitates locating the group/movement/scholar with reference to prevailing configurations of labour and discourse.

The notion of strategic essentialism, despite its ambiguity, has been used productively by researchers in unpacking the ways in which women can create forms of identification in workplaces in the context of substantive differences amongst them (Edley, 2000). It also has pedagogical potential in the Josie Bullock case. In this line of thinking, discourses of indigenous groups of people should be rendered strategically essential depending upon the discursive configurations within which the scholar is herself complicit. For instance, the claim by Hindu fundamentalists in India that Hindus are the indigenous people of India should be treated very differently from the claim that Maori are the indigenous people of Aotearoa New Zealand because the colonial discursive formations that surround the expressions of indigenousness are powerfully different. In the case of India, the dominant cultural binary between Hindus and Muslims privileges Hinduism, which occupies a dominant space in culture and politics. In the case of Aotearoan New Zealand, the dominant colonial binary is between Maori and Pakeha, and Maori cultures, while vibrant, do not occupy a similar dominant space.

Consequently, a key pedagogical task for an instructor in Aotearoa New Zealand is to begin to deconstruct the category Pakeha itself and to ask how other cultural formations are strategically positioned by it. If one does so, what is immediately visible is that the term *Pakeha*, with all its cultural baggage, systematically excludes cultural groups who are not European or White. Consequently, strategically essentializing Indian or Fijian-Indian or Chinese in the multicultural and postcolonial classroom needs to take this dynamic into account. In discussing the Josie Bullock case to engender classroom debates in Aotearoa New Zealand, one needs to move beyond calling students' identities into existence at the intersection of contemporary discourses on gender, culture, ethnicity, and age. I have sometimes been successful in doing so by using the case to push students to reflect upon how their own identities are summoned in terms of their relationship with the dominant Pakeha, thereby creating possibilities for students to reflexively reorganize and reinterpret how they might understand their own intersectional identities.

Such reflexivity and reorganization was evident both in class and in tutorial discussions with students, where I was able to watch students discuss and unpack the exclusionary and raced constructions of Pakeha-ness as they are evident in myriad organizational contexts across the country, including the Corrections department. This message resonated for some Chinese and Indian students who felt that they had slipped between the cracks of the Maori-Pakeha binary. An awareness of the strategic character of their own identities was evident in an emerging irony in their use of terms such as *the Indian experience* or *the Chinese experience* in New Zealand and in an emerging willingness to examine those categories. This in turn helped a few students articulate, identify, and ultimately deconstruct their own latent sense of resentment about what they felt was the Maori's position as a privileged minority, in the context of their own experiences of feeling discriminated against as they applied for jobs, while they were at work, or while they were studying at universities.

Thus, in the larger scheme of things, such pedagogical moves are clearly necessary for us to substantively address issues of difference in classrooms as a first step toward enhancing students' own understandings and experiences of difference. However, despite its obvious potential for postcolonial perspectives in helping to understand, deconstruct, and reposition historical cultural formations in pedagogy in Aotearoa New Zealand, there is a point beyond which the term *strategic essentialism* fails to capture the need for ethical commitments on the part of scholars and teachers as they engage with pedagogical issues of difference. In order to engage the reader with a picture of what such ethical transcendence might look like in relation to the Josie Bullock case, I now move to unpack the potential for a Levinasian perspective on engaging with difference in classrooms, and then I tie it to the Josie Bullock case by employing the metaphor of disorganizing.

❖ TRANSCENDING STRATEGIC ESSENTIALISM: DIALOGUE AND RESPONSIBILITY IN CLASSROOMS

The ambiguity in Spivak's use of the term *strategic essentialism*, referred to earlier, can also be understood as a tension between the language of ontology it invokes and the ethical stance that it prescribes. Here, Emmanuel Levinas's work becomes remarkably useful in providing a vocabulary that moves from ontology to a protoethics that treats what we might ordinarily call *ethics* in foundational and fundamental terms. In many ways, Levinas's critique of Husserl's phenomenology of presence is analogous to Spivak's critique of the subaltern studies collective; however, the Levinasian critique allows us to treat issues of identity, immanence, difference, and ultimately transcendence, in ethical rather than ontological terms.

Levinas moves the notion of transcendence to a level deeper than the received Husserlian view that sees it as the standing-over-against of the object in the act of perception. Levinas specifies that transcendence is not the simple reduction of the ontological difference between being and beings; the act of transcendence is, for him, primarily ethical, and he unpacks the protoethics of transcendence in terms of the notions of responsibility and dialogue with the neighbour (Levinas, 1969). Levinas's concern in theorizing transcendence is to establish the exteriority of the other, and such exteriority implies an intelligibility that cannot be reduced to thought. "Exteriority," he said, "occurs when one term is affected by that which it cannot assume, by the Infinite" (Levinas, 1998, p. 118). The other thus referred to is not just a Derridean other (Derrida, 1992) referred to and negated through discourse, but an *immemorial* and *transcendent* other. Levinas said the following:

> There is an intelligibility older than what is manifested as a comprehension of being, embraceable and thus constitutable by consciousness, and which reigns as world. This is a signification by way of transcendence, older than what governs *esse*, even if, in its turn, the former lets itself be shown in the language it summons and gives rise to in order to enter into propositions of an ontological and ontical form. (Levinas, 1998, p.121)

Through these ideas of transcendence, Levinas invited us to rethink consciousness in terms of ethics. A discussion of transcendence in terms of responsibility and proximity helps us move toward greater reflexivity in understanding the ways in which difference is organized, reorganized, and disorganized.

Dialogue itself is central to Levinas's work. For him, in many ways, dialogue *is* ethics. Accordingly, dialogue is not to be conceived of in terms of reason alone because, as he puts it, "Reason is One. It has no one left with whom to communicate; nothing is outside of it." (Levinas, 1998, pp. 124–125). Reason has, as its centre, the ego, and to try and think of dialogue from an egocentric point of view is to negate the idea of dialogue itself.

The *you* that Levinasian dialogue implies is radically exterior to the ego, and it is this exteriority that Levinas has in mind when he refers to the "absolute distance" between the I and the you. As such, the other is immemorial: it exists outside our consciousness, and therefore, it *cannot be conceived of in terms of consciousness.* In the context of such absolute distance, Levinas (1998) spoke of transcendence as follows:

> The extraordinary and immediate relation of dia-logue . . . transcends this distance without suppressing it or recuperating it, as does the gaze that crosses the distance separating it from an object in the world, while comprehending and encompassing that distance. Here is a way of acceding to the other different from that of knowing him [sic]: to approach the neighbour. (p. 141).

The saying of *you* that comprises dialogue is what sets it apart from the *said* of consciousness, and it allows us to think of the other in terms of proximity: the *dia-logue* is the constitution of the self by the other. The saying of *you* implies no reciprocity, no ontological synchronicity, but rather an ethical obligation. If one must think of dialogue, one must conceive of it through such unequalness, in terms of such radically exterior constitution of selfhood, where we do not even consider students who do not have visible voice in the classroom as othered; rather, students are themselves othered by the very subject positions that post-colonial discourses oblige them to occupy.

Further, if the self is dialogically indebted to the other, the issue of responsibility as a primary ethical consideration comes to the fore. For Levinas, the protoethics of responsibility is a phenomenological move beyond consciousness to *conscience.* To apprehend otherness in these terms is to disengage from consciousness as a category and in awakening, mark the proximity of the other as "the soul within the soul." (Levinas, 1998, p. 151). This interiority of mental life, where the *I* is constituted by the *You*, is depicted by Levinas as a "bad conscience" or a prereflective and nonintentional conscience, which describes the passivity of selfhood in the face of the other. Such passivity at its heart bears *response*-ability to the demand of the other that summons it. In this sense, our constitution, our very being, can be read as a response to the other, as premised upon the other. The need to accede, to respond to the call of the other, is deeper than the subjectivity of self-hood: herein lies Levinasian responsibility.

Levinasian ethics thus allow us to transcend our highly particular-ized responsibility to the other by understanding all pedagogical encoun-ters in terms of radical otherness and exteriority, as well as the intimacy that derives from the dialogic other. If postcolonial pedagogy is extraor-dinarily committed to tracing identity, voice, silence, and difference in historical-discursive contexts, such Levinasian concerns should explicitly form the larger (and in a sense, more impossible) terms of reference as we discuss and negotiate critical and vexed notions of cultural identity in our classrooms. At least three possibilities emerge if we consider the Josie Bullock case in terms of Levinasian responsibility and dialogue.

First, I would suggest that to usefully engage classes in debates about multiculturalism in Aotearoa New Zealand, instructors begin by engaging in a radical deconstruction of their own cultural selfhood. Such processes are often problematic, painful, and solipsistic. For instance, my own self-understanding is always partial, in that the *me* that I interrogate is always a product of a range of foreground experi-ences, as it is impossible to understand how every single experience I have had has served to construct the identities that I perform. My own identity is understood as multicultural in the context of my experiences in Aotearoa New Zealand, and as such, interrogating why and how I am positioned as multicultural and the political cost and opportunities that these constructions provide are a first start to understanding how such processes may also construct my students. Indeed, that the former sharply informs the latter was brought home to me quite resoundingly as I grew to increasingly question my initial impressions about the Josie Bullock case. This sort of painful self-learning, I am realizing, is a lifelong process, a first step toward both responsibility and dialogue.

Second, it is important to understand student voices and silences as products of discourse that are themselves radically exterior. A student's identity as male, Pakeha, and straight, for instance, is contingent upon the context of the discussions and discourses in classrooms that call and position those identities against each other. Thus, in addition to consid-ering student identities as permanently intersectional, one also needs to comprehend them as contingent and exteriorized by discourses. And it is also in this sense that, as we envision dialogic possibilities and impossibilities in classrooms, we must consider discourses as speaking through students, as much as students giving voice to discourse. In the Josie Bullock case, this would mean successfully pushing reflexivity on the issue much further, enabling an understanding of how our own cul-tural identities might simultaneously privilege and other us.

Third, such an approach would treat broad discourses themselves as historical and subject to deconstruction, and the act of deconstructing discourses would help move toward a contingent and mutual awareness of the ways in which they have constructed all of us—and as such, this is an important step toward understanding the contingence of response-ability in the Levinasian sense. For instance, using the Josie Bullock case to deconstruct and reconstruct categories such as Pakeha could give a classroom community a collective awareness of how we are all positioned with reference to it. Indeed, one might productively begin by reconstructing the term *Pakeha* as one that involves a range of cultural and ethnic identities, not just White identities, and doing so might help creatively reimagine the colonial history of biculturalism in Aotearoa New Zealand itself.

❖ CONCLUSION

By way of a conclusion, I would like to reiterate the three lenses that highlight the complexities of identity and difference that are embedded in the Josie Bullock case and that might work together as both analysis and strategy as we attempt to create progressive pedagogy on cultural identity issues. I hope I have demonstrated the productivity of envisioning cultural identity politics summoned by the case at three levels: *organizing, reorganizing,* and *disorganizing.* The idea of organizing in relation to difference has been unpacked in vastly more complicated and nuanced terms by organizational communication scholars (Ashcraft & Mumby, 2004), and I have used it here in a more traditionally Weickean sense (Weick, 1996). Thus, the term *organizing* comes into play when I consider the vigour of student responses to the Josie Bullock case in the classroom as students begin to understand intersections among gender, culture, and space that are accentuated as they contemplate the significance of asking a Pakeha woman to move to the back of a room. Yet as my analysis has shown, it oversimplifies issues of voice, identity, and silence in classrooms, and in some ways, it prevents deeper and more reflexive understandings of cultural identity.

The term *re-organizing,* which I have fleshed out using Spivak's work, helps focus my attention upon moments, fewer and further between, when some students become aware of deeper historical connections and tensions between their own specific cultural identities and those of the dominant cultural binary. Such reorganizing can help students reflexively and creatively reinterpret their own sense of historical connection or disconnection with bicultural politics in Aotearoa New Zealand, and it can significantly and productively help create a reinvigorated sense of multicultural investment in Aotearoa New Zealand's bicultural identity.

Finally, the notion of *disorganizing* is much more fleeting, and I have seen only traces of it as I have discussed the Josie Bullock case in various classes. If the term *organizing* is rooted in an ontology of organizations, perhaps we should consider, albeit playfully, how disorganization might be rooted in a protoethics of organization.[2] I sensed such disorganization most profoundly in one instance, when a student in my postgraduate class remarked on how the case and subsequent discussion sparked her thoughts on how shallow the term *connection* was as a means of describing collectivities, cultures, and our communal existence. I also sometimes experience a "Levinasian moment" when I pause to question why I feel a slight nervousness on my part when I prepare to discuss the case with students. And sometimes I sense that a student has taken their reflexivity on the issue to a much deeper level than an awareness or reinterpretation of the historically contingent character of their cultural identity, and has begun to ask profound questions about how ways in which they speak about culture and politics might simultaneously empower, compartmentalize, and even other them.

These three lenses work well in helping me sort through the nuances of the Josie Bullock case and meaningfully understand difference in my classrooms. In closing, and in the spirit of sparking conversation, I invite the reader to consider how they might approach the very same case, whether my experiences with it might resonate with theirs, and if so, what possibilities that raises for a transcendent pedagogy of difference.

❖ NOTES

1. Aotearoa is often considered a more culturally appropriate name for New Zealand, derived as it is from a Te Reo description of the country as "the land of the long White cloud." However, the term itself is of colonial origin (King, 2003), and when I utilize the term *Aotearoa New Zealand* it is to draw attention to the cultural significance of Maori-Pakeha biculturalism, rather than to refer to New Zealand as a sovereign territory.

2. In this sense, my tentative appropriation of the term *disorganizing* differs significantly from Bisel (2009).

❖ REFERENCES

Ashcraft, K. L., & Mumby, D. K. (2004). *Reworking gender: A feminist communicology of organization.* Thousand Oaks, CA: Sage.
Bisel, R. S. (2009). *The (dis)organizing property of communication.* Paper presented at the annual meeting of the NCA 94th annual convention, TBA,

San Diego, CA. Retrieved April 5, 2010, from http://www.allacademic
.com/meta/p276796_index.html

Bullock, J. (2006, 5 March). Politically correctness (sic) a la the The Office Of
Proceedings. *NCZPR Forum*, from http://www.nzcpr.com/Guest25.htm

Derrida, J. (1992). How to avoid speaking: Denials. In H. Coward & T. Fosbay
(Eds.), *Derrida and negative theology* (pp. 73–142). New York: SUNY Press.

Durie, M. (2003). *Ngā kāhui pou launching Māori futures.* Auckland, New Zealand:
Huia Books.

Eagleton, T. (1995). Where do postmodernists come from? *Monthly Review,*
47(3), 59–70.

Eagleton, T., Jameson, F., & Said, E. (1990). *Nationalism, colonialism, and literature.* Minneapolis: University of Minnesota Press.

Edley, P. (2000). Discursive essentializing in a woman-owned business: Gendered
stereotypes and strategic subordination. *Management Communication
Quarterly, 14,* 271–306.

Husserl, E. (1962). *Ideas: General introduction to pure phenomenology* (W. R. B. Gibson,
Trans.). London: Collier-Macmillan.

Jones, D., Pringle, J., & Shepherd, D. (2000). "Managing diversity" meets
Aotearoa/New Zealand. *Personnel Review, 29*(3), 364–380.

King, M. (2003). *The Penguin history of New Zealand.* London: Penguin.

Levinas, E. (1969). *Totality and infinity: An essay on exteriority* (A. Lingis, Trans.).
Pittsburgh, PA: Duquesne University Press.

Levinas, E. (1998). *Of God who comes to mind.* (B. Bargo, Trans.). Stanford, CA:
Stanford University Press.

Orange, C. (1990). *An illustrated history of the Treaty of Waitangi.* Wellington,
New Zealand: Allen & Unwin.

Papastergiadis, N. (1998). Identity and alterity: A conversation with Gayatri
Chakravorty Spivak. In *Dialogues in the diasporas: Essays and conversations
on cultural identity* (pp. 53–65). London: Rivers Oram Press.

Smith, L. T. (1997). *The development of Kaupapa Maori: Theory and praxis.*
Auckland, New Zealand: The International Research Institute for Maori
and Indigenous Education.

Smith, L. T. (1999). *Decolonising methodologies: Research and indigenous peoples.*
Auckland, New Zealand: Zed Books.

Spivak, G. C. (1988a). Can the subaltern speak? In C. Nelson & L. Grossberg
(Eds.), *Marxism and the interpretation of cultures* (pp. 271–313). Urbana:
University of Illinois Press.

Spivak, G. C. (1988b). Subaltern studies: Deconstructing historiography. In R. Guha
& G. C. Spivak (Eds.), *Selected subaltern studies.* Delhi: Oxford University Press.

Spivak, G. C. (1993). *Outside in the teaching machine.* New York: Routledge.

Weick, K. E. (1996). *Sensemaking in organizations.* Thousand Oaks, CA: Sage
Publications.

Part III

Applying Difference to Organizational Change

9

Different Ways
of Talking About
Intervention Goals

John G. McClellan, Stephen Williams, and Stanley Deetz

❖ DIFFERENT WAYS OF TALKING
ABOUT INTERVENTION GOALS

Difference is an increasingly important issue in organization studies. Many contemporary organizations attempt to promote difference among participants by engaging in various intervention strategies to encourage diversity, equity, advancement, and development of underrepresented groups. In addition, with many organizational communication scholars embracing constitutive perspectives of communication, attention is increasingly being placed on studying discourse as productive of organizational life (e.g., Grant, Hardy, Oswick, & Putnam, 2004). Thus, paying attention to the ways in which difference is discursively constructed is key to understanding difference-oriented intervention programs.

   This chapter attends to difference as enacted and enabled through particular forms of talk about changing aspects of organizational life. Specifically, this chapter aims to explore the consequences of different ways of talking about intervention goals related to difference and opportunity. To accomplish this objective, we focus on workplace diversity programs aimed at supporting the careers of women in university and corporate settings. Our interest is to reveal how varied ways of talking about intervention objectives might influence both the strategies and outcomes of difference-oriented change programs. We will examine four distinct forms of talk about the objectives of such initiatives to show how talk enables some possibilities for engaging difference while simultaneously excluding alternative strategies and outcomes.

We begin this chapter by providing a theoretical foundation for our claim that different ways of talking matter. In particular, we review how language serves as the principal mediator of experience and position communication as a political activity that directs attention to particular ways of understanding organizational life. We then use specific case studies to identify and review four selected discourses associated with intervention programs attempting to promote difference by supporting the careers of women. Here we aim to reveal how various ways of talking about the goals of organizational intervention encourage different logics that then guide unique understandings of organizational life and strategies for change. We then review the potential consequences of each way of talking about difference by discussing the implications for intervention activities, resistance to such initiatives, and challenges for transformation efforts based on each discourse. We conclude this chapter with some implications for attending to the talk about intervention goals as a political activity and encourage those interested in difference to attend to the various ways people talk about difference.

❖ CONSEQUENCES OF ORGANIZATIONAL TALK

Most contemporary organizational communication scholars agree that communication is a practice that is constitutive of organizing and its attendant meanings. These ideas are often grounded in principles of philosophical hermeneutics, furthered by Berger and Luckmann's (1966) social construction of reality, and complemented by Weick's (1979) work on organizing as a social process. Critical researchers in the field have worked with the politics of the construction process for the past 30 years. More recently, the Montreal School (Cooren & Taylor, 1997; Taylor, 1999) developed a constitutive perspective of organization that helped solidify the idea that communication constitutes organization in the everyday vernacular of organizational communication studies. This perspective, following the lines of Giddens's (1984) structuration theory, proclaimed that communication not only reflects reality but also creates and maintains the meanings that guide organized life and motivate particular actions.

These principles are complemented by other works that explore the many ways talk is an important and meaningful aspect of organizational life. For instance, Boden's (1994) work exploring organizational talk as a principal business activity, Tompkins's (1993) insight into the ways in which talk creates and maintains decisional premises, and Barker's (1993) work on concertive control all show the consequences of the constitutive character of communication and illustrate how organizational talk has meaningful implications for organizational life by creating a potentially unified and homogeneous whole. As Kuhn and Ashcraft (2003) explained, all organizational rules, practices, norms, and other properties are developed and maintained through discursive practices; in short, "organization emerges in conversation" (p. 41).

However, with a focus on difference as an organizational practice, our attention is directed away from the creation of "sameness" through talk toward initiatives enacted to promote difference. Thus, we are motivated to explore another aspect of this constitutive perspective. Specifically, we aim to reveal the complexities of organizational talk that result in *this* being constituted in talk, rather than *that*. In addition, with a focus on exploring the consequences of talking about intervention goals in particular ways, we are interested in taking the constitutive perspective a bit further by directing attention to the consequences of talk.

If communication constitutes organization, then the consequence of talking differently about intervention goals enables some possibilities and precludes others. By recognizing language use as a relational process of self-world production, we can explore an alternative way to understand why different ways of talking matter. Specifically, we can see language use as a sociohistorical, political process with meaningful consequences for organizational realities and human responses.

Relational Understandings and Language Use

The ways in which intervention goals are talked about has consequences for understanding difference. Founded on the notion that language use is a relational process, this concept is rooted in the phenomenological idea that experiences emerge in relation with the things of the world and that particular understandings of experience subsequently become embedded in systems of language. This idea purports that knowledge and understandings are created through intricate and complex relationships among individuals and things (Gergen, 1994), where understandings of human experience arise within the relationship between a positioned subject and a not yet determined thing toward which the subject is directed (Deetz, 1992). All personal experiences, as well as worldly objects, are consequentially inseparable from the presubjective, preobjective relationships within the constitutive activities that brought them into being (Deetz, 2003). Thus, the meaning of a thing is defined in terms of its set of relations. And it is language that solidifies particular relationships with the things of the world.

Thus, as we talk about the things of the world, we put forth particular *relational intentions,* and continued talk establishes and re-establishes preferred values for relating to the world. As such, talk enacts particular ways of understanding the self in relation to the things of the world. From this perspective, the people and objects of the world are not *out there* to be discovered, but are the outcome of relationships among people and the indeterminant external space waiting to be constituted as a world through the use of language (Deetz, 1992, 2003). Language is thus the keeper of relational possibilities where meanings, knowledge, and understandings of the world and the self can be produced and reproduced. The practice of talk puts into play the particular worlds we know and live. This "linguistic turn" directs attention toward communicatively based and socially produced understandings of the world and the self.

Embracing this notion removes consciousness as the keeper of meaning and replaces it with socially created language systems. As a result, consciousness is not something found inside the heads of individual people to be shared with others but is found in the language of society. As such, organizations, social norms, personal attitudes, and emotions are not psychological phenomena but are created through communicative interactions. We ground our discussion of talk about intervention goals in this idea that language is the keeper of meanings and talk is the producer of understanding. Embracing this idea directs attention to talk as a political activity that simultaneously produces particular meanings and precludes others.

Talk as a Political Activity

As meanings become embedded in language, alternative ways to know experiences often become reduced, suppressed, ignored, or otherwise made inconsequential. Through the processes of naturalization (Foucault, 1972) and institutionalization (Berger & Luckmann, 1966), some meanings become dominant and preferred understandings of reality, ultimately suppressing the conflicts inherent in the initial formation of meaning. When this occurs, particular logics, values, and preferences for understanding the world are treated as natural and normal and become presented and reinstated through talk. As a consequence, understandings of the world (and the self in relation to the world) are predefined and offered to us through language use. Communication is thus a political activity because talk always expresses some intention, value, or perspective that naturalizes some understandings and hides or obscures conflicts inherent in the relational formation of meaning.

Language use is political because it can result in conflicts inherent in the initial formation of meaning remaining hidden or unknown and can result in value-laden understandings being presented as unified, coherent, and value-free. Through mechanisms such as systematically distorted communication (Habermas, 1984, 1987) and discursive closure (Deetz, 1992), particular ways of talking produce certain interpretations, definitions, meanings, values, and vocabularies of action while simultaneously precluding alternative understandings. This notion that everyday talk is political is illustrated in Acker's (1991) work on the gendered quality of organizational concepts such as the job, Alvesson and Willmott's (2002) exploration of organizational identity as related to neutrally presented managerial values, and Trethewey's (2001) analysis of the narrative of decline among midlife working women. This type of work embraces language as the producer of the very institutional forms that direct and constrain organized life and focuses attention on the ways in which talk is performed among organizational participants to enable and restrict social meanings.

Understanding talk as a political activity directs attention to the relationships inherent in talk—on what is expressed as well as what is suppressed, hidden, or closed-off from discussion. In the next section, we present four different ways of talking about intervention goals associated with programs aimed at supporting the careers of women. By explicating four different ways of talking about the objectives of such programs, our aim is to show the ways this talk emphasizes different strategies for intervention and results in particular ways of understanding difference in the workplace.

❖ TALKING ABOUT INTERVENTION GOALS

Many universities and private organizations have initiated programs to support women in their careers. For instance, in 2002 the National Science Foundation (NSF) began an initiative that provided grants through their Advance Program to universities in the United States to study and enhance the careers of female faculty members in the science, technology, engineering, and math (STEM) disciplines. Through financial awards to universities, the Advance initiatives sponsor creative approaches to facilitate women's advancement to the highest ranks of academic leadership (NSF, 2009). Many corporate organizations have also initiated their own programs to assist the careers of women in various ways. For instance, PepsiCo, a major U.S.-based soda and snack company, has for many years been talking about increasing the number of women and culturally diverse individuals working for the organization. While there are myriad potential ways to talk about intervention strategies, tactics, and goals for these types of programs, we argue that how the objectives are discussed by change agents can generate unique vocabularies, sponsor particular logics, and motivate different intervention activities and outcome measures.

In reviewing various intervention programs, we have identified four ways of talking about intervention goals: (1) as diversity, (2) as equity, (3) as advancement, and (4) as development. Critically reviewing each of these ways of talking to reveal their implicit logics, guiding strategies, and outcome measures will help illustrate how each of these discourses influences the ways difference is enabled in practice. We are not claiming that these are the only ways in which intervention programs that promote difference talk about their goals or that there is only one ideal way to talk about intervention goals; we are saying that by revealing the differences among these distinct discourses, we can see the consequences of talking about intervention goals in different ways. Our aim in exploring these four discourses is to show how each way of talking promotes a particular vocabulary for intervention and serves as a temporary formation of meaning about difference. Our analysis aims to reveal the hidden interests or political motives that become naturalized and positioned beyond contestations. By exposing the consequences of each way of talking, we hope to reclaim the conflicts that have been moved beyond critique.

Recognizing that actual talk of interventions involves a mixing, layering, and overlapping of many vocabularies of change, we hope that in examining four prototypical ways of talking we can expose some of the complexities of talking about difference that are frequently overlooked. In much the same way as Ely and Meyerson (2000) discussed the importance of maintaining constant discussion of gender during intervention programs designed to enhance gender equity, we hope to reveal how talking of difference in various ways may serve to close off discussion related to the core issue of gender within intervention programs that are specifically designed to encourage a better working environment for women. The following is a table that reflects four ways of talking about intervention goals.

Figure 9.1 Ways of Talking About Intervention Goals

Talk	Intervention Objective	Implied Logic	Intervention Strategies	Outputs/Measures
Diversity	Increase the diversity of the organizational members making decisions in the organization.	Increased diversity enhances organizational decision-making and creativity.	• Actively recruit underrepresented people • Complicate the notion of difference beyond superficial group differences • Assure real differences in decision teams • Promote cultural events	• Increased numbers of underrepresented employees • Creativity of decisions • Decision-making that addresses diverse constituents
Equity	Inscribe equity into organizational policies and practices.	We are all created equal, thus out of moral concern for fairness, we should all be treated equitably.	• Promote equitable pay structures • Tout equity as the basis for organizational policies and practices • Promote equity events to sponsor a moral stance • Measure perceptions of equity/inequity	• Equitable pay structures • Equal opportunities in hiring, promotion, and other practices • An emergent culture of equity • Expression of moments of inequity

(Continued)

Figure 9.1 *(Continued)*

Talk	Intervention Objective	Implied Logic	Intervention Strategies	Outputs/Measures
Advancement	Hire and promote underrepresented people to top hierarchical positions.	Dominant groups cannot advance underrepresented people's interests. Thus, underrepresented people must be in positions to do so.	• Engage in targeted hiring and promotion efforts • Provide advancement opportunities • Develop mentoring relationships and networking opportunities	• More minorities in top-level positions • Improved performance of underrepresented groups • Increased salaries for minorities—marking increased promotion rates • Existence of formal networking/mentoring
Development	Share information and develop skills to increase institutional transparency and knowledge.	Everybody lacks knowledge or skills, and if we teach everyone it will advantage underrepresented people more because they lack the most knowledge.	• Provide training and workshops • Promote transparency in hiring and promotion procedures and organizational polices • Engage in formal mentoring and coaching programs	• Increased knowledge of existing policies • Transparent organizational practices • Better skilled organizational members • Easy access to policies and procedures

Diversity

Workplace *diversity* is one common way to talk about difference as an intervention goal. Talk of diversity as the objective of intervention programs often includes discussion about increasing the number of women (or other underrepresented groups) in a given organization. When people talk about diversity, it enables particular logics that engender particular relationships. The implicit logic undergirding this talk assumes that increased diversity will enhance the ability of an organization to accomplish its overall objectives. Talk about diversity often embraces the notion that we live in an increasingly global and diverse society, and because the world has changed, the organization must match the diversity of the world in order to creatively and astutely meet the challenges of this increasingly pluralistic world.

Organizations that talk about promoting difference as diversity often take the stance that having more women and people from other underrepresented groups will enhance the organization. Specifically, because organizational stakeholders, consumers, employees, and other constituent groups are comprised of an ever-wider range of different people, the organization should represent the same diversity among its participants to be able to address the challenges associated with a pluralistic society. This can be thought of as a particular kind of *requisite diversity*. As environmental diversity increases, decision-making ability needs to align with the decisions of a more plural environment. For instance, in the university context, as the problems being addressed through research increase in complexity, the differences present among members of research teams must also increase.

Intervention programs that talk about difference as diversity have specific strategies for success. Inputs for this approach often center on aggressively increasing requisite variety by actively recruiting under-represented groups (such as women), emphasizing retention programs, enacting quotas, and providing diversity training for employees and managers. These efforts align with classic attempts of affirmative action but are aimed at improving outcome performance for the organization rather than overcoming past disadvantages to particular groups. Successful interventions are measured by identifying the number of women in the workplace or through other means, such as hiring quotas. In addition, success might also be marked by a reduction in issues associated with underrepresented groups and in decisions reflecting diverse concerns. The desired long-term outcome of this type of talk is a more diverse organization that is better suited to meet the challenges of an increasingly diverse and global society.

A good example of diversity-oriented talk can be found at PepsiCo. In 2001, as a part of a long-term emphasis on supporting the careers of women and culturally diverse individuals, PepsiCo mandated that half of all new hires must be women or minorities, and it began offering managers bonuses for recruiting and retaining such individuals (Yang, 2006). This diversity logic is reflected on PepsiCo's website: "We value the unique contributions and perspectives people of different culture bring to our business" (PepsiCo, 2009a). In addition, in talking about engaging diversity, PepsiCo (2009b) claimed the following on its website:

> In our business, diversity and inclusion provide a competitive advantage that drives business results. Our brands appeal to an extraordinarily diverse array of customers and they are sold by an equally diverse group of retailers. To truly understand the needs of our consumers and customers—and to succeed in the marketplace— PepsiCo must reflect that diversity in our supplier base and in everything we do.

This type of talk expresses a logic that correlates success with an organization that reflects the same diversity as the marketplace. This logic assumes that a more pluralistic organization will be better suited to meet the needs of diverse consumers and shareholders.

The vocabulary of diversity also appears in relation to the academic tenure and promotion process. While academic promotion processes have been exposed as contributing to sex inequality resulting in academic life being especially problematic for women (Martin, 1994), tenure is generally presented as a neutral, performance-based evaluation process for assessing the promotion of faculty. Its apparent neutrality, however, masks the inherent masculine, White, middle-class interests upon which the tenure process is based. Diversity programs at universities often focus on increasing the number of women successfully navigating the tenure process, and talk of diversity explicitly links increased demographic representation targets with positive benefits for the university. For example, Ohio State University claims that the specific goals of their initiative

> include retaining to promotion and tenure all of the current female assistant professors in STEM disciplines; achieving 30 percent representation by women among the 80 faculty hires anticipated over the next five years . . . hiring at least six new faculty who are either African-American, Hispanic, Asian-American or Native-American women; appointing at least three additional women as associate

deans and chairs; and increasing entrepreneurial activity by women by 50 percent. (Herbers, 2008)

The expressed aim of this diversity initiative is to "reach aggressively across our college boundaries and work together to create change that will make this a better institution" (Herbers, 2008). As such, the vocabulary of diversity encourages increasing the number of women in tenured university positions as the way to improve the quality of the organization as a whole.

Equity

Another way of talking about difference in organizations is to talk about *equity*. Based on principles of social justice, intervention programs that promote equity as an organizational objective typically view the development of differences among organizational participants as morally responsible. Equity is primarily concerned with the principle of fairness. Equity-oriented talk embraces differences among participants (e.g., between men and women), but then leverages those differences to arrive at a "fair" resolution. The exact policy advocated may not be exactly the same between each group, but each group is empowered to pursue stated goals in a manner that is most effective for them, so long as each group has an equitable opportunity for advancement. The implicit logic enabled by talk of equity is that different people deserve equal opportunities, and these opportunities should manifest in ways that are best suited for each constituent group.

Intervention programs that espouse equity engage in specific strategies to meet the morally obligated aim of fairness. Specifically, equity is enabled by inscribing fairness into organizational policies and practices and modifying formal and informal organizational structures to meet the moral standard of equity. For instance, ensuring equal pay for equal work or touting equity as the guiding principle for organizational policies may help instill fairness into a range of organizational practices. In addition, talk of a healthy work-life balance may culminate in the implementation of an equitable human resource policy of maternity leave for women and family leave for men. Outcomes of equity talk can include equal opportunities for hiring and promotion as well as the open expression of inequity. As a result, equity talk often engenders a culture of fairness embraced by members of organizations.

This logic of equity can be seen in the ways members of Case Western Reserve University talk about promoting difference. Receiving grant money from the NSF Advance initiatives to help promote the careers of women in the STEM disciplines, talk about support for women is framed as an issue of equity. For instance, their Provost recently said:

> Case Western Reserve University's institutional transformation is a result of a multifaceted initiative to promote a campus-wide culture characterized by equality, participation, openness and accountability— precisely the kind of collective effort we need to build upon to truly make this topic a constant, campus-wide imperative. (Case Western Reserve University [CWRU], 2008a)

This statement reflects an explicit promotion of a culture of fairness that coincides with the logic of equity—that equity is a moral obligation that is culturally based. Similarly, material explicating the various activities associated with the program focuses on equitable policies. For instance, Case Western's website states that the "university also has improved its overall institutional policies and benefits to encourage diversity" and that "the university offers automatic tenure extension, partner hiring and work release and has approved a paid parental leave policy" (CWRU, 2008a).

This vocabulary of equity, when associated with the tenure and promotion process, promotes a logic of fairness in all practices associated with tenure. For instance, the manner in which Case Western addresses tenure does not directly challenge the legitimacy or bias of the tenure process; rather, it ensures that the structure, access, and benefits of tenure are readily available to all faculty members. Consequently, talk of equity reestablishes the logics of existing organizational structures and seeks ways to work within the system by cultivating a climate of inclusion, participation, and flexibility. Overall, this type of talk promotes the logic that treating different faculty members equitably is a moral obligation.

Advancement

A third way of talking about initiatives that promote difference is through the goal of *advancement*. Advancement talk is a more politically active approach to difference intervention. This way of talking attempts to initiate difference by increasing the number of influential leaders. The objective of this approach is to hire and promote people of underrepresented groups to top-level positions in the organization.

These programs often emphasize that a more supportive environment for minorities can be attained if there are other organizational members of their same group in leadership roles. When advancement is focused on women, the implied logic of this talk is that men cannot best advance the interests of women and, therefore, women must be in positions to do so. In this sense, women need to be in positions to become role models so other women can learn, model, and advance.

Strategies that employ the logic of advancement tend to include targeted hiring practices and active promotion of underrepresented individuals to higher ranks in the organization. Active mentoring programs are also encouraged, along with developing networking opportunities to share insights, skills, and wisdom and provide ongoing support in a manner that only women can accomplish. Outcomes of these initiatives can be measured by an increased number of women in high and influential positions and improved performance among women and other underrepresented groups in the organization.

Advancement talk is evident at another NSF Advance program at the University of Michigan. This initiative sponsors active hiring and promotion of women to high levels of administration and encourages mentoring by senior faculty. For instance, in an effort to try to engage the goal of advancement, a committee was created, called STRIDE (Strategies and Tactics for Recruiting to Improve Diversity and Excellence), that "provides information and advice about practices that will maximize the likelihood that diverse, well-qualified candidates for faculty positions will be identified, and, if selected for offers, recruited, retained, and *promoted* at the University of Michigan" (University of Michigan, 2009, emphasis added). The program also emphasizes mentoring initiatives for senior faculty to coach and mentor women in the organization. For instance, its best practices for mentoring recommend that senior faculty "set up a series of informal lunches with new women faculty" to provide "a chance for them to say, 'Gee, I'm worried about X, Y, or Z,' and to get some feedback that might be helpful" (Waltman & Hollenshead, 2007, p. 4). The logic found in this type of talk is that "mentoring helps insure that no one—especially junior, women, and minority faculty—is allowed to 'fall through the cracks'" (p. 4). This program illustrates how talk of advancement directs attention to placing women in higher positions in order to then connect with and guide other women and how this will ultimately lead to improved careers for women overall.

This talk of advancement positions success in the tenure and promotion process at the University of Michigan as being accomplished through mentoring programs, informal lunches, and other activities outside of standard organizational interactions. The vocabulary of advancement that emerges with regard to promoting difference translates into talk of networking, official and unofficial ways of learning, and leveraging the ability of women already in key positions to assist newcomers in successfully navigating the existing tenure system.

Development

A final way of talking about intervening in organizations to promote difference is *development*. When initiatives are talked about in terms of development, the emphasis is on providing the necessary knowledge and skills to succeed within the existing organizational system. Talking about development as the goal of intervention typically involves discussion of how the acquisition of knowledge or pertinent skills will help members navigate current practices and processes to promote difference. Unlike some of the other ways of talking that emphasize gender identity, a discourse of development deemphasizes identity politics and relies exclusively on information sharing and training as the catalyst for promoting difference. The implied logic embedded within this form of talk is that underrepresented individuals lack the most knowledge and thus will benefit more from any information or improved skill development. In other words, a "rising tide raises all ships." The development approach is more evolutionary than revolutionary as it allows ample space for members of majority population groups to actively participate and attain the same benefits.

Strategies to implement a development objective place attention on information sharing and skills development that will help all organizational members navigate the existing organizational structures, policies, and practices. Emergent from these logics are training sessions and workshops as well as formal mentoring and coaching programs. The aims of these activities are to promote transparency in organizational practices, including the hiring and promotion process, as well as foster the development of necessary management or other skills to navigate such practices. The outcomes of these initiatives are marked by a more educated and skilled employee base, universal knowledge of policies and procedures, and enhanced transparency in hiring and promotion practices.

Intervention programs that sponsor development encourage learning-based activities. For instance, leaders at the University of

Colorado at Boulder talk about their program as a development initiative. Explaining that "a primary focus of the program is developing a cadre of effective leaders who will move both the institution and their particular fields of expertise forward" (LEAP, 2009), the initiatives at this institution involve workshops, training, and active mentoring programs for all faculty to enhance their ability to successfully navigate the tenure and promotion process. The aim is to work with all university faculty members to

> develop their leadership abilities and provide them with opportunities to apply those skills at the highest level of the university's administration. Provide coaching and team building skills to existing faculty members through training and supervised application. Provide faculty with skills they will model through their behavior in everyday interactions for members of their own departments. (LEAP, 2009)

This type of talk encourages all faculty members to participate in knowledge-building activities and exalts knowledge as a neutral resource to be acquired and used to successfully navigate organizational processes.

The vocabulary of development promotes a script that implicitly endorses the existing system by seeking to prepare underrepresented people for success through extensive coaching and leadership development. When considering the four ways of talking about intervention goals as they relate to the tenure and promotion process, each way of talking offers particular vocabularies of understanding and logics for action. While diversity initiatives seek to increase the numbers of women completing the process, equity initiatives seek to encourage fairness and transparency in the process. And advancement initiatives encourage mentoring relationships between members of underrepresented groups, while development talk sponsors training efforts for all members to successfully navigate the tenure system. These various discourses of difference each have consequences for organizations and organizational members.

❖ CONSEQUENCES OF INTERVENTION TALK

Exposing the talk of difference as diversity, equity, advancement, and development reveals embedded logics, consequent strategies, and outcome measures to assess the success of difference-oriented initiatives. Not only does talk constitute particular relational understandings of difference, but each way of talking about diversity goals is inherently political in that it obscures alternative ways of understanding organizational difference. Thus, evaluating the consequences of these particular ways of talking about intervention goals allows for consideration of what each perspective directs our attention to and subsequently away from. In this section, we first discuss the consequences of talking about intervention goals as a constitutive and relational activity that generates particular human responses to the logics embedded in the talk. We then focus on the politics of talk and consider potential implications for resistance and for intervention initiatives overall.

Different Actions

Because organizational talk constitutes relational understandings of organizational reality, we must first consider how the ways of talking about difference promote particular values or perspectives for relating to the world. These relational intentions simultaneously promote particular human responses that correspond with the logics embedded in talk. Thus, each way of talking about intervention goals has meaningful consequences for intervention activities. To help explicate these implications, we offer two dimensions through which to assess these respective discourses of difference: direction of action and objective of action. By *direction of action*, we refer to whether the activities of the initiative are focused on select groups or all groups associated with the organization. By *objective of action,* we refer to whether the goals of intervention activities are directed at promoting a better functioning organization or at more equitable numbers of underrepresented people or organizational procedures.

Figure 9.2   Intervention Actions

		Direction of Action	
		Specific Groups	*All Groups*
Objective of Action	*Organizational Performance*	Diversity	Development
	Equity in Numbers or Treatment	Advancement	Equity

First, consider the direction of action. When intervention goals are discussed, the logics embedded in talk direct attention toward either select groups or the collective organization. The discourse of *diversity*, for instance, emphasizes increasing the number of under-represented people, placing emphasis on particular groups. Actions are thus directed toward hiring and retaining particular groups of people. Similarly, the aim of *advancement* is to promote particular groups of people to top-level positions. While both discourses focus activities on particular groups, the embedded logics imply that these groups will have beneficial implications for the entire organization. Alternatively, talk of *equity* and *development* direct attention to all members of the organization. Whether ensuring that every organizational policy and practice promotes fairness or providing development opportunities for all organizational members, the embedded logic supports the notion that attention to all will benefit the careers of select groups. The relational understanding of difference is consequently understood as something that is enabled by focusing on the few for the benefit of the whole, or focusing on the whole for the benefit of the few. With regard to tenure and promotion processes, diversity and advancement talk encourages promotion and advancement of women or other underrepresented groups, while equity and development talk directs attention to all faculty members participating in the tenure processes.

Second, consider the objective of action. When the goals of difference initiatives are talked about, the logics that guide activities aim at either enhancing organizational performance or promoting fairness. For instance, the discourse of *diversity* attempts to improve organizational performance through enhanced decision-making. Key to this logic is that requisite variety resulting from increased difference results in more creativity and improved organizational actions. Similarly, a discourse of *development* promotes the dissemination of information and skills to ensure a more effective workforce. In both cases, attention is placed on enhancing the performance of the organization as a whole with improved careers for underrepresented groups as an additional benefit.

On the other hand, the discourses of *advancement* and *equity* attempt to promote fair representation or practice. While an *advancement* discourse emphasizes equal representation in positions of power, an *equity* discourse aims to ensure fair treatment and access to organizational opportunities. While not primarily concerned with the performance of the organization, the embedded logic in these forms of talk is that fairness in numbers or practice will ultimately promote the careers of women or other underrepresented groups. When talk of intervention occurs, a relationship with difference emerges that favors either organizational performance or fairness.

Overall, the methods of talking about intervention goals frame difference in various ways. These frames articulate scripts used by organizational members for talking about and understanding difference in particular ways. The meanings of the intervention become embedded in the language used to talk about it. As such, when the idea of promoting difference is expressed in any of these ways, it produces particular relationships with the intervention program itself as well as the organization implementing it.

Resisting Difference

Another consequence of talk about intervention programs is that each type of talk promotes particular politics. When intervention programs are conceived, a decision is made about how to talk about difference. Continued talk of difference in these particular ways naturalizes the discussion and can suppress important conflicts of meaning or reduce resistance by closing off opportunities to engage initiatives in different (and potentially more useful) ways. Thus, the conflictual moment of meaning-making about difference is not revisited or exposed. It remains hidden as talk of intervention continues to be discussed in one particular way. As talk continues, particular motivating logics become institutionalized as taken for granted ways to understand and engage difference in organizations. In much the same way as systematically distorted communication or discursive closure, any initial conflict in establishing meanings about the aims, strategies, or outcomes of intervention becomes lost, forgotten, or suppressed.

For instance, consider programs that talk about difference as *diversity*. Diversity talk establishes a relational understanding that different people in organizing practices will enhance organizational decision-making abilities. The problem being addressed by such an initiative is that the organization is not meeting the needs of a plural society and the logical solution is to make the organization more plural. This logic assumes that by simply including differences in decision-making, a more productive organization will emerge. The assumption embedded in this logic, and promulgated through talk of diversity, is that requisite variety among organizational participants will generate better decisions. Applying this logic to tenure and promotion processes appeals to the logic that more diversity will enhance the research or teaching capability of the university. However, these initiatives often do not provide organizational members with training on enhanced decision-making skills. Thus, this way of talking directs attention toward hiring individuals and away from potential challenges members in those organizations may face when engaged in decision-making processes.

As this way of talking about difference is continually repeated and discussed in a particular way, the logics embedded in the talk become institutionalized and communication about difference can become systematically distorted. Many feminists have critiqued this systematic distortion. Analogous to the feminist criticism of the "add women and stir" approach, Ashcraft and Allen (2003), for instance, explain that this approach is fundamentally flawed because regardless of the emancipatory intentions, scholarly research using this approach only serves to reify the very structures and processes that cultivate racial oppression in organizations in the first place. In this sense, the powerful interests of the organization become embedded in the logic and naturalized in the ongoing talk of diversity. These feminist critiques argue for a paradigm shift in how we understand organizational life by recognizing our personal constitutive role in the processes that place gender or race as a core constituent of all organizing processes. This perspective brings attention back to gender or race in attempt to initiate conflict of meanings hidden by distorted forms of communication.

Resistance can be challenging in these cases of diversity talk. As long as gender or race are seen as the logically necessary components adding value in the form of more creativity in decision-making, attention will be directed away from other potential issues. In other words, while the distorted logics re-presented in this way of talking focus on introducing more underrepresented people in an organization, it leaves these individuals to their own devices to succeed in the "normal" way of being in the organization. When considering this in relation to the tenure and promotion process, more underrepresented people may be hired into the organization; however, these individuals' careers may not be well supported once there. Thus, intervention programs that talk about difference as diversity may ignore existing organizational structures, policies, or practices as problems that directly impact the careers of women and other underrepresented groups. As a consequence, members of these minority groups (assumed to have different perspectives, attitudes, and values) either fail to succeed in constraining environments or conform to existing processes and practices that alter the values they may represent. As long as women and minorities are precluded from participation in the creation of meaning about difference, this way of talking about difference will obscure other ways of understanding the problem of difference.

Similar distortions and closures occur with intervention programs that talk about difference as equity. Talk of equity can hide important conflicts in meaning about difference, yet in different ways. For instance, equity attempts to address difference by rectifying the problem of unfair policies preventing people from getting the necessary opportunities to succeed, and it embeds the logic that by treating everyone in the organization equitably, the careers of women and other minority groups will be enhanced. Applying this logic to the tenure process appeals to the notion that equitable processes will enable more underrepresented peoples to attain promotion. Talk of equity subsequently directs attention toward abstract, neutrally represented organization policies and away from individual people or actual instances of discrimination, problematic practices, or other issues associated with the organization.

This attention on policies and practices, however, serves as a form of discursive closure. Specifically, the claim of neutrality and fairness closes off the ability to question the initiative, the policy in general, or the individuals who make the policy. Considering that all language use is political, any policy or practice—no matter how fair, objective, or neutral—will have some intended purpose. Acker (1991) reminded us of the problem of attempting to treat any organization policy or practice as a neutral concept by exposing their inherent gendered quality. If potentially problematic organizational processes, policies, and structures are treated as neutral, then this talk serves as a discursive closure deflecting and obscuring any discussion of any alternative organizational practices.

Resistance to equity-oriented intervention programs becomes challenging because any object of resistance disappears into a cloud of fair policies—how can one resist something that is considered fair for everyone? Thus, alternate ways of talking about and subsequently understanding difference are precluded from conversations that might better support women or minority groups. When considering this in relation to the tenure and promotion processes, it may become difficult for underrepresented people to talk about systematic distortions of meaning in the process because the process is considered fair for everyone. Overall, intervention programs that talk about difference as equity may fail to expose the complexities of gender, race, or class issues by effectively making talk of difference a neutral and unproblematic topic for discussion. As a consequence, the conflict inherent in the decision to talk of difference as equity may be left hidden and obscure.

Intervention programs that talk about difference as advancement can also serve to distort and close off conversation about alternatives.

Talk of advancement establishes a relational understanding that promoting a select few individuals will enhance the capabilities of many other similar types of people. Talk of this type distorts understandings by tacitly indicating that the problem of underachievement resides in current leadership groups who are unable to advance the needs of women or members of other minority groups. The logic embedded in this type of talk is that only underrepresented people can support their own interests. With regard to tenure, the logical solution of promoting underrepresented individuals into top leadership roles directs attention toward particular individuals and away from taken-for-granted aspects of the tenure process or promotion practice that may play a more significant role in precluding advancement. This tacit logic distorts talk of difference as it assumes minority leaders will have the capability, interest, or ability to act in ways that are significantly different from existing leaders.

This talk of advancement assumes that individuals promoted will succeed within the existing structures and system. However, it fails to consider issues often associated with women and minorities who reach top-level positions. For instance, Benschop and Doorewaard (1998) explained that treating members of a minority group as representatives of that minority group exacerbates the gendered quality of organizations. They explain that while being a "token" has some potential benefits, such as enhanced visibility, the drawbacks include having to take on many more responsibilities because they represent an underrepresented group. Women in these positions, they claim, "need to break a critical boundary and they need to match the profile of the ideal worker" and as such "women need to fight extra hard to prove their potential and to refute stereotypical prejudices about women and careers" (p. 793). The extra efforts of being a token present significant challenges for women and other minorities as they continue to be evaluated on the same criteria as represented groups; however, institutions often fail to take into consideration the additional efforts required of a token.

Resistance to talk of difference as advancement can, consequently, be quite challenging. Because advancement promotes underrepresented individuals to positions of influence, failure to succeed in these positions becomes an issue of individual failure rather than of larger systemic problems. Individuals, and not organizational practices or additional token work, become the focus of attention for any failure. When associated with the tenure process, women who have advanced through the tenure process may be precluded from talking about problems with the tenure process because stating that there is a problem with tenure is effectively admitting that other women cannot succeed in the organization. The closing off of conversations about other ways of understanding difference hides any inquiries or discussion about potentially problematic policies, practices, or individuals currently unsupportive or problematic for underrepresented people. Intervention programs that talk about advancement may place too much attention on minority leadership and hence ignore other existing problems that preclude the continued advancement of women or other minority groups.

Finally, consider programs that talk about difference as development. Development can also suppress important conflicts about ways of understanding difference. In particular, the logic embedded in this system of talk assumes women and other underrepresented individuals lack the knowledge to succeed in the existing system and that by providing organizational transparency and skills training to all organizational members these minority groups will use the enhanced knowledge to advance themselves. Applying this logic to the tenure process results in an understanding that more transparency and training about the promotion process will help underrepresented groups to better navigate the process. This type of talk constitutes difference in a way that positions individuals as not having the requisite skills to navigate the organization. The solution of providing information or training to all individuals assumes that women and underrepresented people lack the most knowledge or skills and will benefit proportionally more than others. This logic directs attention toward workshops and educational programs for all organizational members and away from any problems inherent in the existing organizational structures, policies, or practices. This type of talk distorts understandings of differences as a personal problem and not systematic in organizing practices. Thus, the continued efforts at training and education distort communication by treating the problem of difference as an individual issue. The powerful interests of the organization are not called into question, and discussion about other potential issues associated with difference is ignored.

In this way of talking about difference, resistance becomes a problem in much the same way that it does in advancement initiatives. Attention is directed toward individual skill and knowledge development while potentially problematic organizational structures, policies, and practices are ignored. With conversation about difference shifted toward individual ability and away from the organization, any question of an inability to succeed becomes either embraced as an issue that can be resolved through training or deferred as an individual's inability to succeed. The gender issue associated with this initiative becomes lost while promoting leadership, time management, and other "gender-neutral" positions. Similar to the consequences of talking of difference as equity, talk of skill development serves to suppress initial conflicts of meaning as to why women or other minorities are not found in senior leadership positions. When associated with the tenure process, individuals engaged in skills-based training might be precluded from talking about problems with the tenure process because the problems with the process are assumed to be problems with the individual and not the system, process, or organization.

Overall, each of these four ways of talking about difference serves a particular political function. Each discourse emphasizes certain ways of constituting difference while ignoring others. Further, as the goals of these programs continue to be expressed in terms of diversity, equity, advancement, and development, the logics that motivate action and preclude resistance become institutionalized. Power imbalances become embedded within the talk and are treated as the natural way of understanding difference in these organizations. Naturalization in these cases serves as a mechanism for distorting communication by precluding ways of talking that might generate alternative understandings. Other meanings of difference, actions to promote difference, or outcomes for the organization consequently fail to provide a clear and direct focus on the issue of gender (or race, class, or other characteristics that define underrepresented groups) and, thus, the initial issue of concern may become lost, unclear, or forgotten.

❖ CONCLUSION

Revealing the consequences of each way of talking is intended not to find one best way of talking about intervention goals, but to encourage many different ways of talking about enhancing work environments for women and other underrepresented groups. Despite our exploration of four distinct intervention discourses, in practice, talk is a dynamic and complex process that often crosses boundaries and combines many different ways of talking about difference. The main purpose of this chapter is to elucidate not just the implications of each distinct way of talking, but to advocate an informed, reflexive approach toward combining elements from multiple areas for more effective intervention programs. By directing attention to talk of intervention goals as a relationally constitutive and political activity we hope to show how different forms of intervention talk have meaningful consequences.

As universities and corporate organizations continue to talk about intervening in organizations to promote difference, we hope that organizational communication scholars will pay particular attention to how these initiatives talk about difference. In particular, we hope that the ways in which talk is practiced will be critiqued, revealing taken-for-granted logics embedded in the systems of language that enable particular human responses. Key to this discussion is recognition that one way of talking can preclude other ways of knowing, and continued talk of intervention in one particular way can distort or close off alternative relationships with difference. Talk about intervention is always a political decision; being aware that there are always alternatives is a powerful tool for enabling and engaging organizational difference. Thus, attending to difference only through training workshops or new hiring policies may direct attention away from hidden aspects of organizational policy or practice that hinder opportunities for women and minorities.

Overall, we recognize that all discursive processes generate tacit logics that tend to promote homogeneity and sameness rather than difference and creativity. Thus, we understand the complexity of attempting to promote difference in organizations. Any talk of difference potentially disrupts the stability desired from organizing systems. By attending to difference, however, we hope that disruptions, conflict, and dissensus will be encouraged and embraced rather than repressed, closed, or hidden. Thus, when attempting to intervene on behalf of difference, we encourage creativity in conversation by finding alternate ways of talking about intervention goals rather than simply taking for granted existing ways of talking.

❖ REFERENCES

Acker, J. (1991). Hierarchies, jobs, bodies: A theory of gendered organizations. In R. J. Ely, E. G. Foldy, & M. A. Scully (Eds.). *Reader in gender, work, and organization* (pp. 49–62). Oxford, UK: Blackwell Publishing.

Alvesson, M., & Willmott, H. (2002). Identity regulation as organizational control: Producing the appropriate individual. *Journal of Management Studies, 39*, 619–644.

Ashcraft, K. L., & Allen, B. J. (2003). The racial foundation of organizational communication. *Communication Theory, 13*, 5–38.

Barker, J. R. (1993). Tightening the iron cage: Concertive control in self-managing teams. *Administrative Science Quarterly, 38*, 408–437.

Benschop, Y., & Doorewaard, H. (1998). Covered by equality: The gendered subtext of organizations. *Organization Studies, 19*, 787–805.

Berger, P. L., & Luckmann, T. (1966). *The social construction of reality: A treatise in the sociology of knowledge.* New York: Random House.

Boden, D. (1994). *The business of talk: Organizations in action.* Cambridge, MA: Polity Press.

Case Western Reserve University. (2008a). Case Western Reserve University sees significant improvement in women in science and engineering. *CWRU News Center.* Retrieved January 15, 2009, from http://blog.case .edu/case-news/2008/11/03/womeninscience

Cooren, F., & Taylor, J. R. (1997). Organization as an effect of mediation: Redefining the link between organization and communication. *Communication Theory, 7,* 219–260.

Deetz, S. (1992). *Democracy in an age of corporate colonization: Developments in communication and the politics of everyday life.* Albany, NY: State University of New York Press.

Deetz, S. (2003). Reclaiming the legacy of the linguistic turn. *Organization: The Interdisciplinary Journal of Organization, Theory, and Society, 10,* 421–429.

Ely, R. J., & Meyerson, D. E. (2000). Advancing gender equity in organizations: The challenge and importance of maintaining a gender narrative. *Organization, 7,* 589–608.

Foucault, M. (1972). *The archaeology of knowledge* (A. S. Smith, Trans.). New York: Pantheon.

Gergen, K. (1994). *Reality and relationships: Soundings in social construction.* Cambridge, MA: Harvard University Press.

Giddens, A. (1984). *The constitution of society: Outline of the theory of structuration.* Cambridge, MA: Polity Press.

Grant, D., Hardy, C., Oswick, C., & Putnam, L. (Eds.). (2004). *The SAGE handbook of organizational discourse.* London: Sage.

Habermas, J. (1984). *The theory of communicative action: Vol. 1. Reason and the rationalization of society* (T. McCarthy, Trans.). Boston: Beacon.

Habermas, J. (1987). *The theory of communicative action: Vol. 2. Lifeworld and system* (T. McCarthy, Trans.). Boston: Beacon.

Herbers, J. (2008). Improved culture for women in science is target of NSF grant. *The Ohio State University News Room.* Retrieved February 18, 2008, from http://www.osu.edu/news/newsitem2147

Kuhn, T., & Ashcraft, K. L. (2003). Corporate scandal and the theory of the firm: Formulating the contributions of organizational communication studies. *Management Communication Quarterly, 17,* 20–57.

LEAP. (2009). About LEAP. Retrieved January 15, 2009, from http://www .colorado.edu/facultyaffairs/leap/

Martin, J. (1994). The organization of exclusion: Institutionalization of sex inequality, gendered faculty jobs, and gendered knowledge in organization theory and research. *Organization, 12,* 419–425.

National Science Foundation (NSF). (2009). ADVANCE: Increasing the participation and advancement of women in academic science and engineering careers (ADVANCE). *National Science Foundation.* Retrieved January 12, 2009, from http://www.nsf.gov/funding/pgm_summ .jsp?pims_id=5383

PepsiCo. (2009a). Diversity and inclusion. Retrieved January 15, 2009, from http://www.pepsico.com/Purpose/Diversity-and-Inclusion.aspx

PepsiCo (2009b). Supplier diversity. Retrieved January 15, 2009, from http://www.pepsico.com/Purpose/Diversity-and-Inclusion/Supplier-Diversity.aspx

Taylor, J. R. (1999). What is "organizational communication"? Communication as a dialogic of text and conversation. *The Communication Review, 3,* 21–63.

Tompkins, P. K. (1993). *Organizational communication imperatives: Lessons from the space program.* Los Angeles: Roxbury.

Trethewey, A. (2001). Reproducing and resisting the master narrative of decline: Midlife professional women's experiences of aging. *Management Communication Quarterly, 15,* 183–226.

University of Michigan. (2009). Committee on Strategies and Tactics for Recruiting to Improve Diversity and Excellence (STRIDE). Retrieved February 18, from http://sitemaker.umich.edu/advance/stride

Waltman, J., & Hollenshead, C. (2007). Creating a positive departmental climate: Principles for best practices. Retrieved February 18, 2009, from http://www.umich.edu/~advproj/BestPracticesReport_FINAL_Aug07.pdf

Weick, K. (1979). *The social psychology of organizing.* (2nd ed.). New York: McGraw-Hill.

Yang, J. L. (2006, September 4). Pepsi's diversity push pays off. *Fortune Magazine.* Retrieved January 19, 2009, from http://money.cnn.com/magazines/fortune/fortune_archive/2006/09/04/8384712/index.htm

10

Intersecting Differences

Organizing [Ourselves] for Social Justice Research
With People in Vulnerable Communities

Patricia S. Parker, Elisa Oceguera, and Joaquín Sánchez, Jr.

The focus of this chapter has evolved somewhat from our original intent. In the beginning, we wanted to produce a poly-
vocal, multilayered account of our research praxis and
community organizing with young women of color and other activists
in and near two public housing neighborhoods, Regal Gardens and
University Heights[1], located in the southeastern United States. We
were (and still are) sure that our ongoing project serves as a prime case
of how differences emerging from historically and politically produced social locations operate as a communicative apparatus for
enacting collective leadership and transformative change. Also, we
saw this as an opportunity to add to the growing literature on
engaged scholarship in organizational communication, emphasizing
the critical importance of co-constructed research involving "academics and practitioners." (See Ganesh, Zoller, & Cheney, 2005; Simpson
& Shockley-Zalabak, 2005; and the August 2008 special issue of the
Journal of Applied Communication Research.)

However, nagging questions about (re)presentation caused us to
redirect our focus to how we (Pat, Elisa, and Joaquín), as Black and

brown members of elite educational institutions, positioned (and still are positioning) ourselves to critically engage and do social justice work *with* members in vulnerable communities, such as those interpellated by discourses of poverty, criminality, and violence—and in many ways lacking in voice, status, and representation in the larger context of democratic process. Our concern is with what Michele Fine (1994) referred to as *working the hyphens*, ". . . the hyphen that both separates and merges personal identities with our inventions of Others . . . [invoking] a messy series of questions about methods, ethics, and epistemologies as we rethink how researchers have spoken 'of' and 'for' Others while occluding ourselves and our own investments, burying the contradictions that percolate at the Self-Other hyphen" (p. 70).

As we pondered what a polyphonic text would look like in *this context*, which falls squarely on *this* side of the hyphen in the academic-community collective, we began to question whether we could truly maintain solidarity, confidentiality, and respect for members in the community and refrain from mis/re/presenting or othering them in a scholarly (read *authors-as-experts*) academic book about organizing difference. We count ourselves among the burgeoning cohort of critical ethnographer/activists who not only reject "the positivist notion of an objective social science that produces value-free ethnographies . . . but also [work] the divide between the powerful and the powerless . . . [and attend to] the sentiments and struggles of various oppressed peoples" (Foley & Valenzuela, 2005, p. 217). Like many others doing activist research, we are aware that there are a range of choices to be made about the kind of critical ethnographers we aspire to be, the epistemologies we use, and the tales that are to be told by whom, to whom, and in what context (Foley & Valenzuela). We have discovered that deciding to present a narrative about our work for a traditionally academic venue (versus the various community-based spaces at which we have presented numerous times) seems to bring these choice points into sharp focus. However, it is precisely the interrogation of those choices that we believe can reveal some important insights about organizing difference in vulnerable communities.

So rather than focusing on the project, per se, we choose to present a prequel to this work. That is, we present our reflections about how we came to do this project in the first place and the questions it raised and continues to raise for us as academic researchers and social activists. How did or should we position ourselves to "do difference" in collaborative social justice work? How did or should we prepare ourselves to be able to move between theory and life on the ground (Fine & Weis, 2005), to create theory in the flesh (Moraga, 1981). What does or should collaboration look like? How, if at all, should this work be (re)presented in a traditionally academic text? We believe that this questioning of purpose, positionality, collaboration, and writing styles can reveal much about organizing differences that emerge at the intersection of academic-community research.

Following, we present an overview of the project and the theoretical framing that guided us in positioning ourselves as activist researchers in the traditions of a dialogic, decolonizing research praxis. Then, we present themes that emerged from our reflexive conversations held over the past two years that reveal the radical adjustments we made and are making to our identities as critical ethnographers and new members in a community doing social justice work together. We end the chapter with a discussion of some implications for research, theory, and practice.

❖ OVERVIEW OF THE PROJECT

We launched the project in June of 2007, as a collaboration of differently situated co-researchers: Pat, Elisa, and Joaquín as faculty and student activists with ties to three different academic institutions; seven high-school-aged women of color and their families from Regal Gardens and University Heights; other university students[2]; and three local community activists who lived or worked in the community. During this time, Pat was serving as faculty research mentor to Elisa and Joaquín, who were completing an eight-week research apprenticeship (EWRA) that was funded by a national foundation. Joaquín was finishing up his undergraduate studies at Eugene Lang College in New York, and Elisa was in her senior year at Humboldt State University in California. Both Joaquín and Elisa had been immersed in activism in their respective communities. Joaquín was working with youth in Brooklyn and had recently helped initiate a gang intervention group made up of youth activists in a high school in the Bushwick (Brooklyn) community. Elisa had been doing feminist activism work with women of color in California and participating in Accion Zapatista, a collective committed to theorizing and practicing Zapatismo—a movement emphasizing the relationships among action, dignity, and resisting neoliberalism locally.

Meanwhile, Pat's work in the area of race, gender, and leadership (Parker, 2001, 2003, 2005) was shifting toward questions of critical resistance as a form of leadership learning among girls and young women of color in vulnerable neighborhoods (Parker, 2006, 2007). She had begun volunteering in Regal Gardens and University Heights in 2004, organizing various events that engaged mothers and daughters in the neighborhoods in community dialogues about their gifts, assets, and wisdom. Also, she had been helping out with afterschool programs, establishing relationships with the youth, parents, and volunteer/activists in the neighborhood, and learning about its history. Regal Gardens and University Heights are among five low income housing projects that are virtually hidden in inconspicuous spaces throughout a predominantly White, prosperous city (PWPC) of about 50,000 residents in the southeastern United States. It is not unusual for even longtime residents to express surprise that there are "low income housing projects" in PWPC.

Regal Gardens and University Heights are situated in the historically African American part of town (called Southridge) in PWPC, just two blocks from the fashionable main street that forms the center of the city. The housing complexes were built on a sloping hill, separated by a rather busy street that slices through the neighborhood as a route to more affluent neighborhoods in the city. University Heights sits at the top of the slope and is made up of 15 newer duplex units with a large courtyard and playground in the center. Regal Gardens is much older, constructed in the early 1950s, and consists of four buildings with 10 two- and three-bedroom apartments that continue down toward the bottom of the slope and are surrounded by a thick wooded area. There is also a public park in the wooded area behind Regal Gardens where homeless people sometimes spend the night. There is a path that leads from the park to a small play area at Regal Gardens that people use as a shortcut to get into the center of town or elsewhere. For cars, however, there is one way in and one way out of each of the complexes, and police responding to residents' calls for assistance regularly lock down the entrances, restricting access in and out of the neighborhoods (while their "suspects" find many routes for escape through the park and other paths through the woods). A Family Resource Center (FRC), federally funded in part by a TANF (Temporary Assistance for Needy Families) block grant, is housed in one of the apartments in Regal Gardens, near the bottom of the slope. The FRC is managed by a director of community development who is responsible for planning and staffing community programs. An afterschool program for elementary children is offered relatively consistently throughout the school year and is generally well-attended. Other programs that target middle school youth and families are offered more sporadically and are less well-attended.

Some residents believe that there are tensions in Southridge because of differences that exist between African Americans who are homeowners and African Americans who live in public housing. There are signs of growing tensions related to other potential divides as well. For example, there is a growing Latino/Latina population in Southridge, and local activists are beginning to attend to possibilities and challenges for building African American and Latino/Latina coalitions in the area. Also, in University Heights and Regal Gardens, older, longtime residents have expressed concerns about the lack of activities that engage the older youth and young adults in the community.

Over time, conversations with residents and activists in University Heights and Regal Gardens about these issues engendered support for Pat's desire to create a youth-adult action project that would engage high-school-aged women in the neighborhood working with adult allies to design, implement, and evaluate community-based social change projects. A collective vision emerged to use this initial project as a model for creating similar ones across the Southridge community, engaging residents across the divides of race, class, gender, and age. It is a vision that follows the traditions of community work in African American and Latina women's history that focuses on empowerment, resistance, and civic activism (The Latina Feminist Group, 2001; Parker, 2005; Ransby, 2003; Springer, 1999).

In May 2007, Joaquín and Elisa arrived in PWPC to help launch the project, which eventually unfolded as eight weeks of intensive workshops and dialogues with the young women and adult allies and formed the basis for the existing ongoing collective project that builds on the strengths of people, place, the past, the present, and visions for the future. The young women created a group name to signal their increasing agency, their interests in creating connections as powerful young women in their community, and their willingness to speak *against* injustices and *for* the gifts and positive assets in the community. Currently, the group is one of two youth components of the nonprofit organization Pat created to help generate public and private funding for collective projects. As of this writing, the collective has completed three major community based projects: (a) the "Dumpster Project"—a campaign initiated by the youth to address problems with public works management and waste disposal in their community; (b) the first annual community street festival organized by a major portion of the youth and adults from both communities that focused on encouraging positive youth engagement and highlighting the positive assets of its residents; and (c) a community-based two-day conference on intergenerational organizing for social justice with communities in resistance, co-organized with students from two nearby universities. In addition, the collective has co-produced numerous internal texts, such as our regular meeting agendas, interpretive notes, and visual/media mappings of our critical engagement with various community concerns about state and institutional power (including a rather dramatic meeting with the local police chief). Also, we have done public performances that were jointly created and enacted by a cross section of project members, including presentations to a sociology class on human rights and a women's studies class on leadership at two nearby universities, as well as a presentation to the local town council. As of this writing, the collective is organically shifting in size, make-up, and geography. We are planning summer workshops to engage rising ninth graders and other youth who recently moved into the neighborhood to help organize the next street festival and intergenerational conference. Also, new collective projects are underway that connect the community to others in the region. These projects relate to creating "harm free zones" in neighborhoods that do not rely on police intervention for resolving interpersonal and state-based conflict.

❖ THEORETICAL FRAMING OF THE PROJECT

Before the initial project launch in late June 2007, we engaged in a series of theoretically informed conversations among the three of us and in weekly roundtables at the Family Resource Center with the three other adult allies who lived or worked in the University Heights and Regal Gardens community. End-of-school activities precluded direct participation in these initial conversations by any of the young women. However, they were aware that a new youth project was about to be launched that would include the entire cohort of high-school-aged young women who lived in the two housing projects. (All ten were invited; seven were able to actively participate in the eight-week summer training.) The roundtable discussions focused on the community's needs and our varying ideas about leadership in the community. From these discussions, we identified an overall goal that would frame our collaboration with the young women: youth and adult allies working for positive community change. The initial guiding question was as follows: What does "positive community change" mean to individuals with varying perceptions of community, diverse experiences and histories, and distinct gifts?

Framing Concepts

Our conversations with the community allies were informed by a set of framing concepts that we believed were important for developing a critical/decolonizing praxis that would constitute our collaborative research with youth and adult allies in the University Heights-Regal Gardens community. We drew upon the writings of Louis Althusser (1971), Antonio Gramsci (1971), and Michel Foucault (1979, 1980) to envision a rather eclectic but useful framework for imagining a political praxis of resistance and transformation in low income communities of color. With these writings, we explored concepts of power, knowledge, hegemony, praxis, and ideology. A critical component linking these concepts is the dialectical relationship (political struggle) between power and domination on the one hand, and resistance and transformation on the other (Mumby, 1997). Recognizing the coercive control of state power in low income communities of color, we incorporated theoretical lenses that allowed us to imagine a political praxis of community-based resistance and transformation.

Althusser's (1971) (neo-Marxist) theory of ideology provided a starting point because it articulated a view of state power as ideological apparatuses (e.g., discursive/social structures) that function to further the agendas of capitalism and neoliberalism through various and pervasive means (including complicity by individual actions). For example, the neoliberal discourse of an "authoritarian" state to solve "social problems," perpetuated, for instance, through the media and state agencies, interpellates a particular understanding of "welfare mothers" as threats to capitalist elites (see Lubiano, 1992). This view of power exposes the raced and classed subtext of bureaucratic social policy implementation in low income communities of color where "Citizen-clients are subject to processes of dehumanization and social control [and] not as undifferentiated recipients of state intervention" (Naples, 1998, p. 305).

Althusser's overdeterministic view of state power provides only a partial view of the domination/resistance dialectic because it limits the possibilities for individual or collective resistance. Gramsci's more dialectical/organic understanding of power brought both power and resistance into view. Mumby (1997) clearly articulated this dialectic, especially as it was derived from a particular view of hegemony and its implications for organizational communication:

> Gramsci's concept of hegemony—as framed within his philosophy of praxis—. . . [positions] social actors [neither] as unwitting dupes who unreflectively produce the status quo, nor as individuals who, by virtue of their marginalized status, can create a pristine space of resistance that subverts the dominant order. Gramsci's philosophy of praxis recognizes both the possibilities for social change *and* the

tenacity of the dominant hegemony that resists such change. In this sense, Gramsci's notion of hegemony sets up the critical problematic not of uncovering the truth that underlies an ideologically constructed reality, but rather of identifying *"the mechanisms and procedures by which truth and true realities are produced and imposed (Cocks, 1989, p. 83)."* (Mumby, 1997, p. 366, italics added)

In a 2007 interview, Stuart Hall elaborated a similar view, but emphasized the importance of linking the mechanisms and procedures of hegemony to particular historical junctures, requiring an analysis of culture and the state and a broader sense of what politics is about (Macabe, 2007, p. 24). Hall's references to a broader sense of politics points to the Gramscian tensions between the public and the private domains of civil society and the struggle for the transformation of the "common sense" of the state into the "good sense" of the people (Davidson, 2008, p. 72). Here, for our purposes, Foucault's (1979, 1980) view of power/knowledge and resistance is instructive. Foucault (1980) contended that "there are no relations of power without resistances; the latter are all the more real and effective because they are formed right at the point where relations of power are exercised . . . hence, like power, resistance is multiple" (p. 142). In this context, power functions not simply as ideological domination of one group by another, but is "a dynamic conception of the lived relations of social groups and the various struggles that constantly unfold between and among these groups" (Mumby, 2001, p. 598).

These concepts helped us imagine ourselves as *organic intellectuals* (Gramsci, 1971) in the struggle for social transformation *with* the youth and adult allies at Regal Gardens and University Heights. We saw our roles as helping members of vulnerable communities see their own knowledge, strength, and leadership in constructing models for social change. We were and are positioning ourselves to see the circuits of power (Clegg, 1989) coursing through the lived experiences of the people in the community and joining them in naming and contesting the mechanisms and procedures by which truth and true realities (e.g., the story of this community) are produced and imposed.

Decolonizing Research Praxis

The power/resistance dialectic supports our commitment to a decolonizing/participatory action research praxis with the youth and adult allies at Regal Gardens and University Heights (Bishop, 2005; Fine, Weis, Weseen, & Wong, 2000; Freire, 2000; Smith, 1999,

2005). Decolonizing research represents a challenge to the institution of academic research; it is a "purposeful agenda for transforming . . . the deep underlying structures and taken-for-granted ways of organizing, conducting, and disseminating research and knowledge (Smith, 2005, p. 88). Traditionally, research has been a prime medium for the exploitation of the other for the benefit of the hegemony of autonomous individualism (Fine et al., 2000). Paraphrasing Said (1978), Smith (2005) asserted that research is "a corporate institution" that has made statements about indigenous peoples, "authorizing views" of us, "describing [us], teaching about [us], settling [us] and ruling over [us]" (p. 88). Thus, in keeping with a decolonizing research praxis, we knew that our approach called for a framework that afforded an analysis of our own complicity with oppression and demanded that we remain accountable to all involved in the research (Bishop, 2005). Our personal histories, prior research, and educational experiences compelled us to want to do activist research, to move beyond the confines and constraints of the academy, and to work *with* community members in the struggle for social justice. According to Hale (2001), activist research does the following:

> a) helps us better understand the root causes of inequality, oppression, violence, and related conditions of human suffering; b) is carried out, at each phase from conception through dissemination, in direct cooperation with an organized collective of people who themselves are subject to these conditions; c) is used, together with the people in question, to formulate strategies for transforming these conditions and to achieve the power necessary to make these strategies effective. (p. 13)

In keeping with this approach, we wanted to establish and refine a research protocol where both participant and researcher shared lived experiences and standpoints en route to a shared praxis. Participatory action research (PAR) provides such a protocol; however, we were (boldly) interested in moving beyond the varieties of action research to a more critical interpretive activist PAR that emphasized a continuous process of dialogic practice and reflection (Kemmis & McTaggart, 2000).

Thus, in weekly conversations among the three of us throughout the summer of 2007, our goal was to engage in focused and applied learning about doing decolonizing, activist research and to keep at the forefront questions about our own complicity with oppression. We found inspiration in the varied critical/interpretive perspectives in Denzin and Lincoln's (1994, 2000, 2005) *Sage Handbook of Qualitative*

Research, especially those that provided insights about doing PAR as activist research. Also, we immersed ourselves in works by postcolonial and critical feminist scholars whom we believed had forged a path for us to follow, including Smith (1999, 2005), Paulo Freire (2000), bell hooks (1984), Chela Sandoval (2000), Patricia Hill Collins (1998), Brenda J. Allen (2004), Gloria Anzaldúa (1987), and Audre Lorde (1984).

We were especially influenced by the dialogic approach pioneered and practiced by the social theorist and Gramscian intellectual, Paulo Freire. Freire (2000) argued that absolute wisdom or absolute ignorance are nonexistent because all humans possess knowledge and, thus, possess power. Researchers partnering with community members, then, must be catalysts for the development of knowledge across all races and classes because hegemony can silence the intellect of marginalized people. Freire suggested that a collective ideology originates from a praxis that creates a discourse embodying all aspects of the culture produced while cognizant of the present reality. Out of the discourse evolve "culture circles," which express the knowledges developed, thereby creating an infrastructure for what we call *critical circles* that merge the experiences of all participants and create a new culture; namely, an oppositional culture, a third space.

At the same time, we recognized that whatever our desire to equalize the power and create dialogic relationships in our community-based research collective, we (Elisa, Joaquín, and Pat) are still yet embodied with our statuses, experiences, and knowledge emerging from being members of élite universities. As Valerie Janesick (2000) noted, "qualitative researchers have open minds, but not empty minds" (p. 384). A starting point for decolonizing engaged research, then, is to interrogate our identities as researchers as we prepare for and take on collaborative projects with vulnerable communities. In the next section, we present an analysis of reflections about our engagement in social struggle with the people of Regal Gardens and University Heights and the questions it raised and continues to raise for us as academic researchers and social activists.

❖ BECOMING MULTIPLY POSITIONED TO DO DIFFERENCE IN COLLABORATIVE SOCIAL JUSTICE WORK

In this section, we draw upon our experiences engaging in this project and the radical adjustments made to our identities as researchers and new members in the community in order to move forward in a collective manner toward social change. In doing so, we attempt to answer the clarion call from Fine and Weis (2005):

> Whether in a school, a prison, a neighborhood, a cultural arts center, a community center, a religious institution, or wherever, we invite researchers/writers to travel between theory "in the clouds," so to speak, and the everyday practices of individuals living in communities as they (and we) negotiate, make sense of, and change their/our positionalities and circumstance. (p. 68)

Elisa: Creating Spaces of Encounter

Community-based research raises questions of positionality. Research itself cannot be neutral or objective. As Donna Haraway (1988) articulated so well, positionality, not objectivity, allows us to engage in the active emergence of situated knowledge. She argued that, "situated knowledges require that the object of knowledge be pictured as an actor or agent, not as a screen or a ground or a resource" (p. 592). As a researcher, a person is automatically authorized and gains some form of power similar to that of the academic in the university. I came to this project hoping to complicate this notion of authorized researcher and to practice what it means to be a public intellectual. My thinking was that my own position in this project would be validated through the academic institution only as long as I identified as an academic/researcher/scholar/student; however, when I identify as a member of a marginalized community and as a subject of controversial research, I lose the accoutrements of a scholar. In order for the project to truly have engaged with the community of women of color, I had to reposition myself constantly. I had to tell my own story, as I hoped the young women would tell theirs. I had to be placed in a vulnerable position in order for the young women to feel comfortable with me, the space, and, most critically, to feel like *they* can claim this project as their own.

During the summer of 2007, we used testimony as a method that would facilitate the emergence of situated knowledge in our research collective. Smith (1999) described the use of testimony as ". . . a form through which the voice of a 'witness' is accorded space and protection" (p. 144). We thought it was crucial to incorporate some form of testimony into this project, recognizing that many young women of color are rarely asked to give their opinion, tell their stories, or share their experiences. *Testimonios* is a particular method of testimony used by the Latina Feminist Group (2001) to theorize across the various Latina identities (*Latinidades*) and experiences. They argued that through this method, complexities of *Latinidades* are revealed, refuting any notions of a homogenized Latina identity or experience. Their use of *testimonio* provides an example of the development of an academic political praxis.

Throughout the summer, we held several testimonio sessions—some in private spaces with the young women and myself, and others emerging during the weekly public education workshops, when one or more members of the collective felt compelled to bear witness to some experience. Each of these spaces of encounter provided a safe space where we got to know each other. In some of the sessions, the young women were surprised at each other's achievements and knowledge, commenting, "You did that?" Also, they expressed awe at the work and struggle of others in the community. One thing I learned from this process is that when you learn something from someone—gaining knowledge that they have that you didn't have—you build a kind of shared respect. Outside of that space, a lot of women are not taken seriously. We learned from each other and recognized the knowledge that we had as powerful. I remember thinking about the young women as activists, and I still do, knowing that the process of sharing our emerging knowledge is evidence of our subjectivities and agency.

Emerging from my own experiences as a Xicana organizer is a penetrating question of the power of difference and engagement between women in a community of color. As young activists in our communities, we as women of color are constantly stigmatized and ridiculed by both dominant culture and our own communities. This lack of belonging informs our stance. We continuously become the other/outsider to those who formulate dominant noninclusive structures. In shaping our own spaces, I argue that we are able to theorize our own situated knowledge that gives certain definitions to resistance. My hopes were to share with others my own experience as a young woman of color trying to discover how to resist hegemonic forces through active engagement in oppositional cultural practices and situated knowledge of my lived experience. During my undergraduate and graduate studies, I remained devoted to actively engaging in my passions outside of the classroom that linked my scholarship to public uses. Through my participation in Acción Zapatista, I contribute to various projects, demonstrating a commitment to facilitating spaces of cross border/ transnational and transgenerational sharing of knowledge that emerges at the grassroots outside of formal institutions[3]. Taking Zapatismo and applying it to the work we do in our communities allows us to engage in a politics of listening (Callahan, 2005).

This is what we intended to do in the testimonio sessions—encounter our differences and engage them as a way to theorize our

situation as women of color. In this process of encounter, we were creating relationships in which at first I struggled with my outsider status in the Regal Gardens and University Heights communities. I
realize now that these spaces also generated bonds between individuals and, most important, between communities in struggle, as we
learned greatly from one another. Through this engagement, we were
able to communicate to one another our struggles and knowledge.
This step later enabled us to reflect and take seriously the social justice
strategies that were already rooted in these communities. Each of
these spaces (the *testimonios* and the popular education workshops)
worked together to provide us with facilitation and research skills
that put theory into practice by creating a medium through which
community-based knowledge was generated.

Pat: Getting the Colonizer Out of my Head

> For we have, built into all of us, old blueprints of expectation and
> response, old structures of oppression, and these must be altered at
> the same time as we alter the living conditions which are a result of
> those structures. For the master's tools will never dismantle the
> master's house. As Paulo Freire (1970) shows so well in *The Pedagogy
> of the Oppressed*, the true focus of revolutionary change is never
> merely the oppressive situations which we seek to escape, *but that
> piece of the oppressor which is planted deep within each of us, and which
> knows only the oppressors' tactics, the oppressors' relationships.* (Audre
> Lorde, 1984, p. 117, italics added)

This project is one that, in some respects, flips the script of my
experience engaging hegemonic culture. Throughout my life, I have
experienced predominantly White (primarily educational) institutions
as an "outsider within" (Collins, 1990), developing a double consciousness to learn the language of success in predominantly White
educational systems while remaining self-defined and connected to
Black cultural community contexts that keep me grounded. However,
as I began to join the residents of Regal Gardens and University
Heights in the ongoing struggle of (re)claiming citizenship, agency, and
power and creating meanings of critique and resistance, I had to recognize the colonizer in me—the moments when my actions, words,
thoughts, presence, and absence might be reproducing the deep structure power arrangements that reproduce the injustices that surface
daily in the lives of people in low income communities of color. This
phrase, *getting the colonizer out of my head*, came to me as I reflected on
feelings of frustration I had when events I tried to coordinate in the

community didn't unfold as I had planned, but through some alternative, usually spontaneous way, the ultimate goals were met. I started wondering if my expectations about how things *should* go were my unconscious attempts to impose a universal (colonizing) model of organizing onto our efforts. Also, this frustration seemed to bring to the forefront my status in a relative position of power at an elite university where the most visible and sustaining relationship to local communities of color is through their roles as laborers in its dormitories, cafeterias, and grounds. So one pressing concern for me as we began the collaboration was how to negotiate the aspects of my positionality that simultaneously connect me with and disconnect me from the residents of Regal Gardens and University Heights.

This concern caused me to reflect on my own standpoint about negotiating spaces of difference and what it has taught me about living through and with contradiction. In some ways, it began as a set of questions and answers I developed for myself when, as an eight-year-old girl, I experienced school integration in Atkins, Arkansas, a small, rural southern town, sixty miles west of Little Rock[4]. In 1966, I was among several African American students who integrated Atkins Elementary and Junior High School. In a plan for gradual integration, a few African American students had enrolled in the high school two years earlier, and one of my brothers and two of my sisters had been among them. My memory of the intense emotional climate of that time is firmly entrenched in my mind because of the tragic death of my 16-year-old third cousin who went missing on a warm April evening in 1964. My parents and others had gathered at the two-room segregated Black school to discuss the planned integration. There was some controversy in the Black community as to whether it was safe to send the children to the White school. Reports that Whites in the town were vowing that their children "would never attend school with niggers," naturally created uneasiness and apprehension. However, most parents, including my own, felt it imperative to support the planned integration. The meeting was interrupted by someone bringing news that my cousin, Pete, was missing and that his clothes had been discovered on the banks of a nearby pond where he frequently went swimming. Ironically, it was a White neighbor who used his fishing boat to assist in the search for Pete's body and subsequently dove into the pond to bring his body to shore where his parents, those who had been at the school meeting, and other townsfolk, both Black and White, stood in silent shock. In that moment, the community stood together not as people divided by racial politics, but as a community connected at a profound level of humanity, understanding, and compassion.

At five years old, I was in bed by the time my parents returned home that night. I learned of Pete's death from an older sister who awakened me as she whispered the news through her tears of grief. In my memory of that time, the thoughts of my cousin Pete's untimely death and the transition from my neighborhood school to the White school trigger the same feelings of loss, uncertainty, and apprehension.

Two years later, during my first days at the White school, came the opportunity to begin working through those emotions in context. When someone came to the door of my third grade classroom, pointing, counting, and announcing to my teacher, "OK, you have two," I knew they were referring to my Blackness and that of the other African American third grader in the room. And when my new White friend followed the advice of her old White friend that she shouldn't play with me, it seemed obvious that they, too, were referring to my Blackness. The confusion and hurt I felt in response to those events were real, but yet undefined. Somehow, I sensed at age eight that these (in retrospect) seemingly mundane events were signals for what this strange place represented for me: *outsider; object; Black.* Yet those signals stood in such sharp contrast to what I experienced in my own familiar eight-year-old world. That world was one in which I had begun to think of my family and my community as a wonderful collection of personalities; where I had come to view myself as special as I competed with my 12 brothers and sisters for the attention of my parents and siblings. Most of all, I had come to see life as being filled with hope and infinite possibilities. There was a sense among many of the families in my community that this generation of children would soar to new heights of achievement, and they did everything they could to ensure that their children had educational opportunities, no matter what the sacrifices.

So in my eight-year-old mind, I had the knowledge of my concrete, lived experience grounded in life with my family and my community. And I had the reality of some intense negative emotional responses I was experiencing as I interacted with the teachers and students at the White school. Those two realities stood in stark contradiction. Out of necessity, I worked through those contradictions by developing a set of premises for which I was the reference point. I began with the answers—I *knew* who I was—the strangers in my new world had to learn who I was; and from their interactions, they obviously did not have a clue. From that personal truth, I developed a posture of critical questioning based on the fundamental premise that in experiencing the world, it is possible, and perhaps even probable, that a particular social context will be in contradiction to my concrete experience. It is up to me to determine the salience of my concrete experience in the situation. But my experience gives me the vision to see the contradictions, gaps, and unstated assumptions that make a particular social context work to fulfill a particular ideology or interest.

So it is this stance of critical questioning that guides my work with the residents of Regal Gardens and University Heights and keeps me conscious of how connections and differences surface in our organizing. There are aspects of my identity(ies) that simultaneously connect me to and disconnect me from the residents. I am a Black/female/tenured associate professor/single mother/with an elite educational background/of low income family of origin/middle-class income/with access to privilege. What I have learned and am learning is that I must take seriously the premises of taking a dialogic/decolonizing approach to this research. Frank (2005) was persuasive in his arguments about how a dialogic/decolonizing praxis unfolds in research when he said that "the core ethical demand of the [dialogic] relationship is that neither party ever *finalizes* the other (p. 967, italics in the original). For me, this means not creating final categories about what organizing or resistance looks like, but remaining open to influence by others in the community and being willing to engage in critical dialogues about our activities.

Smith (2005) asserted that a decolonizing, localized critical praxis can work if the goals of critique, resistance, struggle, and emancipation are not treated as if they have "universal characteristics that are independent of history, context, and agency" (p. 229). In our work, we have attempted to take a decolonizing approach to dialogue that is open ended, goes beyond mere perspective taking, and seeks to understand what is being created intersubjectively in that moment. "Am I missing something?" is a question that guides our meaning-making processes, especially if there is some conflict or point of tension. Also, we directly engaged the youth about "limit situations" (Freire, 1982): the naming and interpretation of the material consequences of raced, gendered, and classed spaces that they must negotiate at school and other public institutions.

Joaquín: Bridging Difference, Building Alliance

I began this project much like my ancestors, the Nahua people, began their journey when they migrated from the northern states of México (the present day U.S. Southwest) to the South (presently, the central-basin of México). One of our historical accounts says the Nahua were a people born of the earth. My ancestors' gods demanded that they migrate from the north to the south to search for fertile lands where they could grow food to sustain the growth of their civilization. Similarly, I made a seasonal migration from the North, New York, to the South, North Carolina, in search of fertile land where I and my people could grow. What does *growth* look like for a conscious and socially accountable world citizen? How can I and others, *we*, grow together? I traveled from New York City with a desire to work in "marginalized" communities in the south, to continue my education of understanding, firsthand, the issues that communities of color deal with in our society and find ways to connect and deepen relationships across difference.

As an individual who is not an African American woman, nor a member of the Regal Gardens and University Heights community—as a Xicano—how do I negotiate my role in a research endeavor that looks at community activism and social change for and by a group of African American women? As a queer Xicano who grew up in a homophobic Chicano culture, I learned how to survive. As a working-class Xicano at a predominantly wealthy, White, and colorblind college, I learned how to survive. As neither "top" nor "bottom" in a sexuality that often operates on heteronormative values, I know how to survive and to claim my queer positionality. As an activist and scholar at an elite institution that reproduces many injustices in society, I learned ways to intervene and redirect resources into marginalized communities to build political power indigenous to those communities.

Through PAR methodology, I wanted to answer the pertinent questions about what it means to be an activist researcher, a member of multiple communities, a close ally to the causes of specific communities, and what it means to do so while maintaining a center that honors the many elements of my personal identity. Linda Tuhuwai Smith (1999), in *Decolonizing Methodologies*, sums up this entanglement for indigenous researchers:

> There are a number of ethical, cultural, political, and personal issues that can present special difficulties for indigenous researchers who, in their own communities, work partially as insiders, and are often employed for this purpose, and partially as outsiders, because of their Western education or because they may work across clan, tribe, linguistic, age, and gender boundaries. Simultaneously, they work within their research projects or institutions as insiders within a particular paradigm or research model, and as outsiders because they are often marginalized and perceived to be representative of either a minority or a rival interest group. (p. 5)

On June 21, 2007, when we began our collaboration with the activists and young women from Regal Gardens and University

Heights, I helped to focus our events on deconstructing and reconstructing a safe and critical space that previously did not exist. This space was constructed through self-reflection and allowed us to identify the dynamics that encouraged, worried, disturbed, and enlightened us as individuals. Before we could move forward in our activism to change the community, it was imperative that we unify as a collective, build collective-esteem, and tap into our personal strengths to contribute to the process of coming in to our own skins as members of an activist and research collective.

We created this space by facilitating political education workshops. We created multimedia presentations about youth and women activism and analyzed and discussed the philosophies, issues, activities, and key players in the media we studied. We asked ourselves to identify the ways in which we could relate. In keeping with PAR methods, it was important that we maintained a space where all participants felt their interactions and contributions to the discussion were valid and carried equal weight. Only in such a space would we be able to go deeper in our thinking about ourselves, each other, and our collective vision for change. Rather than impose definitions of *history* and *community*, we utilized collaborative activities to draw from our personal funds of knowledge. We facilitated workshops to help map our collective understandings of history and community. We asked ourselves to draw upon our own experiences and historical perspectives; we analyzed the areas where our individual narratives overlapped; from our similarities, we produced a collective narrative while honoring the tenderness of our differences.

The environment we created allowed the participants to engage in critical conversations. As a queer Xicano, I engaged in the discussions with others and asked critical questions of myself. In order for me to shuttle from my space of difference to a space of alliance and political power building with people that were "unlike" me, I needed to embrace and utilize what Gloria Anzaldúa (1987) called *la (my) consciencia de la mestiza (a mestiza consciousness)*. I am neither indigenous, European, nor African, but all of these traditions and cultures combined, fastened historically and anatomically. At first, recognizing difference within myself and among others felt threatening. Countless times I asked myself, "How is my gender expression, my masculinity, implicated in my contributions to this collective of women working for social change? How is my presence silencing others in this work?" Or, "Is the language I use to express my ideas and political positions understood by the others I am working with on this project?" "Does my sexuality pose a challenge to others to build solidarity with me?

How and when do I address these questions?" All of these questions challenged my positionality. If I were to bridge difference and build alliances with the women in Southridge, I needed to ask these self-reflexive questions, recognize them, and consciously move forward. The moments I felt too masculine, I scaled back my masculinity and allowed my body and mind to reflect on my history with these questions. I allowed myself to examine the past and present and to center myself with a recognition of the chaotic beauty of humanity. With this deeper spiritual awakening of my humanness and love, I forged ahead.

❖ DISCUSSION

Positionality, collaboration, and narrative representation are three important issues that confront critical activist ethnographers (Foley & Valenzuela, 2005). In this chapter, we have presented our reflections about how we negotiated these issues as academic researchers and social activists collaborating with youth and adult residents in a vulnerable community. In the sections that follow, we reveal some themes emerging from our reflections that we believe are instructive for organizing difference.

Do the Self-Reflexive Work and Use it to Transform Silence Into Language and Action

We argue that a crucial aspect of organizing (ourselves) to do difference is reflecting on our own positionality in relation to the collective with whom we are engaged in the struggle for social justice. We are not advocating simply inserting biographical information into a text. Rather, what we are describing is a route to co-producing knowledge situated in a collective with multiple histories, varied (self/othered/invented) identities, and diverse political standpoints. Critical reflexivity is a transformative process that recognizes that "it is not difference that immobilizes us, but silence" and that we must transform silence into language and action (Lorde, 1984, p. 44). The silences that hyphenate self and other are sustained through unarticulated fear, and "each of us draws the face of [our] own fear—fear of contempt, of censure, or some judgment, or recognition, of challenge, of annihilation" (Lorde, 1984, p. 40).

As researchers engaging people in vulnerable communities, it is especially important that we probe the silences behind investigative, interpretive, and writing practices that invent "subjugated Others as if they were a homogeneous mass (of vice or virtue), free-floating and severed from contexts of oppression, and as if we were neutral trans-mitters of voices and stories" (Fine, 1994, p. 74). The transformation of silence into language and action is an act of self-revelation, and it begins a process of co-creating situated knowledge. However, situated knowledge cannot be produced by an individual; instead, it is rooted in a collective identity, a community (Haraway, 1988). It begins with deep reflection by persons conscious of their active engagement across difference becoming aware of the many silences to be broken.

Search for Compelling Ways to Co-Construct Research

> I would emphasize the importance of retaining the connections between the academy of researchers, the diverse indigenous commu-nities, and the larger political struggle of decolonization. . . . This is not to suggest that such a relationship is, has been, or ever will be har-monious and idyllic; rather, it suggests that the connections, for all their turbulence, offer the best possibility for a transformative agenda that moves indigenous communities to someplace better than where they are now. (Smith, 2005, p. 88)

This quotation aptly sums up the critical importance of co-constructing research with vulnerable communities. It also points to the difficulties of making such connections. Fine (2007) observed that, by widening the base of researchers, it is inevitable that "differences of interpretation, critique, vulnerabilities, and conflict will erupt" (p. 466). Therefore, we must craft strategies for how "these differences, both healthy and troubling, are resolved or allowed to flourish . . ." (Fine, p. 466). In our work, we have offered compelling ways for making those connections: namely, encouraging testimonios and other spaces of encounter; participating in relational development; and dialoguing with people about the "limit situations" in which they navigate their lives (Fine, Weis, 2005, p. 66).

Critique and Redefine What Forms Representation Should Take in Academic Settings

The process for presenting decolonizing participatory action research for publication brings up questions of validity, reliability, and repre-sentation. Work produced for the academy must coincide with certain academic standards, whereas research for the community must appeal to the betterment of the participants. It is the latter that PAR researchers adhere to: "Has the research produced knowledge that helps to resolve the problem, to guide some transformation, which formed part of the research objectives from the start? Is the knowledge useful? If so, to whom?" (Hale, 2001, p. 15). Action research findings that may serve the betterment of a particular community do not necessarily have the kind of generalizability sought by traditional academic research. However, such findings are no less important for a community seeking to find self-defined pathways to transformation. Ultimately, PAR researchers in vulnerable communities should remain accountable to the people they engage, not just with dialogic methods and other spaces of encounter, but also in creating and reporting research outcomes.

❖ CONCLUSION

When Dennis Mumby approached us about writing this chapter, we expected that it would be produced in the traditions of postcolonial and participatory action research and (re)present the collective labor and polyphonic voices of the co-researchers in the project of doing difference as we pursued our social justice work. After all, since the beginnings of our collaboration with youth and adult activists in the University Heights/Regal Gardens community, we have co-produced numerous internal texts and public performances. This chapter would have been our first attempt at creating a text for a wider, more traditionally academic audience. However, we questioned whether and how we could produce a text in *this venue* that would reflect the collaborative efforts of our project. In turn, this questioning about representational issues led us to broader and deeper questions about our overall attempts to do difference in a community-based research project. Our purpose in writing this chapter evolved as an investigation of difference that emerges at the intersections of categories such as researcher-researched, elite-other, and academy-community. However, we chose to focus on the less interrogated (former) side of the hyphen to emphasize the importance of academic researchers becoming critically conscious of how our own subjectivities co-produce difference when doing engaged research (especially) with vulnerable communities. We see this chapter as part of the growing decolonizing project in organizational communication that is committed to contesting and subverting the unquestioned sovereignty of Western logics (Ashcraft & Allen, 2003; Broadfoot & Munshi, 2007a, 2007b; Grimes & Parker, 2009; Mumby & Stohl, 2007; Parker & Grimes, 2009; Prasad, 2003).

❖ NOTES

1. Pseudonyms are used for places, participants, and organizations.

2. Jennifer Mease was Pat's graduate advisee who joined the project in July after the initial launch in June 2007.

3. Accion Zapatista de Humboldt focuses a great deal of attention on facilitation as a critical dimension of a politics of encounter.

4. This section is adapted from Parker, P. S. (2009). Always at risk? African American women faculty, graduate students, and undergraduates. In D. Cleveland (Ed.), *When minorities are strongly encouraged to apply: Diversity and affirmative action in higher education* (pp. 119–134). New York, NY: Peter Lang.

❖ REFERENCES

Allen, B. J. (2004). *Difference matters: Communicating social identity.* Long Grove, IL: Waveland Press.

Althusser, L. (1971). *Lenin and philosophy.* New York: Monthly Review Press.

Anzaldúa, G. (1987). *Borderlands/La frontera: The new Mestiza.* San Francisco: Aunt Lute Books.

Ashcraft, K. L., & Allen, B. J. (2003). The racial foundation of organizational communication. *Communication Theory, 13*(1), 5–38.

Bishop, R. (2005). Freeing ourselves from neocolonial domination in research: A Kaupapa Maori approach to creating knowledge. In N. K. Denzin & Y. L. Lincoln (Eds.), *The Sage handbook of qualitative research* (3rd ed., pp. 109–138). Thousand Oaks, CA: Sage.

Broadfoot, K. J., & Munshi, D. (2007a). Afterward: In search of a polyphony of voices. *Management Communication Quarterly, 21,* 281–283.

Broadfoot, K. J., & Munshi, D. (2007b). Diverse voices and alternative rationalities: Imagined forms of postcolonial organizational communication. *Management Communication Quarterly, 21,* 249–267.

Callahan, M., (2005). Why not share a dream? Zapatismo as political and cultural practice. *Humboldt Journal of Social Relations, 29*(1), 6–38.

Clegg, S. (1989). *Frameworks of power.* Newbury Park, CA: Sage.

Collins, P. H. (1990). *Black feminist thought: Knowledge, consciousness, and the politics of empowerment.* New York: Routledge.

Collins, P. H. (1998). *Fighting words: Black women and the search for justice.* Minneapolis: University of Minnesota Press.

Davidson, A. (2008, November). The uses and abuses of Gramsci. *Thesis Eleven, 95,* 68–94.

Denzin, N. K., & Lincoln, Y. S. (Eds.). (1994, 2000, 2005). *Handbook of qualitative research.* Thousand Oaks, CA: Sage.

Fine, M. (1994). Working the hyphens: Reinventing self and other in qualitative research. In N. K. Denzin & Y. S. Lincoln (Eds.), *Handbook of qualitative research* (pp. 70–82). Thousand Oaks, CA: Sage.

Fine, M. (2007). Expanding the methodological imagination. *Counseling Psychologist, 35*, 459.

Fine, M., & Weis, L. (2005). Compositional studies, in two parts: Critical theorizing and analysis on social (in)justice. In N. K. Denzin & Y. L. Lincoln (Eds.), *The Sage handbook of qualitative research* (3rd ed., pp. 65–84). Thousand Oaks, CA: Sage.

Fine, M., Weis, L., Weseen, S., & Wong, L. (2000). For whom? Qualitative research, representations, and social responsibilities. In N. K. Denzin & Y. S. Lincoln (Eds.), *Handbook of qualitative research* (2nd ed., pp.107–131). Thousand Oaks, CA: Sage.

Foley, D., & Valenzuela, A. (2005). Critical ethnography: The politics of collaboration. In N. K. Denzin & Y. L. Lincoln (Eds.), *The Sage handbook of qualitative research* (3rd ed., pp. 217–234). Thousand Oaks, CA: Sage.

Forum (2008). *Journal of Applied Communication Research, 36*(3). 243–297.

Foucault, M. (1979). *Discipline and punish: Birth of the prison.* (A. Sheridan, Trans.). New York: Vintage.

Frank, A. W. (2005, February). "What is dialogical research and why should we do it?" Keynote address presented at the sixth international Advances in Qualitative Methods Conference, Edmonton, Alberta, Canada.

Freire, P. (1982). Creating alternative research methods. Learning to do it by doing it. In B. Hall, A. Gillette, & R. Tandon (Eds.), *Creating knowledge: A monopoly.* New Delhi, India: Society for Participatory Research in Asia.

Foucault, M. (1980). *Power/knowledge.* New York: Pantheon.Freire, P. (2000). *Pedagogy of the oppressed.* New York: Continuum.

Ganesh, S., Zoller, H. M., & Cheney, G. (2005). Transforming resistance, broadening our boundaries: Critical organizational communication meets globalization from below. *Communication Monographs, 72*(2), 169–191.

Gramsci, A. (1971). *Selections from the prison notebooks,* (Q. Hoare & G. Nowell Smith, Trans.). New York: International Publishers.

Grimes, D., & Parker, P. S. (2009). Imagining organizational communication as a decolonizing project: In conversation with Broadfoot, Munshi, Mumby, and Stohl. *Management Communication Quarterly, 22*(3), 502–511.

Hale, C. R. (2001). What is activist research? *Social Science Research Council, 2* (1–2), 13–15.

Haraway, D. (1988, Autumn). "Situated knowledge: The science question in feminism and the privilege of partial perspectives." *Feminist Studies, 14*(3), 575–592.

hooks, b. (1984). *Feminist theory from margin to center.* Boston: South End Press.

Janesick, V. (2000). The choreography of qualitative research design: Minuets, improvisations, and crystallization. In N. K. Denzin & Y. S. Lincoln (Eds.), *Handbook of qualitative research* (2nd ed., pp. 379–400). Thousand Oaks, CA: Sage.

Kemmis, S., & McTaggart R. (2000). Participatory action research. In N. K. Denzin & Y. S. Lincoln (Eds.), *Handbook of qualitative research* (2nd ed., pp. 567–607). Thousand Oaks, CA: Sage.

Latina Feminist Group (2001). "Introduction. *Papelitos guardados:* Theorizing *Latinidades* through *testimonio,"* In *Telling to live: Latina feminist testimonio* (pp. 1–3). Durham, NC: Duke University Press.

Lorde, A. (1984). *Sister outsider: Essays and speeches.* Trumansburg, NY: Crossing Press.

Lubiano, W. (1992). Black ladies, welfare queens, and state minstrels: Ideological war by narrative means. In Toni Morrison (Ed.), *Race-ing justice, engendering power: Essays on Anita Hill, Clarence Thomas, and the construction of social reality* (pp. 323–361). New York: Pantheon Books.

Macabe, C. (2007, December). An interview with Stuart Hall. *Critical Quarterly, 50*(1–2), 12–42.

Moraga, C. (1981). Entering the lives of others: Theory in the flesh. In C. Moraga & G. Anzaldúa (Eds.). *This bridge called my back: Writings by radical women of color.* San Francisco, CA: Aunt Lute Press.

Mumby, D. K. (1997). The problem of hegemony: Rereading Gramsci for organizational communication studies. *Western Journal of Communication, 61*(4), 343–375.

Mumby, D. K. (2001). Power and politics. In F. M. Jablin & L. L. Putnam (Eds.), *The new handbook of organizational communication: Advances in theory, research, and methods* (pp. 585-623). Newbury Park, CA: Sage.

Mumby, D. K., & Stohl, C. (2007). Response to Broadfoot and Munshi: (Re)disciplining organizational communication studies. *Management Communication Quarterly, 21,* 268–280.

Naples, N. (1998, Fall). Toward a multiracial, feminist social-democratic praxis: Lessons from grassroots warriors in the U.S. war on poverty, *Social Politics, 5*(3), 286–313.

Parker, P. S. (2001). African American women executives within dominant culture organizations: (Re)conceptualizing notions of instrumentality and collaboration. *Management Communication Quarterly, 15,* 42–82.

Parker, P. S. (2003). Control, power, and resistance within raced, gendered, and classed work contexts: The case of African American women. *Communication Yearbook ,27,* 257–291.

Parker, P. S. (2005). *Race, gender, and leadership: Re-envisioning organizational leadership from the perspectives of African American women executives.* Mahwah, NJ: Lawrence Erlbaum.

Parker, P. S. (2006, June). *Building capacity for leadership development and community activism among low-income African American teen girls and young women.* Presented at the Moore Undergraduate Apprenticeship Program (MURAP) Seminar. Chapel Hill, NC.

Parker, P. S. (2007). *Still lifting, still climbing: Young women of color practicing leadership through community activism.* Unpublished Manuscript. The University of North Carolina at Chapel Hill.

Parker, P. S. (2009). Always at risk? African American women faculty, graduate students, and undergraduates. In D. Cleveland (Ed.), *Minorities are especially encouraged to apply* (pp. 119–134). New York, NY: Peter Lang.

Parker, P. S., & Grimes, D. S. (2009). "Race" and management discourse. In F. Bargiela-Chiappini (Ed.), *The handbook of business discourse* (292–304). Edinburgh University Press.

Prasad, A. (Ed.). (2003). *Postcolonial theory and organizational analysis.* New York: Palmgrave MacMillan.

Ransby, B. (2003). *Ella Baker and the black freedom movement: A radical democratic vision.* Chapel Hill: The University of North Carolina.

Said, E. (1978). *Orientalism.* New York: Vintage Books.

Sandoval, C. (2000). *Methodology of the oppressed.* Minneapolis: University of Minnesota.

Simpson, J. L., & Shockley-Zalabak. (Eds.). (2005). *Engaging communication, transforming organizations: Scholarship of engagement in action.* Cresskill, NJ: Hampton Press.

Smith, L. T. (1999). *Decolonizing methodologies: Research and indigeneous peoples.* London: Zed Books.

Smith, L. T. (2005). On tricky ground: Researching the native in the age of uncertainty. In N. K. Denzin & Y. L. Lincoln (Eds.), *The Sage handbook of qualitative research* (3rd ed., pp. 85–107). Thousand Oaks, CA: Sage.

Springer, K. (1999). Still lifting, still climbing: African American women's contemporary activism. New York: New York University Press.

11

Problematizing Political Economy Differences and Their Respective Work-Life Policy Constructions

Patrice M. Buzzanell, Rebecca L. Dohrman, and Suzy D'Enbeau

Organizational communication scholars have used different lenses to understand workers' everyday experiences, organizational cultures and structures, and organizing globally with particular attention to social change and applied scholarship (e.g., Frey & Cissna, 2009; Papa, Singhal, & Papa, 2006). Of these lenses, discourses of difference including gender, class, race, institutional, and their intersections have been most prominent (e.g., Ashcraft & Allen, 2003; Ashcraft & Mumby, 2004; Buzzanell, 1994; Buzzanell, Meisenbach, Remke, Sterk, & Turner, 2009; Nicotera, Clinkscales, Dorsey, & Niles, 2009). These lenses reflect, underlie, and guide work-life theories, policies, and practices (see Kirby, Golden, Medved, Jorgenson, & Buzzanell, 2003; Kirby & Krone, 2002). To these lenses of difference, we add political economies as a means of further questioning and making sense of work-life policy construction and implementations.

Political economies define mutually enforcing relationships among sociopolitical-cultural and economic discourses, structures, policies, and practices. In short, theories of political economies embed sociopolitical-cultural dimensions within economic contexts, in effect delineating markers of difference depending on what type of economic framework is privileged. In using political economies as an analytic lens for describing work-life policies and everyday consequences, we develop two goals: (a) to interrogate the discourses and material consequences of two main political economies—neoliberal and social welfare—on work-life issues; and (b) to display how work-life policies and practices are ironic depending on which outcomes are considered desirable (and by whom) in today's world. In doing so, we both contest political economic logics and also explore the vulnerabilities, opportunities, and constraints with which organizational and societal members operate.

To achieve our goals, we lay out differing political economic contexts of caregiving by drawing upon empirical research and popular media reports. We admit our selectivity in the texts used for our analyses. Google searches alone for work-life policy and political economy yielded 323,000,000 and 63,300,000 hits, respectively. To narrow down our texts, we drew upon the most recent books, articles, and media reports that dealt with both topics, that surfaced repeatedly in online searches, and that relied upon empirical data gleaned from labor force demographics and national statistics as well as interviews and focus groups. Of utmost concern was that texts represent arguments and assumptions underlying policies in diverse national and political economic systems. As such, we do not claim that our texts represent all work-life policy and political economy intersections but, rather, that they provide some broad and frequently occurring claims and assumptions.

Throughout, we adjudicate among varied decision criteria and frames whereby people both choose and fail to consider work-life alternatives. By taking a discursive approach to work-life talk (discourse) and macrostructures of policy generation/implementation within contemporary political economies (Discourse), communication researchers can contribute uniquely to theoretical and pragmatic possibilities for global quality of (work) life initiatives (Cheney, Zorn, Planalp, & Lair, 2008; Fairhurst, 2007; Kuhn et al., 2008). Examining the talk and broader societal Discourses that underlie everyday action enables us to consider how difference in the forms of race/ethnicity, class, gender, nationality, and culture shape how people think about, respond to, create, and resist particular work-life possibilities. Destabilizing these macrostructures forces us to consider the strengths and weaknesses of alternative possibilities. By critiquing how political economies are implicated in work-life difference, we do not simply consider diversity in a representational sense, that is, by inclusion of different group members in the construction, implementation, and revision of policy, but see difference as deeply embedded in policy language and structures and participation of stakeholders in policymaking processes and uses.

For us, then, difference is implicated in the intersections among various lenses, including the political economic, as we survey and critique work-life policies. In doing so, we respond to and expand the call to (1) investigate "empowered participation . . . that dispels gender hierarchies; (2) define well-being as equitable access to material and symbolic resources . . . ; (3) suggest alternatives to normative, gendered communication processes across contexts; and (4) promote fulfilling human relationships" (Buzzanell et al., 2009, p. 182).

❖ WORK-LIFE AND CAREGIVING CHALLENGES

Much of the work-life balance literature in organizational and family communication centers on two main strands that have different assumptions and theoretical approaches. In the first, researchers consider the challenges of balance, particularly with regard to raising families and creating time for different interests and people. In the balance approach, researchers talk about their own and other's experiences with caregiving and paid and unpaid work through writing-stories, cases, analyses of interview and focus group data, and textual or feminist critiques of linguistic choices and decision premises in men's and women's discourses in chat rooms, popular media, and other sources (e.g., Buzzanell & D'Enbeau, 2009; Kirby, 2000; Medved & Kirby, 2005; Townsley & Broadfoot, 2008). These materials not only create awareness of the difficulties, joys, and complexities involved in balance but also problematize the metaphor itself (MacDermid, Roy, & Zvonkovic, 2005) and enlarge its boundaries to include aspects such as unpaid work (Medved, 2009) and non-kin family care (e.g., Lucas & Buzzanell, 2006). Through this first approach, researchers expand definitions and examine means for stakeholders' empowerment and care as a social necessity (e.g., Arthur & Rousseau, 1996; Buzzanell & Liu, 2005; Kirby et al., 2003).

In the second communicative approach to work-life issues, the ideological structures that maintain and provide potential fissures in everyday thinking are explored. These ideologies are gendered, raced, and classed insofar as work-life management itself is viewed as a

female- or, at best, a communally-oriented approach to enable engagement in both paid labor and home work (Buzzanell, Meisenbach,
Remke, Liu, Bowers, & Conn, 2005). Work-life balance is seen as feminine in organizing imperatives (Mumby & Putnam, 1992), fraught with
gender taboos and sexuality (Martin, 1990, 1992), and primarily geared
to White, middle-class, heterosexual, married families (Kirby et al.,
2003). Misra, Moller, and Budig (2007) argued that work-family policies
provide a unique lens into a nation's assumptions about women and
gendered roles, which is why looking first at policies is a useful way to
see how gender is conceptualized in a particular country or, as we
argue in this essay, a particular political economy. In this strand of literature, exposure of restrictive assumptions and inequities for national
and global labor force participation has led to legal solutions, such as
inclusion of same sex partner benefits, family leave policy amendments, and corporate benefits expansions to encourage wellness and
retention of workers after family leaves (Sabattini & Crosby, 2008).
Intersections of career and work-life concerns come into play as ideological analyses examine how people in different cultures and occupations frame their labor and work-life possibilities (Watt & Eccles, 2008).

These two strands operate on levels of discourses and Discourses,
meaning that they function within and across microlinguistic choices
or talk-in-interaction as well as the cultural formations and ideologies
in particular collectivities that give meaning to, and are shaped by,
ongoing interactions (for discourse/Discourse, see Alvesson & Kärreman,
2000; Fairhurst, 2007). However, they rarely address the ways in which
political economies create and inhibit opportunities to think, behave,
feel, resist, and generate policies and practices in work-life realms (for
an exception, see Medved, 2007.) Increasing cross-national evidence
points to processes whereby political economies shape work-life possibilities (Edlund, 2007; Hamington & Miller, 2006; Mandel & Semyonov,
2005) and changing terminology and practices related to political
economies alter or modify these structures.

❖ INTERSECTIONS OF CAREGIVING, ECONOMY, AND EQUITY

Studies on discursive and socioeconomic caregiving aspects inade-
quately address the material inequities that result from dominant
Discourses (Buzzanell, Meisenbach, Remke, Sterk, & Turner, 2009;
Cheney & Cloud, 2006; Clair & Thompson, 1996). One consistent finding of longitudinal research on carework is that women do most of the

unpaid care work in the home. Even when paid and regardless of the sex of the individual caregiver, caregiving work is seen as feminine, meaning that it does not have high status in society and therefore is not well-paid or secure (Barker, 2005). Given increases in elder care needs, the U.S. Department of Labor predicts that by 2016, the second-fastest growing job will be home care or personal aide ("Caring for the caregivers," 2009). Aides are most likely to be women and from less affluent regions of the world (see Townsley, 2006). Despite their global labor force entry and men's increased domestic work participation, women still do most household labor (Medved, 2009; Tucker, 2006).

Theories of political economy serve to bracket thinking and behaviors with regard to caregiving and other work-life issues. These theories consider the meso- and microlevels of particular economic ideologies as they shape institutional, organizational, and political policies and practices as well as the mundane interactions of ordinary lives (Riordan, 2002). Although economic ideologies are contested, they appear fixed in their political influence about what is viewed as feasible, what serves the greatest need (as defined by the particular economic ideology), and who benefits or is sanctioned by such policies (Mosco, 1996). Embedded within governmental Discourses, resource allocations, and lobbying efforts, work-life policies and implementations influence day-to-day life considerations (e.g., poverty reform, family leave, health care, microeconomic funds, human rights reforms; economic stimulus packages; see Buzzanell, Meisenbach, Remke, Sterk, & Turner, 2009; Trethewey, 1997).

Current conceptualizations of political economies focus on capitalistic, neoliberal or neocapitalist, socialist systems with capitalist overtones, and social welfare states. The core of each is a view of labor and human capital worth for individual and nation. For our essay, political economies direct stakeholders' responsibilities. They preferred identities, and adapt responses to work-life issues. In addition, political economies promote and create specific ways of thinking that then influence and infiltrate the organizations and individuals that make up that economy. For example, capitalist Discourses assume and instantiate individual agency, ethics of hard work and opportunity, market economy, and individuals' primary roles as producers and consumers of goods and services (Kuhn et al., 2008; Bernstein, 1997; Scott & Hart, 1989). In the process, options for flexible work arrangements and alternative barometers of work success are overlooked and undervalued (Wieland, Bauer, & Deetz, 2009).

In this Discourse, the fittest or most attuned to capitalist entrepreneurial activities and values reap benefits, whereas those who are least fit through individual or familial characteristics do not find employment gains, economic self-sufficiency, or accumulation of capital. In capitalism, the role of the family is to produce additional workers and consumers who, in turn, drive greater capitalist gains. The issue of work-life balance does not enter into laborer roles but becomes isomorphic with consumer roles, meaning that consumers purchase goods, including caregiving services, for themselves and others. Consumers also expend considerable time and effort in locating the best products and surveying possible purchases. That purchased goods and services may serve only symbolic purposes at times (Hochschild, 1997) is unimportant. What is important is that consumers enact the consumerist role which, in large part, aligns with the *life* or spiritual, family, leisure, volunteer, or other nonwage work aspect of their existence (see du Gay, 1996). As such, capitalist political economies bifurcate *work* and *life* into two separate spheres and envision the life aspects as providing time and other resources for the more effective production of both worker and consumer roles and for future labor forces (see Hoskyns & Rai, 2007).

While there are many economic frameworks through which to conceptualize caregiving, our analysis considers two prominent but contrasting ideologies: neoliberal and social welfare approaches.

❖ NEOLIBERAL POLITICAL ECONOMIES AND SOCIAL WELFARE APPROACHES

Caregiving in a Neoliberal Economy

Neoliberalism, also known as *the new capitalism*, envisions human welfare as contingent on free trade, individual property rights, and deregulated markets (Ayers & Carlone, 2007). Neoliberalism is a fragmented ideology whose form is dependent upon the context in which it is embedded. Despite its diverse manifestations, neoliberalism constructs capitalism as "natural, inevitable, and beneficent" (Barker, 2005, p. 2195) to the extent that it affects the way society is structured and infiltrates the way people think about themselves and social issues (Ayers & Carlone, 2007). Key factors are growth, favorable business climates, and educational-community resource alignments for corporate interests.

The premise that economic competitiveness promotes the common good is unquestioned. Economic and individual competitiveness align and often are manifest in careerism. The assumption that career is the central defining experience of a person's life (Wieland et al., 2009) is visible in extreme jobs, broadly defined as jobs with a high salary, demanding hours, and unpredictable work demands (Hewlett & Luce, 2006). Careerist ideologies are reinforced by seemingly innocuous conversational openers, such as, "What do you do?" Indeed, the ideology of careerism can be a destructive and debilitating force as individuals and families manage work and care responsibilities (Wieland et al., 2009).

Thus, neoliberalism coincides with the opportunities and efficiencies afforded by high technology and the knowledge economy on the one hand, and with fragmentation of communities, global employment insecurities, erosion of work boundaries and social rhythms, and 24/7 work intensities on the other (Perrons, Fagan, McDowell, Ray, & Ward, 2006). Feminist research critiques neoliberalism's hypercompetitive global business landscapes, shifting spatio-temporal work configurations, and increasing division between wealthy and vulnerable world citizens. Specifically, feminist analyses link the private sphere of reproduction to economic processes, thus problematizing a favoring of the public sphere (Bergeron, 2001). This privileging augments pressures for those on permanent contracts to forego family-friendly entitlements to breaks, time off for holidays, and other benefits; yet without a permanent contract, these entitlements are often not even offered or available (Perrons et al., 2006). This erosion of social welfare policies and practices accompanies accelerating economic strategies.

Recent research and popular media document work-life trends that demand that workers take responsibility for integrating their public and private lives and adapt to dominant enterprise Discourses of individualism, competitiveness, and self-reliance (Ainsworth & Hardy, 2008). For example, Johnston and Swanson (2003) found that contemporary magazines offer women powerful identity Discourses of motherhood and then subsequently condemn those identity representations. Academe is not immune to these struggles. When women take family leaves, departments must resolve financial challenges, such as handling teaching loads, paying adjunct faculty, and covering some faculty members' full salaries for 80% of their work (Aubrey et al., 2008; Kramer, 2008). Chronicled in interdisciplinary writings are the complexities of single parenting (Sotirin, 2008) and health-work intersections such as having cancer (Manning, 2008), caring for a child with autism (Louis, 2008), dealing with a child's death (McAlister, 2008; Short-Thompson, 2008), and other work-life issues (Monosson, 2008; Rees, 2006). These personal accounts reflect a widespread underutilization of corporate and institutional policies because in academic culture, anything short of complete work dedication is problematic (Townsley & Broadfoot, 2008).

In these and multinational statistical analyses of organizational and labor force data, the Discourses of rights, gender, and choice color perceptions of appropriate policy use (Brandth & Kvande, 2006; Hayden & O'Brien Hallstein, 2010; Kirby & Krone, 2002). Use of policy implementations, such as onsite childcare, becomes problematic when working mothers' maternal caregiving roles are reinforced in employment contexts (Hoobler, 2007). Only when the act of caregiving becomes valued for men and women will we see cultural assumptions shift.

Popular representations of work-life issues exacerbate these same obstacles to sustaining work-life spheres and enacting gender equitable caregiving practices. In a recent episode of *Lipstick Jungle* (Goldstick, Busfield, & Bushnell, 2009), a main character decided upon oocyte cryopreservation, freezing some of her eggs to address her biological clock, her single relational status, and her ambitious career track. The show portrayed the possible physical complications of her decision (e.g., hormonal imbalance) but not the emotional consequences of delaying childbearing for one's career. D'Enbeau and Buzzanell (2009) noted that while reproductive technologies such as egg freezing can offer some women the appearance of greater choice in managing work-life tensions, individuals pursuing such alternatives ignore possible institutional changes that could allow better integration of work and life. Moreover, egg freezing is a costly procedure ($9,000 to $14,000), making it an unlikely choice for many.

Thus, neoliberal Discourses reinforce individual responsibility for caregiving practices and work-life tensions. Individual responsibility is linked to "choice," especially private, non-state work-life management options, and neglects sustained gender change.

Caregiving in Social Welfare Systems

Social welfare systems position the state as the provider of caregiving and social services. Caregiving practices are outlined as rights and policies to which individuals are entitled. We outline U.S. welfare policies informed by neoliberalism and social welfare policies abroad to present the gender equity obstacles of each.

Welfare has been the predominant state-funded resource for lower income U.S. families. Its purpose is to provide adult recipients with work positions and to enforce consequences for not working (Weigt, 2006, p. 332). However, because U.S. economic policies are informed by neoliberal ideologies, welfare has been reframed as a "market relationship" where "one must now exchange labor for a benefit" (Weigt, 2006, p. 337). Carework is often redefined and refashioned as a result of this framing (Little, 2006). In her interviews with welfare recipients, Weigt (2006) found that individuals were forced to take jobs with low wages and long working hours that had adverse effects on their ability to care for their children. Instead of questioning the problematic wage and time structures of these positions, mothers voiced their personal inabilities to effectively care for their children. In essence, Discourses of what it means to be a good mother diverted "attention from low wages, long hours, and inflexible schedules, and [aided] in the assignment of 'personal responsibility' for carework to mothers" (p. 343; see also (Buzzanell, Meisenbach, Remke, Liu, Bowers, & Conn, 2005). This reframing strengthened neoliberal Discourses guiding these welfare reforms by positioning the individual as ultimately responsible for carework and personal outcomes.

Moreover, intersections of neoliberalism and welfare privilege Discourses of work enforcement to the detriment of carework. Discourses of work enforcement argue that welfare mothers need to model strong work ethics for their children at any cost (Hamington & Miller, 2006). A strong work ethic may be constituted as paid work outside of the home, not necessarily caring for children. This intersection masks the financial, time, and caregiving struggles of working mothers in low-wage jobs (Weigt, 2006). In short, welfare reform policies reframe adequate caregiving practices to mean paid work outside of the home.

Based on her fieldwork in welfare-to-work programs, Little (2006) found that welfare employees reframed caregiving so that children's needs were in conflict with mothers' needs and wage labor was the best way to care for children. Domestic caregiving practices were portrayed as trapping women, while paid work outside of the home promised them liberation from welfare. However, paid work offered inadequate wages and inflexible hours—in effect, forcing women to bypass all caregiving responsibilities. Findings lead to the conclusion that women's empowerment through participation in the paid workforce can no longer be assumed (Barker, 2005). Indeed, mothers continue to be perceived as less competent and committed to paid work because it is assumed that they are not the primary earners or that they are the primary caregivers. Correll, Benard, and Paik (2007) labeled this phenomenon the "motherhood penalty" because the difference in perception only negatively impacts mothers, and in fact, fathers are at times more positively perceived than male non-parents. In the end, an underlying assumption of neoliberal welfare and work policies is that individual women, no matter what their material circumstances, will assume full responsibility for carework with little institutional and organizational support (Weigt, 2006).

While it may come as no surprise that U.S. welfare-to-work programs, informed by neoliberalism, are beset with obstacles to developing gender equitable caregiving practices, research from other countries,
including those with developed welfare states, presents obstacles as
well. Mandel and Semyonov (2005) noted that wage gaps between men
and women are typically more pronounced in liberal-market
economies, like the United States, than in corporatist economies characterized by more social and family welfare policies. As a result, many
incorrectly conclude that social welfare policies lead to a less pronounced gender wage gap. However, in their analysis of gender-
based earning inequalities across 20 advanced societies, Mandel
and Semyonov found that while "mother-friendly" policies increase
women's labor force participation, these same policies reinforce gendered occupational inequalities. Women are more likely to be concentrated in female-typed occupations and less likely to hold managerial
positions. In fact, it is the egalitarian wage structures of welfare states
that lessen the gender wage gap, *not* the presence of social and family
policies purported to ensure adequate caregiving services.

Other research has considered father-friendly welfare states.
Brandth and Kvande (2006) described two care policy reforms in
Norway: the fathers' quota and the cash-for-care scheme. The highly
successful fathers' quota, a state-provided right given to employed
fathers, offers four weeks of paid leave for fathers. Designed to be gender neutral, the cash-for-care program offers parents with small children cash payments with the intended goal of encouraging more time
spent with children and offering parents a choice with respect to childcare. The authors found that because the fathers' quota was viewed as
a right, fathers were more likely to take advantage of this program
because a right was a reasonable excuse for work absence. However,
the cash-for-care scheme did not challenge existing social structures
and gender inequalities because mothers were more likely to change
their labor participation and increase their caregiving. Similar research
also found that "choice" most often translates into women choosing
between working and caring for children, rather than increasing
father's time in caregiving (Ellingsaeter, 2007). In this regard, particular linguistic selections and their assumptions render seemingly gender-neutral policies to be predicated on difference.

Underlying this structure are the central assumptions of earning
and caring that Misra et al. (2007) used to articulate the impact of various work-life policies. The various assumptions relate to whether
women and/or men are assumed to prioritize earning or caring in a
home. A caring strategy would mean that women prioritize caring

work and are valued for that work by social policies; other strategies are the earner strategy, the choice strategy, and the earner-carer strategy (see Fraser, 1994). Misra et al. (2007) noted that welfare states are often premised on the man as earner, woman as caregiver model, although, to some extent, current welfare policies identify women as caregivers and earners. The United States employs the earner strategy in which both men and women are equally involved in and privilege paid work, but the state does not provide caregiving support. Within this strategy, it is left to individual families to negotiate who will or should care for children. As a result, individuals may choose to not have children.

In contrast, the earner-carer strategy promotes men and women's equal involvement in paid work and unpaid care work through state and organizational support. Misra et al. (2007) noted that this strategy decreases the poverty levels of women while challenging traditional gender stereotypes. The carer, earner, and choice strategies all result in higher poverty rates for women, partly because they reify gendered assumptions. For instance, the choice strategy includes additional leave for women when children are young but does not challenge the feminization of carework. Higher or lower rates of poverty for women are just one of many unexpected consequences of work-family policies that are designed to help women but that rely on gendered assumptions that lead to higher poverty rates and associated health and safety issues for women and children.

Finally, Gheaus (2008) critiqued the Western assumption that strategically links feminism to welfare states in response to neoliberal and global capital expansion. Some Western feminists call for a redistribution of care, articulating caregiving as "a common good" (Tracy, 2008) and an essential duty of every citizen to ensure that the next generation of citizens is prepared to enter society as adults. Redistributive care is framed as either shifting care from families to society or from women to men (Ellingsaeter, 2007). This view of care as justice and, therefore, in the public's best interest is intended to combat pervasive neoliberal policies that increase poverty in women by "destroying traditional industries on which they used to rely and so forcing them into the informal economy" and increasing women's financial dependence on men (Gheaus, 2008, p. 188). Using Romania and postcommunist Hungary as case studies, Gheaus argued that although both of these countries inherited massive welfare states with institutions that were supposed to provide adequate social services support, the people of these countries had good reasons to mistrust the state since the communist state relied on privileged women as caregivers. Furthermore,

Gheaus warned that welfare states could potentially create too much state dependency and further mask gender inequities in private, as well as public, spheres.

Thus, it appears that although the challenges posed by neoliberalism might seem best met by public expenditures for carework, a more welfare-state approach, while certainly needed in terms of adequate state-subsidized childcare and family leave provisions, has an uneasy relationship with gender equality (see DeMartino, 2000; Mandel & Semyonov, 2005). Perrons et al. (2006) concluded by questioning motivations, outcomes and implications, necessary related changes, and ironic consequences of current policies. Furthermore, the state's role is questionable because theorizing the nation-state as women's primary source of resistance to global capitalism, neoliberal politics, and gender inequities overlooks state governments' complex connections to transnational capital (Bergeron, 2001).

❖ DISCUSSION

Throughout our chapter, we show how difference is implicated in and reproduced by macrostructures of political economies and at the microlinguistic levels through particular linguistic choices. Thus far, difference logics underlie consequences that seem unintended but support current societal systems. However, once made visible, difference can also operate as a Discourse for making policymakers and implementers accountable. To continue our discussion along these lines, we first elaborate upon our theoretical contributions to the literature on work-life issues. We conclude by noting the practical implications of our findings, focusing specifically on three policy areas that require transformation.

Looking Forward: Caregiving as Choice, Policy, and Practice

Through governmental, corporate, institutional, and not-for-profit organizations' work-life policies, individuals and groups of people are constructed in certain ways for policy use and exclusion. Intersections of work and life discourses, processes, and policies become sites for articulating social identities along difference lines of race, class, gender, sexuality, and nation. By interrogating the everyday discourses and material consequences of work-life policies in particular political economies, we display how these policies and practices have unintended, indeed ironic, consequences.

Neoliberal choice masks significant inequalities because "the logic of the market is a logic of opportunity and choice for the privileged few and a logic of inequality and exploitation for the rest" (Barker, 2005, p. 2204). Neoliberalism situates causes and remedies for work-family management problems in the individual who operates within a global and local landscape of hypercompetition, privatization, and privileging of corporate needs. To use family-friendly benefits, when available, means that workers are neither enterprising nor committed to their work. Conversely, under social welfare states, workers have rights to and use a variety of family-friendly policies, yet women still do most caregiving and are located in feminized occupations with lower pay and little advancement potential. If policies are framed as choice, then they are associated with weakness, the feminine, and lack of use by men.

It seems, therefore, that neither political-economic situation can fully ease the strain of work-family considerations in a competitive global marketplace. Neither can to gender equity and quality of (work) life, and provide human services and maintain the importance of work in individuals' well-being (for an overview of the importance of work in human well-being, see Cheney et al., 2008). Future policies should be informed by both people's experiences and talk (discourses) and by economic frameworks and other cultural formations (Discourses) that can more fully address issues pertaining to country wealth and modernization (Edlund, 2007).

If policy is to move forward, it is imperative that the ways in which individuals and nations discursively and materially construct care-work begins to transcend public-private divides. Neoliberal political and economic theories assume that care is an individual responsibility. In this context, care for children and the elderly defaults to individuals in familial networks, rather than to mutual interdependences and communities or, as Tronto (2006) argued, making care a public good that is subsumed with citizen and national identities. The individual focus on care negates one's environment. Furthermore, socioeconomic status impacts the level of care provided and received (Tronto, 2006). In contrast, a focus on familial networks masks the increased and unequal amount of caregiving that women continue to provide in most heterosexual families (Coltrane, 2000).

When work-life policies are framed as rights, they are more likely to receive organizational and governmental support. They are also more likely to be embraced by men and might lead to more gender equitable caregiving practices in the home (Brandth & Kvande, 2006). This notion of rights is largely rooted in Western morality and "shapes what we mean when we define citizenship and what we expect of each other and our government. It defines our narratives of good and bad" (Hamington & Miller, 2006, p. xv). Yet Hamington and Miller also argued that

> notions of rights and rules have not been sufficiently formulated, for example, to overcome narratives of free market liberalism to argue for the alleviation of homelessness. Care may not fare any better, but it starts with a concern for others and self that is less susceptible to being hijacked by abstract formulations. (p. xiii)

In terms of organizational support, Tracy (2008) called this idea "care as common, collective good" (p. 171) where care is one element of organizational social responsibility. Employees have a right to receive and enact care based on needs interpretations (Fraser, 1989) with continued analyses and reassessments of justice and care Discourses in workplaces (Buzzanell & Liu, 2005) and other contexts. These contexts and this analysis afford the kinds of continuous assessments that can sustain the necessary dialectic tensions among neoliberal-social welfare political economies and discourses-Discourses.

A second possibility for change that transcends public-private divides is to consider household, reproductive, and care labor in economic terms (Hoskyns & Rai, 2007). Hoskyns and Rai defined social reproduction as

> biological reproduction; unpaid production in the home (both goods and services); social provisioning (by this we mean voluntary work directed at meeting needs in the community); the reproduction of culture and ideology; and the provision of sexual, emotional, and affective services (such as that required to maintain family and intimate relationships). (p. 300)

These are resources that contribute socially and economically to society and are provided mainly by women from diverse socio-economic backgrounds. Within a neoliberal economy, this unpaid work is translated into money and assigned market value (Hoskyns & Rai, 2007).

Policy prescriptions informed by social welfare regimes only succeed if socialized care provides "universal family allowances, state-supported day care, paid family leave, universal health care, an increased minimum wage, limitations on work hours, and more housing subsidies" (Little, 2006, p. 136). However, these policies do not transform wage work into care work nor unseat the gendered inequities in life.

Across the globe, as transnational flows and capital enact power over nation-states and their abilities to provide state-supported care, ethical globalization practices are needed. Robinson (2006) noted that "the integration of the values and practices of care into social policy, as well as into the workings of private organizations, may be helpful in alleviating the deep gender and racial imbalances—in terms of access to wealth, resources, services, and power—caused or at least exacerbated, by globalization" (p. 164). Furthermore, ethical globalization requires challenges to the illusion that globalization economics is unified, with purpose, and without contradiction, as well "as the more or less inevitable outcome of a drive to accumulate on a worldwide basis, or even as an outcome determined solely by powerful international institutions" (Bergeron, 2001, p. 996). By recognizing that globalization does not have to naturally coincide with neoliberal policies, this relationship is socially and discursively deconstructed. We must be wary of associating women's independence and ability to navigate work-life tensions with having the same access to independent incomes lest we combine feminist interests with those of global capital (Barker, 2005). Indeed, if globalization continues on its current course, then additional jobs may become low-paid and not secure, thus providing the employee with less and less flexibility (Barker, 2005).

These problematic situations have differential effects on global and political economic sectors. Specifically, Edlund (2007) explained that modernized countries are more likely to push for gender equality. They are most likely to have high levels of mass education, and have more skilled than unskilled workers. Thus, a country's wealth does impact work-family balance. However, "although the overall probability increases with economic wealth, the relative disadvantage for women compared to men persists" (Edlund, 2007, p. 466).

Practical Implications: Looking Forward to Pragmatic Policy Change

In this section, we begin a list of pragmatic suggestions for discursive and material change because "policymaking involves more than a competition over policy emphasis; it is also a struggle over legitimate interpretation of policy rationales" (Ellingsaeter, 2007, p. 58). We suggest that the unique challenges that women face in terms of caregiving are supplemented with policy talk and changes that address issues of working *parents* to encourage men to talk more about work-life issues. This would create an expectation that men become more involved in daily routines of parenting.

We suggest national dialogues to learn more about the caregiving practices and strategies of ordinary individuals. For instance, prior to recrafting policy and finalizing stimulus package funds distributions, we recommend listening tours around the country where political and organizational leaders can meet with individuals from diverse contexts and resources. The issue is not simply that members of different stakeholders have representation. They also need to have voice or participation in the decision-making, content, structure, and implementations of revised work-life policies (see Haas & Deetz, 2000). A second part of this listening tour could occur online. Leading a discussion could highlight how policies impact mundane lives as well as provide a platform to change work-life conversations.

We also offer a set of pragmatic suggestions for material changes to account for diverse economic backgrounds. These particular suggestions largely pertain to the United States; however, they could be adapted for diverse political, cultural, and economic contexts throughout the world. Indeed, we argue that context is incredibly important in laying out suggestions to address intersections of work-life and difference. First, we recommend a national task force with expertise in different political economic systems, charged with examining policies and practices and their intersections with difference (e.g., class, race, gender). We recommend a national imperative to insure that the next generation begins life in a situation where single-parent and dual-parent households are less stressed. For example, this task force could investigate the Family and Medical Leave Act (FMLA) and consider its expansion to account for all workers (rather than, for example, excluding small companies). Many hourly workers, who receive less vacation time, must choose between caregiving in the home and engaging in paid work outside the home. Insuring that everyone has, for instance, two weeks of paid leave as a "right" of employment would encourage more fathers to take a full two weeks and reduce the chance that they will not take leave because of financial constraints. For this recommendation, governmental assistance to offset the financial considerations of small companies would be a necessity.

A second policy would establish government-sponsored childcare. Full day kindergarten and preschool, with some weekend and evening programs, could help reduce the caregiving responsibilities of parents by providing them with a place for their children to thrive and learn while they work. An important element of this childcare system must be arrangements for individuals who work nonstandard work hours. Because single mothers work nonstandard hours more often than married mothers, it is particularly important to provide provisions that account for the variety of shifts in which a family may need childcare (Hertz, 2004). Certainly, childcare is one of the most pressing and important issues related to working families, so it is essential to work toward improving the institutionalized childcare structure in the United States.

A third suggestion would solicit creative solutions to resource allocation. Working families struggle with the amount of time required to financially provide for their family, engage in paid work, and spend time caring for children. Because time is a limited resource, allocation of this resource can cause significant logistical and emotional stress on working parents. Despite the lack of institutionalized policies for working families in the United States, many working families are finding solutions that work at their local level. For instance, some single mothers develop a strong familial community with other single mothers in close proximity. In some cases, this is more formalized (Bazelon, 2009), and in others, it is more informal. In other cases, neighborhoods set up childcare co-ops to provide community members with quality childcare without the exchange of money. For instance, the "Yes we can!" program, funded by the W. K. Kellogg Foundation (2009), provides resources to set up a neighborhood childcare co-op in the Battle Creek, Michigan, area. In soliciting strategies like these from the bottom-up, and determining if and how they can be institutionalized, researchers, policymakers, and activists may develop stronger, more nuanced, and gender equitable solutions to work-life dilemmas.

❖ REFERENCES

Ainsworth, S., & Hardy, C. (2008). The enterprising self: An unsuitable job for an older worker. *Organization, 15,* 389–405.

Alvesson, M., & Kärreman, D. (2000). Varieties of discourse: On the study of organizations through discourse analysis. *Human Relations, 53,* 1125–1149.

Arthur, M., & Rousseau, D. (Eds.). (1996). *The boundaryless career: A new employment principle for a new organizational era.* New York: Oxford University Press.

Ashcraft, K. L., & Allen, B. J. (2003). The racial foundation of organizational communication. *Communication Theory, 13,* 5–38.

Ashcraft, K. L., & Mumby, D. K. (2004). *Reworking gender: A feminist communicology of organization.* Thousand Oaks, CA: Sage.

Aubrey, J. S., Click, M. A., Dougherty, D. S., Fine, M. A., Kramer, M. W., Meisenbach, R. J., Olson, L. N., & Smythe, M. (2008). We do babies! The trials, tribulations, and triumphs of pregnancy and parenting in the academy. *Women's Studies in Communication, 31,* 186–195.

Ayers, D. F., & Carlone, D. (2007). Manifestations of neoliberal discourses within a local job-training program. *International Journal of Lifelong Education, 26,* 461–479.

Barker, D. (2005). Beyond women and economics: Rereading "women's work." *Signs, 30,* 2189–2209.

Bazelon, E. (2009, January 29). 2 Kids + 0 husbands = family. *The New York Times.* Retrieved February 1, 2009, from http://www.nytimes.com/2009/02/01/magazine/01Moms-t.html

Bergeron, S. (2001). Political economy discourses of globalization and feminist politics. *Signs, 26,* 983–1006.

Bernstein, P. (1997). *American work values: Their origin and development.* Albany: SUNY Press.

Brandth, B., & Kvande, E. (2006). Care politics for fathers in a flexible time culture. In M. Hamington & D. C. Miller (Eds.), *Socializing care: Feminist ethics and public issues* (pp. 148–161). Lanham, MA: Rowman & Littlefield.

Buzzanell, P. M. (1994). Gaining a voice: Feminist organizational communication theorizing. *Management Communication Quarterly, 7,* 339–383.

Buzzanell, P. M., & D'Enbeau, S. (2009). Stories of caregiving: Intersections of academic research and women's everyday experiences. *Qualitative Inquiry, 15,* 1199–1224.

Buzzanell, P. M., & Liu, M. (2005). Struggling with maternity leave policies and practices: A poststructuralist feminist analysis of gendered organizing. *Journal of Applied Communication Research, 33,* 1–25.

Buzzanell, P. M., Meisenbach, R., Remke, R., Liu, M., Bowers, V., & Conn, C. (2005). The good *working* mother: Managerial women's sensemaking and feelings about work-family issues. *Communication Studies, 56,* 261–285.

Buzzanell, P. M., Meisenbach, R., Remke, R., Sterk, H., & Turner, L. H. (2009). Positioning gender as fundamental in applied communication research. In L. Frey & K. Cissna (Eds.), *The Routledge handbook of applied communication research* (pp. 181–202). New York: Routledge.

"Caring for the caregivers." (2009, January 27). [Editorial]. *The New York Times.* Retrieved February 4, 2009, from http://www.nytimes.com/2009/01/28/opinion/28wed1.html?th&emc=th

Cheney, G., & Cloud, D. (2006). Doing democracy, engaging the material: Employee participation and labor activity in an age of market globalization. *Management Communication Quarterly, 19,* 501–540.

Cheney, G., Zorn, T., Planalp, S., & Lair, D. (2008). Meaningful work and personal/social well-being: Organizational communication engages the meanings of work. In C. Beck (Ed.), *Communication yearbook 32* (pp. 136–185). New York: Routledge.

Clair, R. P., & Thompson, K. (1996). Pay discrimination as a discursive and material practice: A case concerning extended housework. *Journal of Applied Communication Research, 24,* 1–20.

Coltrane, S. (2000). Research on household labor: Modeling and measuring the social embeddedness of routine family work. *Journal of Marriage and the Family, 62, 4,* 1208–1233.

Correll, S. J., Benard, S., & Paik, I. (2007). Getting a job: Is there a motherhood penalty? *American Journal of Sociology, 112*, 1297–1338.

DeMartino, G. F. (2000). *Global economy, global justice: Theoretical objections and policy alternatives to neoliberalism.* London: Routledge.

D'Enbeau, S., & Buzzanell, P. M. (2009). Efficiencies of pregnancy management: From penciling in pregnancy to elective c-sections. In S. Kleinman (Ed.), *The culture of efficiency* (pp. 3–19). New York: Peter Lang.

du Gay, P. (1996). *Consumption and identity at work.* Thousand Oaks, CA: Sage.

Edlund, J. (2007). The work-family time squeeze: Conflicting demands of paid and unpaid work among working couples in 29 countries. *International Journal of Comparative Sociology, 48*, 541–480.

Ellingsaeter, A. L. (2007). "Old" and "new" politics of time to care: Three Norwegian reforms. *Journal of European Social Policy, 17*, 49–60.

Fairhurst, G. T. (2007). *Discursive leadership: In conversation with leadership psychology.* Thousand Oaks, CA: Sage.

Fraser, N. (1989). *Unruly practices: Power, discourse, and gender in contemporary social theory.* Minneapolis: University of Minnesota Press.

Fraser, N. (1994). After the family wage: Gender equity and the welfare state. *Political Theory, 22*, 591–618.

Frey, L., & Cissna, K. N. (Eds.). (2009). *The Routledge handbook of applied communication research.* New York: Routledge.

Gheaus, A. (2008). Gender justice and the welfare state in post-communism. *Feminist Theory, 9*, 185–206.

Goldstick, O., Busfield, T., & Bushnell, C. (Producers). (2009, January 2). Chapter 19: Lovers' leaps [Television program]. New York: NBC.

Haas, T., & Deetz, S. (2000). Between the generalized and the concrete other: Approaching organizational ethics from feminist perspectives. In P. M. Buzzanell (Ed.)., *Rethinking organizational and managerial communication from feminist perspectives* (pp. 24–46). Thousand Oaks, CA: Sage.

Hamington, M., & Miller, D. C. (2006). Introduction: A modern moral imperative. In M. Hamington & D. C. Miller (Eds.). *Socializing care: Feminist ethics and public issues* (pp. xi–xxii). Lanham, MD: Rowman & Littlefield.

Hayden, S., & O'Brien Hallstein, L. (Eds.). (2010). *Contemplating maternity in the era of choice: Explorations into discourses of reproduction.* Lanham, MD: Lexington Press.

Hertz, R. (2004). The contemporary myth of choice [Review of the books *Competing devotions: Career and family among women executives; It's about time: Couples and careers; Working in a 24/7 economy: Challenges for American families;* and *Families that work: Policies for reconciling parenthood and employment*]. *The Annals of the American Academy, 596*, 232–244.

Hewlett, S. A., & Luce, C. B. (2006). Extreme jobs: The dangerous allure of the 70-hour workweek. *Harvard Business Review, 84*(12) 49–59.

Hochschild, A. R. (1997). *The time bind: When work becomes home and home becomes work.* New York: Henry Holt & Co.

Hoobler, J. M. (2007). On-site or out-of-sight? Family-friendly child care provisions and the status of working mothers. *Journal of Management Inquiry, 16*, 372–380.

Hoskyns, C., & Rai, S. M. (2007). Recasting the global political economy: Counting women's unpaid work. *New Political Economy, 12,* 297–317.

Johnston, D. D., & Swanson, D. H. (2003). Undermining mothers: A content analysis of the representation of mothers in magazines. *Mass Communication and Society, 6,* 243–265.

Kirby, E. L. (2000). Should I do as you say or do as you do? Mixed messages about work and family. *The Electronic Journal of Communication/Le Review de electronique de Communication, 10*(3–4). Available from http://www.cios .org/www/ejcmain.htm

Kirby, E., Golden, A., Medved, C., Jorgenson, J., & Buzzanell, P. M. (2003). An organizational communication challenge to the discourse of work and family research: From problematics to empowerment. In P. Kalbfleisch (Ed.), *Communication yearbook 27* (pp. 1–44). Mahwah, NJ: Lawrence Erlbaum Associates.

Kirby, E. L., & Krone, K. J. (2002). "The policy exists, but you can't use it": Negotiating tensions in work-family policy. *Journal of Applied Communication Research, 30,* 50–77.

Kramer, M. (2008). The year of the newborns: A department chair's reflections. *Women's Studies in Communication, 31,* 196–202.

Kuhn, T., Golden, A., Jorgenson, J., Buzzanell, P. M., Berkelaar, B., Kisselburgh, L., Kleinman, S., & Cruz, D. (2008). Cultural discourses and discursive resources for meaning/ful work: Constructing and disrupting identities in contemporary capitalism. *Management Communication Quarterly, 22,* 162–171.

Little, D. L. (2006). From "giving care" to "taking care": Negotiating care work at welfare's end. In M. Hamington & D. C. Miller (Eds.), *Socializing care: Feminist ethics and public issues* (pp. 121–141). Lanham, MA: Rowman & Littlefield.

Louis, M. M. (2008). Walking the walk: My autistic son and the scholarship of empathy. *Women's Studies in Communication, 31,* 233–239.

Lucas, K., & Buzzanell, P. M. (2006). Employees "without" families: Discourses of family as an external constraint to work-life balance. In L. H. Turner & R. West (Eds.), *The family communication sourcebook* (pp. 335–352). Thousand Oaks, CA: Sage.

MacDermid, S. M., Roy, K., & Zvonkovic, A. M. (2005). Don't stop at the borders: Theorizing beyond dichotomies of work and family. In V. L. Bengston, A. C. Acock, K. R. Allen, P. Dilworth-Anderson, & D. M. Klein (Eds.), *Sourcebook of family theory and research* (pp. 493–516). Thousand Oaks, CA: Sage.

Mandel, H., & Semyonov, M. (2005). Family policies, wage structures, and gender gaps: Sources of earnings inequality in 20 countries. *American Sociological Review, 70,* 949–967.

Manning, L. D. (2008). Parenting and professing in cancer's shadow. *Women's Studies in Communication, 31,* 240–248.

Martin, J. (1990). Deconstructing organizational taboos: The suppression of gender conflict in organizations. *Organization Science, 1,* 339–357.

Martin, J. (1992). The suppression of gender conflict in organizations. In D. M. Kolb & J. M. Bartunek (Eds.), *Hidden conflict in organizations* (pp. 165–185). Newbury Park, CA: Sage.

McAlister, J. F. (2008). Lives of the mind/body: Alarming notes on the tenure and biological clocks. *Women's Studies in Communication, 31,* 218–225.

Medved, C. (2007). Investigating family labor in communication studies: Threading across historical and contemporary discourses. *Journal of Family Communication, 7,* 225–243.

Medved, C. (2009). Crossing and transforming occupational and household gendered divisions of labor: Reviewing literatures and deconstructing divisions. In C. Beck (Ed.), *Communication yearbook 33* (pp. 457–484). Thousand Oaks, CA: Sage.

Medved, C., & Kirby, E. (2005). Family CEOs: A feminist analysis of corporate mothering discourses. *Management Communication Quarterly, 18,* 435–478.

Misra, J., Moller, S., & Budig, M. J. (2007). Work family policies and poverty for partnered and single women in Europe and North America. *Gender and Society, 21,* 804–827.

Monosson, E. (Ed.). (2008). *Motherhood: The elephant in the laboratory: Women scientists speak out.* Ithaca, NY: Cornell University Press.

Mosco, V. (1996). *The political economy of communication.* Thousand Oaks, CA: Sage.

Mumby, D. K., & Putnam, L. L. (1992). The politics of emotion: A feminist reading of "bounded rationality." *Academy of Management Review, 17,* 465–486.

Nicotera, A. M., Clinkscales, M. J., Dorsey, L. K., & Niles, M. (2009). Race as political identity: Problematic issues for applied communication research. In L. Frey & K. Cissna (Eds.), *The Routledge handbook of applied communication research* (pp. 203–232). New York: Routledge.

Papa, M., Singhal, A., & Papa, W. (2006). *Organizing for social change: A dialectic journey of theory and praxis.* Thousand Oaks, CA: Sage.

Perrons, D., Fagan, C., McDowell, L., Ray, K., & Ward, K. (Eds.). (2006). *Gender divisions and working time in the new economy: Changing patterns of work, care, and public policy in Europe and North America.* Cheltenham, UK: Edward Elgar.

Rees, T. (2006). Promoting equality in the private and public sectors. In M. Hamington & D. C. Miller (Eds.), *Socializing care: Feminist ethics and public issues* (pp. 229–240). Lanham, MA: Rowman & Littlefield.

Riordan, E. (2002). Intersections and new directions: On feminism and political economy. In E. Meehan & E. Riordan (Eds.), *Sex and money: Feminism and political economy in the media* (pp. 3–15). Minneapolis: University of Minnesota Press.

Robinson, F. (2006). Ethical globalization? States, corporations, and the ethics of care. In M. Hamington & D. C. Miller (Eds.), *Socializing care: Feminist ethics and public issues* (pp. 163–182). Lanham, MD: Rowman & Littlefield.

Sabattini, L., & Crosby, F. J. (2008). Ceilings and walls: Work-life and "family-friendly" policies. In H. M. G. Watt & J. S. Eccles (Eds.), *Gender and occupational outcomes: Longitudinal assessments of individual, social, and cultural influences* (pp. 201–223). Washington, DC: American Psychological Association.

Scott, W. G., & Hart, D. K. (1989). *Organizational values in America.* New Brunswick, NJ: Transaction Books.

Short-Thompson, C. (2008). A parenting odyssey: Shouldering grief, welcoming joy. *Women's Studies in Communication, 31,* 249–257.

Sotirin, P. (2008). Academic momhood: In for the long haul. *Women's Studies in Communication, 31,* 258–267.

Townsley, N. C. (2006). Love, sex, and tech in the global workplace. In B. J. Dow & J. T. Wood (Eds.), *The Sage handbook of gender and communication* (pp. 143–160). Thousand Oaks, CA: Sage.

Townsley, N. C., & Broadfoot, K. J. (2008). Care, career, and academe: Heeding the calls of a new professoriate. *Women's Studies in Communication (WSIC), 31*(2).

Tracy, S. J. (2008). Care as a common good. *Women's Studies in Communication, 31,* 166–174.

Trethewey, A. (1997). Resistance, identity, and empowerment: A postmodern feminist analysis of clients in a human service organization. *Communication Monographs, 64,* 281–301.

Tronto, J. (2006). Vicious circles of privatized caring. In M. Hamington & D. C. Miller (Eds.), *Socializing care: Feminist ethics and public issues* (pp. 3–25). Lanham, MD: Rowman & Littlefield.

Tucker, J. S. (2006). Care as a cause: Framing the Twenty-First-Century mothers' movement. In M. Hamington & D. C. Miller (Eds.), *Socializing care: Feminist ethics and public issues* (pp. 183–203). Lanham, MD: Rowman & Littlefield.

Watt, H. M. G., & Eccles, J. S. (Eds.). (2008). *Gender and occupational outcomes: Longitudinal assessments of individual, social, and cultural influences.* Washington, DC: American Psychological Association.

Weigt, J. (2006). Compromises to carework: The social organization of mothers' experiences in the low-wage labor market after welfare reform. *Social Problems, 53,* 332–351.

Wieland, S. M. B., Bauer, J. C., & Deetz, S. (2009). Excess careerism and destructive life stresses: The role of entrepreneurialism in colonizing identities. In P. Lutgen-Sandvik & B. Davenport Sypher (Eds.), *The destructive side of organizational communication* (pp. 172–212). New York: Routledge.

W. K. Kellogg Foundation. (2009). *Yes we can!* Retrieved February 4, 2009, from http://www.wkkf.org/yeswecan

12

The Worlding of Possibilities in a Collaborative Art Studio

Organizing Embodied Differences
With Aesthetic and Dialogic Sensibilities

Lynn M. Harter and William K. Rawlins

T he 2000 United States Census estimated that 49.7 million Americans over the age of five live with a disability (Waldrop & Stern, 2003). The experience of disability emerges in part from living in a body that becomes a site of struggle over the meaning of *difference.* People with disabilities often fall short when measured with the yardsticks of "normalcy," and they are responded to as body-objects as they enter an array of institutions and are inscribed by their medical, legal, and normalizing discourses (see Foucault, 1973/1994). Not surprisingly, disability remains strongly imbued with definitions of separation and exclusion. Although the 1990 Americans with Disabilities Act (ADA) and the 2001 New Freedom Initiative sought to redress inequities and ensure access to organizational life, legislation alone cannot disrupt patterns of isolation lived by those marked as disabled. For several years, we have witnessed alternative performances of disability that draw their vitality from aesthetic sensibilities, or what Lakoff and Johnson (1980) might term *imaginative rationality* (see Harter, Leeman, Norander, Young, & Rawlins, 2008; Harter, Scott, Novak, Leeman, & Morris, 2006). By fostering collaborative art among people with and without medically recognized disabilities, Passion Works offers into circulation edifying ways of acknowledging and organizing embodied differences.

Passion Works is a nonprofit studio housed within a sheltered workshop sponsored by the Athens County Board of Mental Retardation and Developmental Disabilities (ATCO). ATCO provides vocational and habilitative services for 160 adults. More than half of its clients rely on a wheelchair for movement, and nearly all of them live with full-time care providers or in medical facilities. Passion Works employs an artistic director, business manager, and volunteer coordinator, as well as several staff and production artists. Staff artists maintain a safe environment for art work, make the aesthetic process accessible to clients by providing resources, share ideas with artists, and directly collaborate in the art-making process. Production artists primarily prepare artwork for sale and manage the on-site gallery. The client artists engage in two interrelated activities: what they call *fine art* and *production art*, with roughly equal time dedicated to each activity. The inspirations for production art (e.g., the painting of mirrors) emerge from fine art processes. In turn, revenue generated from production art supports ongoing fine art collaborations.

Since its inception in 1998, Passion Works has provided employment opportunities, participated in over 40 gallery exhibitions, and realized a steady growth in sales. It serves as a rich context for exploring the dialogic and liberating potential of art. Although the studio does not explicitly invoke dialogic theory, its organizing practices embody key dialogic themes. Drawing on the work of Bakhtin and Buber, we understand dialogue as characterized by the celebration of difference and singularity, continuous acknowledgment and consummation of another, and openness to emergent possibilities. As such, dialogic and aesthetic sensibilities offer organizing logics to foster humanizing social change. At the studio, art-making involves not only the communicative activities of a marginalized group, but also a collaborative perspective rendered subordinate in cultures that reward solo artists and seemingly independent work. The collaborative ethic of the studio vigorously calls into question societal illusions of independence and separation as artists choose attunement with others in lieu of isolation.

Passion Works realizes in practice what several philosophers have endorsed: Art, if answerable to life, can be harnessed to develop fuller and richer relational and institutional life (see Burke, 1931/1968; Bakhtin, 1990). Burke (1931/1968) understood the corrective potential of aesthetic processes as articulated in his manifesto, or what he identified as The Program, "It [The Program] would define the aesthetic as effecting an adjustment to one particular cluster of conditions, at this particular time in history" (p. 121). Art, for Burke, remains eternal in the sense that it deals with constants of humanity (i.e., recurrent emotions, experiences, attitudes). Meanwhile, art is historically specific, fluctuating with the pressing cluster of conditions experienced by creators and contemplators. Bakhtin (1990) also advanced an understanding of art as answerable to the ongoing events of living—a symbolic system for disrupting cultural orientations in the ongoing fashioning of our worlds.

Most Americans remain insulated from the experience of Mental Retardation and Developmental Disabilities (MRDD) and those who live it. Disability-rights movements have raised consciousness and fostered legislative initiatives (see Longmore & Umansky, 2001), yet policy shifts have not significantly altered the disabling aspects of bureaucratic logics that fail to demystify the embodied differences separating people. Moreover, people with disabilities remain less likely to be either fully employed or underemployed and more likely to live in poverty than individuals without medically diagnosed disabilities (Waldrop & Stern, 2003). Passion Works opens up new possibilities for disability narratives as subtle, surreptitious, and multidimensional forms of protest surface that bespeak the power of artful beliefs and practices. Through art, the studio is proposing and shaping the worlds people inhabit together.

In this chapter, we move between our ethnographic experiences with Passion Works[1] and dialogic theory to develop a communicative understanding of aesthetic rationalities as knowledge producing resources for organizations that do the work of social movements. To begin, we situate our work amidst emergent literature on the aesthetic dimensions of organizing. We then explore the convictions and practices composing a dialogical aesthetics that, taken together, constitute a heartening form of organizing—*a worlding of possibilities*—that actualizes contemplative spaces for inventing other worlds. The coupling of dialogic theory and the aesthetic practices of Passion Works is instructive in its ability to *answer* difference rather than simply *normalize* or *accommodate* it, the latter of which remains deeply entrenched in deficit driven models of social service organizing.

❖ AESTHETICS AND ORGANIZING

Instrumental and objectivist logics maintain a hegemonic place in organizing and organizational theory, reasoning skills powerfully equipped to address certain dilemmas even as they may obscure and even diminish other ways of knowing. The aesthetic dimensions of organizing represent a modest but growing strand of interdisciplinary research (e.g., Eisenberg, 2007; Gagliardi, 2006; Strati & Guillet de Montoux, 2002). Although such approaches to inquiry differ, scholars are coupled loosely by desires to assign knowledge value to aesthetic experiences and stretch dominant understandings of rationality. We join and enrich this conversation by offering an aesthetic view of knowledge as vital for organizing embodied differences in humanizing ways. We understand rationalities as *modes of reasoning*, knowledge producing resources that guide organizational actors' daily choices and actions, the processes they engage in the production of knowledge, and the value judgments they make about knowledge claims (see also Harter et al., 2008). In turn, we position aesthetic rationalities as logics of possibility that cultivate individuals' capacities to imagine otherwise.

Actors' experiences of organizational life remain sensory ones. Organizations and relationships selectively develop our senses, enhancing some of our perceptive capacities at the expense of others. The writings of Dewey (1934/1980) leveraged aesthetic experiences as ways of knowing. Writing at the turn of the twentieth century, Dewey positioned instrumental rationalities as narrow views of reason and recognized dimensions of human experience constricted by routinization. Even as he acknowledged the value of rules and patterned interactions, Dewey sought to develop individuals' creative capacities to foster a full and free interplay of ideas in organizational contexts. Decades later, Strati (1999) argued that aesthetic sensibilities constitute a form of human knowledge—sensemaking yielded by the perceptive faculties of hearing, sight, touch, smell, taste, and the capacity for aesthetic judgment (see also Clair, 1998; Gagliardi, 2006). Aesthetic rationalities form knowledge by relying primarily on individuals' *intuition* and *imagination*. From this perspective, the imagination is a "muscular mechanism" (Charon, 2006, p. 12) by which we enter another's reality. Aesthetic experiences invite us to imagine events befalling others and fashion previously unimagined possibilities. To exercise our creativity is to affirm our capacity to move beyond the boundaries of our own bodies and truths, appreciate other's experiences, and interrupt automatic patterns reinforced through organized living.

Passion Works regularly calls into question taken-for-granted assumptions about the human potential of those living with medically diagnosed disabilities. Most efforts of disability rights movements have focused on legislative solutions (Longmore & Umansky, 2001). Even so, such efforts remain limited engines of change if policy shifts fail to attend to the larger task of re-orienting how society understands and organizes embodied differences. It requires imagination to realize openings through which we can perceive, write about, paint about, sculpt about, and go about things as if they could be otherwise. To tap into the imagination is to become able to break with what is supposedly rigid or fixed and to carve out new orders. Passion Works realizes in action what Weick (1995) conceptualized as an aesthetics of imperfection—a fresh mindset that allows us to see deviations from socially constructed norms as opportunities rather than threats. Weick urged us to stretch beyond the language and images of perfection in an effort to acknowledge and develop each other's creative capacities.

From this perspective both *I* and the *other* make all action and creativity possible, revealing complex interrelationships between selfhood, co-authorship, and representation. While composing or painting are typically conceived of as the activity of one person, aesthetic selves are so linked with other's lives that meaningful expression can be seen to derive intertextually from the relationships that comingle during each person's lifetime. Passion Works acknowledges this interactive potential and consciously organizes around a collaborative ethic. Dialogic theory provides a useful lens for making sense of the aesthetic rationalities of Passion Works and the relationships developed through the studio. In concert, dialogic theory and Passion Works further reveal the worlding potentials of responsive relationships in which individuals acknowledge and remain answerable to others in creating together. In the remainder of this chapter, we move between our account of the communicative patterns of Passion Works and dialogic theory to reveal the liberating potential of aesthetic rationalities in organizing embodied differences.

❖ CONVICTIONS AND PRACTICES
OF DIALOGICAL AESTHETICS

"I'm in an artistic rut. I'd like to do something different, Casey," exclaimed Jessie. "But I don't have a vision." "You don't have to start with a clear vision, Jessie. Most artists don't," Casey suggested. "How about painting a background? The line work could come later." Casey brought over a piece of black foam-board and encouraged Jessie to paint strokes of color, moving the brush across the page to create fields of blue, green, and red. "I like that idea, it is different for me. My work usually begins and ends with hard edges, hard

lines," reflected Jessie. Casey gave Jessie a choice of working with two different types of brushes, explaining that flat brushes allow for broader strokes
and round brushes allow for detailed work. Jessie swirled different hues of
paint together, creating a multicolored background. Occasionally, he asked
Casey or I [Lynn] to open a different color of paint or put a different paint-
brush in his hand. Forty minutes later, Jessie had an idea. "I had a crappy
weekend. So I want to title this 'laughing in the face of anger,' and I want to
draw a face and torso. The face of someone laughing." "You haven't really
drawn faces or torsos before," mused Casey.

Casey got out several blank pieces of paper and talked with him about
how to draw faces. "When I was in school and learned to draw faces, I was
taught to draw an oval shape like this and cut it in half three different
times. So you draw a line in the middle of the oval. Right below the line is
approximately where the eyes go. And then you draw another line halfway
between the eyes and the bottom of the oval. And the bottom of the nose
ends on that line. And then you draw another line between the nose and
the bottom of the oval. And that is where the mouth goes. So the lines help
you to learn how to place things on the face." To illustrate how the artist
can exercise creative license, Casey drew the second face with a Mohawk
stripe of hair. She then placed a marker in Jessie's hand and encouraged
him to try. Jessie's first attempt looked like a crescent moon. On his second
attempt, Jessie drew an oval, followed by two lines, eyes, and a nose.
Repeatedly, Casey affirmed Jessie's vision and abilities. "This second face is
a hallmark moment. And the more you do this, the better you will get
Jessie." (Field notes)

The artful activity of Passion Works demonstrates several features
of a dialogical aesthetics. First, *the staff strongly recognizes the value of singularity and celebrates the embodied differences composing each human being.*
They are committed to the unique potentials of each participant who
spends time in the studio. As such, their regard for client artists exem-
plifies Bakhtin's (1981, 1984a, 1984b) conviction that authentic respect
and ethical action are rooted in responsiveness to "the radical singularity of each person at every moment" (Morson & Emerson, 1989, p. 16)—
that is, to *each* other. Bakhtin drew much of his insight about dialogue
and aesthetics from understanding the discourse of novels and how
authors act toward characters. The moral demand of dialogue is that
individuals grant authority to each other's voices. These are never cat-
egorical actions; Bakhtin's (1993) concept of once-occurrence insists
that every single moment of the responsibly lived life has ethical
import. As conscious and purposeful human beings, we are addressed
continuously by the events of our world in our radical singularity and

in once-occurrent moments. During these continuous yet evanescent occasions, we define ourselves and others simultaneously by how we respond to them and how they respond to us in our particularity. In the field notes provided earlier, Casey affirmed Jessie's inclination to stretch his artistic horizon and drew on her own experiences to engage him in the process. Both Casey and Jessie released in each other something that might otherwise remain dormant.

Claire, an artist herself and the artistic director of Passion Works, described in detail during an interview the studio's dedication to singularity in its work with client artists:

> One of the challenges is just the physical issues that people have and making art accessible to those guys and making them feel as though they can do it. But we have to be creative. You know, sometimes it works with a headstick, sometimes it works by holding an elbow up. God knows what . . . . There is no rule about how it's going to work. You have to pay attention to each individual person and figure out how to make it work. Which is really exciting, especially when we have breakthroughs. It's enormous. For some of these guys, it's absolutely life-changing. That now they can communicate.

The corporeal experiences of clients are acknowledged as staff artists creatively enable clients to participate fully in their craft. Consider the following excerpt from Lynn's field notes:

> "I want to be back," declared Tom, as he rolled into Passion Works studio. "We want you to be back in the studio, Tom, and we hope this special device made just for you will get you back to work," stressed Claire as she clamped the arm of the Versatile Painting Solution to the side of Tom's wheelchair. The Versatile Painting Solution, developed by biomedical engineering students in a collaborative effort between two universities, consists of an adjustable arm support and a wrist attachment that holds writing devices. This adaptive technology was inspired by a desire for Tom to use his wrist, rather than his fingers, to paint. Claire gently lifted Tom's arm and placed it on the padded arm rest. "Should this be higher, Tom?" asked Claire. "Yes, higher." She followed cues from Tom as she adjusted the height of the armrest to maximize comfort. Next, she slipped the wrist support onto Tom's left hand and placed a marker into an aluminum tube designed to hold writing devices. As Lynn held a flower petal, Tom moved his wrist from left to right, up and down. With each move of his wrist, Tom added a stroke to the petal, creating a multi-layered image full of depth and texture. "I'm back, I'm back," exclaimed Tom. "You are back, Tom," affirmed Claire.

Staff artists make the aesthetic process accessible to clients by organizing and sharing materials, including canvases, paints, and glitter. They also engage in conversations about particular mediums client artists wish to explore, offer suggestions (e.g., colors that might enhance images), and demonstrate techniques (e.g., drawing a house). Sometimes, staff manually guide and support the arms and hands of clients or place paintbrushes in clients' hands. In other cases, staff artists use adaptive technologies to help clients enter into the creative process. The Versatile Painting Solution, for example, is designed to allow Tom to be creative—to paint, draw, express ideas, and "be back" in the studio as an artist. "We work to make art accessible. And we don't ask our clients to reinvent themselves. Instead, we try to provide resources and support for clients to fully realize who they are and artistically express their impulses," shared Claire. "In return, we ask that our artists, like all artists, struggle through the artistic process." As a result, many interviewees commented on the studio's success in drawing on and developing previously untapped gifts and interests of clients. Amy, a production aid, shared, "When Passion Works began, it was so powerful . . . It was new. But it was also different. It was things coming out of an individual that we weren't able to draw out of them through programming or whatever." In the studio, creativity stems from the profound moral obligation artists bear toward others—their responses to individuals in specific moments. For Bakhtin (1990), too, creative work involved answering another. As such, answerability contains the moral imperative that the artist must *answer* life, must remain engaged with life. In Bakhtin's (1981) formulation, creativity presupposes that life itself is dialogic.

The studio understands that *being a person is itself a ceaseless aesthetic project undertaken, of necessity, with others.* Viewed aesthetically, the existential mandate for all persons is to give meaningful form to our experiences, what Burke (1931/1968) termed "the element of self-expression in all human activities" (p. 52). Even so, at the same time that our creative efforts of self-fashioning propose a shape for our lived moments, they embody a call to others to confirm our actions, our bodies, and our very existences. In the preceding anecdote, the interactions between Casey and Jessie embody the dialogic creativity that is unfolding constantly at Passion Works. The goal is to keep everyone involved in exercising their imaginations. This is accomplished with a constant eye toward each other's capacities. Artists in the studio are reminded that they are "unfinalizable" and capable of outgrowing where they are today. In Bakhtin's (1993) terms, each person embodies "answerable, risk-fraught, and open becoming through performed actions" (p. 9). Jessie's and Casey's differences make creative breakthroughs possible. Jessie's capacities and horizons grew that day in the studio, as did Casey's vision and experience of faces, Jessie, and collaborative possibility.

Bakhtin (1990) distinguished between our inner experience of our body and the crucial role other's responses play in shaping it:

> There is an equally profound difference between my inner experience of my own body and the recognition of its outer value by *other* people . . . . The plastic value of my outer body has been as it were sculpted for me by the manifold acts of other people in relation to me, acts performed intermittently throughout my life: acts of concern for me, acts of love, acts that recognize my value. . . . In this respect, the body is not something self-sufficient: it needs the *other*, needs his recognition and his form-giving activity. (pp. 49, 51, emphasis original)

As important, just as we require the responses of others to complete ourselves, we are also the sources of their moments of consummation. Even as staff artists elevate a table to accommodate wheelchairs, they also are affirmed by clients' curiosity and accomplishments.

Casey is convinced of the client artists' aesthetic potentials and remains troubled by the limiting perceptions that they often experience:

> Everybody sees the disability first and doesn't realize there's just this whole, complex, working person working inside them just like everyone is. So they're bound by this anchor that is their body or their disability. And you know art has been a way to really break that bondage. And I don't even really understand why except that art is really true and when it's done with true intentions, um, beauty comes out of it and that is just the essence of it in my mind. And so with the making of art, they were able to, they were able to rise above their disabilities, you know, they're no longer limited to be a person in a wheelchair. They can be anyone they want. And that's where my role comes in, to feed their imagination, to get those things working. That they have confidence to do whatever they choose to do. . . . And that's so huge in our studio because people are full of depth and beauty and imagination and whimsy and they have as much going on as any one of us has going on, you know. They just, unfortunately, have not been given the opportunities that we have. Until now, I think. I think that's what is happening in the studio is that they are actually receiving things that they haven't received before.

As suggested by Casey, the disabled body is often inscribed with meanings such as damaged and defective, and people with disabilities are rendered subordinate and often sheltered from the fullness of community life. "These guys are traditionally excluded from the public, from work," stressed Claire. "In our culture we are so identified through work. Once I realized this [collaborative art-making] could mean work for our guys . . . it became a moral obligation to provide it." Staff artists at once recognize the unique embodied experiences of clients and the need to make art accessible and yet refuse to anticipate (or limit) possibilities based on (dis)ability. Ultimately, we are reminded of the importance of revaluing the mind and body as a source of *difference*. At Passion Works, collaborative aesthetics allow participants to explore the edifying potentials of differences in embodied living. Meanwhile, aesthetic experiences provide a scaffold for the achievement of other goals, including paid labor and self-advocacy.

There are several dynamic contingencies in Bakhtin's (1990) account of how the aesthetic accomplishment of meaningful wholes, that is, consummated forms, transpires in human interaction. For one, as mentioned previously, each one of us occupies a unique place and time in the history of human becoming throughout every moment of our respective lives. During each instant, no one ever has or ever will view the world in the precise manner and from the exact vantage point of our lived experience—a human privilege and imperative termed "the Law of Placement" by Holquist (1990) in reading Bakhtin. Indeed, Bakhtin (1993) argued that we have no alibi in being—no right to evade the answerability of our "once-occurrent Being that is unique and never-repeatable, a place that cannot be taken by anyone else" (p. 40). Meanwhile, we constantly live the ongoing fashioning of our moments as both self and other. As self, our inner experiences of our body's features and expressions open outward into the world. But we can never truly experience these self-fashionings apart from our own activities of rendering them; we can never truly get outside of ourselves. The openings we create in our attempts to express ourselves cannot be closed by us. We require responses from others to give our activities closure and significance. It is therefore the other who consummates and accords value and beauty to our doings, or deems them worthless and ignores them—that is, who authorizes all increments of their significance between esteem and indifference.

This "response-ability" is imposed upon the other—and ourselves *as* others—in light of the other's capacity to perceive more of self than self can achieve. For example, a person can never actually witness the figure one cuts in the context of one's life; one never sees one's own face nor hears one's own voice in an unmediated way. Experiencing self directly from elsewhere, evaluating and rounding out the significance of one's deeds are the provenance of the other. Bakhtin (1990) calls this crucial capability to apprehend each other as a completed whole "the excess of seeing," which gives the other the capacity "to unify and order" (p. 24) another self's works, actions, and fashionings of possibilities.

For Bakhtin, each of us as a person is incomplete without the response of the other, just as our works of art must also be consummated by the other in the artifacts' ongoing potential for creating meaning. His aesthetics describe active and ongoing triadic interrelationships of creators, contemplators, and human works. The integrated whole of aesthetic activity involves all facets of this process. The existential mandate to create is tightly wedded to the expressive mandate to communicate, and both are connected to "the perceptual mandate to consummate" (Holquist, 1990, p. xxx). These mandates shape and reflect art/aesthetic activity as communication, communication as art/aesthetic activity, and both creation and communication as offering and requiring consummation. Such a dialogical aesthetic insists that our respective wholeness emerges through our consummation by the/each other. It celebrates the ongoing aesthetic activity of creative collaboration among singular beings—fashioning together meaningful wholes that open outward and invite the regard of others.

Claire is adamant about the creative well-springs residing in all human beings. For her, collaboration, affirmation, and encouragement are key responses for teasing out and consummating everyone's potentials for creating beauty. Accordingly, she rejects deficit-driven models that undergird social service organizing and insists instead on providing concrete opportunities for self-expression:

> I just want this to be an opportunity to make stuff—to express themselves. That's it. We just really want people to work from where they are at, from their own lives, from their hearts. And that's the amazing part. Because there is no shame in it. Or whatever it is that keeps folks from even expressing themselves at all. I can't tell you how many people who don't have so-called disabilities walk into the studio and say, "Oh, I'm not artistic. I have nothing creative to share." And I think, wow, you have really convinced yourself that you are not a creative being. And hopefully if they are hanging out with Mary Ellen and Cassie for a little while they will realize, you know, what kind of disability they have given themselves in assuming they can't be creative.

The aesthetic rationalities and practices composing the studio create possibilities for emancipatory dialogue and meaningful community.

Sarah is a client artist who has a knack for inscribing narratives about Smokey Robinson on collaborative art projects. Her mother, Suzanne, spoke warmly of the impact these aesthetic activities and Claire's encouragement have had on her daughter:

> We really do appreciate Claire. We think she's wonderful. She's made a huge difference in Sarah's life. It's a generosity that is kind of rare, you know. That generosity of spirit where you say, "Oh, you like to write compulsively about Smokey Robinson forever and forever? Great! You're an artist. Start writing." You know, (laughter) it's brilliant. I never would have predicted or ever imagined it. It's fabulous.

We hasten to emphasize that aesthetic consummation of self and one's expressive efforts remain an ongoing dialogical activity at Passion Works—the capacity for affirming beauty flows both ways between collaborators. For example, here Casey discusses the positive impact she witnesses her confirming responses having on the client artists when they work together in the studio. Even so, notice how their responses to her artful activity also confirm her well-being and consummate her efforts as "a blessed job":

> They're recognized for their own thoughts. Not for doing good on a job, you know, not for completing a task that they were told to complete, but for choosing and deciding on their own and then seeing, seeing it through to the end. And you know, I really have a blessed job because I get to, I'm always at the triumph end, I get to help with recognizing their potential for completing these paintings and sculptures and so, you know, I guess, I constantly get, I get in on the good parts of their art-making. And that's what I see my job is to do, is to just to help them, compliment them, help them to get their painting to the stage they want to call it complete. And they make those calls, you know. They tell me when it's done. They tell me if they are going to paint or draw. It's you know, I try to give them as many options as possible.

The client artists' responses and their active choices in the aesthetic process reciprocally consummate the validity and beauty of Casey's work in offering them creative possibilities, as revealed earlier in our observations of her and Jessie's collaborative drawing of faces.

Staff members realize that the imagination offers vibrant modes of being, and they craft environments in which clients can exercise their pliable capacities to imagine. In turn, staff artists also experience the liberating potentials of creativity. Consider Casey's testimony, "Our mission is to inspire and liberate the human spirit through the arts. They've had a lifetime of not. What we find is that it lifts us too. There is this constant elevation of who we are as a people."

> *Jackson, Alexandra, Jan, and Connor were creating prayer flags using pillowcases as canvasses. The artistic expressions were as diverse as the flags' previous uses: Jackson drew birds, Connor constructed houses, Jan proudly created a flower, and Alexandra narrated a drawing of two kissing yaks saying, "I do." "Take out the papers and the trash. Or you don't get no spending cash," wrote Alexis, "Yakety, yak, yakety, yak. Don't talk back." Claire invited two visiting monk-artists from Drepung Gomang Monastery, Sopa and Tsultrim, to join in the collaborative process. Sopa curved Tibetan words in an arc around the birds drawn by Jackson. Tenzin translated the meanings, "For all beings to have the freedom for peace in their hearts,""For success and purification,""A lifelong blessing for Passion Works." Pillow cases were passed around so each artist could contribute a different layer to the art, and the energy in the room was felt by all. Tsultrim drew a wind horse and Tenzin revealed its symbolism: a prayer for purification. Ultimately, the flags will be hung so that prayers can be carried by the wind.*
>
> *The next day, the monks were kneeled on pillows and working on a "Buddha Mandala," a sand painting. "Teach me, teach me," exclaimed Ross. A few minutes later, Tenzin, a bilingual resident artist of Drepung, translated an invitation from the Monks for Ross and Jamie to participate in the craft of sand art. "See what happens, Ross, when you ask to learn something— magic," exclaimed Claire. Reva and Christy quickly set up a table accessible by Ross and Jamie in their wheelchairs as Tenzin placed materials in front on them including rubber mats, colored sand, and chakpurs of various sizes. Chakpurs are metal tools cylindrical in shape, hollow and ridged. Tenzin patiently helped each artist figure out how to hold and use the instruments. Fifteen minutes later, in the midst of rhythmic motions of Chakpur rubbing against Chakpur, Tenzin declared "Ross and Jamie, you are naturals. You are sand painters!"(Field notes)*

Affirming the validity of dialogical aesthetics, Passion Works emphasizes collaboration among its artists and challenges an individualistic conception of artistic creation and labor. Artists consciously make space to encounter the world through other's eyes and voices. In *Toward a Philosophy of the Act* (1993), Bakhtin urged readers to live themselves into another's ideas in order to clarify and deepen their own. In a Bakhtinian sense, artists at Passion Works live themselves into another's lifeworld in order to enrich the creative process. The artists of Drepung and Passion Works reside in different cultures and speak different languages, practice spirituality in diverse ways, usually are separated across time and space, and yet remain united with one another by aesthetic impulses. Throughout the duration of the monks' visit, Passion Works artists explored new subjects and genres of artwork and learned about cultural similarities (e.g., the role of detail in artwork) and differences (e.g., spirituality). Likewise, the monks were transformed through the presence and energies of Passion Works's artists. "Though we didn't understand each other's language, painting and art was language enough to become friends," emphasized Tsultrim Sherab.

The studio insists that works expressing viewpoints on life emerge between and among artists with differing talents and experiences. The studio's practices seem to ask the following: Why can't works of art be embodied and rendered as active interhuman performances—as collaborative engagements expressing the differences composing our worlds? Why not incorporate radical differences in apprehending existence—what Buber (1937) and Bakhtin (1990) each call "bodying over against" others—directly into the creative process? Perhaps reluctance to do so stems from a limiting conception of what it means to be a self or to express oneself. It also may reflect a need to convert self and one's works into commodities produced by and identified with one solitary person. In contrast, Bakhtin (1990) insisted upon the necessity for more than one participant in aesthetic activity, as well as the imperative for difference in creating "something new." He asserted, "If there is only one unitary and unique participant, there can be no aesthetic event" (p. 22), later adding:

> There are events which are in principle incapable of unfolding on the plane of one and the same consciousness and which presuppose two consciousnesses which never merge. Or, in other words, what is *constitutive* for such events is the relationship of one consciousness to *another* consciousness precisely as an *other*. Events of this kind include all of the *creatively* productive events—the once-occurrent and inconvertible events that bring forth something new. (pp. 86–87, emphasis original)

Artists are enjoined to transcend their self-defined limits and preoccupations through giving themselves to enveloping aesthetic activity. Participants are richly connected as they respond to one another in nonlinear, unpredictable fashions. Such *a dialogical image of aesthetic collaboration demands that participants surrender their ego-involvement with their own contributions to emerging creations.* Working with Gregory

Bateson's ideas in *The Aesthetics of Change*, Keeney (1983) remarked, "In this interactive dance, a whole pattern of organization rather than conscious intent or purpose triggers action" (p. 194). With the studio dedicated to aesthetic activities that transcend specific individuals' conscious intents, several artists and staff members have commented on the joy of doing artwork in this manner. One of the guiding assumptions of Passion Works is that *both the process and the products of such shared artful activity can be aesthetically pleasing.*

Reflecting the classic dialogical conceptions of Gadamer (1989) and Buber (1937), these collaboratively created works of art are the unfinalized, physical embodiment of *the between.* The works embody collective expressions of difference that are palpable results of everyone's participation without being reducible to any single person's contributions. As such, they constitute the emergent and shared subject matter of dialogical relating that supplants a dominating focus on individuals (Gadamer). Instead, singular and irreplaceable persons relate to each other in affirming ways mediated through their connections with the shared creative work. In responding to each other's creative activity, works and human beings are continuously acknowledged and consummated.

In describing her experiences in the studio, McKibben, a production artist, reflected on the unique features of such a creative process:

> We can pull something out that we thought was done like a week ago and someone will say, "I'll draw an elephant on that," and we'll be like, "Okay." It's never really done. We are always adding stuff and the more the merrier. It's not territorial art. It's community art. They don't care if somebody else draws on it—they are like, "Great, we're putting it together." If it were me I'd be like, "Dude, you're painting over that thing I just drew last night and I loved it, and you're ruining it—I'm not collaborating any more!" But it's just a different deal here and I like that they are all about each other . . . I love that. It is different from the outside art world.

Client artist Alexis's father, Billy, also commented on her enjoyment of the process and her lack of possessiveness about her Smokey Robinson stories:

> What's cool to me is that she writes it out on a piece of flat sheet metal and then down in the workshop, they just cut it up. And then it becomes the calligraphy and the stories are gone and it doesn't bother her at all. She's just into the process more than of writing for her. She doesn't hang on to them so much.

The constant opportunity for such unselfish contributions and participation by artists with and without disabilities produces an array of
unique artworks for exhibition and sale. But Casey is just as convinced
of the aesthetic value of the collaborative process itself, asserting:

> And really so much of the art is the process, I mean, there's where so
> much of the beauty lies and why they are so rich and so special and
> so intricate and so worked because it spent a month on a table with a
> dozen hands on it. I mean, it can't deny being rich and full and full of
> life and thought because it has tons of it in it.

Indeed, the studio's collaborative ethic is one of its most distinctive
characteristics, which we believe deserves an extended personal definition from Casey to provide a sense of its dialogical qualities and nuances:

Casey: Oh, my own terms. (Pauses). What I believe. In the studio,
         yeah, it's, we collaborate physically because we all physically
         work on the work. We also collaborate mentally and emotion-
         ally, and we, you know, we have that open dialogue, what's
         going on, and there's this, again it's back to this reassurance,
         that they're seeking it, we're giving it out. Um, all of that
         plays, plays a part in getting the piece done. And, 'cause you
         know Harry will start something out of his own thinking, out
         of his own brain. He'll come in the morning and say, "I have
         a new idea." He'll tell me a little bit about the new idea; I'll
         ask a few questions. He'll start in on a painting and he'll get
         to the point where he's fearful, "Oh, like, I can't draw any-
         more. This is too hard."

Lynn: I've seen it.

Casey: And so then I have to come over and say, "It's not too hard.
         You got it. Two wheels, you got this going on. You got this
         going on. Tell me what else is going on in this scene. Now
         think about it again." And then he'll say, "Oh, there's sup-
         posed to be this person and this person." "Okay, what do you
         do with these people? Where do they go?" "They're there."
         "Well, go put those in there." And he'll say, "No, you do it."
         And I'll say, "You do it. It's your piece. You believe that you
         can. You know the confidence is in you. You need to know
         that you can get in there and draw that." It's just a little push
         but that's all he needs. And then he puts that in. And when
         I come back, and he says, "Come see it." And he shows a

couple other people. And he wants to talk about it, and someone new comes in and he brings them into it too. It really is just
a full on, I don't know how to put it, collaboration at its max.
It's all of our being involved in the room sometimes. It's our
heads and hearts and our hands. And it's—they never come
in a particular order. They all kind of just come in on the side.
I just see it as a big ball in that way. I think about the collaboration in there, and you see it as a sphere where we all just roll
around and rock back and forth and sometimes someone's up
and someone's on the bottom and you know, and it never gets
stuck in the corner. It's always just rocking around.

Ironically, participants' expressions of individuality become
sources of solidarity and connection with others. When art is answerable to the ongoing events of living, the creative act inspires connections between self and others. As a result, Jessica reflected, "It makes
people feel less separate. I don't think it makes them feel like less of an
individual, but less separated, closer to others, closer to community
and closer to the world, than like doing something on their own."

❖ WORLDING OF POSSIBILITIES

Taken together, the convictions and practices composing the dialogical
aesthetics of Passion Works constitute a heartening form of worlding;
that is, a collective arrangement of activities and works proposing edifying spaces for the human spirit. Several touchstones concerning
ways of thinking about art support our recognition of this ongoing
invitation by Passion Works. Lakoff and Johnson (1980) maintained
that both metaphor and art involve "imaginative rationality," which
"permits an understanding of one experience in terms of another"
(p. 235). Different imaginings are juxtaposed and combined to produce
new possibilities. Meanwhile, the fresh comprehensions that result
engender novel realities that are not solely linguistic matters.
Regarding art in particular, the authors argue:

> Each art medium picks out certain dimensions of our experience and
> excludes others. Artworks provide new ways of structuring our expe-
> rience in terms of these natural dimensions. Works of art provide new
> experiential gestalts and, therefore, new coherences. From the experi-
> entialist point of view, art is, in general, a matter of imaginative ratio-
> nality and a means of creating new realities. (pp. 235–236)

Other authors also acknowledge the vital contributions of art as a potentially edifying way of worlding—giving form to persons and works that presuppose and are consummated through belonging to altered and encouraging worlds. Brown (1959) found art to be crucial for persistently forging vivifying meanings in the face of mortality and invokes Rilke's conception of "art as a way of life . . . 'the sensuous possibility of new worlds and times'" (1959, p. 66). And Bakhtin's (1990) observations are once more definitive:

> What needs to be understood, however, is not the technical apparatus, but *the immanent logic of creative activity,* and what needs to be understood first of all is the value-and-meaning structure in which creative activity comes to pass and in which it gains an axiological awareness of itself—that is, the context in which the act of creation becomes meaningful . . . The fundamental problem is to determine first of all the artistic task and its actual context, i.e., that axiological world in which the artistic task is set and actualized. (p. 194, emphasis original)

Determining and shaping such axiological worlds is what we intend by the worlding potentials of aesthetic activity. Accordingly, when Claire speaks of the studio as engaged in "civil rights work," she is speaking of artfully *creating new realities* (Lakoff & Johnson, 1980) and *axiological worlds* (Bakhtin, 1981) within which diverse persons can express themselves, earn money, and experience connection through the processes and products fashioned at Passion Works. Don, the manager of ATCO, also invoked notions of social change as he spoke of the studio's mission:

> Our goal is to use art as a way to empower the people we serve and to educate our community. As we got this thing rolling, I thought of it as a civil rights movement. It wasn't enough to make art. . . . Art ended up being the right vehicle to express what goes on in people who don't have a good way to communicate. It draws people in, makes people step closer. Then you can talk to them about other issues that affect their lives.

> Aesthetic experiences foster inventive expression. For individuals with MRDD, it is difficult to endow events with meaning through language. The arts offer a range of media for self-expression, inviting creators and contemplators to envision otherwise.

This civil rights work is achieved using imaginative rationality and collaborative self-expression. The selves expressed here are enlarged senses of self (Rawlins, 2009). The works of art and the social/workaday circumstances through which they are created are interlinked aesthetic achievements requiring consummation by others. As such, the aesthetic endeavors of Passion Works occasion consummations of the collaborative relationships between artists with and without disabilities, between the studio and its support staff, and between the ongoing activities and products of Passion Works and its appreciators, consumers, funding agencies, and visitors. Thus, this collaborative art studio is itself an ongoing aesthetic achievement—a living, vulnerable, delicately balanced composition of activities. At the same time, it facilitates the creation of various works of art that are themselves aesthetic achievements and enables the self-expression, confirmation, and consummation of diverse human beings qua artists. Both the creative works and the studio's collaborative processes invite recognition and participation by others in the surrounding community. In doing so, they simultaneously propose a possible world where the works they create and the ways they do so are deemed desirable and worthy of notice.

Client artist Sarah's parents each described positive consequences of Passion Works's worlding activities. During an interview in their home, Suzanne observed:

> People want to accept handicapped people but they really don't know how. Passion Works gives them a way to know how to relate. It's like somebody isn't really comfortable approaching someone in a wheelchair and talking to that person. But if they go to an opening of a show and that's somebody in a wheelchair and they can say, "Oh. That's your painting." Then there is a way to communicate, to connect with people.

And Billy shared with us a copy of a letter he wrote in support of a state award recognizing the studio's artistic achievements. In the letter appear these words:

> It's amazing to me how the aura of that studio has begun to permeate this community. First of course through the art works and the public events like the parades and the poetry readings, but also through the magnet of direct interaction with the people on so many levels that go beyond the ordinary "mainstreaming" of the disabled. The communication is profound, and the medium is art.

Invoking another world of aesthetic activity and human becoming with others, Passion Works's endeavors challenge routine notions of taste and artistic production. We already have noticed how the myth of the solitary artist is displaced and socialized by the studio's collaborative ethos. These practices in themselves have occasionally created some problems for the studio in terms of how its works are perceived (and therefore consummated) by other artists, judges, exhibitions, and endowments supporting the arts. Widely varying skills, standpoints, aesthetic understandings, and preferred images of artists with and without disabilities also are embodied in the artworks themselves. Consequently, the artwork produced by the studio tends to exhibit distinctive attributes and stylistic features—some would say *spirit*. An array of responses to the artifacts is possible, but such diverging and converging responses are constitutive features of aesthetic worlding. The matter of taste is pivotal in joining worlds.

Passion Works's aesthetic activities continually raise the question: What do we want to make of ourselves and our co-constructed and shared worlds? The works produced embody activities of worlding— bodying forth a possible world (Anton, 2001). The ethical and political turn of this aesthetic involves placing these works fashioned through mutual recognition in a public forum as exercises of inclusion. The aesthetic also addresses the terms under which that inclusion is insisted upon—not as reduced to a person's disability—but as collaborative art and as civil rights. It emerges as and from a recognition of the roles that each person plays in the creation, composition, and production of the works.

❖ CONCLUDING OBSERVATIONS/OPENING INTERPRETATIONS

We have shared and theorized actual moments and practices of dialogical aesthetics serving social change. We have characterized the dialogical aesthetics of the studio as (1) celebrating the value of singularity and the embodied differences composing each human being; (2) understanding personhood itself as involving ongoing aesthetic activity and mutual consummation necessarily pursued with others; (3) emphasizing artistic collaboration and emergent creative works, thereby challenging individualistic notions of artistic production; (4) regarding both the process and the products of collaborative artful activity as potentially beautiful; and (5) performing convictions, practices, and works as dedicated worlding, that is, as proposing edifying spaces for the human spirit.

We find Passion Works instructive in its aesthetic celebration of embodied differences as artists exercise their imaginations in order to enter the worlds of others. In daily acts of living, these artists link imaginative capacities to a sense of possibility and ability to respond to other human beings. The studio offers a set of relational and organizing rhythms worthy of modeling, in which those often categorized as other for whatever reason (e.g., age, race, ability, gender) share in humanly fabricated worlds. Rather than disregarding or rendering invisible embodied differences that remain consequential (e.g., inability to use one's hands or voice for expression), artists at Passion Works are imaginative enough to be present in and contribute to what Bakhtin (1981) called the "heteroglossia" or multiple discourses of relational living. All told, a salient lesson taught by Passion Works together with dialogic theory is to *answer* difference rather than simply *normalize* or *accommodate* it—the latter two practices remaining deeply embedded in the restitution or deficit-driven narratives sponsoring mere assistance for those living with disabilities. Sheltered workshops, like many government-sponsored social service agencies, easily succumb to deficit models that position clients as flawed and passive recipients of care (see also Trethewey, 1997). By embracing aesthetic and dialogic sensibilities, Passion Works has made a social service organization more responsive to the interests of its clients.

Reaching beyond the context of Passion Works, we propose here that all relational and organizing acts constitute aesthetic endeavors. Social living continually offers occasions for aesthetic consummation of otherness. The extent to which we grasp another's lifeworld largely depends on poetically exercising our imagination. While we do not necessarily need to approve of or even ultimately embrace all diverse standpoints (Ashcraft & Mumby, 2004), we must extend our experience sufficiently to grasp them as authentic possibilities. Meanwhile, to tap into the imagination is to break with what is supposedly rigid or fixed and to carve out new orders. The aesthetic worlding of possibilities is a first step in acting on a belief that conditions can be changed. Through artful activities, we can articulate common imaginings and demystify differences that separate us. In a Burkean sense (1954/1984), artful activity can disrupt the trained incapacities and fossilized institutions that hem us in. Achieving momentary or more enduring community involvements can be understood as intersubjective, relational, and aesthetic accomplishments—activities of worlding, the ongoing creation of new interpretive orders.

❖ NOTE

1. See Harter et al. (2008) for an overview of the research design.

❖ REFERENCES

Anton, C. (2001). *Selfhood and authenticity.* Albany: State University of New York Press.

Ashcraft, K. L., & Mumby, D. (2004). *Reworking gender. A feminist communicology of organization.* Thousand Oaks, CA: Sage.

Bakhtin, M. M. (1981). *The dialogic imagination: Four essays* (C. Emerson & M. Holquist, Trans.). Austin: University of Texas Press.

Bakhtin, M. M. (1984a). *Speech Genres and other late essays* (M. Holquist, Trans.). Austin: University of Texas Press.

Bakhtin, M. M. (1984b). The hero, and the position of the author with regard to the hero, in Dostoevsky's art. In C. Emerson (Ed. & Trans.), *Problems of Dostoevsky's poetics* (pp. 47–77). Minneapolis: University of Minnesota Press.

Bakhtin, M. M. (1990). Author and hero in aesthetic activity (V. Liapunov, Trans.). In M. Holquist & V. Liapunov (Eds.), *Art and answerability: Early philosophical works by M. M. Bakhtin* (pp. 4–256). Austin: University of Texas Press.

Bakhtin, M. M. (1993). *Toward a philosophy of the act* (V. Liapunov, Trans.). Austin: University of Texas Press.

Brown, N. O. (1959). *Life against death: The psychoanalytical meaning of history.* Middletown, CT: Wesleyan University Press.

Buber, M. (1937). *I and thou* (R. G. Smith, Trans.). Edinburgh: T. and T. Clark.

Burke, K. (1931/1968). *Counter-statement.* Berkeley: University of California Press.

Burke, K. (1954/1984). *Permanence and change* (3rd ed.). Berkeley: University of California Press.

Charon, R. (2006). *Narrative medicine: Honoring the stories of illness.* New York: Oxford University Press.

Clair, R. (1998). *Organizing silence: A world of possibilities.* Albany: State University of New York Press.

Dewey, J. (1934/1980). *Art as experience.* New York: Perigree.

Eisenberg, E. (2007). *Strategic ambiguities: Essays on communication, organization, and identity.* Thousand Oaks, CA: Sage.

Foucault, M. (1973/1994). *The birth of the clinic: An archeology of medical perception* (A. M. Sheridan Smith, Trans.). New York: Vintage Books/Random House.

Gadamer, H. G. (1989). *Truth and method, 2nd revised edition.* (J. Weinsheimer & D. G. Marshall, Trans.). New York: Continuum.

Gagliardi, P. (2006). Exploring the aesthetic side of organizational life. In S. Clegg, C. Hardy, T. Lawrence, & W. R. Nord (Eds.), *Exploring the aesthetic side of organizational life* (pp. 701–724). Thousand Oaks, CA: Sage.

Harter, L. M., Leeman, M., Norander, S., Young, S. L., & Rawlins, W. K. (2008). The intermingling of aesthetic sensibilities and instrumental rationalities in a collaborative arts studio. *Management Communication Quarterly, 21,* 423–453.

Harter, L. M., Scott, J., Novak, D., Leeman, M., & Morris, J. (2006). Freedom through flight: Performing a counter-narrative of disability. *Journal of Applied Communication Research, 34,* 3–29.

Holquist, M. (1990). *Dialogism: Bakhtin and his world.* London: Routledge.

Keeney, B. P. (1983). *Aesthetics of change.* New York: Guilford Press.

Lakoff, G., & Johnson, M. (1980). *Metaphors we live by.* Chicago: University of Chicago Press.

Longmore, P. K., & Umansky, L. (Eds.). (2001). *The new disability history: American perspectives.* New York: New York University Press.

Morson, G. S., & Emerson, C. (1989). Introduction: Rethinking Bakhtin. In G. S. Morson & C. Emerson (Eds.), *Rethinking Bakhtin: Extensions and challenges* (pp. 1–60). Evanston, IL: Northwestern University Press.

Rawlins, W. K. (2009). *The compass of friendship: Narratives, identities, and dialogues.* Thousand Oaks, CA: Sage.

Strati, A. (1999). *Organization and aesthetics.* Thousand Oaks, CA: Sage.

Strati, A., & Guillet de Montoux, P. (2002). Introduction: Organizing aesthetics. *Human Relations, 55,* 755–766.

Trethewey, A. (1997). Resistance, identity, and empowerment: A postmodern feminist analysis of clients in a human service organization. *Communication Monographs, 64,* 281–300.

Waldrop, J., & Stern, S. M. (2003). *Disability status 2000: Census 2000 brief.* Washington, DC: U.S. Department of Commerce/Economics and Statistics Administration.

Weick, K. (1995). Creativity and the aesthetics of imperfection. In C.D. Ford & D.A. Gioia (Eds.), *Creative action in organizations: Ivory tower visions and real world voices* (pp. 187–194). Thousand Oaks, CA: Sage.

Author Index

Subject Index

Academe and caregiving, 251–252
Academic tenure/promotion, 202–203
"Accenting" discourses, 160
Accion Zapatista, 239
Accommodator style, 90
Accountants, 9
Activist researchers, 226–228
  See also Regal Gardens/University Heights project
ADA (Americans with Disabilities), 267–268
Added value, difference as, 34–35
Administrative evil, 133
Advancement, talking about difference as, 198, 200, 204–206, 209–210, 213–214
Aesthetic endeavors and social living. *See* Passion Works
Airline pilot analysis, 17–18, 165–166
Alliance building, 69–72
Alpha biases, 32
Alpha females, 81–82, 87–91
Alpha males, 81–86
Alpha Male Syndrome (Ludeman and Erlandson), 78–93
Americans with Disabilities (ADA), 267–268
Aotearoa/New Zealand cultural identities
  background/context, 176–179
  Josie Bullock case details, 174–176
  organizing/reorganizing/disorganizing, 188–189
  pedagogical problems, 179–181
  strategic essentialism, 182–188

Apparel industry, 66–67
Archives of Internal Medicine, The, 139
Aristotle, 37
Art of torture, 80–81
Asset, difference as, 34–35
Assumptions for class interactions, 117, 124–125
Authenticity, 88–89
Authoritarian state of power, 225
Authority in teacher-student relationship, 111–113
Autobiographical writing, 63–64
  See also Reflective exercises
Autonomy/control tension, 46–47, 49

Balance of behavior and jobs, 166
Balance of caregiving and work, 247–248
Beta males, 94
Bias
  beta, 32
  institutional, 169–170
  institutional classism, 141–143
  institutional racism, 133–134, 138–141
  institutional sexism, 136–138
  invisible, 135
  questioning, 168–169
Biography, subtext of, 91–93
Blacks hearing prejudicial comments, 40
"Blessed job," 278
Borderlands, 60
Bounded emotionality, 39

295

About the Editor

Dennis K. Mumby (PhD, Southern Illinois University, Carbondale) is Professor and Chair in the Department of Communication Studies at the University of North Carolina at Chapel Hill. His research examines the relationships among discourse, power, and identity in work settings. He has published several books, including *Communication and Power in Organizations* (Ablex, 1988), *Reworking Gender* (Sage, 2004, with Karen Ashcraft), and *Engaging Organizational Communication Theory and Research* (Sage, 2005, with Steve May). He is on the editorial board of numerous journals, including *Human Relations, Organization Studies,* and *Management Communication Quarterly.* He is a former chair of the Organizational Communication Division of both the National Communication Association and the International Communication Association. He is a five-time winner of NCA's Organizational Communication Division Annual Research Award for outstanding scholarly work. When he's not working, he loves to read good fiction, play golf, and run (but not all at the same time).

About the Contributors

Brenda J. Allen (PhD, Howard University) is an associate dean in the College of Liberal Arts and Sciences and a professor in the Department of Communication at the University of Colorado–Denver, where she also is the master mentor of the Tenure Track Faculty Mentoring Program. Her research and teaching areas are organizational communication, diversity, and critical pedagogy. Among her numerous publications is a groundbreaking book titled *Difference Matters: Communicating Social Identity* (2004, Waveland Press). She presents keynote speeches and conducts workshops for various groups on a range of topics, including diversity, empowerment, mentoring, presentational speaking, and teamwork. She was recently designated as a Master Teacher by the Western States Communication Association.

Karen Lee Ashcraft (PhD, University of Colorado–Boulder) is a professor of Organizational Communication at the University of Colorado at Boulder and an associate editor for *Human Relations*. Her research examines gender, race, and sexuality in the context of work, particularly as these relations intersect with organizational forms and occupational identities. She specializes in qualitative methodologies, and her research has appeared in such forums as *Communication Monographs*, *Management Communication Quarterly*, *Administrative Science Quarterly*, and the *Academy of Management Journal*. She co-authored a book with Dennis Mumby, *Reworking Gender*, which explores the contributions of feminist scholarship to critical studies of work and organization. Among her current projects is a five-year study of U.S. commercial airline pilots—an empirical case that illuminates how an occupation's institutional status as "professional" develops in relation to social constructions of gender and race.

Jane Stuart Baker (PhD, Texas A&M University) is an assistant professor in the Department of Communication Studies at the University of

Alabama. She has co-authored chapters in several books, including *Research Methods for Studying Groups: A Behind-the-Scenes Guide* (in press), *Managing Organizational Crises* (in press), *Rhetorical and Critical Approaches to Public Relations* (2008), and *Applied Health Communication* (2008). In 2006, she was awarded the John "Sam" Keltner Inspiration Award for the Most Outstanding Student Paper by the National Communication Association's Peace and Conflict Division. She studies diversity, dialectics, conflict, and group communication in organizations.

Patrice M. Buzzanell (PhD, Purdue University) is professor and the W. Charles and Ann Redding Faculty Fellow in the Department of Communication at Purdue University. Her research centers on leadership, work-life issues, and careers, particularly gendered careers and those associated with science, technology, engineering, and math (STEM). Buzzanell has edited *Rethinking Organizational and Managerial Communication From Feminist Perspectives* (2000), *Gender in Applied Communication Contexts* (2004, with H. Sterk and L. Turner), and *Distinctive Qualities in Communication Research* (2010, with D. Carbaugh). Author of approximately 100 books, articles, and chapters, she has also edited *Management Communication Quarterly* and has held key leadership positions in communication associations. A former Research Board member for the National Communication Association (NCA) and president of the Organization for the Study of Communication, Language, and Gender (OSCLG), she is currently Immediate Past President of the International Communication Association (ICA) and current president of the Council of Communication Associations (CCA).

Marthe L. Church (MA, University of Cincinnati) is a Homeless Education liaison for Project Connect, Cincinnati Public Schools.

Stanley Deetz (PhD, Ohio University) is professor of Communication, director of the Center for the Study of Conflict, Collaboration, and Creative Governance, and a President's Teaching Scholar at the University of Colorado. He is author/co-author of numerous articles and twelve books, including *Leading Organizations through Transitions, Doing Critical Management Research,* and *Democracy in an Age of Corporate Colonization.* His research focuses on corporate governance and communication processes in relation to democracy, micropractices of power, and collaborative decision-making. His current work investigates native theories of communication and democracy and their consequences for mutual decision-making. He was a Senior Fulbright Scholar and is a National Communication Association Distinguished Scholar and an International Communication Association Past-President and Fellow.

Sarah E. Dempsey (PhD, University of Colorado–Boulder) is assistant professor in the Department of Communication Studies at the University of North Carolina–Chapel Hill, where she teaches organizational communication, communication theory, and critical/cultural approaches to globalization and civil society. She is interested in problems of communication, collaboration, and representation within nonprofit, community-based, and gendered forms of organizing. Her research has appeared in *Management Communication Quarterly, Communication and Critical/Cultural Studies, Feminist Media Studies, Communication Monographs,* and *The International and Intercultural Communication Annual.* She is currently writing about the rise of social entrepreneurship, including how it is impacting meanings of work within the nonprofit sector.

Suzy D'Enbeau (PhD, Purdue University) is an assistant professor in the Department of Communication Studies at the University of Kansas. Suzy studies work-life issues, popular culture, and feminist organizing processes, particularly the branding of feminism in a neoliberal economy. Her work has appeared in *Feminist Media Studies* and *Qualitative Inquiry.* She has also co-authored book chapters that explore intersections of class, parenting, and work.

Rebecca L. Dohrman (PhD, Purdue University) is an assistant professor of communication at Maryville University. Rebecca's research interests include the discursive construction and material-symbolic intersections within several high-tech careers, such as engineering, computer science, and entrepreneurship. Additionally, Rebecca does research on gender and work-life intersections. Her dissertation focused on the discourses of high tech entrepreneurship for young people and the materiality of entrepreneurial work.

Gail T. Fairhurst (PhD, University of Oregon) is a professor of communication at the University of Cincinnati. Her research interests include organizational communication, leadership, and organizational discourse. She has published over 60 articles in communication and management journals as well as book chapters. She is the author of three books, including *Discursive Leadership: In Conversation With Leadership Psychology* (Sage, 2007) and *The Power of Framing: Creating the Language of Leadership* (Jossey-Bass, 2010). Her work has received numerous awards. She is also a Fulbright Scholar, an associate editor for *Human Relations,* and serves on a number of editorial boards.

Shiv Ganesh (PhD, Purdue University) is an associate professor in the Department of Management Communication, at the University of

Waikato in Aotearoa New Zealand and is editor of the *Journal of International and Intercultural* Communication (Vols. 4, 5 and 6). His research, which focuses upon issues of globalization, transnationalism, and technology in the context of social movements and civil society organizing, has been published in several outlets, including *Communication Monographs, Communication Yearbook, Human Relations, Journal of Applied Communication Research, Management Communication Quarterly,* and others. He is co-author of the book *Organizational Communication in an Age of Globalization: Issues, Reflections, Practices,* now in its second edition.

Danielle Hagen (MA, University of Cincinnati) is an adjunct instructor of Public Relations and Effective Public Speaking at the University of Cincinnati and an account executive at Wordsworth Communications.

Lynn M. Harter (PhD, University of Nebraska–Lincoln) is the Steven and Barbara Schoonover Professor in the School of Communication Studies at Ohio University and the senior editor of *Health Communication.* Her scholarship focuses on the discourses of health and healing and organizing processes, feminist and narrative theory-praxis. She has published over 50 journal articles and book chapters and several books and edited volumes. She lives in Athens, Ohio, with her husband, Scott, daughter, Emma Grace, and basset hound Ned.

Jody L. S. Jahn (MA, University of California–Santa Barbara) is a doctoral student in the Department of Communication at University of California–Santa Barbara. Her research focuses on organizational socialization, membership negotiation, and gender in high reliability organizations.

Erika L. Kirby (PhD, University of Nebraska–Lincoln) is a professor and chair of Communication Studies at Creighton University. A teacher-scholar of organizational communication, her teaching and research interests emphasize how differing social identities (especially gender) assimilate into↔collide with organizations. Broadly speaking, she is interested in the everyday intersections of work and personal life, and she has published widely in that area. She co-edited *Gender Actualized: Cases in Communicatively Constructing Realities* with Chad McBride and has published in outlets such as *Communication Monographs, Journal of Applied Communication Research, Management Communication Quarterly,* and *Communication Yearbook.* She is president of the Organization for the Study of Communication, Language, and Gender and vice-chair of the Organizational Communication Division of the National Communication Association. She has trained and consulted for multiple constituencies within Creighton University as well as in organizations outside of academe. She lives in Omaha, Nebraska, with her partner Bob, daughters Meredith and Samantha, and cat Otis.

Joe Levi (MA, University of Cincinnati) is a supply chain specialist for Total Quality Logistics.

John G. McClellan (PhD, University of Colorado, Boulder) is an assistant professor of communication at Boise State University. With an interest in communicative approaches for living and working together in an increasingly pluralistic society, his work attends to collaborative practices that might enable more sustainable and mutually beneficial ways of organizing. His recent collaborative work appears in *The Handbook of Business Discourse* (2009) and *The Oxford Handbook of Critical Management Studies* (2009). His current research explores the discursive quality of organizing with attention to issues of knowledge, identity, collaboration, and organizational change. As a former organizational change strategy consultant, his research focuses on organizing discourses that simultaneously enable and constrain opportunities to transform the ways we understand and engage organizational life.

Jennifer J. Mease (PhD, University of North Carolina at Chapel Hill) is an assistant professor in the Department of Communication at Texas A&M University. Her research focuses on organizations as sites of cultural production, addressing how social bias is built into organizational structures and theorizing the process of organizing to create social change. This focus has lead her to study a variety of organizational contexts and processes, including the regulation and construction of race in public school board meetings, teaching about whiteness and human differences, and diversity consultants' strategies for social change.

Elisa Oceguera (MA, San Francisco State University) is a doctoral student in Cultural Studies at the University of California–Davis. She is an active participant in several horizontal collectives that engage in the politics of encounter, action, and dignity. Her research interests focus on women of color feminisms, cultural studies, autonomous social movements, food politics, and community-based research methods. Her current work looks at the links between food security discourse, race, and the neoliberalization of urban commons. She currently resides in San Francisco.

Patricia Parker (PhD, University of Texas–Austin) is associate professor of communication studies at The University of North Carolina at Chapel Hill and the founder and executive director of The Ella Baker

Women's Center for Leadership and Community Activism, a venture supported by a Kauffman Faculty Fellowship for social entrepreneurship. Her work uses critical/feminist and postcolonial frameworks to explore questions at the intersections of race, gender, class, and power in organization processes. The primary focus of her research is girls' and women's leadership communication practices as constitutive of resistance and transformative social action. Her publications include a book on African American women's executive leadership in dominant culture organizations (Erlbaum, 2005), as well as several articles and book chapters appearing in edited volumes and journals.

Linda L. Putnam (PhD, University of Minnesota) is a professor in the Department of Communication at the University of California–Santa Barbara. She was the George T. and Gladys H. Abell Professor and Regent's Professor in the Department of Communication at Texas A&M University prior to this appointment. She has published seven co-edited books, including *Building Theories of Organization* (2009), *Organizational Communication: Major Works* (2006*), The Sage Handbook of Organizational Discourse* (2004), and *The New Handbook of Organizational Communication* (2001). She is a Distinguished Scholar of the National Communication Association, a Fellow of the International Communication Association (ICA), and the 2005 recipient of the ICA Steven H. Chaffee Career Productivity Award. Her scholarship focuses on gender and negotiation, organizational conflict, dialectics, and language analysis in organizations.

William K. Rawlins (PhD, University of Delaware) is Stocker Professor of Communication Studies at Ohio University, Athens, Ohio. His latest book is *The Compass of Friendship: Narratives, Identities, and Dialogues* (Sage, 2009), which received the 2009 David R. Maines Narrative Research Award from the Carl Couch Center for Social and Internet Research. His book, *Friendship Matters: Communication, Dialectics, and the Life Course,* was designated a 1993 *Choice* Outstanding Academic Book and received the Gerald R. Miller Book Award in 1994 from the Interpersonal and Small Group Interaction Division of the National Communication Association. In 2002, he received The Theory That Has Left a Legacy Award: "The Dialectical Perspective" from the Communication Theory Interest Group of the Central States Communication Association. He presently serves on the editorial boards of six scholarly journals and continues to study how communicating as friends facilitates the well-lived life for persons and societies.

Joaquín Sánchez, Jr. (BA, Eugene Lang College, The New School for Liberal Arts) hails from Aztlán by way of La Villita on Chicago's

Southwest Side. The son of an immigrant father and a Chicana mother, he understands intimately the struggles of working-class, immigrant, people of color. As a good mestizo, he balances this history and his art as a radical, Xicano, Queer poet with his organizing and movement-building work in the ongoing struggles for environmental and LGBTQ justice in NYC. He received his B.A. in Education Studies at The New School. Joaquín is a founding member of the Ella Baker Women's Center for Leadership and Community Activism in Chapel Hill, where he also conducted graduate research at the University of North Carolina–Chapel Hill. He gives big ups to all the mentors, elders, and ancestors who have offered guidance and paved the way.

Stephen Williams, MA, is a PhD candidate in communication at the University of Colorado. His research interests are in exploring communication processes that cultivate micro-emancipation and collaborative decision-making in organizations experiencing change. He is a practicing organizational change and enterprise resource-planning (ERP) technology consultant to international corporations and government organizations globally. He has worked with organizations such as the United Kingdom Department of Work and Pensions, Genus Plc., Qualcomm, Daiwa Capital Markets Europe, Roadrunner Sports, General Dynamics, and numerous small- to medium-sized businesses. His work is influenced by applied research approaches and explores the intersection between theory and practice. His current research focuses on corporate governance, collaboration, power, and technology in relation to sustained organizational change.

Supporting researchers for more than 40 years

Research methods have always been at the core of SAGE's publishing program. Founder Sara Miller McCune published SAGE's first methods book, *Public Policy Evaluation*, in 1970. Soon after, she launched the *Quantitative Applications in the Social Sciences* series—affectionately known as the "little green books."

Always at the forefront of developing and supporting new approaches in methods, SAGE published early groundbreaking texts and journals in the fields of qualitative methods and evaluation.

Today, more than 40 years and two million little green books later, SAGE continues to push the boundaries with a growing list of more than 1,200 research methods books, journals, and reference works across the social, behavioral, and health sciences. Its imprints—Pine Forge Press, home of innovative textbooks in sociology, and Corwin, publisher of PreK–12 resources for teachers and administrators—broaden SAGE's range of offerings in methods. SAGE further extended its impact in 2008 when it acquired CQ Press and its best-selling and highly respected political science research methods list.

From qualitative, quantitative, and mixed methods to evaluation, SAGE is the essential resource for academics and practitioners looking for the latest methods by leading scholars.

For more information, visit **www.sagepub.com**.